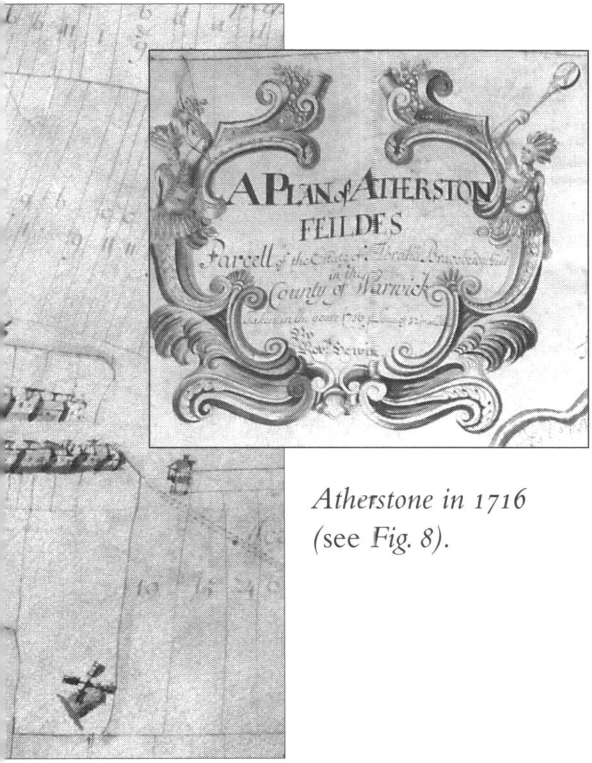

Atherstone in 1716 (see Fig. 8).

Atherstone in 1786 (see Fig. 7).

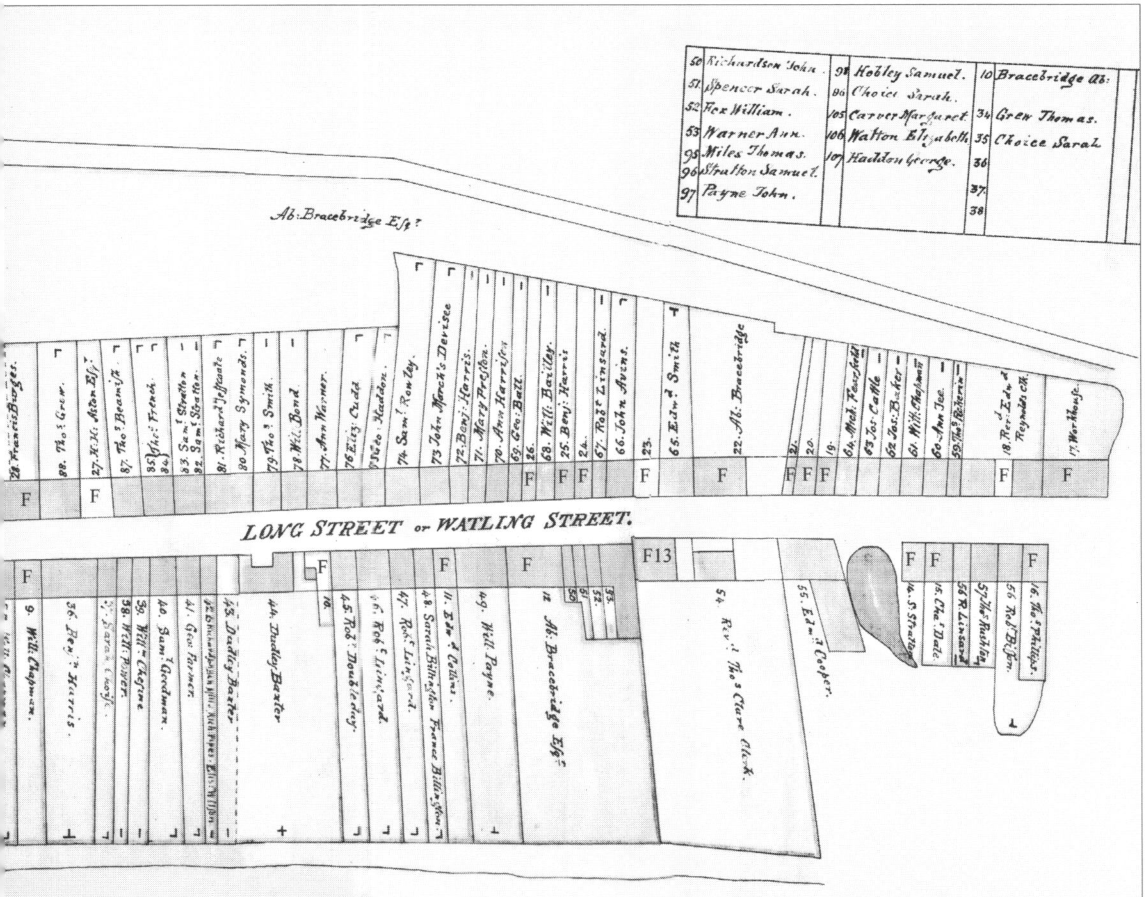

Atherstone

A Pleasantly Placed Town

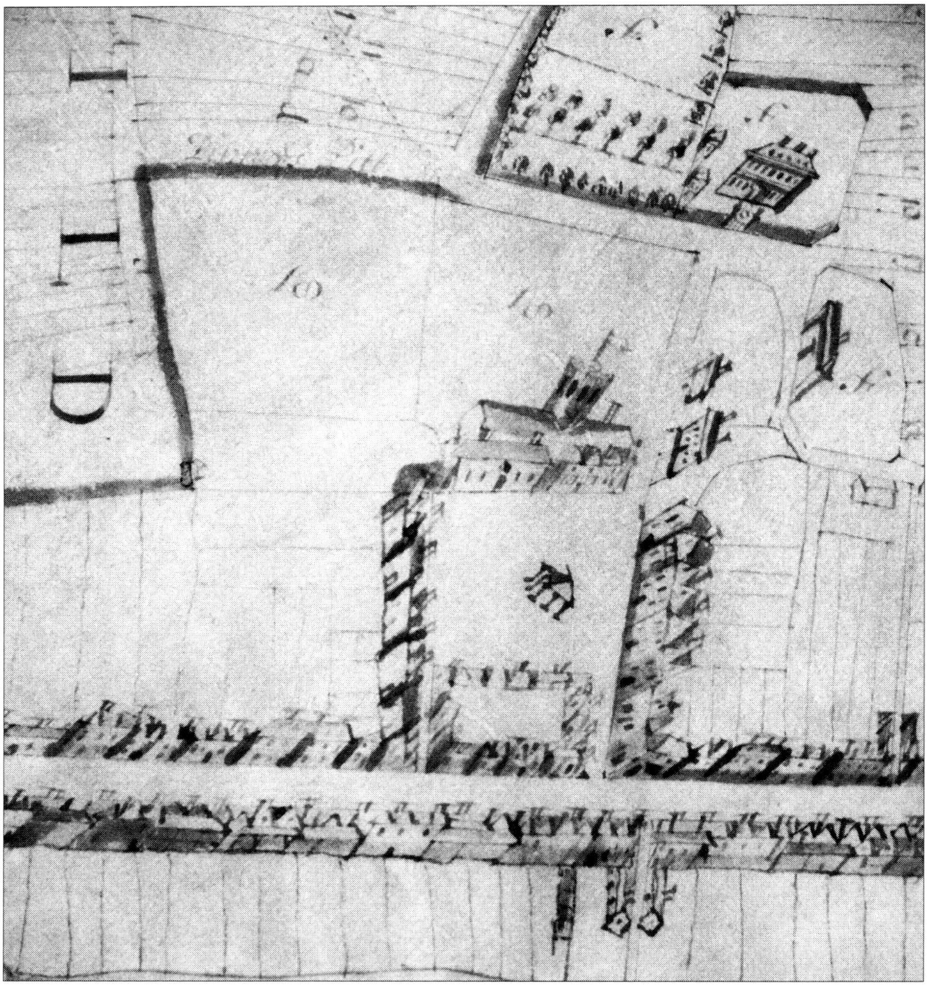

Atherstone Market Place in the 1716 map by Robert Hewitt (Warwickshire County Record Office, P7, reproduced with permission).

THE TITLE OF THIS BOOK ALLUDES TO THE DIARY OF THE HON. JOHN BYNG, QUOTED IN BUILDING HISTORY TWO.

Hence we journey'd in a pleasant evening, without any occurrence, till our crossing of the little River Anker, (which divides the counties of Leicester and Warwick) now so swelled by the late rains, as to make my passage unsafe, even by the help of a bridge; for my boots were well soaked. – T.B. was sent forward to the Swan Inn *at Atherstone, a neat clean house, in this pleasantly placed town.*

(John Byng, *Torrington Diaries, 1789*, Eyre Spottiswood, 1935, Vol. II, p. 97)

Atherstone

A Pleasantly Placed Town

Edited by

Nat Alcock
and
Margaret Hughes

Phillimore

2008

Published by
PHILLIMORE & CO. LTD
Chichester, West Sussex, England
www.phillimore.co.uk
www.thehistorypress.co.uk

ISBN 978-1-86077-493-5

Printed and bound in Great Britain

Contents

List of Illustrations

Tables

Illustration Acknowledgements

N. W. Alcock, 48, 50, 51; J. Beechey, 10, 13, 28, 29, 53, 56, 57, 58, 59, 60, 62, 68, 69, 70; Birmingham City Archives/Aylesford Collection, 33; Friends of Atherstone Heritage, 22, 23, 55, 61, 67; David Gilbert, 49; T.J. Laight, 1; Bob Meeson, 24, 25, 31, 32; Ordnance Survey/1888 1:500 map, 20, 38; 25-in map, 37; Charles Tomlinson, *Illustrations of Useful Arts and Manufactures*, SPCK, London, 1858, 34; M. Trye, 11, 12, 14, 15, 16, 17, 18, 19, 21, 26, 27, 28, 29, 30, 52, 54, 63, 64, 65, 66, 71; T. Slater, 3, 4, 5, 6; Archives of Vero & Everitt Ltd, 35; J. Vero, 36; Warwickshire County Record Office, P7, frontispiece, 8; CR1130/18, 9; P26 CR2511/21, 7; L2/8, p 424, 39; PH213/3, 41; PH213/5, 44; PH213/23, 42; PH213/25, 40; PH213/28, 45; PH213/34, 43; PH352/14/30, 47.

Foreword

People often say a town has 'real character', but what is it that is bound up in that description? They say it about Atherstone, but what do they mean? 'Character', too, is only recognised by people who are experiencing it at that time, in their lifetime.

What they are recognising, though, is something which has evolved over centuries. It is the history of the place, the people and what they built to adapt to the needs of each age, to service the life of the town as it developed.

This book is an important document of that history, and the result of three years of delving into local and county records, town surveys and other historic documents by the History of Atherstone Research Team. It shows who owned the land, what they built, how they worked and why it changed. It describes the power struggles between those families which rose to the top; it shows the struggles of others just to live. It is a wonderful and highly readable record of the life of the town told through the history of its buildings.

Atherstone began with an exceptional situation, set on a famous Roman road which allowed easy access for trade, with mineral-rich hills and woods to the south to give people shelter and warmth, and fertile, well watered land to the north to give them food. Development, expansion and change were always part of its makeup, and despite the disappearance of the industries for which it became famous, the town has lived on and put its resources to good use. Nowadays, the industrial estate is a major source of employment, and an important part of its success is the very existence of that Roman road.

Kay Alexander

Introduction

History is powerful. Chains of cause and effect are perceptible at any given moment. Few witnesses of the 1989 demolition of an arm of Vero & Everitt's Atherstone hatting factory at the end of Long Street would have spared a thought for a 13th-century Norman abbot – let alone an anonymous Roman surveyor of the first century A.D. Yet it was a decision taken by the Abbot of Bec that governed the setting out of burgage plots at right angles to the Roman Watling Street. He had been constrained by geography and the manor boundary, and his decision was governed by the line of the Innage Brook – separating Atherstone from Merevale – whose course along the 'back way' dictated that these plots shortened the further westward they were situated. In time, the abbot's burgage plots determined the shape of the Atherstone Yards, and later the position of the hat factory. Such continuities form the fabric of any town, and *Atherstone: A Pleasantly Placed Town* demonstrates their relevance for this town.

Today, most traffic along the A5 passes around this north Warwickshire market town. But for many centuries it was a regular stopping point along the Watling Street for travellers to and from Wales and the north-west. Our account starts with the prehistory of the region and the arrival of the Romans, whose fort and settlement not only provided the first way-station for travellers but also gave its name (Manduessedum) to the town's mother parish of Mancetter. The history of Atherstone itself begins in the 11th century, and continues with the laying out of a new town by the abbey of Bec. Through the medieval and early modern period, it prospered as a market centre and travellers' stopping place – with close to forty inns in the 19th century. The growth of its hatting industry through the 18th and 19th centuries gave the town's economy a new direction. The ensuing demand for workers in the hat factories led to the need to house them, and the creation of the crowded Atherstone yards. Although slum clearance has swept these away, evocative photographs and documents preserve their memory.

The book has a distinctive central component in its Chapter Five, describing Atherstone's streets and houses and, with the final Gazetteer, exploring the history that is still visible today in the town's buildings. The surrounding chapters, chronicling the town's life over the centuries, provide the background to the interpretation of its topography.

This book is the outcome of a five-year joint venture between Atherstone Civic Society and the Friends of Atherstone Heritage, with substantial financial support from the Heritage Lottery Fund. The research has been carried out by the History of Atherstone Research Team (HART), comprising volunteer researchers, supported by specialists. Their aim has been to research and present Atherstone's history so as to bring together the making of the town and its buildings with accounts of the lives of families and individuals. The research has included both surveys of the actual buildings in the town and searches through a wide range of related documents: wills, inventories, deeds, maps, tax returns and the particularly detailed Manor Court Rolls.

A related HART publication that drew upon this research appeared in 2005: *Once Upon A Time In Atherstone* (M. Hughes), a collection of informal stories dramatising aspects of the town's history. This present volume presents HART's researches in a more directly scholarly way that we hope will be equally appealing.

Novelist and playwright Don de Lillo has commented that history is reducible to the story of men in rooms. The top-down view of history is indispensable – the story of the deliberations of the powerful few, close-closeted together, making decisions that affect the many. Such history finds its way into the account of Atherstone in these pages – the shifting Anglo-Saxon border, the decisions of the abbey of Bec, the effects of Enclosure, the consequences of the abolition of slavery ... However, other forces impact upon those 'men-in-rooms' – the climate, the ecology, the economy, ideologies, disease, wars both near and far, the need for room to live, and more – so that decision-makers and the forces of the age needs must interact. And the men-in-the-street, in our case, the men and women in Long Street, in Church Street ('Bakehouse Lane'), in Market Street ('Butchers Row') – they have their story, too, arising from that interplay. It is their story in particular that we have tried to tell.

History is powerful. It has been said that without its perspective 'men would become little better than the flies of a summer'.[1] We hope this book will help readers to appreciate the long and wide perspective of one pleasantly placed town.

Nat Alcock
Margaret Hughes

I Roots of Atherstone: Geology and Early History

Alan F. Cook

Introduction

The birth of a town is the result of the interplay of many factors. Significant among them is the landscape itself, offering the raw materials that affect human development. This opening chapter deals with Atherstone's geological context, demonstrating the potential of local natural resources to support the town's growth. But first of all, Atherstone's location is pinpointed in relation to England's national map; followed by elements of the area's story prior to its Anglo-Saxon development (*see* Chapter Two). The main theme is then addressed, under four headings:

- Building Materials and Minerals
- Topography
- Soils
- Drainage

Atherstone's Location

Atherstone is situated near the geographical centre of England, as defined by Colonel Sir Charles Arden-Close in 1941;[1] later by the Ordnance Survey,[2] under two categories as follows:

> Lindley Hall Farm, 1.5km east of Fenny Drayton and 5.7km east south-east of Atherstone parish church. This is the 'mainland only' centre of England.
>
> Between Lindley Hall Farm and Lindley Grange, 6.3km east-south-east of Atherstone railway station. This is the centre of England if all surrounding islands are included.

The geographical region known as the Midlands is V-shaped. To the north-west is the Cheshire Gap (or gateway) that provides a link to the Cheshire and Lancashire lowlands; to the north-east is the Midland or Trent Gap (gateway) providing a link to the Vale of York via the broad lower Trent Valley; to the south-west is the Severn Gap that provides a 'gateway' to the Severn estuary and beyond. The Midlands valley town of Atherstone is situated to the east

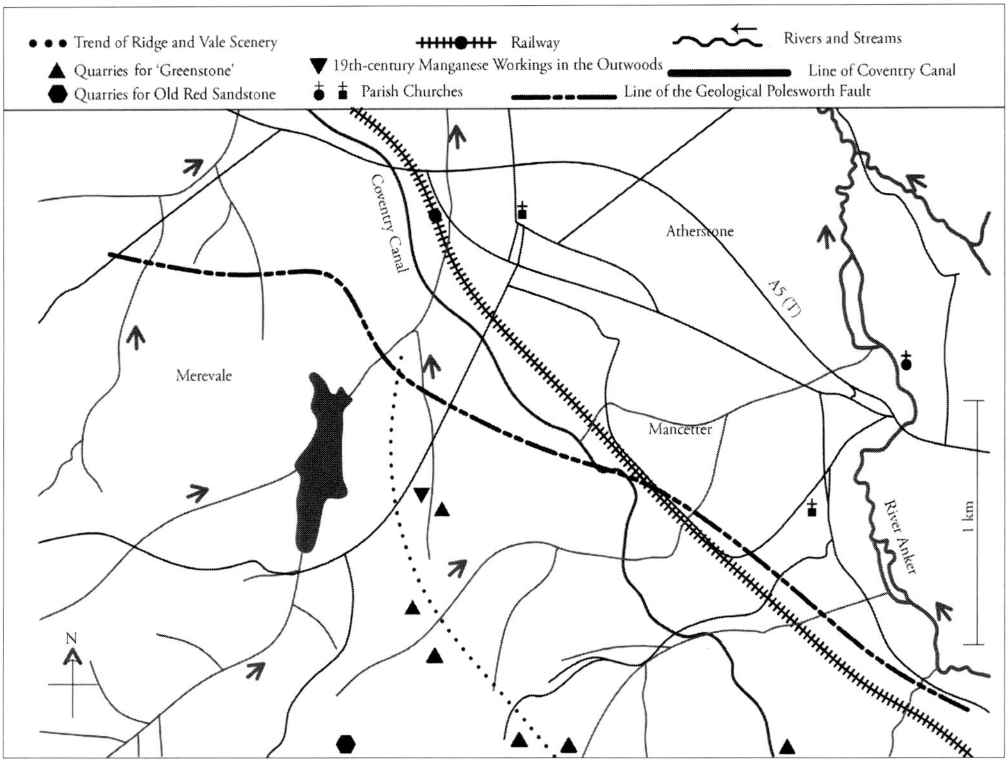

1 *Simplified map of the Atherstone district, with key.*

of the Tees-Exe line (a line between the mouths of those rivers, a useful way of dividing England into lowland and upland). It is reasonable to say that the town is situated in the lowland zone. Post-medieval people knew this area, together, as the Arden and the Wolden.

Earth Story

Over millions of years, 'Atherstone' has sometimes been beneath the sea, and at other times, uplifted land. It has also moved – along a tortuous journey known as Continental Drift – from being near Antarctica 570,000,000 years ago. This drift is driven by powerful plate tectonic forces that cause faults, compressional squeezing and stretching in pieces of the earth's crust. These forces helped create the discontinuities and joints in the various local rock types that make them useful building stones. At that time, a cool, low-oxygen, freshwater sea prevailed. On this seabed, complex life-forms existed in the clayey, silty sediments. These are known as trilobites – segmented relatives of today's king crabs. The Nuneaton-Hartshill-Atherstone Ridge is world-renowned for its fossilised forms, and many species are named after this area, for instance: *Hartshillia inflata*. The sediments attained a thickness of several thousand metres and were compressed and dried out to form mudstones and shales. Colossal forces created a strong trend, or strike, in these rocks. (Trends control the ridge and valley scenery.) Today, the trend of the Nuneaton-Hartshill-Atherstone Ridge is north-west to south-east, but as the ridges near Atherstone they are twisted to lie almost north-south.

The extensive local Carboniferous coal, sandstone, clay, limestone and ironstone deposits were deposited about 300,000,000 years ago, when the area was on the tropical Equator.

One hundred million years after this, the area had moved further north and was a Triassic desert, with sand and mud deposits. These were affected by the Polesworth Fault line, which influences the course of the Anker valley; this in turn influences the road, canal and railway routes. This twist in the ridge and valley trend gives a north-facing hill slope – not as popular as a south-eastern aspect for settlers. The overall slope is also eroded by valleys to form interfluvial spurs.

Early Human History in the Area[3]

Palaeolithic humans left their artefacts behind in the Anker Valley (over 175,000 years ago), then, for millennia, glacial ice sheets prevented human settlement. People had returned by about 7,500 B.C., and from then on there was more or less continued activity in the area – albeit only small family groups of people constantly on the move. Some flints and stone axes have been found, now in Warwickshire Museum. However, there are no permanent pre-Roman buildings, or even structural landmarks, except the Oldbury Hill fort (Bronze and Iron Age) and the associated Hartshill tumulus (possibly Bronze Age).[4]

The story of the occupation of the Oldbury Hill fort is probably one of short tenures.[5] It was never a fully occupied structure as was, for example, Corley Hill, near Coventry. However, there must have been a people who saw the need to dig the huge ditch structure *(vallum/fossa)*; work which would have taken a body of organised manual labour – many men working several months. Yet Oldbury seemingly remained an intermittently occupied site. The lack of freshwater streams on the north-east facing slope may have been a problem. Another conjecture as to why it appears not to have worked invokes the River Anker fogs and mists that reduced visibility – causing difficulties in defending the site. These occur over many months of a year, when atmospheric conditions are right. Moreover, smoking fires in the low Anker valley would easily produce a smog; evidence of this is provided by stubble burning in our own times. Further, mists and fogs are eerie, suggestive perhaps of displeased deities, and could have been off-putting to a fearful and suspicious people. Some recent theories also suggest that many hillforts were not permanent settlements, but seasonally occupied by the surrounding population.[6]

The author studied all datable evidence of human activity as recorded in the SMR (Sites and Monuments Records) for a four-kilometre radius around Atherstone. The average spatial densities were as follows:

Period	*Density of Human Activity (sites per 10km²)*
Stone Age (Old, Middle and New)	2.8
Bronze Age	1.2
Iron Age	1.4
Roman	2.0
Domesday Settlement	1.6
Medieval	3.2

Table 1 *Historic Environment Record finds and sites within a four-kilometre radius of Atherstone. Procedure: All datable traces of human activity derived from the National Monuments Record and the SMR were plotted on to a base map and the density of sites within a four-kilometre radius circle calculated.* [7]

Table 1 portrays, perhaps quite realistically, sparse Bronze-Age human activity in the area;[8] it is estimated the British population at any one time was 14,000 in that epoch (from *c.*2500 B.C. to 600 B.C.). If that population is averaged over available land, it was six persons per 10 square kilometres – and that includes highlands.

The local soils for miles around were not ideally suited to early agriculture or earthwork building. Hence the evidence of genuine tumuli (barrows) is sparse, apart from the one proven at Hartshill. Many of the other so-named tumuli were misinterpretations of other later features, such as post-windmill mounds, sometimes colloquially named 'tumps'. Bloxam, the late-Victorian, Rugby School, amateur archaeologist, had been influenced by Stukeley's publications and his notable visit to Mancetter in 1712.[9] Bloxam and his colleagues set about excavating every mound in the district.[10] His excavation and assessment of these mounds did not seem to cause him to question any alternative explanation for them. He failed to recognise that their construction soils were often dark, damp, stiff, clayey soils – not popular construction soils for early British peoples.

The Roman Presence

The Romans had a strong presence in the area, centred on the settlement of Manduessedum, which straddled the Waetlinga Roman road – the Watling Street – about a mile east of what later became the site of Atherstone parish church, near the crossing of the River Anker.

Manduessedum is overlooked by the high ridge and wooded area of Oldbury, which, as noted, offers indication of earlier occupation, evidencing as it does both Bronze- and Iron-Age establishment of a hillfort.[11] However, Oldbury's role for the Romans is something of an enigma. Although the Romans re-settled Bronze-Age sites, they avoided those of the Iron Age. Yet when Thomas and Taylor excavated part of Oldbury in 1965, Roman mortaria were visible.[12] Maybe Oldbury fulfilled an intermittent purpose for the Romans as a vantage-point?

The present-day name, Mancetter, derives from that Roman place name, which itself has been identified as being composed of two elements, *mandu-* and *-essedo*.[13] The first element is British, mandu-, meaning 'small horse' or 'pony'. The second element, -essedo, is an early Gaulish word imported into Latin, and means 'chariot'. Manduessedum's position on the Watling Street is surely significant in the origin of the name.

The fort at Manduessedum was created around the time of the construction of the Watling Street: local archaeologists have discovered defensive ditches and ramparts. However, it is difficult to be accurate in the absence of documentary evidence. Nor may we gain precise dating from coins and other artefacts; the impressions they give are broad – within decades sometimes, although radiocarbon and cosmogenic evidence can give dates to within five years or so. It may be reasonable to surmise that the southern part of Britain was under Roman rule, and Watling Street built as far as High Cross, by A.D. 47. In A.D. 50, Ostorius Scapula subdued what is broadly speaking now Warwickshire, and it became part of the region known as Flavia.[14]

Early Roman settlements often developed outside larger forts, within embanked precincts appended to those dominant sites – often called *vicus* settlements. The plan usually consisted of a broad street stretching away from the gate, wide enough for a market place and bordered by farm plots leading back to the edge of a surrounding field. The Manduessedum site on the Watling Street is classified as a vicus, close to the fort which stood on the higher land now occupied by Mancetter parish church and its graveyard. A villa existed between the vicus and the fort. Much of our local knowledge on these Roman activities should be credited to the late Keith Scott.

Current understanding of the whole site recognises that early archaeologists, unaware of the adjacent fort, designated the vicus site alone as 'Manduessedum', a limitation that still occurs on some maps. However, opinion is as yet undecided as to whether one site is solely the true Manduessedum: the bigger site under the church, or the vicus, or indeed, both? Care is needed, therefore, in interpreting precisely what is being discussed under references to 'Manduessedum'. We may perhaps avoid misinterpretation by referring to 'the Manduessedum area', or 'Manduessedum and its local settlement area', rather like some modern small town with districts and suburbs. And with their book-keeping mentality in mind, we may well think of the Romans as entering it in their records as all of:

vicus
villa
castrum (fort)

When Boudicca led her followers north-west onto this Roman military road, the Watling Street, after her destruction of Colchester, St Albans and London in A.D. 60, she must have thought she was invincible. Instead, she brought about the end of the 17 years of resistance that had been the British response to the Roman invasion of A.D. 43. The Manduessedum area is a strong candidate for the site of her final battle.[15] A vague description of the battlefield is given by Tacitus: it was approached by a narrow defile, with a wooded area to the rear of the Roman army, who were on a plain with little or no cover to the front – details that certainly apply to Manduessedum.[16]

In the three centuries following Boudicca's uprising, Britain became a settled, wealthy province of the Roman Empire, during which time some five thousand miles of British road were constructed. The Manduessedum settlement, taking advantage of its position on a major road, developed widespread trading links. Evidence has been found of kilns from a pottery-making industry,[17] as well as items of glass and paint.[18] The area is known to have been in the province of Britanniae in A.D. 297, and in the diocese of Praefectus Praetorio Galliarium in A.D. 314.

Roman political and economic activity collapsed in the fifth century, but by this time there had developed a Romano-British culture (quite remarkable in parts of England). General thought is that much of this Romano-British population was a Romanised British population rather than there being a major influx of continental Romans who interbred with the native peoples. Much of the population of Roman Britain would have carried on their daily lives more or less unchanged, with Roman organisation/administration superimposed on top; for example, people carried on farming, but took their crops to the nearest town and paid taxes. In this way, the population of this Romano-British village, Manduessedum/Mancetter, would continue to live, work and survive in the area.

Atherstone Relative to the Roman Watling Street (The Waetlinga)

The actual alignment of the Waetlinga chosen by the Romans has been the subject of much debate.[19] A pre-Roman mineral route existed between North Wales and London, which avoided high land and followed river valleys (for water, easy gradients, etc.). The Roman route used the same design philosophy in many places, but diverged on a more westerly trajectory through the Midlands. The local high points helped surveying and inter-visibility for route surveying.

Over time, Atherstone developed astride the Roman road. Although the siting of the town was not determined solely by geology and the geologically-influenced route of Watling Street, it is interesting to consider the impact of these factors. Consider, for instance, how in the Atherstone area the road and the town sit well above the level of the flood plain (except at the Witherley crossing point). The town has a linear or ribbon settlement pattern,[20] adopted by only a few towns on the Watling Street; most were significantly offset (Tamworth, Nuneaton and Hinckley),[21] as Slater comments in Chapter Three (p.18). But had Atherstone evolved offset to the Watling Street, its site options would have been poor – damp, soft, alluvial flood lands of the Anker or steep-sloping, hard, rocky soils in the Purley-Outwood-Merevale area. Therefore, it may be conjectured that the road and settlement came to occupy a thin corridor of safe land. The corridor itself was not endowed with much mineral wealth.

Building Materials and Minerals

Coal, Sand and Gravel

The Carboniferous Productive Coal Measures (300,000,000-year-old coal, ironstone and clay) are more than one and a quarter miles to the south-west;

younger glacio-fluvial sand and gravel resources are confined to the Anker Valley to the north and north-east.

Stone

The hilly area to the immediate south-west comprises very old shales and mudstones from the Cambrian system of rocks (approximately 520,000,000 years old). In places the shales were intruded by a useful rock, spessartite lamprophyre, also known locally as greenstone, black granite, diorite or Dun Dick. There is 18th-century evidence of greenstone quarrying for road and house building in the Outwoods area.[22] However, there were earlier uses of this hard rock. The Romans and medieval people dug it for construction.[23] It was used extensively in Merevale's Cistercian Abbey,[24] built *c.*1148 (There are other rocks employed in the Abbey, listed in the table below.) This once-molten greenstone was injected approximately 450,000,000 years ago. The tremendous heat and pressure involved in that process helped to concentrate and enrich manganese minerals (*see* below), and others – pyrites, lead and zinc – in the shale.[25]

However, the really useful stones, for architectural purposes, were the grey and red-brown sandstones. The following table details types used in Atherstone buildings.[26] The most recent geological period is at the top of the table, the oldest at the bottom:

Geological time period	*Stone, Colour, Characteristics*	*Sites*	*Instances of use*
Triassic	Sherwood and Bromsgrove Sandstone Formations – light red-brown or buff, easily dressed and carved; tend to occur in blocks. Bond well with mortar, but are not biochemically stable. Polesworth Formation: red-brown coarse sandstone with fine gravel layers, easily dressed.	Nearest outcrop: canal corridor, Mancetter to Whittington	St Mary's Church – ashlar. 9, 11, 19 Market Place buildings – foundations, ashlar, kerbs, and steps, with occasional blocks of sandstone from earlier buildings (perhaps the Old Town Hall). The church of our Lady, Merevale. Merevale Abbey walls – ashlar.
	Hollington Stone	Uttoxeter area	The church of Our Lady, Merevale – ashlar. St Mary's Church – ashlar.

Geological time period	*Stone, Colour, Characteristics*	*Sites*	*Instances of use*
Carboniferous	Halesowen Formation – hard grey-green sandstones, locally reddened. Meriden Formation – sandstones (formerly known as Keele) – dark red-brown, easily dressed and carved; tend to occur in blocks. Bond well with mortar, but are not biochemically stable	Nearest outcrop: Bentley/ Baxterley	St Mary's Church – ashlar. Market Place (Old Town Hall site) – foundation, ashlar, kerbs, steps. Merevale Abbey – ashlar. The church of Our Lady, Merevale – blocks.
Devonian	Oldbury Farm Sandstone Formation (*Upper Old Red Sandstone*) – dark red-brown, white flecks, easily dressed and carved; tend to occur in blocks. Bond well with mortar, but are not biochemically stable	Nearest outcrop: Mancetter Hill Farm	St Mary's Church – ashlar. The church of Our Lady, Merevale – blocks. Merevale Abbey – blocks.
Ordovician	Spessartite Lamprophyre (greenstone, black granite, Dun Dick or diorite) Green, blue-black, brown when rotted. Moderate to very hard. Can be dressed or cut, but with difficulty.	Nearest outcrop: Monks Park Woods, Outwoods	19 Market Place – setts St Mary's Church – blocks. Merevale Abbey – blocks.
Cambrian	Hartshill Sandstone Formation (*quartzite*, or *white granite*) grey-white; very hard, not easily dressed or shaped; tend to occur in rough cuboids. Do not bond well with mortar because of the glassy quartz content	Nearest outcrop: Hartshill	St Mary's Church – NE wall. Coventry Canal towpath dry-stone wall. Merevale Abbey – blocks.

Table 2 *Types of stone used in Atherstone buildings.*

The Augustinian friary, founded in 1375 close to the Market Place (*see* Chapter Three: 'Guild and Friary'), may have used local building stone as well as timber framing.

Brick

The superficial drift deposits sometimes yielded good brick clay. However, brick-making in North Warwickshire was rare before the 16th century (the making of floor and roof tiles, pipes and household goods was not.) Then, around 1770, there was something of a technological explosion in the use of bricks. The physics and chemistry were better understood; kiln designs were improved and clay mixing was better.

Manganese

The manganese referred to above, under 'Stone', may have been discovered as early as the Roman period, because there are traces of it in local Roman pottery. The Merevale Cistercians may have also used this mineral in ceramic and apothecary activities. Cistercians preferred isolated positions; solitude was chosen as a buffer against too much contact with the secular world. Yet their business-sense was very realistic and they would not remain aloof from any local markets or towns. They were good at helping town development on the outskirts, the lay brothers being skilled labourers – both agricultural and industrial. By 1820, there was local manganese exploitation in the Outwoods area, combined with the quarrying of greenstone, noted above, for road and house building.[27]

Topography

The Midlands is often thought of as a flat, rolling plain. However, Atherstone's ground level and physical scenery are variable; this is largely owing to the association of hard and soft rock geology.[28] The River Anker valley is only 219ft (67m) above mean sea level in places, but high ground to the south of the Market Place rises to over 460ft (140m).

Many written works in the last 400 years have attempted to describe the local topography. Drayton's *Poly-Olbion*,[29] a series of songs describing England, written between 1612 and 1622, used poetic verse to describe his birthplace, the Anker Valley:

> His Tamworth at the last, he in his sway doth win,
> There playing him awhile, till Anker should come in,
> While trifleth twixt her banks observing state so slowe.
>
> *(Song XIII, line 243)*

This was followed by a succession of references in antiquarian and more recent works:

1730 Dugdale, vol. II, p.66:[30]

> Nun Eaton. This place hath its name from the Rivulet nigh which it stands, Ea, our Old English signifying water.

1777 Burton, p.314:[31]

Witherley, in old Deedes written Witheredeley, situate vpon the border of Warwickshire on the bankes of the River Anker, neere unto Watling Streete. This Manner was once belonging to the Lord Wake as is evident by this Roule of Edward the first's time.

1795-1815 Nichols, vol. IV, part 2, p.1,007:[32]

... in old deeds written Witheredeley, very pleasantly situated in a fine sporting country, on the banks of the river Anker, on the borders of ...

(Incidentally, in vol. IV, part 2, the plate CLVII shows a mammoth tooth from the Anker at 'Shepey'.)

1904 Doubleday and Page, vol. I, p.6:[33]

The distance from its rise to its mouth is about twenty-five miles. It is everywhere a pretty stream ...

1908 Doubleday and Page, vol. 2, p.383:[34]

There is no pack of otterhounds kennelled in Warwickshire, nor is there any trace of county pack having existed in the past; but packs from other districts have long paid occasional visits to the shire. The streams hunted include the Arrow, Avon, Leam, Itchen, Anker and Blyth.

However, in 1950 The British Association improved upon such general descriptions,[35] defining the Atherstone area as belonging to:

Primary Region	*Sub-region*	*Local region*
The Trent Valley System a highly influential area of tributaries excavating valleys into the plateau.	*The Tame Valley* this divides the Birmingham Plateau into two distinct areas; part of the valley is underlain by a much older valley structure, eroded by the Proto-Tame river.	*Anker Valley* nearly 25 miles long; a meandering, low gradient valley source is near Wolvey, 400ft above sea level; at Tamworth it has dropped to 200ft above sea level
The Birmingham Plateau the largest and most important physical unit in the Birmingham district; land over 400ft above sea level.	*The East Warwickshire Plateau* separated by the Tame and Blythe valleys from other plateaux; lying between 400ft and 500ft above sea level and comprising old rocks with strong scenic trends.	*Ansley Plateau* the Bourne valley defines this small plateau area; many streams drain to the west; lying between 400ft and 525ft above sea level and comprising old rocks with strong scenic trends (containing the Nuneaton-Hartshill-Atherstone Ridge)

Table 3 *Geological regions and sub-regions relating to the Atherstone area.*

More recently, in 1996, the Secretary of State for the Environment launched *The Character of England: landscape, wildlife and natural features.*[36] This attempted to standardise the terminology and evaluation of the landscape. It was a summary of 181 areas of England as defined by English Nature and the Countryside Commission. As one might expect, the Atherstone area did not fit neatly into a single category; it was defined as belonging to 'Areas 72 – Mease/Sence Lowlands', and '97 – Arden'. The descriptions refer to gently rolling clay ridges and shallow valleys, becoming virtually flat around the main rivers. There are areas of open agricultural land complemented by copse and spinney on the ridges and occasional groups of trees on the stream sides. In many of the arable areas, hedgerow trees are sparse. The tree cover is due to surviving park lands, which are prominent features of the landscape, often surrounding manorial halls. Many of these park lands were once extensive, with the result that their ancient trees are now isolated within arable or short term ley. In the core of this area is a small-scale landscape of low, rounded hills, steep scarps and small, incised valleys that, with their abundant tree and woodland cover, give a strong sense of enclosure. Broad-leaved woodlands and hedgerow trees lend a well-wooded character to the area. The woods themselves vary in type from 20th-century plantations to species-rich ancient woodlands. Semi-natural habitats, such as species-rich acidic and neutral grassland, along with remnants of heathland, are still present in the area.

Soils

Soil classification is a rapidly-evolving science. Antiquarians would have used simple terms like *loam* (a mixed, humic light soil), and *marl* (a red-brown clayey, damp soil) to describe local soils. But modern soil science recognises many analytical factors when describing soil.

Atherstone is noted today for the following soil types:

> Along the line of the lower Innage Brook, Arrow soils occur; they are permeable, coarse, loamy soils, affected by groundwater;
> the Anker valley and its lower slopes comprise a mixture of Rufford, Whimple and Wick reddish-brown soils; they are derived from more recent sediments and have slowly permeable subsoils with slight seasonal water-logging;
> in Bentley Park Woods, the younger Triassic sandstones comprise Salop soils, reddish mudstone and clay, slowly permeable, with seasonal water-logging;
> the coalfield outcrop from Baddesley to Ansley comprises Bardsey soils; these are slowly permeable and seasonally waterlogged loams on top of clayey, silty soils;
> the ridge and valley areas of Oldbury, with their ancient mudstones, comprise Denbigh and Dunkeswick soils; they are well-drained, fine, loamy, silty soils, with some slowly permeable subsoil, suffering from slight seasonal water-logging.

The free-draining soils have tended to be of light to moderate acidity (pH 5-7), owing to minerals leaching outwards and downwards, in particular those in the Outwoods/Monks Park area.[37] The steep and variable slope gradients hereabouts prohibited pasture and arable farming, hence their use for timber plantations and woodland. The damp Anker washlands developed for dairying pasture – and even sheep grazing in former times. In summary, it has mixed quality agricultural land, with Grade 3 predominating.[38] Rainfall is between 24½ and 26½ inches per annum.

Drainage

It is no coincidence that the Anker Valley is so close to the watershed of England. The Nuneaton–Hartshill-Atherstone Ridge influences the drainage direction of the River Anker, which in turn influences the communication routes.

However, the Anker drainage system did not carve the present day topography. That was achieved by a much greater river, known as the Proto-Soar/Bytham River. On some occasions it flowed to the North Sea; at other times part of the Proto-Soar went south to the Avon/Severn.[39] This 'palaeo' river system appeared several million years ago and its erosion and deposition activity was interrupted by several ice ages and impounded glacial lakes. Around 450,000 years ago, the remnants of several impounded glacial lakes, once known collectively as Lake Harrison, had modified the large valley by way of its thick lake-bottom sediments. The river that established on this fenland was the misfit (or superimposed) Anker:[40] a slow and meandering stream, often prone to severe flooding when rainfall exceeded one inch in 24 hours.

This was never ideal for water-mill turbines. By medieval times, the engineers of the day had dammed local streams for fish ponds and to augment millraces. Thus began the diversion and removal of the old established stream pattern.

With the advent of the 18th-century Coventry Canal construction, a Parliamentary Bill sought powers to use more than 80 per cent of all the local streams as feeders. The canal suffered leakage problems, owing to underlying geological faults and porous jointed sandstones.[41] A reservoir had to be built near Purley Chase to supply the local flight of locks. This was eventually decommissioned in the 1990s because of pollution problems and is now being quarried for its meagre greenstone reserves.

More and more streams have disappeared. With the rapid development of deep mining and quarrying, further groundwater controls have been initiated. Vast amounts of water were abstracted, purely to facilitate ever-deeper mineral extraction. Growing industrial need for water saw boreholes and wells being sunk en masse.[42] The lowering of this permanent water table has caused even more streams and springs to dry up.

The local streams often rise from springs associated with the sandstone aquifers. These can comprise remarkably pure water, hard or soft; for example, the Innage Brook springs from the pure Halesowen Sandstone Formation at Bentley Common/Monks Park Wood. Some of these streams run for miles on clean, sandy soils and rocks. In latter times, groundwater and streams became polluted with nitrates from agriculture and iron-sulphur rich 'minewaters'.[43] Today, the river quality is steadily improving, with local streams scoring 'Fair' to 'Good' on most measured parameters. The local area has lower than average atmospheric pollution levels for NOx, CO2, CO and S2.

Conclusion

To follow this chapter's review of the natural resources available to the town, subsequent chapters refer variously to their exploitation, delineating where relevant the extent to which Atherstone owes what it is to the land on which it stands.

2 A Little Light on the Dark Ages: Atherstone in Anglo-Saxon Times

Terry R. Slater

A Little Light

There is very little historical or archaeological evidence to shed light onto the 600 years between the end of Roman Britain and Domesday Book in 1086. It seems likely that Atherstone was part of the territory of Roman Manduessedum (Mancetter) and that it continued to form part of that territory throughout the Anglo-Saxon period. The evidence for this is that Atherstone, Oldbury and Hartshill were all part of the parish of St Peter, Mancetter, into the later medieval period and beyond. It seems likely from analogies with other small Roman towns, where there is more evidence, that the Roman Manduessedum territory was much larger, extending into what is now Leicestershire, to include at least the parish of Witherley (which embraced Fenny Drayton and Ratcliffe Culey) (*see* Fig. 2), and possibly other parishes as well.

If we were to model the development of such a place in the Anglo-Saxon period, then we might expect a large minster parish to be formed in the seventh or eighth century, based on the territory of the former Roman settlement. This minster parish would contain many subsidiary settlements, and its church would be expected to have one of a limited number of early dedications. The division of Manduessedum's territory by the Danelaw boundary in the ninth century (*see* below, p.14) means that it is much more difficult to prove that this happened at Mancetter. On the one hand, the parish contains other settlements, its church has an 'early' dedication saint – so it may therefore have some call to be considered as a possible minster church. On the other hand, in this part of the Midlands, minster parishes were generally much larger (Aston-juxta-Birmingham, Coleshill and Polesworth are nearby examples). So the case must be judged unproven.[1]

The name of Atherstone derives from a personal name, Aethelred, and means simply 'Aethelred's farm'. We can imagine an Anglo-Saxon landholder with a farming estate on the west side of the Anker valley, not too far from the parish church in Mancetter, giving his name to a small settlement gathered around his farmhouse.[2] Indeed, we may even know precisely who this Aethelred was, though it is always dangerous to attach historically-attested individuals to specific place-names without firm evidence. In 1066, Atherstone was held by Countess Godgifu (Godiva), widow of Earl Leofric of Mercia: in other words it was a Mercian royal estate. Atherstone may well, therefore, have taken its name from the Aethelred who was ealdorman (earl) of Mercia in the early 10th century (whom we will discuss further, below). This suggests another reason for the estate having had an early church, since royal favour enabled the Church to acquire both sites and endowments to support buildings and clergy.[3] It is also no surprise that this estate was in royal hands. The defensive enclosures of both the Roman settlement and the iron age hill-fort at Oldbury provided the means to control the point at which Watling Street crossed the River Anker. This strategic importance is emphasised further by the dramatic ridge marking the eastern edge of the East Warwickshire plateau. Royal control of such a significant location must have been regarded as a necessity.

FROM MERCIA TO WARWICKSHIRE

The next question we need to ask is why Mancetter's territory eventually became smaller than it had originally been. To answer this, we need to raise our sights from the local to the national scene. In the ninth and tenth centuries, Mancetter (and therefore Atherstone), was part of the kingdom of Mercia, which dominated the midlands of England. Indeed, the estate was close to the administrative heart of the kingdom, since the royal court at Tamworth was only a few miles away, and its cathedral church only a few more miles westwards, at Lichfield.[4] However, in the ninth century, Mercia was under attack from Viking raiders from East Anglia and the eastern parts of the kingdom were ceded to the Danelaw by an agreement of A.D. 874.[5]

This was formalised in a treaty between Alfred the Great, king of Wessex, and the Danish leader Guthrum in A.D. 886. The Danes granted the western half of the Mercian kingdom back to Coelwulf – a member of the Mercian court who became king of Anglo-Saxon Mercia – but the eastern half was divided among those Danish leaders who wished to settle there. Thereafter, these eastern parts used Danish law and many farming folk came to settle there from Scandinavia.[6] The boundary between these two parts of Mercia was set along the Roman road of Watling Street, and it was possibly at this time that Mancetter lost that part of its former estate which lay to the east of the Anker. What is also notable is that it is at Mancetter that the new political boundary between Anglo-Saxon and Danish Mercia left Watling Street and followed the River Anker around Atherstone (*see* Fig. 2).

We can only imagine that Coelwulf wanted to ensure that his estate at Mancetter-Atherstone remained within his own jurisdiction, especially given its strategic significance. That significance was, of course, considerably enhanced now that Atherstone lay on the boundary of the kingdom rather than at its heart. Life on a politico-military boundary is never easy, and place-names such as Griff, Copston, Monks Kirby and Thurlaston suggest that a number of Danish lords acquired estates just over the new border, in east Warwickshire.[7] However, this seems not to have happened in the immediate vicinity of Atherstone.

The two Anglo-Saxon kingdoms of western Mercia and Wessex operated as a single unit over the next 50 years, countering the threat of further Danish military incursions. King Alfred's eldest daughter, Aethelflaed of Wessex, was

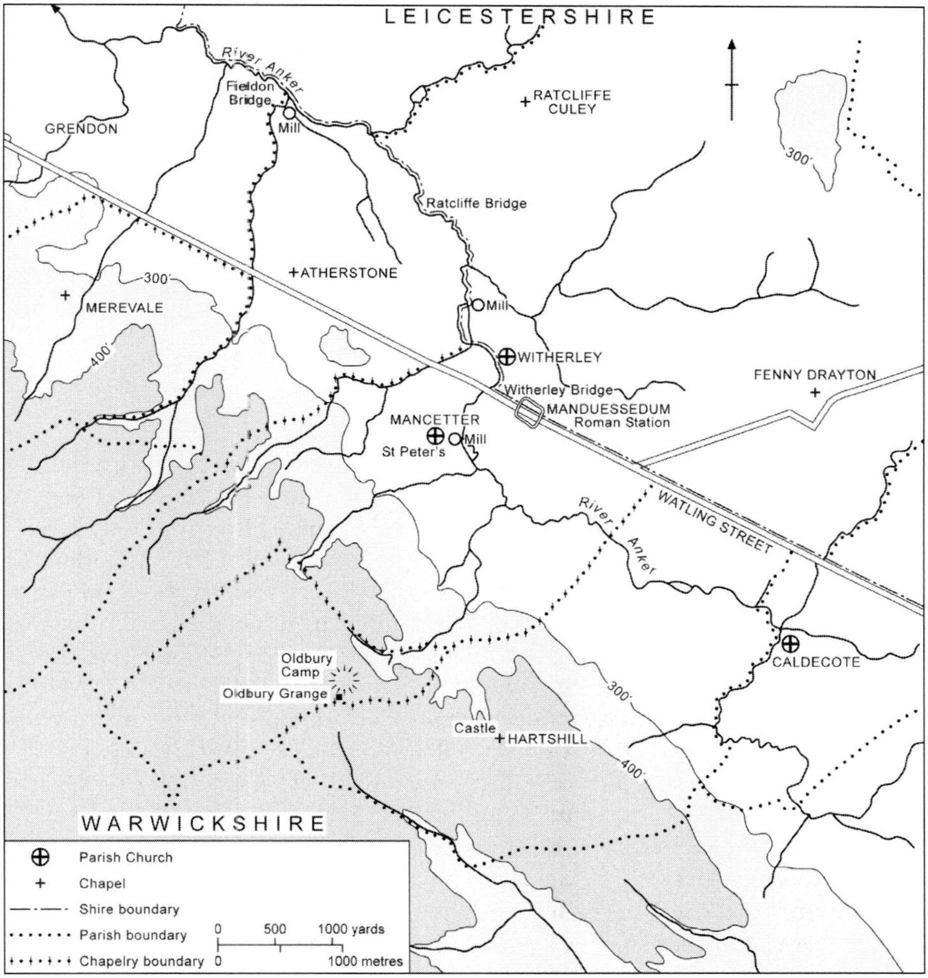

2 *The Anglo-Saxon landscape and parish boundaries of Mancetter district.*

married to ealdorman Aethelred, Coelwulf's successor as leader of Mercia. This helped to cement the alliance. On Aethelred's death in A.D. 911, Aethelflaed, 'Lady of the Mercians', ruled the country for the next eight years, while her brother, Edward the Elder, had succeeded Alfred in Wessex.[8] Together they began the military consolidation of their kingdom through the building of urban fortresses, *burhs*, where all the inhabitants of the locality could trade, where coins were minted, where justice was dispensed, and where those same inhabitants were duty bound to defend their burh in time of military necessity. One of those new fortresses was established at Tamworth in A.D. 913, and here archaeological excavations have shown us exactly what the new timber-laced earthwork defences were like.[9] It seems probable that the men of Mancetter and Atherstone would have come within the ambit of the Tamworth burh and, therefore, have been responsible for helping with its construction and its defence. By A.D. 921 the whole of England, south of the Humber, was back in English hands.

In the early 11th century, the midlands of England were divided into new shires for administrative purposes, probably by Eadric Streona, ealdorman of Mercia between 1007 and 1017.[10] What is perhaps surprising is that the boundary specified in the A.D. 874 agreement between the Danes and the Mercians was used to define the eastern boundary of the new shire of Warwick, which thus followed Watling Street all the way from Clifton-on-Dunsmore, via High Cross, to Mancetter. The new shires effectively (and, some historians think, deliberately) downgraded the status of Tamworth which was left without a supporting shire territory in 1007-17, even though it had been constructed as a burh in A.D. 913. Indeed, the shire boundary ran through the centre of the town, putting half in Warwickshire and half in Staffordshire. For administrative, juridical and military services, Atherstone now had to look much further away, to the new shire town of Warwick. It was now on the edge of civic and political affairs, rather than close to the court at Tamworth, while it had lost its former strategic importance on Mercia's boundary.

Domesday Book

Domesday Book records that Atherstone was one of the estates of Countess Godgifu; she had died sometime between 1066 and 1086, but her estates had not yet been granted by the king to anyone else. Later, they were granted to the Earl of Chester.[11] Hartshill and Atherstone together made a five-hide holding. Mancetter, though it was the parish centre, is not recorded separately. We must therefore assume that it was probably omitted altogether, or, possibly, that it was subsumed within the entries for Atherstone and Hartshill and that the whole estate was held by Godgifu. However, since Mancetter did not follow the same manorial descent as Atherstone and Hartshill after Domesday, this seems much less likely.

There was land for five ploughs in Atherstone and for seven ploughs in Hartshill, but only four were in use in Atherstone and five in Hartshill; in other words, land suitable for arable cultivation was not yet being worked. Each estate had six acres of valuable watered meadowland alongside the Anker, and Atherstone had woodland which was measured at two leagues long by two leagues wide; this must have been located on the hill slopes to the south-west of the settlement. In Hartshill, all the 13 households were of villein status, holding their land through labour services for their lord, while in Atherstone there were 11 villein households, two bordar households (smallholders who often brought new land into cultivation), and a slave. In total, perhaps some 130 people lived on the estate in the various settlements at Atherstone, Mancetter, Hartshill, Ansley and Oldbury (assuming that each household comprised five people), though some of these places were probably no more than single farmhouses. The estate was increasing in value for its owner and seemingly, therefore, had been untroubled by the Norman takeover. Atherstone had increased in worth from £2 to £3, and Hartshill from £4 to £5 in the 20 years between 1066 and 1086. Given the later evidence of a full three-field open-field cultivation system in operation in Atherstone, the likelihood is that this had already been organised before the Domesday Survey. Most scholars today suggest that such reorganisation was well under way in the 10th century, if not before.[12]

3 In the Hands of an Alien Priory: Creating a Medieval Town

Terry R. Slater

Introduction

This chapter begins by narrating the development of Atherstone from Norman times to 1289, at which date large-scale replanning of the settlement effectively established the town-centre street plan as we see it today. A detailed scrutiny of the town plan follows, based on analyses of the 1716 estate plan, the 1786 burgage map (*see* Fig. 7, which derives ultimately from the same sources that underlie the 1547 Survey; *see* Appendix to this chapter), and metrological analysis. It concludes by summarising its development, as indicated by the foregoing evidence.

In the Hands of an Alien Priory

When the lands of Atherstone and Hartshill were granted to the Norman Earls of Chester in 1086, soon after compilation of Domesday Book, the estate passed from one great lordship to another. (*See also* Chapter Four.) Typically for such large estates, the earls of Chester farmed the individual sub-manors to lesser lords. Atherstone, however, was granted by Earl Hugh to the Benedictine abbey of Bec in Normandy soon after he acquired it, a gift that was confirmed by both King Henry II and Henry III.[1] Bec administered its English lands from the Priory of Ogbourne St George in Wiltshire, so that technically Atherstone became a dependent cell of this relatively distant priory.

Atherstone exchanged being part of a great secular lordship for being part of a great ecclesiastical one. Consequently, for the first time, the settlement got its own church. The monastic cell, or grange, would have had its own chapel where the monks could celebrate the daily offices. To begin with, this would not have been available for use by the secular residents of Atherstone, who would still have used St Peter's at Mancetter. However, *c.*1125 the rector of Mancetter made an agreement with the monks to celebrate mass for the people of Atherstone in the chapel three times a week, on Sundays, Wednesdays and Fridays. Residents also gained permission for baptism and burial to take place in the Atherstone chapel.[2]

The monks would have been responsible for administering the open-field system; for collecting the tithes from those who farmed the fields and sending the produce on to market, or to Ogbourne St George; for enforcing the law; and for collecting the rents in cash, or kind, or as labour services from the tenants of the manor. Monasteries were never the most popular of lords, since the literacy of the monks meant that their estates were usually administered efficiently and effectively. However, alien priories were even less popular and this was especially so when England was at war with France. It was for this reason that the abbey of Bec made sure its possessions were confirmed by successive English kings.

An Agricultural Landscape

Atherstone was unusual for a north Warwickshire township in having a full three-field system.[3] Early 18th-century maps make it clear that two of the fields ran across Watling Street, though the southernmost furlongs may have been later enclosures from the pastures and Outwoods which lay on the slopes on the southern boundary of the township. In the 18th century, these fields were known as Windmill, Middle and Aldermill Fields.[4]

The 1716 estate map enables the full pattern of furlongs and arable strips to be reconstructed (*see* Fig. 3),[5] together with the trackways that gave access to them and the meadows which provided hay for the livestock and which stretched along the banks of the River Anker. A great cow pasture occupied land to the south, with the Outwoods beyond. The Anker and the little streams that formed the eastern and western boundaries of the township provided sites for mills. To the east was the mill of Witherley, over the county boundary in Leicestershire. Atherstone's mill was close to Fieldon Bridge in the northern extremity of the township, hence Aldermill (old mill) Field. By the early 18th century there were two windmills, one close to Aldermill and the other at the southern end of the town, but there are no early references to these windmills, so we are unsure just how old they are. Nationally, the earliest windmills date from the 12th century and are documented in East Anglia, but by 1200 there was one at Wigston Parva, not too far from Atherstone.[6]

Common field systems were usually accompanied by nucleated villages, not by scattered farmsteads. The little village of Atherstone appears to have stood just to the north of Watling Street where the market square is today. The present parish church marks the site of the priory, the domestic buildings of which were probably on the chapel's north side. The later Market Place might have been a small village green with farmhouses around it. One or two properties might already have faced on to Watling Street. Such a location was extremely unusual in midland England, and even on today's Ordnance Survey map Atherstone is still the only settlement in Warwickshire/Leicestershire that bestrides the Roman road (*see also* below, p.21). Anglo-Saxon settlements tended to avoid Roman roads, as they were considered rather dangerous places for farming, since armies continued to use them for rapid movement across the country.[7] This was certainly so for Watling Street, which had been an important political boundary between the Danelaw and Anglo-Saxon England for several hundred years (*see* Chapter Two). Normally, it was only in the 12th and 13th centuries that more peaceful conditions and the need for transport of trade goods encouraged traders and craftsmen to settle beside these roads. At Atherstone, it may have been the organisation of the open-field system in the 10th or 11th century that led to the building of a group of farmsteads just to the north of the road, but since we have no archaeological dating evidence, we really do not know.

3 *The central part of the 1716 open-field estate map of Atherstone parish redrawn.* (See *Fig. 8)*

THE MARKET AND FAIR

It was precisely the socio-economic changes of the 12th and 13th centuries that were no doubt instrumental in encouraging the abbey of Bec to seek market and fair charters from Henry III in October 1246.[8] The market was to be held on Tuesdays and the fair on the three days around the feast of the Nativity of the Blessed Virgin Mary (7-9 September), suggesting that this was the dedication of the parish chapel, fairs normally being established on the patronal festival.[9] The 1716 estate map shows a furlong north-east of the church called Horse Fair Butts (*see* Fig. 3), which suggests the probable location of the fair (discussed below, p.23). The Tuesday market was in competition with another at Nuneaton, only six miles away, while the market at Atherstone was the last to be chartered in the area (though that at Polesworth had been granted only four years previously, in 1242).[10] Such matters were often important in determining the success of a new market. However, the north Warwickshire economy was flourishing and there was clearly room for a new town in this corner of the shire, since it was Polesworth, not Atherstone, that failed to develop urban characteristics.

One way in which Atherstone differed from Polesworth seems to have been that the Prior of Ogbourne St George granted new tenements with burgage tenure around the Market Place and along Watling Street. At least thirteen and a half burgages were recorded soon after the market was granted, but the major laying out of the street-town with which we are familiar today seems to date from 1289, when the Prior carried out a large scale replanning of the settlement.[11] First, 18 tenants with plots already established along Watling Street were granted their land in burgage tenure; secondly, seven other tenants with land around the Market Place and on Watling Street gave up their land and it was reorganised to make 12 new burgages; thirdly, in the next five years a further six burgages must have been laid out, since 36 free tenants were recorded in the manor in 1294.[12] Despite the language of the surveys and charters, it is clear from later sources and the transfers in the court rolls (starting in 1334) that these 'free' tenants were, in reality, copyholders.[13] (*See* Appendix to this chapter, p.31.)

In most 13th-century new towns of this kind the well-established custom was that the normal burgage rent was 12d. per year. However, the priory rental in 1294 records revenue of £6 0s. 9d. from the free tenants of Atherstone, rather than the £1 16s. 0d. that 36 times 12d. would have produced. It seems likely that the free tenants not only had their burgage tenements but also held agricultural land for which additional rent was paid, as is recorded in 1547. Later documents certainly refer to the inhabitants of Atherstone making their living from agriculture.[14]

No doubt the restriction to copyhold tenure for the burgages was one of the ways in which the Prior of Ogbourne St George hoped to keep reasonably close control over the inhabitants of the little town. An extent of the manor in 1379 shows that the rent was exactly the same as a century earlier, suggesting that the rents agreed upon when the borough was founded were fixed and levied on a defined group of properties. The same arrangement is known to have applied in Henley-in-Arden, another Warwickshire new town.[15]

Later documents, however, demonstrate that the original burgages were being sub-divided. The survey of 1547 (*see* Appendix to this chapter), shows that the majority of people holding land along Long Street and around the Market Place held fractions of a burgage (a quarter, a half or three-quarters, or, in one case, only one eighth), and also in multiples (one and a half, or two burgages).[16] The estate map of 1786 uses the same proportions (*see* Fig. 7).[17] What is interesting here is that neither the 1547 rents, nor the area or frontages of the holdings shown on the 1786 map, are proportional to some notional 'standard' burgage. The rents for half a burgage vary from 6d. (what one would expect), to several shillings, whilst the average is some 3s. for a full burgage, but with very substantial variations. Since these are rents to the lord (in 1547 it was the Marquis of Dorset, Thomas Grey), it suggests that as each burgage was divided at some time in the later Middle Ages, one or more of the successive lords of Atherstone took the opportunity to increase the burgage rent on such properties. The 1547 survey indicates a total of some 70 full burgages, nearly double the 36 recorded in 1289. While the priory rental might suggest that the burgages were fixed in number, the 1547 survey indicates either that the town had been doubled in size sometime between 1400 and 1550, or that it was twice as big when founded in the 13th century as the priory documents suggest.

Guild and Friary

It is perhaps no surprise to find that the abbey at Merevale took an increasing interest in the developing town on its doorstep and began to build up its land holdings in the district. In 1343, the abbey at Bec obtained permission to sell its Atherstone estate to Merevale. It is clear, however, that this sale was not completed, since Atherstone was still a possession of Bec in 1369, when property belonging to the alien (foreign) priories was seized by the king on the resumption of war with France.[18]

Nonetheless, it was the abbot of Merevale who founded both a guild of the Holy Trinity and a chantry in Mancetter church, to which the tradesmen and merchants of Atherstone belonged. The guild owned rents worth £10 10s. at the Dissolution, including 10 full burgages (15 properties) in Atherstone, while the chantry owned another four burgages.[19] It was the abbot of Merevale, too, who obtained a grant of pontage in 1332 for the repair of Fieldon bridge which allowed goods being taken over the bridge to be taxed for three years.[20] (*See also* p.41)

The 1369 confiscation of the possessions of the alien priories saw the cell at Atherstone granted to Ralph Basset, lord of nearby Drayton Basset. Soon thereafter, he founded an Augustinian friary in the town. The existing chapel was remodelled and a new nave added west of the tower for the townspeople, *c.*1385. Basset left 500 marks (£333 6s. 8d.) in his will for the completion of the church. The Dissolution (1538) led to further ecclesiastical disruption; the chancel of the church was given over to the town's grammar school, founded by Sir William Devereux in 1547, and the nave became the parochial chapel (*see* p.50).[21]

THE TOWN PLAN

Atherstone's town plan is absolutely ordinary, but at the same time very interesting! First, the town falls into the most common category of English medieval town plans – the single street plan. In such town plans, equal-sized burgages are laid out at right angles to a main road. In some towns there is a back lane that provides access to the rear of the properties. The market place is often simply a widening of the street in its middle portions – or it can be a rectangular space along the length of the street, or, less frequently, it can be at right angles to the street. The church (or more usually the chapel) is away from the main street, sometimes central to the plan, sometimes at one end of the street. Often the borough is differentiated from the rural township from which it was formed by a boundary tightly enclosing the burgages and thus running along the back lane, or the rear, of the properties. Bar gates often marked the start and finish of the borough, so that tolls could be collected on market days.[22] There are a number of other such street-towns in Warwickshire, most notably Henley-in-Arden and Coleshill. The focus on the main road was, of course, because it was the road which brought in the traders on market day and travellers daily, who needed food and drink, and sometimes accommodation overnight.

So, what is distinctive about Atherstone? First, it is the only town located on the midland section of the Watling Street. As we have seen (above, p.18), Roman roads were generally shunned by settlements altogether and very few midland towns are located on major Roman roads. (Brinklow and Moreton-in-Marsh on the Fosse Way, and Bidford on Ryknield Street, are all tiny places; only Stratford-upon-Avon is of any size and that is on a minor Roman road.) By contrast, in the south-east of England, quite a large number of street-towns were established as medieval new towns on the Roman roads which fanned out from London.[23] Secondly, the borough has no well-marked boundary. There is no doubt that burgage tenure was established at Atherstone but, unlike Henley and Stratford, those with the privilege were not contained within a defined area of the township differentiating freeholders from manorial tenants.[24] Thirdly, the documentary references (*see* Notes 11 and 12) to the replanning of the tenements in 1289 are exceptionally rare and provide us with new insights, demonstrating how the planning of some of these one-street towns was far from the simple act that it is easy to assume. Finally, few other examples of such street-towns have surviving 17th- or 18th-century maps which show how the towns nested into open-field farming layouts, and which allow us to ask questions about field strips and burgage layouts.

Analysis of town plans begins with discerning 'plan units', areas of the plan which are internally homogenous and which often correspond to developmental phases.[25] At Atherstone, the simpler part of the plan is that on the south-west side of Long Street. Here, the plan divides into two long plot series separated by Coleshill Street: plots to the south-east of Coleshill Street are longer than those to the north-west (*see* Fig. 4).

A broad back lane runs along the rear of both plot series (now Station Street and South Street). To the north west of Coleshill Street it forms a broad triangular space which, at the time of the first edition large-scale (1:500) Ordnance Survey plan (1887-8),[26] had a pond at its centre. The 1716 estate plan shows this lane to have been an original element of the town plan (*see* Fig. 3). However, it also shows that this back lane fails to link to Long Street at either end of the two plot series, as we might normally expect for such a plan feature. What we have with this lane is rather a part of the open-field system, and its purpose was originally to link the town to the great cow pasture field to the south-west of the town. It enabled occupants of burgages on the south-west side of the highway to get livestock into the rear of their

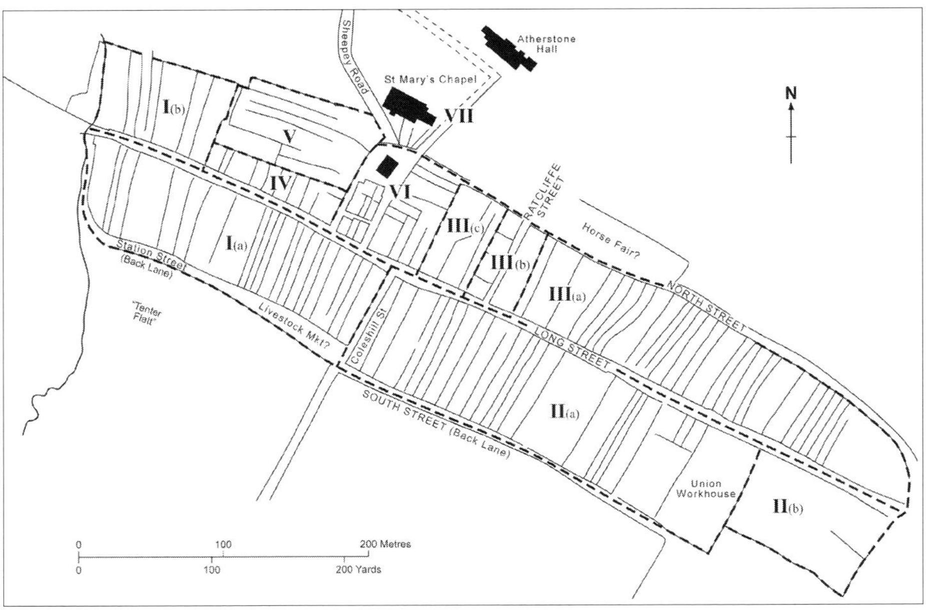

4 *The plan units of Atherstone based on the 1888 first edition 25-inch Ordnance Survey.*

plots, without having to take them along the main street. The pond provided drinking water and it may be that this triangular space was used as a livestock market on market days, so as to keep livestock out of the provisions market. Warwick and Stratford each had a separate space for livestock on market days, so there were local precedents from which Atherstone townspeople could learn. The other thing worth noting is that Coleshill Street is a narrow lane between two burgages; plots are not aligned along it and it fails to enter Long Street opposite the Market Place so as to make a rather grander cross-roads in the centre of the town. It is almost as though the contact with Coleshill has been deliberately down-graded because this was a nearby competitive market.

The part of Middle Field which backs on to these two plot series, beyond the back lane, has furlongs with strips which are aligned with the burgages, but there is little indication that the burgages have been derived from earlier field strip boundaries (*see* Fig. 3). These field strips are much broader than elsewhere. One notable component is the most northerly furlong, called 'Tenter Flatt', being the place where late medieval cloth-makers spread out their cloths to dry on tenter racks (*see* Chapter Six, p.126). Southwards are 'Tyle House Flatt', 'Tyle House Close' and 'Flatt on ye Clay Pitts', providing the location for another of Atherstone's 16th- and 17th-century industries (developing as houses were converted from thatch roofs to tiled roofs in the interests of fire prevention [*see* Chapter Six, p.127]).[27] Finally, we need to note the three larger blocks of land at the southern end of the plot series, where a large mansion, its garden and the town windmill were located (*see* Fig. 4, Units II[a] and [b]).

A third major plan unit consists of those plots on the north-east side of Long Street and south of what was to become Ratcliffe Street and which, like the plots on the other side of Long Street, had a distinctive back lane, North Street on the 1888 Ordnance Survey plan. However, comparison with the 1716 plan demonstrates that this is a tidying-up. In 1716 there were three blocks of plots, and North Street can be seen to be part of the access system to the fields on this side of the town (*see* Fig. 3). It terminated where a small stream ran between the plots, which then formed the boundary between Middle and Windmill Fields. The stream also caused the distinctive curved boundaries in the middle of this plot series. Only a narrow footway continued the alignment of North Street to the manor house behind the church. The third block of plots (Unit III[c] on Fig. 4) did not terminate on this lane or footway at all, since, in 1716, a large close with a fenced enclosure stood at its end. It may be that this enclosure was the site of the horse fair named in 'Horse Fair Butts' on the other side of the footway – the broad grassy access way which was the predecessor of North Street would certainly have allowed easy access to this large enclosure from Watling Street.[28] Within the burgage layout, it meant that the plots that backed on to this enclosure were rather shorter than others and had no rear access other than across this close. The whole area was reorganised in 1765, when the open fields were enclosed and the burgages extended backwards over the close; in 1797, a regular street – North Street – was laid out,[29] and Ratcliffe Street was later widened. A simple plan unit thus proves to have had a complex developmental history. We might also note that the broad green-way, which was the predecessor to North Street, may well have been the link between the pre-urban village, Watling Street and Mancetter church, given that 'Town Flatt'

5 *The Market Place plot pattern based on the Ordnance Survey 1:500 map, 1888.*

of Windmill Hill Field aligns at right angles to it, producing a broad triangular green at the junction (*see* Fig. 3).

The area of the plan which encompasses plots on the north-east side of Long Street, from the north-west end of the town as far as the Market Place, also divides neatly into three plot series. The westernmost are similar to the other plot series thus far considered, in terms of length and breadth. They seemingly have no relationship with the Aldermill Field furlong to the rear, since its strips are oriented south-east/north-west, while the burgages run north-east/south-west. Secondly, the plots (Unit IV on Fig. 4) fronting Long Street between Unit I[b] and the Market Place are short (only one third the length of those in Units I[a] and [b]) and they back on to a common boundary. This boundary is part of a block of four or five plots at right angles to Long Street and fronting onto the north-west side of the Market Place (Unit V on Fig. 4). These plots are the longest in the town and are oriented with the furlong strips of Aldermill Field to the north. Their rear boundary is marked by a track which crosses Aldermill Field to Fieldon Bridge (*see* the account of the *Angel*, in Chapter Five), but by 1716, the track joined the road behind the churchyard (*see* Fig. 3). The implication of the layout of these three plot series is that the short plots facing Long Street have been taken from one or more long plots originally facing the Market Place and that the north-western plot series (Unit I[b] on Fig. 4) was laid out subsequently. In other words, a clear chronological sequence is embedded in this plan division, though, whether the chronology covers a few years or many decades unfortunately is not clear. It is in this part of the plan where we can see evidence of the reorganisation of plots as recorded in the priory documents.

Finally, there is the Market Place and the block of plots between the Market Place and Ratcliffe Street (*see* Fig. 5 and Units VI and III[c] on Fig. 4). The first thing we must note here is the similarity of plan between the market places of Atherstone and Coleshill. Both open on the north-east side of the main street; both link the main street and the town church. It must be a strong possibility that Coleshill provided the model for Atherstone, when the prior decided to develop a town at the latter. The Ordnance Survey map shows three blocks of property in the market space (*see* Fig. 5). The northernmost is the market hall: town property on town communal space, which is extremely common in small boroughs from the 16th century onwards. The southern portion, separating Church Street and Market Street, and itself divided by Derby Lane, is made up of what are called market place accretions: blocks of building that have infilled the Market Place at some later stage, usually in the later middle ages. Most of this infilling was deliberate, by the lord of the manor, in order to increase his rent roll, and such buildings were often preceded by blocks of temporary market stalls. The lord could levy a rent on these too (normally 4d.), but permanent buildings commanded a higher rent. We should also notice that the Market Place is not geometrically regular, but that its sides curve gently.

Sheepy Road, which enters the northern corner of the Market Place, dates from the reorganisation of roads at the enclosure of the fields in 1765 (*see* Fig. 4). Its realignment provided more privacy for Atherstone Hall by replacing the road that ran on the north side of the church. The block of plots on the south-east side of the Market Place is carefully arranged in an interlocking herringbone pattern, so that the plots facing the market square and Long Street are of more or less equal status (*see* Fig. 5). Such plot patterns are common at important road junctions in many towns, and are always an indication of careful planning. This was usually carried out by an individual, who purchased two or three plots on the corner (here, probably originally facing Long Street) and then subdivided them in this herringbone pattern to gain maximum rental from roughly equal-sized properties, here facing onto Market Street and Long Street.[30] The alternative 'unplanned' way of organising corner plots is well shown on the corner of Church Street opposite (*see* Fig. 5). Here, as more and more properties were sub-divided, a narrow common lane was created, running back at 45 degrees to provide access to the rear of the properties, with entrance via a covered passage. Despite considerable reorganisation, the remaining plots between Market Street and Ratcliffe Street can be seen to be a continuation of the plot series further southwards. However, one of these plots has 'captured' the rear half of the neighbouring plot so as to develop a large Victorian garden, while the plots nearest to Ratcliffe Street have been sub-divided transversely, so that new houses could be built facing on to Ratcliffe Street after it had been widened in 1765. All of these property development processes can be 'read' from the large-scale Ordnance Survey plan.

Metrological Analysis

Descriptions of two-dimensional town plans, such as that given above, can seem rather arid and difficult to follow. However, they are essential if the complexity of a plan is to be properly appreciated. The purpose of studying the subtleties of the town plan is to discover whether the few documentary references we have can be recognised in the plan interpretation, and whether a coherent story can be told about the evolution of Atherstone as a planned medieval town.

Before doing that, however, one more technique can be applied, that of metrological analysis – measuring the modern plot frontages and relating those measurements to the historical plot pattern provides another strand of evidence. It has proved especially useful where medieval charters give the dimensions of the burgages when they were first laid out, as is the case in Stratford-upon-Avon. These dimensions can be in perches (one perch equals 16½ statute feet), as they were in Stratford where dimensions of 3½ x 12 perches were stipulated; or they can be in feet as, for example, in Beaumaris (Anglesey) where Edward I specified plots 60 by 80ft; or they might be in acres, as in Thame (Oxfordshire), where one-acre plots were specified.[31]

Metrological analysis is usually most successfully applied to smaller historic towns where modern redevelopment has been limited, but this is unfortunately not the position in Atherstone. The 19th-century infilling of the long medieval plots with back-to-back housing, consequent to the industrial development of the hatting industry in the town, meant that housing conditions were as poor as in inner Birmingham or Coventry (*see* Chapter Nine). As a result, almost all of these yards were swept away in the 1950s slum clearances, often including the shops and inns at the front of the plots. Consequently, for significant blocks of property along Long Street, both buildings and plot pattern are wholly a product of the later 20th century. Nonetheless, some sequences of older properties and plots survive, and so all the building frontages in the town centre were carefully measured (*see* Chapter Five).[32]

The block of properties south-east of Coleshill Street (the earlier Hall Lane) is one of the best preserved in the town, but the measurements demonstrate that it is impossible to discover an underlying pattern of perch-based measurement. They also confirm what is clear from the map alone, namely, that neither the width nor area of the plots are proportional to the burgage proportions stated on the 1786 burgage map (as earlier described in the 1547 rental). Thus, the first two plots moving south-eastwards from Coleshill Street are given as three-quarters of a burgage and a quarter burgage on the map; they have widths of 35ft 10ins and 23ft 7ins respectively (*see* Fig. 6). If these plots were proportional to their burgage size, the larger should be 70ft 9ins wide! A little further on are two plots, both regarded as half a burgage, but one is 75 feet wide and the second 33 feet wide. All these plots are exactly the same length, some 21 perches, or 346ft 6ins. One or two plots do suggest an underlying statute perch based measurement – such as the half burgage that is 33 feet wide (two perches) (*see* Fig. 6) – but that is a rarity and is not sufficient to confirm that the whole pattern of plots was laid out in this way.

A second well-preserved set of buildings and plots are those on the other side of Long Street in the vicinity of the Market Place. The corner block on the Church Street side, to which we have already made reference (p.25 above), is 121 feet deep to the common rear boundary; that is only two feet short of 7½ statute perches, whilst the first four properties along Long Street together measure two feet more than six perches. The block of properties between Church Street and Market Street are together two feet longer than 5½ perches. On the corner beyond Market Street, the first three properties are a little over 4½ perches wide

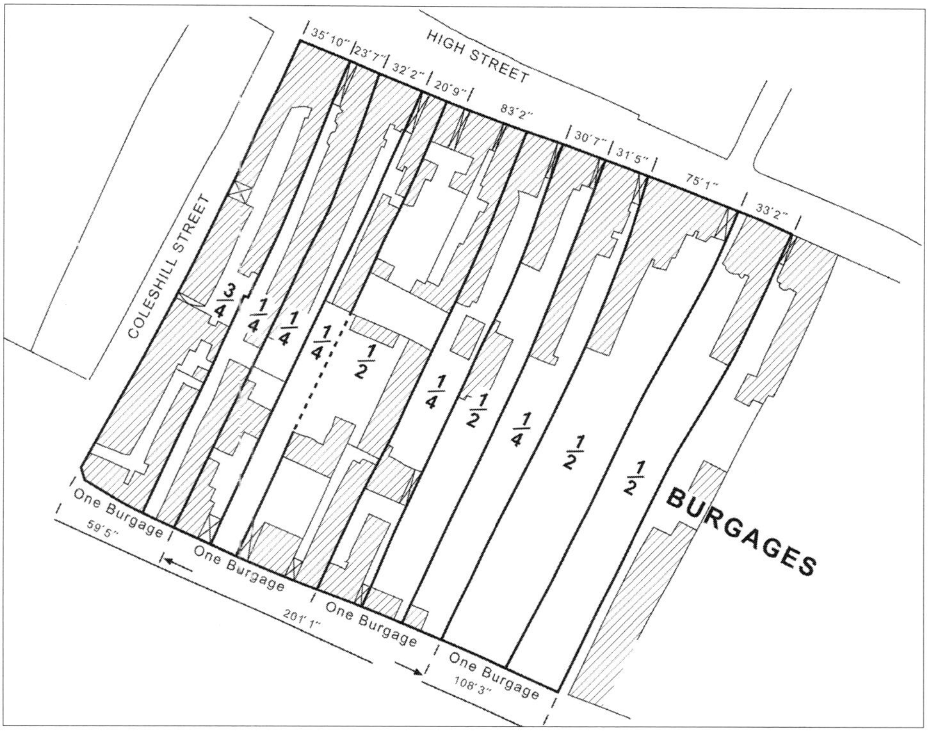

6 *Plot metrology and burgages south of Long Street, based on the Ordnance Survey 1:500 map, 1888.*

and the next four properties some two feet more than 6½ perches. The whole block is some two feet more than 17 perches deep (*see* Fig. 5). All this metrology hints at an underlying perch-based framework for the burgages when first laid out, but it is insufficient to suggest what that framework was. The irregularities are too great and the margins of error in excess of what has been found in other towns, where such a framework can be discerned more clearly.

Another hypothesis is that the town's burgages were derived from field strips (though the pattern of 18th-century strips offers little support for such an idea). That might result in the width of plots being proportional to some base number other than 16½, because we know that agricultural perches in the 13th century and earlier varied quite considerably.[33] Again, however, the surviving metrology offers little support for this idea, though it is not easy to compare base measures of this type.

Developing the Medieval New Town: A Summary

A conclusion might hope to tell a coherent story of the founding and laying out of the little medieval new town of Atherstone, so that is what I shall attempt. However, the reader should be warned that this is a story filled with 'perhaps' and 'may be'. More work on the documents and archaeological excavations might remove some of the uncertainties, or completely overturn this story. Until then, it is the best we can do.

Atherstone began as a small farming community in the parish of Mancetter. It may have had anything from two, to eight or nine farms gathered together on the northern side of the Roman Watling Street. By the 10th or 11th century the farmland had been reorganised into an open-field system, with meadows alongside the River Anker, arable field land stretching up to Watling Street and beyond, then a band of pasture-land with woods on the hilltop above. When the abbey of Bec became lord of the manor, a cell of monks came to live at Atherstone; they built themselves a chapel, almost certainly where the town's church still stands and, by 1125, the villagers began to use it as their church, too. They could use it for baptism, and had a cemetery there. There may have been a 'green' on the south side of the chapel, while the monks had their domestic buildings on the north side.

By 1246, the abbey was aware that the north Warwickshire economy was flourishing and that they could increase their financial return from the manor by running a weekly market, holding a yearly fair, and trying to establish a town where people could make their living from industry, trade and service occupations. The circumstance that made them confident of success was the great road that passed close to their village, though they would have been aware that much of the long-distance traffic from London to the Welsh border went via Coventry and Coleshill at this time, not along Watling Street. The village green became the Market Place and new urban plots were laid out, held by burgage tenure, some in among the farm plots, and some newly-established on the other side of Watling Street. The abbot's surveyor seems to have known of the plan of nearby Coleshill and used this as his model. It is likely that some of the field land would have been taken to make the new burgages, but there may well have been a broad linear common along Watling Street, which would have been easier to commandeer.

In 1289, it was obvious that the town was flourishing, so the abbey's representative decided to reorganise the properties to make the place more urban, especially in the vicinity of the Market Place, where higher rents could be charged. This may be when the area to the north-west of the Market Place was laid out, where a whole block of short properties now line Long Street, backing on to enormously long, rural-looking properties behind. More new burgages on Long Street were also developed, possibly at the south-eastern end of the town. The town was paved and one or more new blocks of burgages may have been established, but it is unlikely that any were added after the mid-14th century, when the Black Death would have ravaged the population. Until the middle of the 18th century, Atherstone people continued to farm the open fields that surrounded the town, where the pattern of furlongs and strips are unlikely to have changed very much from the later medieval period. The Parliamentary enclosure of the open fields in 1765 changed the town dramatically. New roads were laid out around the church (*see* the account of Swan House, in Chapter Five); North Street, Ratcliffe Street and South Street became proper roads in the town. At the same time, an economic revolution was under way as the hatting industry developed (*see* Chapter Eight) – new workers needed houses and the back gardens of the medieval burgages began to fill with rows of cheaply-built cottages (*see* Chapter Nine).

Chapter 3 Appendix: The Burgages of Atherstone from 1547-1926

Nat Alcock and Judy Vero

The 1547 Survey

On 11 and 12 May 1547, the estate surveyors of the Marquis of Dorset undertook a survey of the manor of Atherstone.[1] Although frustrating in some respects, this survey gives the clearest view we have of the town at the moment of the Dissolution of the monasteries; the manor itself had just passed from Mount Grace Priory to the Marquis of Dorset, but the Guild and Chantry of Mancetter still retained their property.

The survey starts by describing the character of the town (*see* Chapter Six), then lists the demesne fields that were held by lease, followed by those that were held at will. Then comes the main series of entries, for each of the customary tenants, with the chief rents they paid for each burgage. Thus, for example:

> Mr Altofte holdeth 2 burg[ages] and an halfe. That is to say first one burg[age] and a quarter lying between a quarter of a burg[age] of John Powers on the one parte, and a burg[age] of the Gilde on the other parte and paith therfore 3s. Also one burg and a quarter being devyded into 2 howses lying between iij quarters of a burg[age] of John Draiton on the one parte and a ½ burg[age] of the Chauntery on the other parte & paith therfore 4s. 5d.[2]

The list of the 65 named tenants is organised according to the total size of their holding, from the Guild with 10 burgages in all (divided into 15 properties), down to Thomas Woode and 13 other tenants each with just one quarter burgage. As seen in the above example, the survey gives the size, the abuttals (the adjoining properties on each side), and the chief rent paid for each property, sometimes with notes, such as its being divided into more than one house. The town also included a number of freehold burgages alluded to in the survey but not themselves described (*see* below).[3]

Reconstructing the Survey

Although the survey is arranged in order of total holding size, the way the abuttals are named is highly consistent from one tenant's property to another.

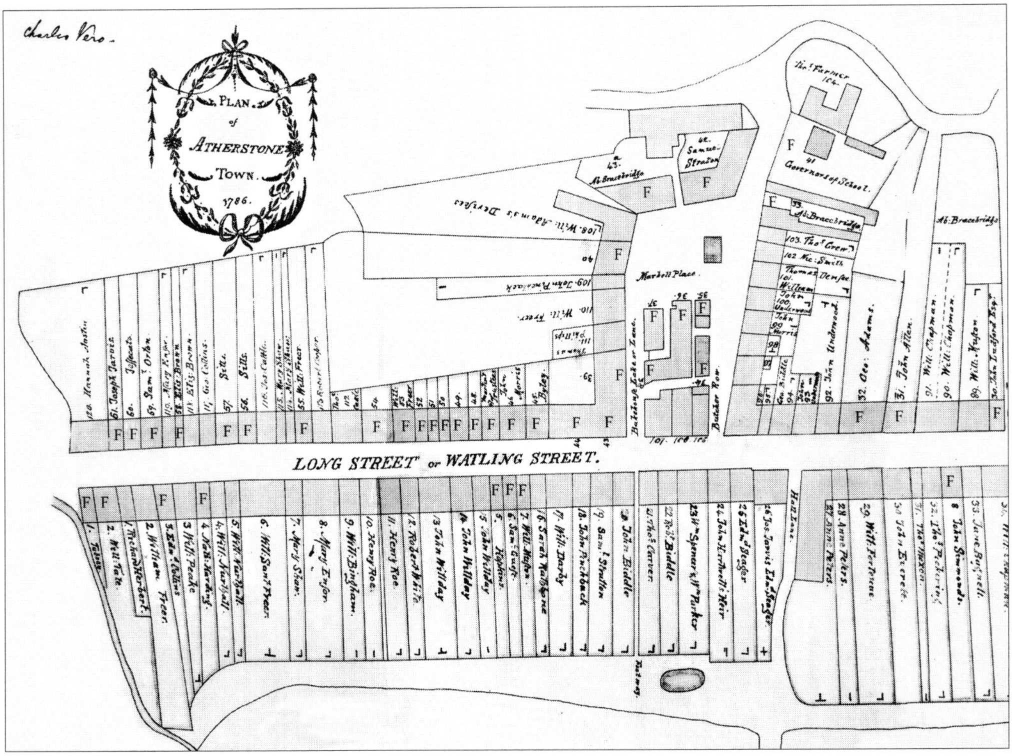

7 *The 1786 Plan of Atherstone. Although somewhat schematic, this map shows all the properties in Atherstone, naming each owner, and indicating whether it is freehold (F) or copyhold. The symbols indicate the size of each copyhold, from '|' for ¼ burgages to '+' for full burgages.*

Thus, it was almost certainly compiled from a list originally drawn up in street order. To a large extent, this order can be reconstructed, by chaining the properties together in the order in which the abuttals are listed. The result of this reconstruction is the grouping of the identified properties into 12 sequences (interrupted by freeholdings). The longest sequences cover 43 and 40 properties; the first can be tentatively located on the south side of Long Street, while the second starts on the east side of the Market Place, with the 'Kidd Gap' (which can be located north of C104 on the 1786 Plan (*see* Fig. 7: Thomas Farmer, the northernmost property on the east side of the Market Place). Its 15th tenement is the 'King's Croft', which is identifiable with F27 on the 1786 Plan.

Fractional Burgages

One of the most notable features of the 1547 survey is its listing of fractions of burgages. It might seem obvious that these had arisen through the subdivision of full burgages. Reconstruction of the sequence of holdings through the abuttals shows that this could indeed have occurred in some cases, for example a sequence of (¼, ¾), 1 (½, ½) (¼, ¾), 1, 1 burgages.

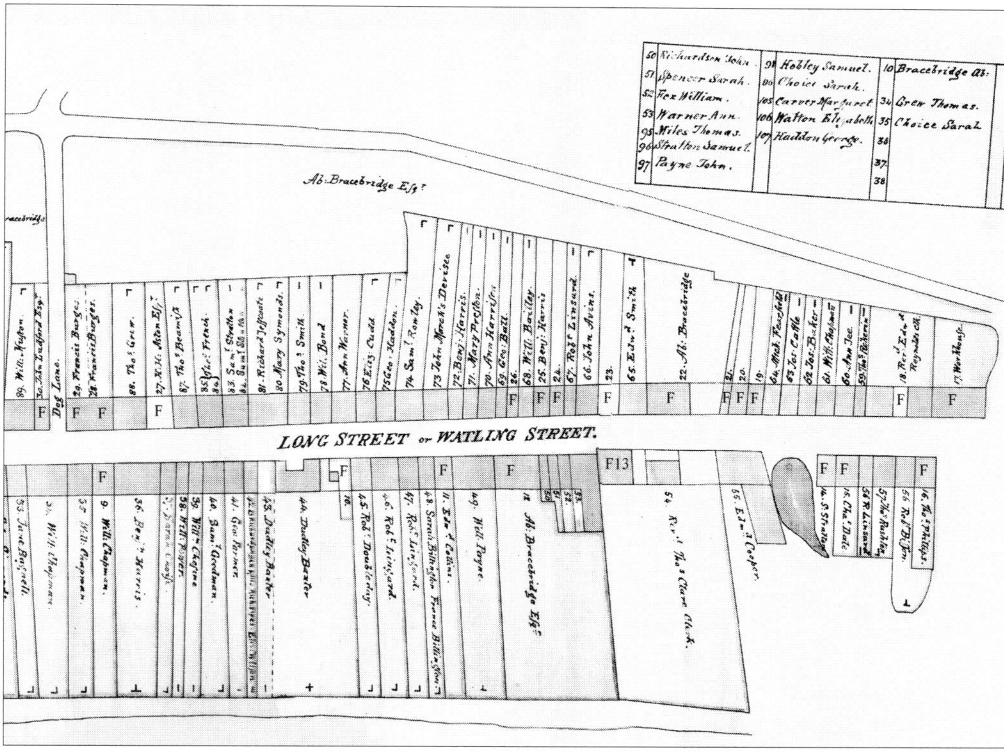

However, it is virtually impossible for others: a sequence of 1, ½, ¼, ½, ¾, ¾, 1, 1 burgages implies 2¾ burgages between three full burgages.[4] It is possible that some of these fractions had been mis-copied over the years (and discrepancies in the values do appear), but it seems more likely that the holdings were laid out as fractional burgages, to suit the needs of the original tenants.

Burgage Rents

A surprising aspect of the rents listed in the survey is that those paid for burgages of identical size are very variable.[5] On average, just under 3s. was paid for a full burgage, but this varied between 1s. 6d. and 4s., while quarter burgages paid between 5d. and 2s. 1d., with no obvious concentration on any one figure. We can be relatively confident about the total burgage rent. For the tenements listed, it comes to £10 5s. 1d.;[6] a summary rental of 1614 gives £10.[7]

FREEHOLDS AND COPYHOLDS

The Copyholdings

The general expectation in medieval towns is that burgages were freehold, transferred by deed (charter). In Atherstone, however, virtually all the property described in the 1547 survey was copyhold.[8] With this form of land-holding, whenever the ownership changed, it was recorded in the manor court rolls (or books), and the new owner was given a copy of the manor court entry – hence he was said to hold the property by 'copy of court roll' – it was a 'copyholding'.

Copyhold tenure was governed by the 'custom of the manor' which varied considerably from place to place; in Atherstone it was of the most liberal type, which was effectively equivalent to freehold. Copyhold land could be inherited, or bought and sold, without the permission of the lord of the manor, by paying a standard fee. However, its 'owner' was still technically a tenant of the manor, and the court rolls or books therefore record changes in ownership. He also had to pay a fixed rent, other manorial dues (e.g. heriots, fines paid on the death of the tenant, consisting of either a sum of money, or the best beast or best possession) and he had to attend the manor court.

Transfers from one owner to another took place in the manor court by a formal procedure. The holding was 'surrendered into the lord's hands' (via his deputy, the steward), 'to the use of' a named person (the key point). It was then granted to this person to hold according to the custom of the manor, paying the usual rent, and he was formally admitted as tenant. If the ownership had changed because of the death of the previous tenant, then the jury would 'present' to the court the name of his heir, and the latter would simply be admitted.

By the end of the medieval period, copyhold transactions sometimes became very sophisticated, so that anything that could be done with freehold land could also be done with copyhold, such as placing it in the hands of trustees in a marriage or family settlement, mortgaging it or bequeathing it. Bequests were made by the owner before his death, surrendering the property 'to the uses of his will'; these were not stated then, but after he died, his heirs would bring the will to court and its terms would be recorded.

For a mortgage, the owner had to attend the manor court and *conditionally surrender* the property to the lord's steward. It was then granted to the use of the mortgagee, and details of the amount lent (and sometimes the interest rate) were usually entered in the records. The *condition* stated that if/when the loan was repaid, the surrender became null and void. Dates when repayments were due were often given and if the mortgagee defaulted, he was likely to lose his property. If all went well and the loan was repaid, the property was *re-surrendered* by the mortgagor to the use of the mortgagee. In principle, though, this was not necessary, since the repayment made the original surrender void.

The Freeholdings

In 1547, only one holding was identified as a possible freeholding; 'Kings Croft', for which the surveyors noted that it was in the lord's hands, and:

> allthough yt lyeth among the burgages yet it is uncertayne whether yt be of the demaynes or customarye tenure.

However, 14 abuttals are also given on tenements (12), ground (one) or land (one) belonging to Lord Ferrers, which are not described in the survey.[9] These can in fact be identified as freeholdings, since in 1540, Sir

Walter Devereux (also known by the title of 'Lord Ferrers and Chartley'), had received a grant of all the lands of the monastery of Merevale in Atherstone. A 1543-4 bailiff's account for the Devereux estates summarises the rents of 16 tenants who had formerly held burgages from Merevale Abbey.[10] These, like all the later free-holdings, seem likely to have originated as manorial copyholds that came into monastic hands. Following the Dissolution, when both the individual properties and the manor itself were in Crown hands, they were apparently re-granted as freeholds (though still subject to the copyhold rents).[11] Two further tenements of the same type were the former property of the Atherstone Friary (and probably adjoined the Friary Church).[12] Thus, we can add some 18 individual freeholdings to the total in the 1547 Survey (probably corresponding to about six full burgages with rents totalling about 15s.).[13]

Enfranchisement and the Extinction of Copyhold

The major change that affected Atherstone property between the mid-17th and early 20th centuries was the gradual conversion of tenure by copyhold into freehold. The identification of some eighteen freeholdings in 1547 has already been discussed, and occasional references to freehold properties are also found in deeds and wills during the 16th and 17th centuries.[14] Most notably, in June 1649 the Marquess of Hertford sold 13 properties in Atherstone to what appears to be a consortium of local worthies. These represent the former Ferrers properties which the Marquess had acquired through marriage, and no doubt they were soon dispersed among individual owners, as indeed we know happened for one house in the following October.[15]

From the mid-17th century onwards, the number of freeholdings began to increase through what is known as enfranchisement. In this procedure, the lord of the manor granted a copyhold tenant the freehold of his copyhold property, for an agreed payment, so that it no longer had to be transferred in the manor court but could be bought or sold by deed; the former tenant would also no longer be responsible for the various payments due to the manor court (though the former burgage rent might still be owed).

One major enfranchisement grant was made in 1740, when Walter Bracebridge, son of Abraham, freed all his property in the town from copyhold tenure, apparently comprising some ten holdings.[16] Further grants were made in the later 19th century, and the final abolition of copyhold tenure came in 1926, following the 1924 Law of Property Act – after which any remaining copyholds were compulsorily enfranchised.[17]

Later Rentals, Maps and Other Sources

Several documents that elucidate the later development of property in the town are summarised in Table 4. The 1716 map (frontispiece and Fig. 8) shows the burgages but does not identify them. More important is the schematic map of the town (reproduced in Fig. 7) that was made in 1786, which is of

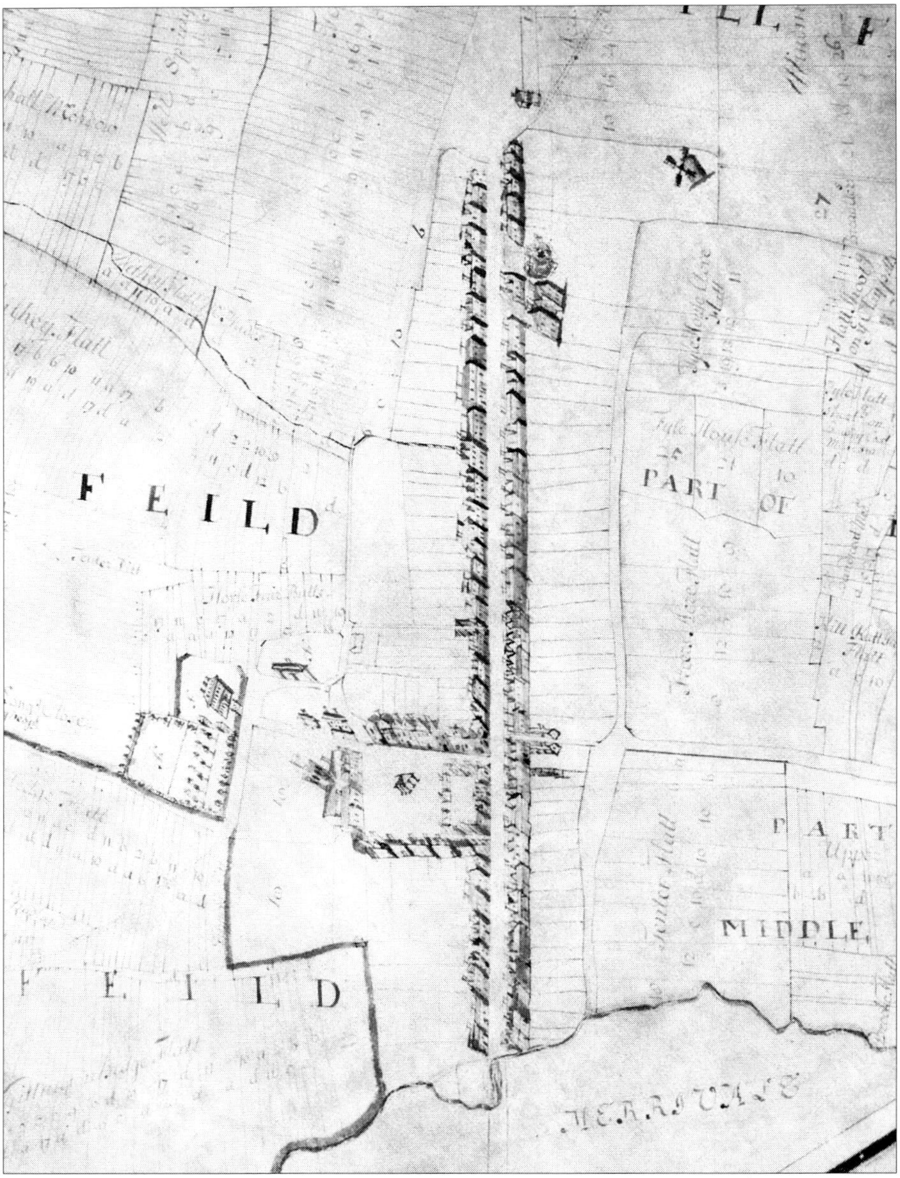

8 *'A Plan of Atherston Feildes Parcell of the Estate of Abraham Bracebridge Gent in the County of Warwick Taken in the yeare 1716 by Robert Hewitt'. From the centre, north is to the lower left corner. (Warwickshire County Record Office, P7.)*

particular significance, since it locates and numbers all the copyholds and freeholds.[18] This map also indicates the conventional size of each of the copyhold burgages (¼, ½ burgage, etc.) and is very useful for locating the copyhold properties referred to in the court books. The total number both of copyhold tenements and of burgages can be estimated from it.

Date	*Nature*	*Ref.*	*Total burgages*	*Properties*	*Owners*	*Tenants/ occupiers*	*Total rent*
1547	Survey	Lambeth	C 66; F 6	C118; F 18	C 65; F 2	C 140; F 18	C £10 5s.; F 15s. (est.)
1614	Summary rental	Dugd. 566					£10
1661	Copyhold rental	WCRO, MR9/11		C 156; F 25?	C 130; F 15		£10 1s. 6d.
1670	Hearth Tax Assessment	WCRO, QS11/23				222	
*c.*1718	Summary rental	Dugd.750					£10
1786	Burgage map (*see* Fig. 7)		C 59; F 10?	181 (C 120; F 61)	*c.*140		
1793	Poor rate assessment	WCRO, HR 38/1			142	538	

Table 4 *Numbers of burgages, tenants and rents at various dates (C = copyhold; F = freehold).*

DEVELOPMENT OF THE TOWN

Burgages

The subdivision of the burgages has led to a large difference between the total number of separate properties in the town and the number of 'full' burgages. The latter numbered about seventy in both 1547 and 1786, with the principal uncertainty being the equivalence in burgages of the freeholdings.

Properties and Owners

The 1547 survey identifies 118 separate copyhold properties, to which we must add the estimated 18 freeholdings. By 1661, further subdivision had increased the number of copyholds to 156, despite a probable increase in the number of freeholdings. Thereafter, further conversions to freehold occurred, but with relatively little additional subdivision, leading to the total of 181 identified properties on the 1786 map. The large blocks of property owned by a few owners in 1547, particularly the guild (15 holdings), Mr Lewas (14), John Drayton (nine) and Lord Ferrers (15-16), mean that the town was in the hands of no more than 70 people as copyholders and freeholders. By 1661, this had more than doubled to 130 copyholders, with perhaps 15 freeholders (assuming that most of the freeholds were owned individually). By 1786, ownership seems to have contracted somewhat, with 112 distinct names given on the map (but with owners omitted for 22 of the freeholds), indicating an overall total close to 140; a few years later, the 1793 rate assessment lists 142 names.

Tenants / Occupiers

The number of individual tenants was much greater than the number of holdings. Even in 1547, the survey identifies 140 tenanted properties, allowing for subdivisions, apart from the 17 freeholdings. In the 1661 rental, 156 names are listed, with perhaps 20 freeholders. By the time of the 1670 Hearth Tax assessment, 222 households are identified (34 of these unnamed, described as living in 'town houses and receiving collection'). By 1793, the development of the yards, the origin of which is noted in Chapter Seven and which is the theme of Chapter Nine, was well advanced, and the rate assessment includes some 540 separate properties, though at least 30 of these were vacant.

Rents

It is clear both from the tabulated statistics and from the evidence of the court books for individual properties that, throughout the period, the burgage rents remained as standard payments.[19] The copyhold rents in 1547 totalled about £10, with a further 15s. due for freeholds. The chief (copyhold) rents in 1661, and *c.*1718, totalled just over £10; this corresponds very closely to the summary figures of £10 in the 1614 manorial rental for 'Coppyhold rents & Cheife rents'. By the 17th century, the chief rents due from the freeholds had almost certainly been extinguished, as discussed above.

4 Standing in the Great Highway: Atherstone, Medieval Market Town

Andrew Watkins

Introduction[1]

The town of Atherstone, like its nearest small town neighbours Coleshill and Nuneaton, developed from an existing peasant settlement. Today, it is most famous as a former centre of hat making. Consequently, its role as a market town in the middle ages has often been overlooked. Atherstone was one of the 600 or so small market towns founded in England during the economic upsurge of the 12th and 13th centuries and, as Slater recounts in Chapter Three, its creation came about through the vision and commercial acumen of the abbot of Bec or his agents. These small market towns were to form the frame of a national trade and marketing network which has endured until recent times.

This chapter draws upon a range of detailed evidence to create an account of life in Atherstone during the 13th, 14th and 15th centuries. Aspects of the town's location are presented first, followed by a review of Atherstone's lordship up to the time of the Dissolution. The chapter continues with an explanation of the obligations and rights of the manor's tenants, before demonstrating the growing success of the newly founded town. Next, certain over-arching influences on the townsfolk are considered – the manor courts and the church (including the guild of Mancetter). Food and drink and the agriculture that underpins them comprise the final topic.

Location

The town was well sited to attract merchants and traders travelling along the important long-distance routeway of Watling Street, and, of course, was also supported by peasant cultivators and craftsmen from the surrounding countryside. Its early development was undoubtedly helped by its position between two distinct agricultural landscapes, the rolling champion (arable) Feldon lands of western Leicestershire and the wood pasture of the Forest of Arden in Warwickshire (*see* Chapter One, p.6: the 'thin corridor of safe land'). Many acres were given over to growing crops in the Arden, but, particularly after the mid-14th century, both lord and peasant increasingly concentrated on cattle grazing. The natural resources of the Arden woodlands allowed peasants access to wood, both for fuel and for the opportunity to dress timber acquired from seigniorial reserves, and to trap game (albeit illegally), as well as to gather fruit, nuts, wax and honey. Many peasants were involved in industrial processes within the woodlands – charcoal and ash burning, tile manufacture and stone quarrying – while coal mining was recorded at Merevale and Nuneaton at this period. (*See* below, Colepit Field, p.47.) All these commodities were sold in Atherstone market, as were the grain and wool produced in west Leicestershire.[2]

That this was an advantageous location for a market town was appreciated by contemporaries. The compilers of the rental of 1547 (*see* Appendix to Chapter Three) commented that Atherstone 'standeth in the great hye way called Wattling Strete, on the border of the Felden countrey joyninge to the Woodlande', while around a hundred years later Dugdale wrote that Atherstone 'stands so opportunely both to the Woodland and the Feildon'.[3]

Atherstone's Lordships 1066-1536

As Slater details in Chapter Two, Atherstone was owned by Countess Godgifu in 1066. Domesday Book for 1086 shows that 11 villeins, two bordars, and a serf lived on the estate, which was worth an annual 60 shillings to the countess. Domesday's record of two leagues of woodland emphasises that much of the forest of Arden had yet to be cleared. Countess Godgifu's lands passed to the earl of Chester, a powerful Norman lord and possessor of many estates throughout England. By 1100, he had granted Atherstone to the abbey of Bec. This was a rich and prosperous Norman house with extensive estates both in Normandy and in England. It was a centre of religious life and a seminary for numerous bishops and abbots, and today is probably best known for providing Lanfranc and Anselm – the first two post-conquest archbishops of Canterbury.

The manor remained formally in the abbey's ownership until 1414, when it was confiscated by the Crown, as were other properties belonging to 'alien priories' – these were monasteries which had once been in the French Empire of the English kings, but by this stage of the Hundred Years War lay in areas once again in the hands of the kings of France. However, some considerable time before this, it had been sequestrated (taken into Crown hands) and, in 1406, Atherstone was leased to Henry IV's son John, Duke of Bedford, 'for his life or as long as the war lasted'.[4] The Duke then sub-let it to William Brinklow and Peter Prilly, the lord of part of the manor of Mancetter. On the death of Bedford in 1438, Atherstone was leased to the duke of Buckingham, but by 1444 it had passed to Henry VI's newly founded King's College, Cambridge. This grant was soon rescinded, as was another one made in April 1453 to Edmund, earl of Richmond, the father of the future Henry VII (revoked in July of the same year). Finally, in early 1462, it was granted by Edward IV to Mount Grace Priory, a Carthusian house near Thirsk in Yorkshire. Nevertheless, it was in the hands of the earl of Warwick in 1463, as is evidenced by the precept he issued through the constable, that the people of Atherstone were not to take livery of any one but the earl; however, it soon reverted to Mount Grace Priory, remaining in their hands until the Dissolution.

Obligations and Rights of Manorial Tenants

A survey made in the mid-13th century reveals much about Atherstone at this time, listing all the tenants of the abbey of Bec and giving details of the customs, or services, they owed the abbot in exchange for their lands.[5] Adam, the son of Elye, was the first peasant recorded in this custumnal, and his services were typical of those owed by most of the tenants. He held a yardland, probably about thirty acres, in the fields of Atherstone, and he paid the abbot 4s. rent annually in two payments: at the Feast of St Martin (11 November) and at the Nativity of St John the Baptist (24 June). In addition, he owed labour services, by which he worked on the abbot's land as part of his obligations as a tenant. At the sowing of the winter and Lenten fields, he had to plough one acre of the abbot's demesne, and if he used his own plough he received food for his efforts. He was also obliged to spend two days weeding and hoeing the abbot's crops, and another two days mowing his meadows. For lifting and carrying this hay he was rewarded with bread, cheese and ale. Along with two men that he must bring, he had to reap for two days at harvest time, and he owed a third day's reaping with all his family. When his daughter intended to marry he had to pay a *merchet* for the lord's permission, and on his death he owed the abbot a heriot – this was a kind of death duty, for which peasants had to surrender their best beast or its cash equivalent. Finally, when he brewed ale to sell he had to give four gallons to the abbot. The social controls exercised by lords over their tenants in the Arden were usually weak; by comparison these extensive feudal rights claimed by the abbot of Bec over his peasants at Atherstone were unusually harsh and far more typical of those he would have exerted over his French tenants.[6]

It is the same mid-13th-century custumnal that provides the earliest indication of the origins of the town. In 1246, the abbot of Bec had bought a market charter from Henry III, giving him the legal right to hold a weekly market in Atherstone on Tuesdays, and a three-day Fair on the Eve, Feast, and Morrow of the Nativity of the Blessed Virgin Mary (7-9 September) (For more on the market charter, *see* p.19). This market and fair were an important source of revenue for the abbot, allowing him to receive monies from the trade and commerce generated in the Market Place, such as stall rents and tolls on goods coming into the town, and the profits of jurisdiction. The latter came from amercements (fines) levied on traders breaking the regulations of the market.[7] Contemporaries would have recognised Atherstone as a borough, that is to say, a settlement where land was held by burgage tenure. Fourteen burgesses, or people who owned their burgages, appear among the rural tenants in the mid-13th-century custumnal. One of the most important distinctions between town and countryside at this time was that burgesses had special privileges compared to peasants on rural manors. At Atherstone, those who held their land by burgage tenure paid the lord 2s. 6d. annually. This gave them the freehold of their property, special rights of access to the town's market without paying tolls and, most important symbolically, they paid this rent to the lord instead of working on his land. The existence of the 14 burgesses holding 13½ burgages reveals a nascent urban community of craftsmen and traders and, as Slater narrates in Chapter Three, is part and parcel of the town's foundation around the time of the acquisition of the market charter in 1246.[8] In a final concord of January 1246, the abbot of Bec released five of his tenants from paying merchet, tallage, and their other villein services, and this can best be seen in the context of the abbot changing the tenurial conditions of some of his tenants around the time of the borough's creation.[9]

Development of the Town

The newly founded town was successful. The abbot encouraged migrants and craftsmen to settle, enticed by the opportunity of making money and the social and legal advantages burgage tenure offered. The vibrancy of the town is shown by a bailiff's account of September 1289.[10] The manor then was worth £30 12s. 7½d. to the abbot. Rents brought in £7 19s. 3d., and the leasing of the manor's oven yielded £2 14s. However, the perquisites of the court, that is to say the fines levied on traders in the market, amounted to £5 3s. 8d., or nearly a sixth of the manor's income, demonstrating a handsome reward for the abbey's investment in creating the town. By 1294, following the abbot's extension and reordering of the settlement in 1289, there were 36 free tenants in the town, over double the number mentioned in the mid-13th century.[11]

The great survey of rights of private jurisdiction made for Edward I in 1284, known as the *Quo Warranto*, provides a further indication of the town's development.[12] The abbot enjoyed extensive rights that were typical of those found in a small market town, rather than on a rural manor. He claimed the rights of gallows, that is to say, the right to hang criminals, and pillory. He had the market and fair, the right to take tolls on goods coming into the market, and the Assize of Bread and Ale. The settlement evidently flourished and by the time of the Lay Subsidy of 1327, there were 21 tax-payers in the town, who paid £1 19s. 8d. between them.

Prior to the early 14th century, surnames were non-hereditary and reveal much about the occupation of their owners. The surnames for Atherstone indicate a wide range of trades in the town: millers, fishermen, cloth workers, tailors, dyers and weavers, woodworkers, coopers, and merchants – all are recorded in the late 13th and early 14th centuries. Studies of other small towns have shown that peasants who migrated from the countryside to better themselves often came from villages within the five- to 10-mile area served by the market of that town. Atherstone surnames similarly suggest that many of the townsfolk came from local villages such as Ansley, Combe, Hinckley, Wyken, and Pooley in Polesworth.[13]

Medieval Atherstone had a thriving market, with a wide range of goods and commodities being made and sold there. Once a week the Market Place (usually referred to as the 'marketstede' or 'le marketplace' in late medieval sources), filled with stalls – butchers, bakers and ale sellers setting out their goods for sale.[14] Their importance is reflected in the medieval town's street names, such as Bakehouse Lane, to the west of the Market Place, and Butchers' Row to the east. In the 16th century, the Bull Ring, another place associated with butchery, lay to the north of the church. The Market Place held a stone cross and a whipping post, and nearby was the meeting place of the community: the Court Hall, or Court House.

The town's craftsmen sold their wares either on the stalls of the market or from workshops in their homes. They also sold from separate shops, places of both manufacture and retail, which fronted onto the Market Place. Although not recorded until the 16th century, these are likely to have existed before that. Merchants from Coventry and other towns came to sell their goods to the people of Atherstone and buy up commodities in the market. Peasants from the surrounding settlements brought in their in ale, butter, cheese, grains, vegetables, fruits, honey and livestock. Some sold game: Simon Mason and William Bredon, for instance, who in 1421 had used nets and snares to trap rabbits and hares. Others brought in the products of the Arden woodlands, such as the seven cartloads of charcoal sold in the market in 1370 or the 200 kyddes (faggots) mentioned in 1463. There were also more exotic transactions, as when Agnes le Colier and Robert le Taylor were in dispute over a 'pipe' and 12 gallons of wine in 1370.[15]

The monks of Merevale Abbey owned a burgage in the Market Place, giving them direct access to the commercial heart of the town. During the 1490s they were frequent shoppers in Atherstone, buying leather goods, iron pots and utensils. In 1498, they bought six pairs of shoes from Matthew Corviser of Atherstone to give to the abbey's servants, one of whom was 'James of the Kitchen', and in the following year they purchased four bullocks and four cows at the September fair. The monks also bought building materials, such as guttering, 12,000 stone nails, 400 'syxpenne nayle', 400 'foworepenn nayle' and 400 'pennenayle', in 1498.[16]

Although the majority of buyers and sellers in Atherstone came from the settlements of the Arden and western Leicestershire, some travelled from much further afield. There were traders from the small Leicestershire towns of Ashby-de-la-Zouche, Hinckley, Lutterworth, and Market Bosworth. Others came from towns in Warwickshire, from Tamworth astride the Warwickshire/Staffordshire boundary, and from Lichfield in Staffordshire. Merchants, drapers and weavers from Coventry came. Travellers, waggoners, drovers with their herds of Welsh cattle and men with strings of pack animals passed through the heart of the town as they journeyed along Watling Street.

Also, traders from Atherstone went to other towns. In 1427, Richard the Spicer of Atherstone was recorded as being in debt to a London merchant at Melton Mowbray, while in 1523 Thomas Booth of Atherstone had visited Market Bosworth regularly enough to bequeath 40 pence to the Lady Guild in the church there.[17]

Various grants were obtained from the crown to help Atherstone's development. In 1319, Edward II granted pavage to the 'bailiffs and good men' of Atherstone for four years. This gave the right to take a toll on all commodities coming into the town – specifically a farthing on every quarter of corn – the money to be used to improve the pavement or road through the settlement. Fourteen years later, in 1343, a further grant of pavage was made for five years, because it was complained that the town 'lies low and in wintertime and in wet weather is dirty, whereby merchants with goods and wares come only in small numbers at such time', suggesting something of the seasonal nature of medieval trade. As mentioned in Chapter Three (*see* p.21), in 1332 the abbot of Merevale obtained a grant of pontage from Edward III, giving him the right to take tolls on goods carried over the river Anker by the Feldon Bridge, to be used for its repair. This was a shrewd move by the abbot as it allowed him to make money from visitors to Atherstone as they passed by his grange at Pinwall.[18]

Courts

Life in the town was regulated by two distinct courts, whose magnificent surviving records are a key source for the period.[19] A dozen or so 'Little Courts' were held throughout the year, meeting about once a month. These oversaw trade among the townsfolk and peasants, dealing with issues such as credit and broken commercial contracts. The major court, the View of Frankpledge, met twice a year and enabled the community to regulate victuallers, enforce rudimentary sanitary regulations, punish sharp commercial practice and report and punish violence. Calling upon long held practices and local memory, the community of Atherstone passed ordinances and made bylaws to regulate all aspects of town life. The court had the responsibility for enforcing law and order, through the officers called constables and tithingmen. They had to report crimes and apprehend law breakers. Both courts recorded property transactions, specifically the transfer of copyhold properties.[20]

Every frankpledge court heard reports of assaults, with the protagonists often having drawn weapons. Frequently blood was spilled, and occasionally events got so out of hand that there was raised the *hue and cry*: the alarm following the witnessing of a robbery, violent act, or murder. Everybody in the neighbourhood was then obliged to abandon whatever they were doing and help pursue and capture the miscreant. The court rolls include numerous examples of such incidents, as in 1471 when Richard Smyth attacked Thomas Weaver, a servant of John Blackgreen, with a stick and drew blood, or, when in the same year John Smith, a baker, drew a dagger on Clement Nightingale. Violent attacks were not confined to men. In 1334, the wife of Hugh le Weir drew blood in an attack, and Alice Roper made an attack on Denise Hyde and drew her blood in 1456. Although the View of Frankpledge reminded people that no one was to carry weapons, this was often ignored, as in 1454 when Walter Warrener and Richard Smith, wearing jacks (protective jackets) and with their swords drawn, attacked Thomas Roper and Thomas Pratchett.[21]

Strangers were welcome to buy and sell in the town; nevertheless, the ordinances of the court reflect distrust and suspicion of the intentions of strangers. In 1408 and in 1506 it was ordained that no one should give hospitality to strangers. In 1419, a bailiff was instructed to watch over any strangers coming into the lordship, while in the following year the movements of such a stranger were reported to the court. Similarly, William Mitchell and John Parkes were described as common vagrants in 1478. The community also distrusted nightwalkers. These were people who were out and about during the hours of darkness. In 1477 it was agreed that there was to be no loitering by servants around houses at night.[22]

The View of Frankpledge of Atherstone had responsibility for the maintenance of the roads. People were frequently presented for obstructing roads with timber and dung, while in 1423 each tenant was instructed to repair the common pavement before their tenements.

The court also tried to ban games, believed to promote idleness. In 1420, 'le tenys' was banned, and in 1477 chess, bowls and closhing, a kind of nine-pins, were forbidden. It is known that Shrovetide football games in other parts of the country originated in the later middle ages, and it is probable that the famous Atherstone ball game can trace its beginnings to this time, but disappointingly the medieval records make no mention of it.[23]

THE CHURCH

During the middle ages, Atherstone lay in the parish of Mancetter. As noted in Chapter Three (*see* p.17), St Mary's Church in Atherstone originated as a chapel of the abbey of Bec, and indeed is referred to as the chapel of Atherstone in 1349. It was later occupied by the friary of St Augustine, founded in 1375 by Ralph, Lord Basset of Drayton. He endowed it with 12 acres in the fields of Atherstone, and bequeathed 500 marks to the friary on his death in 1383, to help complete its building. Friars were well respected by medieval people because of their frugal lifestyle, attempting to return to the ideal of apostolic poverty. Many people from Atherstone and the surrounding area made bequests to the friars, such as Simon Bacon of Bulkington in 1423, Thomas Bate, gentleman of Pooley Hall, Polesworth in 1459, and Thomas Booth of Atherstone in 1523. On its dissolution in 1535, the friary consisted of the church site, a dovecote, a barn, an orchard and two messuages. Eventually, it came into the hands of the Repington family, who ' built a fair house of Brick upon the ruins of this Friery',[24] while the friary church was preserved as a chapel for the town, its chancel becoming the first home of the Grammar School.

However, the church of St Peter's, Mancetter, was the parish church of the medieval town. It was here that the townsfolk went to celebrate mass, to have their children baptised, to marry and to be buried. The extensive building works at the church during the 14th and 15th centuries, including side aisles and a clerestory, are proof of both the wealth and the piety of the townspeople.[25]

Many of the religious functions of the guild were also celebrated in Mancetter church, and the guild house was located near the church. Although first recorded as the 'brethren of the gild of Atherstone' in 1370, it was subsequently known as the guild of Mancetter. It appears to have been re-founded in 1458 (nothing is known about its history during the intervening period), when the abbot of Merevale obtained a licence to create the guild. The members, termed brothers and sisters, were to elect annually two masters at the Feast of the Holy Trinity, and were to be incorporate and in perpetual succession, with a common seal. Chaplains of the guild were to celebrate mass daily at the altar of the Blessed Virgin Mary, located in a side chapel of the church. The guild was very popular with the people of Atherstone and received many gifts, such as those from Agnes Stretton (who left it 12d. rent from half a burgage in 1463), and John Scarborow (who in 1522 bequeathed 10s. to the guild and a further 6s. 8d. to the guild's altars; his will is noted in Chapter Six, p.120). On the eve of its suppression in 1547, the popularity of the guild was such that it was the second largest landowner in the town after the lord of the manor. It owned 10 burgages in all, divided into 15 properties, and land in the open fields as well.[26]

Mancetter church also contained a chantry, which was probably associated with the guild, where prayers would be said for the dead. The chantry, like the guild, received many gifts, such as a burgage in 1469. In 1547, it was the fourth largest owner of copyhold property in the manor, holding three and three quarter burgages.[27]

Schools often developed from chantries or guilds. Although Atherstone Grammar School was founded in 1558 by Amias Hill, the town clearly had a school well before this date. In 1420, a cloak, three bed coverlets and seven sheets were stolen from Thomas Stretton's house by one Elena, the servant of John Scolemayster of Atherstone. Thus, a school was already in existence by the 15th century.[28]

Food and Drink

One of the most important economic functions of a small town was the exchange of foodstuffs. Many of the townsfolk of Atherstone were involved in victualling: butchering, mongering, baking bread and, most commonly, brewing ale. Ale was the most widespread drink in medieval England. Gallons of this brew were downed by men and women of all ages. Unlike modern beer, medieval ale was not hopped, but was made from water and malt, with herbs and yeast added. The drinking of ale being so very common, its production was widespread. Many peasant households brewed habitually throughout the year, both to slake their own thirst and to sell to generate cash. The brewing and retailing of the ale was frequently undertaken by the women of the household, who were often called alewives.

The View of Frankpledge was responsible for the Assize of Bread and Ale. Originating in the 13th century, this was a law regulating the volume and frequency of the sale of food and drink. It was administered by officials of the court, called tasters, who inspected foodstuffs offered for sale within their jurisdiction. The fines levied on these victuallers were an important source of revenue for the lord of the manor.[29] In late 14th-century Atherstone, large numbers of women were amerced for selling ale; thus, in 1377, 22 women were fined, some for brewing up to sixteen times in the previous six months, while, in 1386, 36 were fined.

The 15th century was a time when drinking patterns throughout England were evolving. As the century progressed, the numbers of brewers recorded in the court rolls declined, probably because brewing was becoming concentrated into the hands of fewer people. As home consumption of ale declined, the numbers of specialist alehouses rose.[30] Atherstone is renowned for its large number of inns and public houses along Long Street and off the Market Place, and it is likely that some of them came into existence during this time. The number of alehouse keepers in Atherstone recorded in the court rolls was increasing during the 15th and early 16th centuries, but unfortunately none of the names of these early establishments have survived.[31] However, it is probable that the *Angel*, *Three Tuns*, *Red Lion* and others occupy the sites of medieval inns and alehouses not recorded by name until the early modern period.

The tasters also regulated the price and quality of bread, including the various types of loaf. These ranged in texture and weight from the wastel loaf of the finest quality, to the coarsest horsebread. Frequent complaints were voiced about bakers who sold bread of poor quality, or white bread that was light in weight. In 1420, John Banwell was fined because two of his loaves – the wastel and the coket – were too light; four other bakers were also fined for similar offences. In 1422 Richard Fale, a prominent baker with scant regard for the community, had the dubious distinction of having an ordinance passed against him by the court ordering him to maintain the quality and weight of the white bread and horsebread he was baking.[32]

The abbot of Bec was anxious to preserve the feudal right of the suit of oven, which compelled all the bakers of the town to bake their bread in his oven, while he charged them for using it. This monopoly was obviously worth a considerable sum to the lord. In 1387, some of the bakers of Atherstone had defied the abbot by building ovens in their homes. The tasters reported that they baked white bread and horsebread without the abbot receiving any of the money due to him. The court instructed that those bakers should be fined, and ordered the ovens removed. In the early part of the 15th century, the common oven located in Bakehouse Lane was leased out to the aforementioned Richard Fale. Another baker, William Milner, objected to this monopoly, and in 1423 the court heard that the strife and discord between Fale and Milner was so great that neither could bake their bread without disturbing the peace. To restore order, Milner was encouraged to buy a licence from the lord to build his own oven of five measures.[33] To compensate Fale for no longer using the common oven, Milner agreed to pay him 6s. 8d. a year. Throughout the rest of the 15th and early 16th centuries the oven continued to be leased out, and by 1547 the common oven, by then referred to as the common bakehouse, was leased to Amias Hill for 30 shillings.[34]

The tasters also inspected meat offered for sale. A frequent complaint against the butchers was that they sold unfit or rotten meat, as in 1421 when three were amerced for selling infected meat. William Hawker was craftier; in 1420 he attempted to sell mutton which the court was told was a ram 'killed by thunder and lightning and not wholesome for human food'.

Another problem for the tasters was the sale of meat by butchers who sold meat from their own homes rather than the stalls in the marketplace. This worried the court, as the meat was not in public view, and therefore could not be inspected properly. In 1387, nine butchers, one the aptly named John Fleshewer, were amerced for selling meat in their own houses and not in the appointed place. They each had to pay 12d. and were warned that if they did not sell meat from their stalls they would forfeit both the meat and its value.[35] Butchers at Atherstone also fell foul of the court for not disposing of waste correctly, as in 1421, when the same William Hawker was fined for dumping offal and waste in the common way.

The church required that each Friday and Saturday and the penitential season of Lent be meatless. Consequently, the demand for fish was great. Fishmongers, whose catches came not only from local rivers, streams and fishponds but also from the coast, were regular visitors to the market, as witnessed by the four fish sellers amerced in 1471.[36]

Town governments were always anxious to keep prices of foodstuffs low so as to prevent social discontent. Therefore they sought to restrict the activities of the hucksters and regraters. These were traders who bought up foodstuffs in the market and then sold them on, causing food prices to become inflated. Atherstone always suffered from large numbers of them, for instance, 18 in 1471, 19 in 1478, and 15 in 1506. The majority were women, such as Alice Nightingale, who was accused of being a common regrater of bread, salt and flour, and Alice Clement, who regrated bread and candles in 1455. To counter this, access to the market by regraters was restricted until after the ordinary townsfolk had visited to buy their foodstuffs at wholesale prices. At Atherstone, regrating was forbidden until the market had been open for a few hours. In 1408, it was ordained that no one was to regrate in the market until 10 o'clock and this was repeated in both 1467 and 1477. In the latter year, a bylaw added that no one was to buy victuals before the commoners of the town had been satisfied.[37]

Agriculture

As with any small town, agriculture remained an important element in daily life, as many of the people of Atherstone combined their crafts and trades with keeping animals and growing crops. (The practice continued into the 16th and 17th centuries, as illustrated in Chapter Six.) The 1289 account offers a glimpse of the working of the abbey's demesne. Their officials had sown 380 acres of arable, predominantly with wheat and oats, with lesser acreages given over to drage (a mix of barley and oats), barley and rye. Wood sales brought in a further £3 15s. 4d., hay from the meadows £1 6s. 8d., and herbage, that is to say the grazing of pasture, seven shillings. The wool of the abbey's sheep flock was worth £1 0s. 3d. Honey from its hives and the cheese and butter from its dairy also were sold. Increasingly during the 13th century, the abbey became less involved in the direct management of its English lands, and by 1344 Atherstone was leased out by Bec to Merevale Abbey.[38] By the end of the middle ages the role of the lord in the agricultural life of the manor had diminished. The abbot of Bec was probably the last lord of the manor to involve himself directly in the agricultural exploitation of the estate.

In the early 15th century the duke of Bedford leased out the manor, as did his successor the duke of Buckingham in 1437. The lands known as Hall Close and Hall Orchard, around what had been the manor house,[39] had been converted to pasture. The 12 yardlands of demesne land scattered throughout the fields of Atherstone were leased out, as was the water mill and horse mill of the estate, for £8 13s. 4d. Many townsmen took on leases of pieces of demesne arable land during the later middle ages, allowing them to expand the size of their own holdings.[40]

In the late medieval Arden, wheat, barley, oats, and peas and beans were the most common field crops and these would have been sown in Atherstone's fields.[41] Many of their names are recorded in the late 15th and early 16th centuries, such as Old Mill Field (whose name had evolved by 1716 into Aldermill Field), Windmill Field, which lay towards Witherley between the town and the river Anker, and Hallsich Field, on the west of the town under the edge of the Arden and the Outwoods. Prior to enclosure (*see* Chapter Seven), these were large open fields divided into strips (selions), with many cultivators. However, other smaller cropping units were part of the field system, such as Rye Butts, Scaffold Close, Barley Croft, and Colepit Field (which interesting name probably referred to early coal workings). The name of a field west of the town – The Stocking – refers to a process common in the 15th-century Arden in which land was improved and reclaimed by clearing trees and bushes from fields which had become overgrown. As elsewhere in the Arden, some land was enclosed into small, hedged fields, or closes. Many of these were the result of clearances of the woodland in the 12th and 13th centuries, and by the later medieval period were often used for keeping livestock. Evidence from the 16th century also suggests that many of the townsfolk kept their animals in closes in neighbouring Mancetter, Oldbury, Merevale, and Bentley.[42] (*See* Chapter Six.)

A tithe account from the late 15th century shows that most of the 149 people who paid tithe in Atherstone to the vicar of Mancetter had at least one, and sometimes two, milk cows.[43] Later, in the 16th century, in 1522 John Scarborow (*see* Chapter Six, p.120) left a yearling heifer to each of his three servants, while in the following year Thomas Booth bequeathed a calf to his godchild and a heifer and bullock to his father-in-law, John Wyke, a weaver. In 1536, Richard Knight left a crop of unharvested barley, as well as barley and wheat in his barns. He had invested in much agricultural equipment, having carts, yokes and hand tools. He also possessed a horse, two mares, two cows, a steer, eight sheep and 24 pigs. His debts listed in his inventory shows he was trading in malt, oxen, lambs and cows with men of the surrounding villages of the Arden and Leicestershire.[44]

The communal agriculture of the town was managed by the court. It decided when fields were to be ploughed and sown, when the harvesting was to take place, when meadows were to be mown and how the commons were to be managed. There was obviously a three-year rotation, with two fields sown with winter and spring crops and a third left fallow. This is indicated for instance in 1547,[45] when it was reported that Hallsich field was to be common every third year; in other words, it was to be fallow and the townsmen could graze their animals on it. Often the court rolls record when peasants tried to assert their individuality against the collective will of the community. In 1395, Roger Miller, who was leasing a mill from the abbot of Merevale, encroached upon the Washbrook.[46] This stream, sometimes referred to as Washford Brook, is an often-mentioned part of the medieval topography of Atherstone. It flowed almost through the centre of the town, and Miller was presumably trying to divert the water for his own purposes and deprive the townspeople of its use. Others also blocked streams and watercourses, although often through neglect of cleaning or scouring ditches. In 1420, the court heard that a watercourse under 'Whetyngham' Mere was obstructed through the negligence of the Rector of Sheepy Magna. Another peasant with little regard for others was Agnes Parker, who was cited in 1419 for putting lime into the marlpit 'where horses and other beasts came to drink'.

By the end of the 15th century, rising numbers of animals put great strain on the common pasture. In 1477, the court was so concerned about the commons being overstocked with animals that it decided that each person could graze no more than three steers. Other peasants allowed their animals to damage the crops of others, as in 1420, when the court heard that William Hawker broke the fences around the fields of Atherstone and allowed his beasts to destroy the crops. Similarly, in 1422, Richard Warner was fined 40 pence for allowing his pigs to trespass in the corn of John Rawlyn. By the early 16th century, the court was seeking to regulate how animals were allowed to graze, and in 1514 it set out bylaws about foals not being fastened between haycocks and about the use of the common bull.[47]

THE TOWN AT THE CLOSE OF THE MEDIEVAL ERA

By the early 16th century, the demesne was entirely leased out and much land had been converted to pasture from arable. The power of the lord of the manor was in decline. The compilers of the 1547 rental (*see* Appendix to Chapter Three) noted that John Rampton, who was leasing the water mill and the horse mill, also had a barn which 'he himself dyd bylde upon the lordes grownde' without the lord's permission. They also voiced the concerns of the community over the pressure on arable land, and they were particularly worried about engrossing (land becoming concentrated into a few large holdings), enclosure, and rights of common. These all mirror national concerns, which within two years were to help provoke the rebellions of 1549.

It is difficult to determine exactly how the town had grown through the middle ages. Domesday Book's record of 11 villeins, two bordars and a serf suggests a population in excess of 60 to 70 persons towards the end of the 11th century. The foundation of the town in the mid-13th century and the growth of the English population in general is reflected in the Lay Subsidy of 1327, where the presence of 21 taxpayers implies some 200-300 inhabitants. By the time of the Lay Subsidy of 1525[48] this had risen substantially, as the 100 payers indicate a population in excess of six hundred. The demand for urban property had become so great in Atherstone during the 15th century that many of the burgages transferred through the court had become subdivided and were held as half and quarter burgages. That rental of 1547 shows that sometimes these were further divided, such as a three-quarter burgage owned by the guild which had four houses built on it, or two burgages which were divided into six houses.

By the end of the middle ages, the town of Atherstone had been in existence for almost three hundred years since the abbot of Bec had created a community of traders and craftsmen alongside Watling Street. It had become both prosperous and populous, visited not only by locals but also by those travelling along the great highway. Trade dominated the settlement; at the same time agriculture remained important. The abbot's commercial gamble had been well rewarded: Atherstone had become a successful and well-established small market town serving the surrounding area of west Leicestershire and the Warwickshire Arden.

The story of the later stages of Atherstone's development is taken up once again in Chapter Six by Marion Alexander, following the next chapter which describes the legacy of Atherstone's historic buildings.

5 Streets and Houses

Bob Meeson, Mike Trye and Judy Vero

Introduction

The historic architecture of Atherstone has received less attention than that of other, more celebrated, Warwickshire towns. An important group of buildings has survived, and the aim of this chapter, which spans development from the end of the middle ages to the early 20th century, is to recognise and celebrate Atherstone's contribution to the county's architectural heritage. The chapter consists of three parts. First, Bob Meeson presents a chronological account of some of the significant buildings in the town (*see* below, 'Historic Buildings in Atherstone'). This is followed by a set of streetscapes by Mike Trye, which capture something of the present character of the town; to these he has appended information on former owners and occupiers. Thirdly, building histories by Bob Meeson and Judy Vero enlarge the history of six selected properties.

Closely linked to this chapter is the Gazetteer, compiled by Mike Trye and Bob Meeson as a guide for a walking tour of the town centre, which forms the final segment of the book.

Historic Buildings in Atherstone

Medieval Buildings

The three main elements that make up the plan of a medieval town are the street system, the tenement plots, and the buildings which stand upon them. Once the street pattern of an urban settlement had been established, this conditioned the sites and the plans of all the buildings subsequently built within it and their relationship with each other. As Terry Slater has shown (p.21 ff.), detailed analysis of the topography of Atherstone yields evidence of a complex development. Nevertheless, in essence it is a town planned along a single street with back lanes, and with a market place offset to one side, rather than astride the main thoroughfare. From the 14th century, the medieval Market Place was bounded by Long Street on its south side and by the Augustinian friary to the north. As they abutted the east and west sides of the Market Place, Market Street and Church Street were likely to have contained some of the better medieval buildings. Although they were inevitably constrained by the sizes and shapes of the tenement plots on which they were built, none of Atherstone's medieval buildings would have rivalled the great merchants' houses of such places as Exeter, Coventry or York. In considering the context of buildings around the Market Place, it should not be forgotten that when the Market Hall and adjoining buildings occupied what is now an open square there would have been fewer long views of the street elevations.

Through a combination of piecemeal rebuilding and wholesale replacement, the medieval buildings of Atherstone have almost disappeared. Only archaeological excavation might enable comparisons to be made between the standard of medieval buildings around the Market Place and those elsewhere in the town. Almost nothing remains standing from that period in Long Street, the one exception being the *Old Swan* public house, where a single blade from a medieval cruck house has been identified (*see* Building History Six, and below, p.53). In most medieval towns, the Market Place was the focus for the best buildings, owned by the wealthiest burgesses. Although in Atherstone the few remaining remnants of 15th- or 16th-century timber-framing around the Market Place belong to relatively modest buildings, they might well have been the best in the town. Generally they were of two or two-and-a-half storeys, most having gables to the street, and with one notable characteristic in common: they all had jettied façades (the upper floors stepping forward of the ground floor walls).

The impetus for change gathered momentum during the 18th century, culminating with the construction of many late Georgian and Victorian buildings, but the process of renewal had begun at an earlier date. The best example of an early replacement of a medieval building is probably 11/13 Market Street, where an entirely new timber-framed structure was assembled in the late 16th or early 17th century, with two tiers of jetties on both the front and rear elevations. At that date, it was probably the tallest and most impressive house in the town. This house has been substantially remodelled, and it now presents a fine three-storeyed Georgian brick façade to the Market Place (*see* Building History Five, and below, p.54). In Long Street, the *Old Swan* (*see* Building History Six) amply demonstrates the process of piecemeal change in timber-framed buildings, but elsewhere in Atherstone most of the evidence of those early changes to the urban fabric have been swept away.

St Mary's Church

In many towns, the most significant medieval building is the parish church. In Atherstone, first impressions gained from the exterior of the nave of St Mary's Church do not set the historian's pulse racing, but there is more to the building than meets the eye. Despite the intrinsic interest of the site, its development has never been subject to detailed archaeological fabric analysis or excavation, and the generally accepted version of the development of the building is open to question. The medieval town of Atherstone fell within the parish of Mancetter, but it had its own chapel by as early as 1125. The location of this chapel of ease is unknown, and on the basis of parallels elsewhere it need not have been on the site of the present church. Presumably, it was built by the abbey of Bec in their role as lords of the manor; following their establishment of Atherstone as a planned town in the 13th century, this chapel would undoubtedly have been enlarged. Most accounts of the former friary church repeat the belief that the present chancel stands over the foundations of the Norman church, and that a west tower had been added by the 13th or 14th century, but no evidence has been cited in support of this, and it runs counter to what is known generally of the planning of Augustinian friaries. The accepted position is that when the Friary of St Augustine was founded *c.*1375 by Ralph Basset, it took over the chapel and remodelled it. In his will of 1383, he left 500 marks for the completion of the church; this, it is argued, prompted the construction of the nave. But as Pevsner points out,[1] the friars' churches in England generally included a nave, then a cross-space in the middle of which stands a tower, often octagonal, and then a chancel. There are no good grounds for supposing that St Mary's Church is the result of adding a 14th-century *de novo* nave west of a pre-existing tower – it is more likely that the tower was also built at this stage, as part of the crossing – the normal arrangement in such friary churches. It stood over the 'walking space' – a north-south passage which separated the nave from the monks' quire.

The post-Dissolution history of the site has resulted in the loss of much of the medieval building. Sir William Devereux, who held the manor in the 16th century, founded the grammar school, and this was sited in the chancel. The chancel arch was walled up, and a new doorway was inserted through the north chancel wall for access to the school. The upper part of the tower was rebuilt in 1782 to a design by Henry Couchman, while the nave and its aisles continued in use as the parish church, but they in turn were rebuilt in 1849 to designs by T.H. Wyatt and D. Brandon. The chancel became disused after 1863, but was restored in 1888 (*see* Fig. 9); a new vestry and porch incorporating a Norman doorway brought from Baddesley Ensor were added to its north side after 1907.

It would be easy, on first sight of the nave, to dismiss St Mary's Church as substantially Victorian, and not particularly good Victorian at that. But

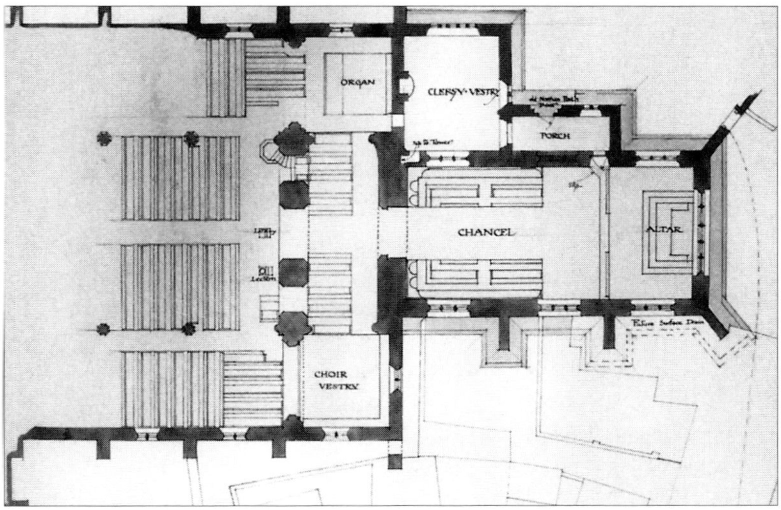

9 *Plan of the chancel of St Mary's Church, c.1907.*

the church building is important for its history, archaeology and, still, its architecture. Furthermore, the replacement of the western arm of the church in 1849 with a large new nave and aisles was probably in response to a major period of population growth in Atherstone. Whether the remains of a Norman chapel lie buried beneath the present chancel is open to question, and only the archaeological deposits now have the capacity to yield the truth about the development of the building. Later medieval fabric remains visible, especially under the crossing tower and in the chancel. The chancel arch – the east arch under the tower – is very narrow, and the tower is itself less than 13 feet square. The responds in the west archway include capitals in 14th-century style. Despite later alterations, a medieval altar recess has survived in the wall south of the east crossing arch; from this it is argued that shallow transepts must have flanked the tower.[2] Quite how much of the tower is medieval is not clear, but it should not be dismissed lightly as a mainly 18th-century rebuild, for the lower portion certainly retains medieval fabric. The tower is an important reflection of the Augustinian plan-form, and of the manner in which the friars intended the building to function, reserving the chancel for their own use, but serving the parishioners in the nave.

The main claim of the church to architectural distinction is that it has one of the oldest parochial chancels to be built in the Perpendicular style anywhere in Warwickshire. The earliest Perpendicular work in St Michael's, Coventry (now the old cathedral) was commenced in 1371, and the chancel at Atherstone was already under construction in 1375. The windows in the north and south chancel walls are attributed to the 14th century,[3] but in each window the middle lancet is taken up with straight mullions into the main arch; this is identified by Pevsner as an early example of Perpendicular tracery.[4] The east wall of the chancel has grey sandstone rubble up to the string course, brown ashlar above, with angle buttresses. The reveals of the east window are late 15th-century, but the tracery has been replaced.

Late Medieval Buildings in and Around the Market Place

(Short multi-phase descriptions of each building are given in the Gazetteer, and the history of some in the Building Histories.)

By around 1600, Atherstone had a 'well-frequented market' and Ogilby described the town as 'well-built',[5] but few remnants of the town's medieval and early post-medieval buildings remain around the Market Place. This is principally because they have been altered piecemeal, not that they have been entirely swept away. However, the alterations have been so thorough that it is difficult even to identify such late medieval fragments as remain in situ. These few surviving remnants are discussed here as a group.

The Angel Inn *(Building History One)*

The chequered history of Atherstone's buildings is amply illustrated by the *Angel Inn*, where it is remarkable that any pre-Georgian building fabric survived behind the *c.*1920s false framing, itself replacing a stucco façade. Despite major alterations, in-situ fragments of the original timber-framing can be seen inside the building. The limited surviving evidence suggests that the oldest parts of the *Angel Inn* could have been built within the couple of decades either side of 1500 (*see* p.77.)

Market Tavern *(Building History Three, 21 Market Street)*

Situated on the opposite side of the Market Place from the *Angel Inn*, the *Market Tavern* is, at first sight, more evidently Georgian, but one has only to step off the street into the bar to find that this was originally two rooms, divided by a timber-framed wall (*see* p.91.) The entry to the right also shows the tell-tale evidence of a former jetty. Thus, this building is also late medieval in origin.

8 Church Street

Not far from the Market Place, at 8 Church Street, only the proportions of the front façade give any clue that this might have been a timber-framed building, but the attic contains the scant remnants of a clasped purlin roof, probably constructed in the 15th or 16th century.

The Old Swan *(Building History Six, 175 Long Street)*

The *Old Swan* is situated some distance east of the town centre, on the south side of Long Street. The only known fragment of a cruck-framed building in the town brings the date of the *Old Swan* firmly into the medieval period. The wide frontage of the house masks an extremely complex sequence of alterations. Detailed analysis (*see* p.109) shows that as well as the cruck remnants, the building contains what appears to be a solar over upper-end chambers, and a second former cross-wing. The western end appears to have been an independent building jettied to the street.

THE END OF THE MEDIEVAL BUILDING TRADITION

The *Old Swan* is a clear example of piecemeal alterations to groups of medieval and early post-medieval buildings, leaving a complicated story to unravel. Even here, a little way out of the town centre, several buildings were crowded together on a relatively small plot of land. However, each element of the buildings comprised a number of bays or rooms in line, each of them only one room deep; both this plan-form, and the stages of development, were rooted in the medieval period. In some medieval town centres, especially around market places, the demand for sub-divided tenements, where trade and profits might be greater, led to tall street frontages and long developments along narrow tenements to the rear. Neither pressure for space nor the profits from trade were great enough in Atherstone to promote the type of cellared and multi-storeyed late medieval buildings that were built in major towns like York or Coventry. Nevertheless, in response to both general architectural trends, and the constraints of narrow plots, some new 17th-century buildings around the Market Place were given plans that were two rooms deep, as at 11/13 and 15/17 Market Street. If there were additional late medieval buildings to the rear they can now be identified only by archaeological excavation.

15/17 Market Street

This pair of houses, each with one big gable on the front elevation, have been ascribed to the 16th century in the Listed Building Description, and that may well be correct, especially as in the entry-way to No. 15 the splayed head of a post might once have been part of a jettied front wall. But how old are the twin brick chimney-stacks? Might they be late 16th-century, or a little later? They appear to have been built as a pair, and in No. 15, a narrow barrel-vaulted passage passes through the base of the stack, preserving the line of an entry. The front elevation of 15 Market Street retains, on the first floor, a timber-framed partition wall with small square panels – but the framing in the gable is a late mock-up. Upstairs in No. 17 what may be the partition wall between the two properties retains one long brace and several poor studs. The interiors have been very much adapted, but the intended late 16th-century plan form suggests that two discrete premises were built together, plausibly as a speculative development. Each property had, on the ground floor, an unheated front room, and a back room with a substantial fireplace – in No. 17 the fireplace retains its timber bressumer behind the mantel shelf.

11/13 Market Street (Building History Five)

Prominently located on the east side of the Market Place, this late 16th- or 17th-century timber-framed building was certainly intended to impress, having been jettied at first-floor and second-floor levels on both the street elevation and to the rear. It was not just its structure, but also its plan-form that might have been new to Atherstone. Despite the size of its plot of land, instead of having a medieval plan-form comprising a main range one room deep, with a wing or back range, it was two rooms deep across the entire width of its plot.

The front elevation of the building has been entirely replaced in brick, but evidence of its timber-framed origins can be seen from the street. The outside walls are all close-studded, but surviving internal partition walls are framed-up in relatively large panels. Several 17th-century features remain, including a balustrade with turned balusters. Early in the 17th century, 11/13 Market Street must have been one of the most impressive buildings in Atherstone, but within two or three generations it would be eclipsed by the new fashion for brick.

New Styles in the Late Seventeenth and Early Eighteenth Centuries

In 1700, Atherstone was still a small market and coaching town; many of the buildings around the Market Place, and those strung out along both sides of Long Street, would have been timber-framed. Change was at first gradual and piecemeal. The first new brick buildings were constructed for two main groups of clients – a few of the more wealthy inhabitants, and the owners of such commercial premises as inns and banks. The new houses, shops and inns still stood at the front of long narrow plots that were relatively open and undeveloped to the rear.

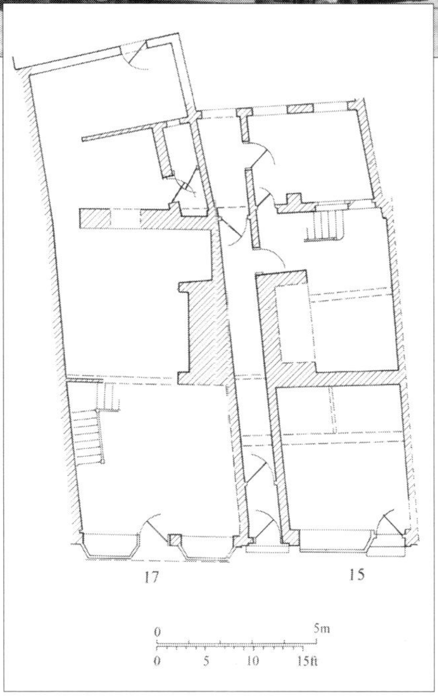

10 *15/17 Market Street.*

11 *Plan of 15/17 Market Street.*

155 Long Street, The Conservative Club

What is probably the earliest, and in its time the grandest, brick building in Atherstone is the present Conservative Club on the south side of Long Street, a little removed from the town centre. However, it was altered in the 19th and again in the 20th century. The harsh rendering on the façade, modern top-hung casement windows, purple brick chimneys, plain-tiled roofs and the single-storey infill between the forward-projecting wings all now detract from what must once have been one of the town's finest historic buildings. Pevsner noted, 'inside, a late 17thC staircase with turned balusters'.[6] Outside, the best indications of the fine quality of this building as first constructed are the quoins, string course and the boldly projecting moulded eaves cornice.

Beech House, 19 Market Street (Building History Four)

Dating from 1708 – the middle of the reign of Queen Anne – Beech House is the oldest remaining brick house overlooking the Market Square, and it is indisputably the finest, even if it has vernacular undertones. It is especially important as one of a very small number of buildings that still retain a high proportion of their early internal fixtures and fittings; many of the rooms are of outstanding quality, deserving careful conservation. The front elevation is of five bays with a basement, two full storeys and an attic, though it was not designed to the very best proportions that could be achieved at this time. Both doorways, and the windows at each end of the first floor, are all sited disproportionately close to the giant corner pilasters – a foible that the contemporary architectural practice run by the Smiths of Warwick would not have condoned, but one which presumably did not offend the owner, William Eyre. Inside, the imposing entrance hall has a fireplace with bolection mouldings, and the fine dog-leg staircase has a continuous moulded string, a heavy moulded handrail, and turned balusters.

It would not be surprising to find the first brick buildings in Atherstone on the Market Place and in Friars Gate – a more fashionable part of the town than Long Street. However, the construction of Beech House in 1708 on a plot overlooking the Market Place apparently did not prompt an immediate architectural response in other properties nearby. However, several new buildings appeared in Long Street at around the same period.

The former rectory (St Mary's House) and Chapel House (*see* p.60), both in Friars Gate, did not follow the Queen Anne Beech House until the early to mid-Georgian period. However, the timber-framed row, 2a-8 Church Street, were largely rebuilt in brick at much the same time, though on a smaller scale. Almost nothing remains of their medieval roof structure, but even from the street this long, low brick façade can be recognised as the rebuild of something older.

The shop fronts are later, the dormers have been altered, and on the first floor none of the windows contain the original sashes. Only the moulded eaves and two windows that have retained their splayed heads with moulded key-stones offer any hint of the 18th century. On the opposite side of Church Street, the *New Swan Inn* was an impressive mid-18th-century addition to the street, but it was remodelled in the 19th century.

In Long Street, the stone plaque on the very long and graceful façade of No. 129 gives the date of construction as 1711 – a mere three years later than Beech House, and much of the brickwork may be of that date, but all of the present doors and windows are replacements of around 1775. Formerly known as Old Bank House, but now part of the district council offices, these large commercial premises were extensively refurbished only about six decades after they were built (*see* below, p.59).

The piecemeal redevelopment of Long Street continued at number 97 Long Street, presently a Lloyd's Pharmacy, which has one of the best façades in the street, but it is also one of the most perplexing to interpret. High above the street, one of its gables is ogee-shaped, and presumably this was intended to impress anyone who approached the building from the west. The effect was spoilt when a

12 *The west side of Church Street, viewed from the south, including Nos. 2a-8.*

higher building was constructed on the adjoining plot. Ogee-shaped brick gables were built at nearby Tamworth Castle before 1600, and others in the general vicinity have been attributed to the 17th century – but on general grounds the Listed Building Description attributes 97 Long Street to the mid-18th century. Whilst the present stuccoed façade and the balustrades on the eaves parapet appear to point to this later period, the sash windows on the first floor are set very low in relation to the eaves; what one sees from the street may well be a remodelling of something older.

On the adjoining plot to the east, the *Red Lion Hotel* might also hide older fabric behind its remodelled façade and refitted interior.

Middle and Late Georgian (1714-1810)

That the HART survey identified few medieval buildings in Atherstone is in large measure due to the extensive replacement of the older building stock, a process which began only slowly in the Queen Anne and early Georgian periods. While the pace of rebuilding did begin to grow during the middle Georgian period – reflecting the changing economic circumstances – even then the process of rebuilding was not nearly as rapid as in the late 18th century and, especially, later during the nineteenth. During Atherstone's most prosperous phase, driven mainly by hatting – but with coal mining and other industries contributing to growth in the area – two main types of new building occurred: that on street frontages, and that on the yards to the rear (for the latter, *see* Chapter Nine).

13 *97 Long Street.*

The yards have been almost entirely demolished, but many of the larger and better-built street frontage houses, shops, inns and banks still stand. Especially in the town centre, however, they have been subject to pressures for change; moreover, many have not been well maintained. In common with some other west Midland towns, most of the late Georgian brick building façades in Atherstone are well-proportioned, but relatively plain and unembellished. These new buildings were constrained by the medieval tenement plots on which they were constructed, leading most commonly to three-bay brick façades, generally of two-and-a-half or three storeys. Most properties were individually owned, so reconstruction was piecemeal.

14 *The* Red Lion Hotel.

Examples from this period include 67 Long Street, which began as a typical mid-18th-century building, but is one of many historic buildings to have been badly treated, now having plastic windows and a concrete tile roof. The late 18th- or early 19th-century 21 Long Street, in Flemish bond red brick, with splayed rusticated lintels with keystones over the windows, brick eaves dentils and a pitched blue tile roof is redolent of its time (apart from the reproduction Victorian shop-frontage). The covered entry doorway to the right is another typical feature of Atherstone buildings. Trent House, at 102 Long Street, appears to have been stripped out to form offices, but the front elevation gives a good impression of a late 18th-century façade (although somewhat over-restored). The façade has three bays set slightly forward, and a fourth recessed bay to the right; it is of three storeys, defined by rendered plat-bands, and is topped by a moulded eaves cornice. The door with fanlight over, in the left-hand corner, is set within a wooden doorcase with Tuscan Doric half-columns under an open pediment. Originally, it had a service or entry doorway in the set-back fourth bay, but this has been replaced by a sash window. All of the 6-over-6 sash windows are set between rendered sills and rendered, rusticated and splayed flat lintels with keystones.

The best mid- to late-Georgian group is at 2a–8 Church Street, where older buildings, probably timber-framed, have been almost totally replaced by a well-proportioned two-and-a-half-storey row of shops with Flemish-bond brickwork (*see* Fig. 12 and Street scenes). Within this group, 4 and 6a Church Street, both with modern shop fronts in mock Victorian style, have retained their moulded eaves cornices. The windows on the first floor have splayed flat lintels with keystones, and the replacement 8-over-8 sash windows still have authentic-looking exposed sash boxes. At both ends of this group, the taller façades indicate later wholesale replacement of the older buildings. One of them, 2a Church Street, was squeezed onto a very narrow plot of land, and is only one bay wide; on the first floor it has a 6-over-6 sash window with a shallow elliptical head, typical of the mid to late Georgian period. At the opposite end, 10 Church Street is a building of three bays and three full storeys, now with a rendered façade. At first glance it might be taken to be early 19th-century – the period of its front elevation – but the story is more complicated, as the attic appears to have been raised. Originally, this building may have been of two-and-a-half storeys, like its neighbours to the south. It retains good sash windows to the first and second floors.

The heightening of the façade at 10 Church Street is illustrative of many of Atherstone's buildings of the later 18th century, a number of which were refurbished not long after they were built. Whether this reflects a response to changing architectural fashion or to the requirements of the owners, it is clear that the late 18th to early 19th century was both a restless and a formative period for the better buildings that lined the streets. Set behind attached railings, 129 Long Street (Old Bank House) is a clear example of a large but formerly plain early 18th-century house that was soon given more refined architectural fixtures.

The building has a date-stone inscribed 1711, but the handsome front elevation is said to have been remodelled *c.*1775. Of the five three-storeyed bays, the best are the projecting middle three. The central doorway is flanked by Tuscan Doric pilasters and topped by a triangular pediment. The six-panel door has a good semi-circular fanlight. On each side of the doorway there are tripartite windows with 6-over-6 sashes in the middle and 2-over-2 on each side – a form that has been attributed to the late 18th century. However, the paterae on the window at Old Bank House would place this example around 1800 or somewhat later. The first-floor windows stand on a sill-band; the middle window now has shouldered stone architraves, and a fluted flat canopy above. In the set-back bay to the right a pair of 8-over-8 sash windows and a handsome doorcase incorporating an over-door fanlight are united by a single flat canopy.

Another building that was subject to early additions and alterations is Chapel House in Friars Gate. If style is any guide, the older four-bay façade, now stuccoed, is of the 1720s. The front (west) elevation is divided in two by a high brick wall between the front and back gardens; the single bay on the north side of the wall is probably an addition. In the corner next to the garden wall, a single Tuscan Doric column carries one corner of an early 19th-century flat portico. The 6-over-6 sash windows have exposed sash boxes and narrow moulded architraves, a moulded eaves cornice, and a blue-tiled roof pierced by flat-topped dormers with casement windows. Originally, there were two good rooms at the front of the house – a big reception room and a more private parlour for the family, and there is a very good staircase with turned balusters. Such internal features as three-quarter-round bead-mouldings on the corners of chimney-breasts, and elliptical arches, belong to a refurbishment after 1800. A good, but steep, service stair with turned end-baluster, thin square balusters and a moulded hardwood handrail probably belongs to this time. In the added north bay, the dining room has pretty shaped cornice boards, unlikely to predate 1800.

15 *Old Bank House: 129 Long Street.*

215-16 Long Street (Hilton House)

This house stands just outside the main study area, but it is included here as it bears close comparison with Bank House. Both buildings stand behind attached railings – a feature that may have been common to many of the better 18th-century houses, providing some slight segregation from the street and a

16 *Old Bank House: detail of doorway and windows in right-hand bay.*

note of quality. Which was built first is uncertain, but Hilton House has two very good tripartite windows with Doric pilasters in the middle bay, one on the ground floor and another above, standing on a sill-band, perhaps dating from some time after *c.*1780. If so, their appearance here might have prompted the slightly later examples at Bank House. Hilton House has a three-bay façade of three storeys. The left-hand door, with fanlight above, has a doorcase with Doric pilasters and an open pediment, but the doorway to the right has a plain round arch containing an over-door light, plausibly denoting the entrance for servants and trade-people. The windows to the left and right on the first floor, and all three on the second, have flat splayed lintels with keystones and sash windows with set-back frames. The façade is topped off with a narrow moulded eaves cornice. The proportion of window to wall is redolent of the somewhat earlier Palladian revival, and the flatness of the façade adds to the sense of restraint. Its location outside the commercial core of the town has ensured the relatively complete survival of this dignified façade.

One of the difficulties in dating relatively simple buildings on their appearance is the level of uncertainty as to how long a given style might have persisted once it became fashionable. Many façades in Atherstone retain windows with flat splayed lintels, either plain, lined or rusticated, and with keystones – those at Hilton House might belong to the end of the 18th century, but apparently, such features continued to be built in Atherstone for most of Queen Victoria's reign. Another method sometimes used to suggest building dates is the observation of the relationship between the front brick wall and the window joinery. In 1709, it was stipulated in the Building Act that window frames should be set at least four inches (*c.* 10cm) behind the wall face; a new Building Act in 1774 required the sash boxes to be set behind the brickwork. At first these rules were introduced as fire precaution measures, but then in some areas sash boxes hidden behind brick reveals became fashionable. Builders in many provincial towns ignored both these strictures and the fashion: in Atherstone, while a few buildings adopted the new style, the majority continued to employ exposed sash boxes, some of them almost flush with the brickwork. In the 1774 Act, it was stipulated that bay windows should not project more than ten inches (*c.*25 cm) into the street. This regulation had been in force for some time before the timber-framed 11/13 Market Street was given a handsome new front elevation as part of a substantial refurbishment. On the ground floor, the multi-pane elliptical bow windows are of relatively shallow projection, apparently conforming with the rules, but the sash boxes on the first and second floors were left exposed. Not far away, at the *New Swan*, the regulations were observed when a new window with sash boxes set behind the brick reveals was inserted on the first floor of the Derby Lane elevation. (*See* below, Fig. 17)

Regency to Victorian

In the late 18th and early 19th centuries the population increase was accompanied by nonconformism, resulting in the construction of several small churches. Trinity Church, Coleshill Road, has been somewhat adapted, having a 19th-century single-storey lean-to front range with a central gabled porch. However, something of the original character of the church can be seen on the brick front elevation at first-floor level. This has a shallow central projection, and in each of the three bays it has retained pointed 'Gothic' windows with cast iron glazing bars intersecting in the arches and, above, a rendered castellated parapet. Inside, cast iron columns support the gallery. The Independent Chapel in North Street, built in 1827, has a three-bay front, the central bay projecting slightly, and rendered parapets hiding a shallow-pitched, hipped slate roof. The wide central double doors and half-round fanlight are set inside a rendered, rusticated arch over Ionic columns; the ground-floor and gallery windows have gauged brick round arches and iron window frames.

The part of the Coventry Canal between Atherstone and Fazeley was opened in 1790, providing a water transport link with Birmingham and the rest of the country. Warwickshire's first railway was opened in 1826, but Atherstone would have to wait until 1845 before prime minister Sir Robert Peel cut the first sod for the Trent Valley railway line from Rugby to Stafford. Both of these initiatives brought better transport for Atherstone's growing industries, but they simultaneously and progressively reduced the once-profitable trade of the coaching inns. The delightful railway station, which remains in use as offices, was designed in Tudor style by J.W. Livock and opened in 1847. It is of brick with limestone dressings, and has several steeply-pitched gables with finials and handsome, tall brick chimneys.

The pace and scale of change increased during this period, driven by the relative prosperity of the town, but even now some buildings were adapted rather than being replaced. Reference has already been made (*see* p.59) to the heightening of 10 Church Street, and that alteration may have prompted the owners to have the façade rendered. Similarly, substantial alterations can be seen at the *New Swan Inn*, Church Street (*see* Fig. 17). Although originally built in the 18th century, most of what can be seen from the street is the result of refurbishment by, or before, the middle of the nineteenth. The front of the public house overlooks Church Street, where a three-bay, three-storey façade has lined rustication to the ground floor, then plain stucco above, with quoins at the corners. The door in the middle is flanked by Doric pilasters that carry a shallow flat entablature. The bay windows to the left and right rise through two storeys. However, on the ground floor the sides of the bays are quarter-round, while those above are flat and canted. Presumably the early 19th-century bay windows on the ground floor were originally of only one storey, and those above were added later. On the south elevation in Derby Lane, the lined rustication returns to a pair of flat Tuscan pilasters and an entablature around an 8-over-8 sash window. Above, on the first floor, the window has sash boxes recessed behind the brick reveals – a later style than the exposed sash boxes almost flush with the wall of the small second-floor window.

17 *The* New Swan Inn, *at the corner of Church Street and Derby Lane.*

Late 18th- or early 19th-century alterations at 97 Long Street included the fitting of an excellent wooden doorcase with three-quarter-round columns supporting an open triangular pediment over (*see* Fig. 13); there is another good doorway to the left, with reeded architraves and corner-blocks.

One of the better, newly-built, late 18th- or early 19th-century façades is just west of the town centre, where it forms part of Atherstone Upper School in Long Street; it stands behind low ornamental railings. The main portion consists of three bays and three storeys with rusticated quoins and moulded eaves, fronting a big double-pile plan building, now without chimneys. On the ground floor, the wide 10-over-10 sash windows are flanked by flat pilasters supporting an entablature; the central doorcase has Tuscan three-quarter-columns and a fluted entablature. The sash windows on the upper floors have bold projecting surrounds. The single-storey bay to the left has a rendered front, and the otherwise plain parapet is broken by a row of balusters above a 10-over-10 sash window, identical to those in the main façade.

The predominant, more conser-vative style is illustrated at 45/47 Long Street, with a brick-sized stone set into the second floor bearing the date 1827. The features that are likely to belong to that date include two windows on the first floor and three on the second, all with plain rendered sills and rusticated splayed lintels with keystones. The original sash windows might have been multi-paned, but even without the date-stone its 19th-century construction date could be deduced from the projecting caps over each keystone. This formerly modest and simple façade was given a new shop window to the right, with classical pilasters and entablature constructed in a manner that places it in the 19th century. A larger shop-front was added to the left, rather later. An Edwardian bay window with canted sides and plate-glass windows was added on the first floor, and the original sash windows were probably replaced at the same time.

18 *45-47 Long Street.*

In an era of pattern books and greater communication, some clients – and their architects (still in the minority) – showed awareness of contemporary architectural styles, as in two buildings that exemplify the late 18th- and early 19th-century penchant for shallow blind arcades. At 74 Long Street, shallow recesses with round heads frame the sash windows, and a Diocletian window is tucked into another shallow recess under a parapet with concave curved ends. In the Market Place, one house has a single-bay brick façade of two-and-a-half storeys with a rubbed brick arch, framing a Venetian window, on the first floor, and a Diocletian window above. On the other hand, the study area does not have a single, decent, early Georgian giant pilaster. The front elevation of 9 Market Street (Ex-Servicemen's Club) of *c.*1830 is tall and impressive, but its giant pilasters are decorated with incised lines after the manner of John Soane, placing its construction nearer to 1830, rather than earlier. The portion of a massive classical column that stands adjacent to the south east corner of 108 Long Street is all that remains of the former corn exchange – but this was not built until 1854.

110 Long Street has been attributed to the respected architect, J.A. Hansom. The designer of the Hansom cab, he was also responsible for the former Dominican Convent in Atherstone, Birmingham's Victorian Town Hall – built like a Corinthian temple – and handsome extensions in Gothic taste at Princethorpe College (Warks). If 110 Long Street was indeed by this architect, its restraint might have been at the behest of the client. The rendered façade is of *c.*1837 although the ground floor elevations have been made over blandly by the former Midland Bank (now HSBC). On the upper floors the moulded surrounds and cornices on the sash windows have survived. Some of Atherstone's plastered or stuccoed façades are almost entirely devoid of elaboration, a type of quiet Regency dignity that is typified by 23 Market Street, done in the wake of Greek revivalism. More vernacular in character, 108 Long Street is another good example of a stuccoed façade, this with an entry to one side, a good shop front, and sash windows on the upper floors.

Several stuccoed or rendered façades in Long Street stand out for their references to the Palladian revival. The style flourished in the great houses from about the 1720s, but in provincial Atherstone its manner of execution and its combination with somewhat quirky later features places this group of buildings in the 19th century. The Old Bakery, 94 Long Street, is one of the best of these – three first-floor windows with bold architraves are topped by elliptical pediments, their shallow arches are broken by elaborate keystones, and the bracketed window-sills break a moulded sill-band. In a similar vein, though more restrained, 82 Long Street – a former coffee tavern – has three first-floor windows with shouldered architraves and triangular pediments on the front elevation. At 95 Long Street (formerly *The Earl of Richmond* public house), the bold window architraves and shaped heads demonstrate how the Victorians could elaborate on a theme and make it their own.

Classical and Gothic references abound in the buildings of this period, especially in many of the shop doorways and windows – work requiring considerable craft skills, and a constant delight for passers-by and customers alike. Examples include the fluted pilasters and Ionic capitals around the doorway at 122 Long Street, and the delightful bow windows at 11/13 Market Street.

Atherstone also has its share of Victorian Gothic buildings, one of the most flamboyant of these being at 63/63a Long Street, with its date-stone of 1875. The Corinthian capitals alongside two doorways seem deliberately Romanesque rather than Roman, but then there is nail-head ornament on the corbelled base of the canted oriel window, which has colonettes in Early English style. Over the smaller first-floor window, a slender two-centred arch contains a diaper panel, accurately done in gauged brickwork.

During the Regency and Victorian periods some of the most refined buildings were constructed for the better-off residents on sites outside the main commercial centre. Standing on the north side of Watling Street just to the west of the town centre, one of the best of them, Grendon Lodge, has retained a fine Regency façade, topped by an octagonal lantern. Built around 1820, it has a three-bay, two-storey perfectly symmetrical front elevation with

19 *Former* The Earl of Richmond: *95 Long Street.*

recessed corners and wings set well back. The porch in the middle of the main front is Greek Revival, and the slender 2-over-2 sash windows on the ground floor are set within shallow arched recesses; it is the finest building of its kind in the town. Built a decade or so later, and standing at the opposite end of Atherstone, 5/7 Witherley Road is less elaborate but equally graceful. Set well back from the road, this pair of houses presents a six-bay red-brick front, with each end bay stepped slightly forward, and with moulded eaves under a shallow-pitched slate roof with rolled lead ridges. The well-proportioned 6-over-6 sash windows have shallow elliptical arches of gauged brickwork, and the panelled doors, with overlights, are protected by wooden trellis porches with concave canopies. A later impressive pair of dwellings at 1/3 Witherley Road have Gothic wooden porches and tall, steep, brick gables with ornamented bargeboards and dog-tooth decoration on the stone sill-band; the stone balustrades over the bay windows have pierced quatrefoils. In Church Walk, The Old Vicarage, of around 1850, was built in English bond brickwork – rare in Atherstone. It is another handsomely gabled house, with mullion and transom windows and other Tudor details.

The Twentieth Century

There is not a single distinguished example of 20th-century architecture within the area of this study. In Long Street, The Memorial Hall, opened in September 1962, and the bland Library are as good as it gets. Also in Long Street, The Arcade, opened in 1985, was kept in scale and proportion with its neighbours, but that is the best that can be said for it. Thankfully, at least from the perspective of the street, Atherstone has retained a high proportion of its 18th- and 19th-century architectural heritage, imparting a comfortable market town image. Unfortunately, many of these buildings have recently been sadly neglected or poorly repaired.

In many small towns, the post-war years saw a lack of appreciation of historic buildings, with little thought being given to how vulnerable the character of a place could be to continuing small changes to its architectural heritage. In Atherstone, this mood was exacerbated by economic factors. Many owners were either unaware of the impact that their decisions were having on the general character of the place, or they simply could not afford to commission a high standard of repairs and conservation. From the 1950s, the situation was made worse by a lack of adequate advice to local planning authorities as to how they might apply existing legislation to control such works. The historic and architectural character of the town was generally undervalued, and many buildings suffered as a result. Typical alterations included the replacement of authentic sash windows on upper floors with either top-hung or side-hung casement windows. Even recently, within the Conservation Area, bland plastic window frames have been inserted into some façades, however inappropriate they may be considered to be in historic buildings. Some moulded eaves have been replaced by cheaper plain boxed eaves, and some roofs that once had old clay tiles have been re-covered with concrete tiles. The loss of chimney-stacks may be less obvious to pedestrians, but it results in bland longer views. Atherstone deserves better, as, unlike neighbouring Tamworth, the great majority of its historic buildings survive. Atherstone should be treated as one of Warwickshire's jewels, employing the best level of understanding to ensure authentic and appropriate repairs.

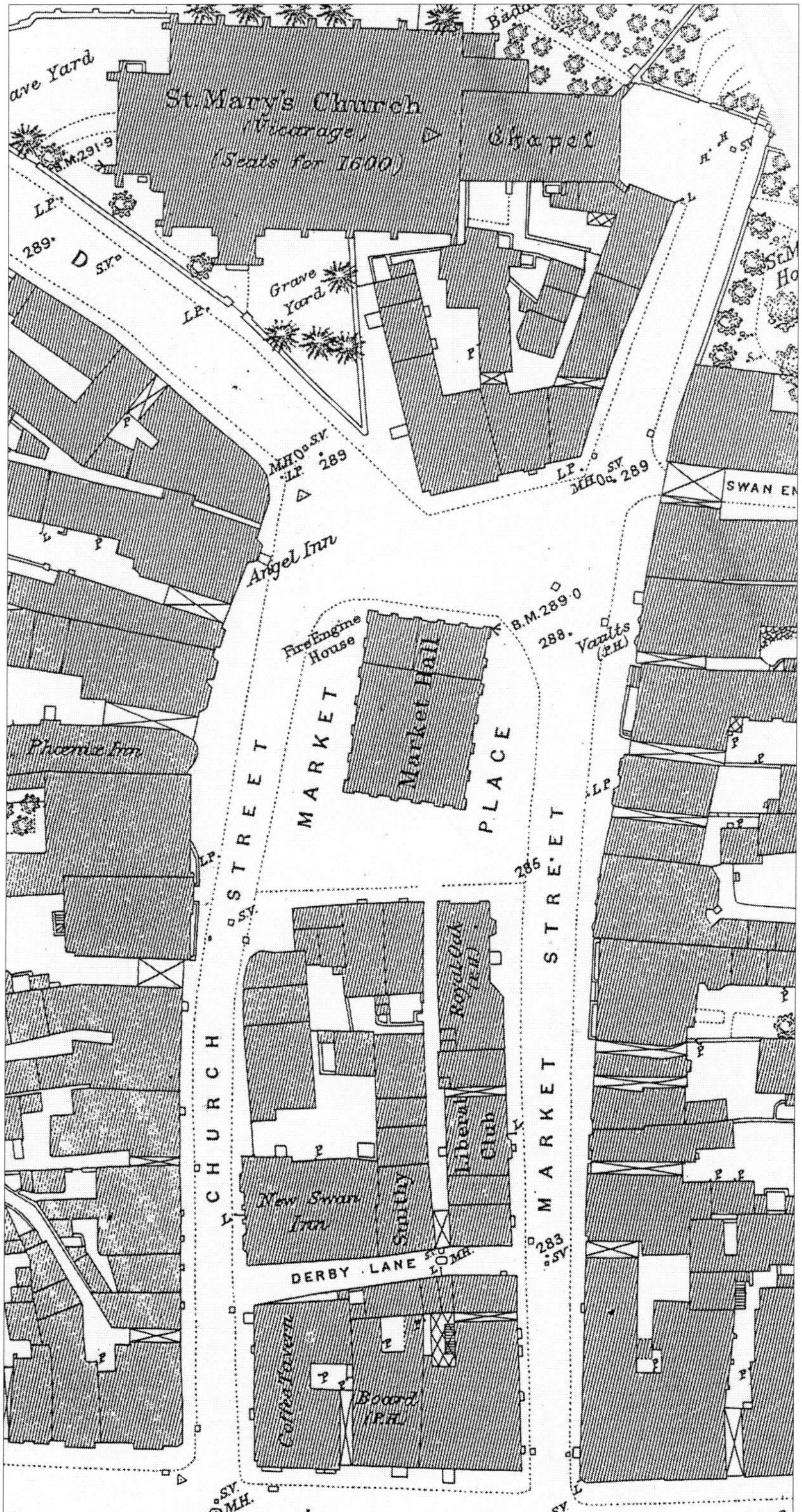
ave Yard
St. Mary's Church
(Vicarage)
(Seats for 1600)
Chapel
B.M. 291·9
L.P.
289
D
S.V.
Grave Yard
M.H. S.V.
L.P. 289
Angel Inn
M.H. S.V. 289
SWAN EN
Fire Engine House
Market Hall
B.M. 289·0
288
Vaults (P.H.)
MARKET PLACE
Phœnix Inn
CHURCH STREET
MARKET STREET
285
Royal Oak (P.H.)
Liberal Club
New Swan Inn
Smithy
DERBY LANE
M.H.
283 S.V.
Coffee Tavern
Board (P.H.)
282 M.H.
S.V.
L
O

The Streetscapes

Mike Trye

The streetscapes present the current elevations of the properties, below which are shown their 2008 street numbers, but also their identifications on the 1786 Plan of Atherstone (*see* Fig. 7), giving each property's designation as either copyhold ('C') or freehold ('F').

Some properties are itemised on one elevation, with the side of the property also shown on another elevation; in this case the details are not repeated.

Below each elevation, a column holds the names of its owners and/or occupiers, from 1912 at the top, down to the earliest identified, at the foot of the column.[1] The copyhold properties are well represented in the manor court rolls for Atherstone. As outlined in the Appendix to Chapter Three, between 1645 and 1871 the manor court recorded the owners, and, in many cases, the occupiers, whenever a property changed hands. The freehold properties, however, were not subject to the lord of the manor, and the details of owners or occupiers are rather sparse. It is generally possible to derive information on a freehold property only when it abutted copyhold premises. In these situations, owners and/or occupiers of the freehold property were recorded, to serve as identifiers for the adjacent copyhold property.

Occupiers from 1841 to 1901 are taken from the census enumerators' records. For 1912, the information comes from Kelly's Directory (WCRO).[2]

20 *OS map 1888: Atherstone Market Place and surroundings. For the Market Place area, it is interesting to compare the present streetscapes with the area as it was in 1888. The mid-1960s saw the demolition of the Market Hall and the group of buildings to the south of St Mary's Church, together with the building to the right of the* Angel Inn. *Some time earlier, the third bay to the left of the* Angel Inn *had also been removed.*

Church Street West Side (South End)

2008	2	2a Curds	4 4CS / 6a Bairstows	6	8	10 Butlers Gery
1786 Map	F43 Freehold	F39 Freehold				C111 Copyhold
1912	(No Information)		George Evans *Confectioner*	Martin Thomas Chapman *Haberdasher*	Edwin Clark *Milliner*	Joseph Woods *Boot & Shoe Maker*
1901		Henry Jones *Foreman Shoe Factory*	James Hopkins *Hat Finisher*	Mary Martin *Hosier*	Edwin Clarke *Milliner*	Joseph Woods *Boot & Shoe Dealer*
1891		Ambrose Twigger *Agent*	James Hopkins *Hat Finisher*	Thomas Martin *Hosier*	Susan Clarke *Milliner*	Unoccupied
1881			George Clarke *Tailor*	Thomas Martin *Hosier*	Mary Clarke *Milliner*	William Starmer *Boot & Shoe Maker*
1871		Samuel Baldwin *Railway Porter*	John Tuckey *Washer Mfr*	Thomas Martin *Hosier*	Susan Clark *Bonnet Maker*	Alfred Clarke *Currier*
1861		Samuel Baldwin *Grocer*	John Tuckey *Nailor*	Thomas Martin *Hosier*	Henry Orme *Cabinet Maker*	Thomas Kimberlin *Currier*
1851			John Tuckley	John Kimberlin *Shoemaker*	William Hatton *Tailor*	John Kimberlin *Boot Maker*
1841			William Allen *Baker*	Joseph Dent *Builder*		Thomas Pullin *Currier*
1786 Owner		Unstated		1768 Mrs Bagnoll; Mrs Biley; John Thomas		Joseph Phillips
1663 Hearth Tax		Widow Hodgkinson Owner		John Wood		Richard Mosse

Church Street West Side (North End)

2008	12 Howkins & Harrison	14	16	18 Serenity	20	*Angel Inn*
1786 Map	C110 Copyhold		C109	F40 Freehold		C108 Copyhold
1912	William Steel *Wholesale beer & Spirits*	Baker Megginson *Furnishing Ironmonger*		William Starkey *Grocer*	Herbert Sandles *Hardware dealer*	Edward Porter & William Whitehead *Cycle agent & Angel Inn*
1901	William Steele *Brewers's Agent*	Baker Megginson *Ironmonger*	John Gretton *Licenced Victualler*	William Harvey *Grocer*	William Wade *Hard Ware Dealer*	Harry Howe *Licenced Victualler*
1891	William Hatwell *Ironmonger's Porter*	Baker Megginson *Ironmonger*	William Rathbone *Innkeeper*	Caroline Orton *Dress-maker*	William Starkey *Grocer's Assistant*	Charles Jackson *Publican*
1881	David Wilner *Solicitor's Clerk*	Baker Megginson *Ironmonger*	William Rathbone *Stone Cutter*	Luke Lakin *Draper*	Thomas Gisbourne *Confectioner*	Mary Buckmall *Innkeeper*
1871	William Ison Retired *Veterinary Surgeon*	John Page *Ironmonger*	John Simonds *Innkeeper & Hatter*	Chas Harrison *Draper*	George Simonds *Confectioner*	Mary Bucknall *Licenced Victualler*
1861	William Willothesse *Retired Farmer*	Being built	Unoccupied	Edward Roberts *Draper*	George Simonds *Confectioner*	Mary Bucknall *Innkeeper*
1851	Unoccupied	Joseph Mellor *Tailor*	Sarah Hawkes			John Ball *Victualler Carpenter*
1841	William Freer	William Freer			1794 Edmund Simonds	Michael & Geo Adams *Hat Mfr & Innkeeper*
1786 Owner	William Freer		John Pinchback	Charles Beale	Charles Beale	William Adams Devisees
						1758 William Adams
1663 Hearth Tax		John Chamberlaine	Henry Shepie	Michael Trayford	Widow Greene	1652 Richard Robinson

Market Street East Side (North End)

2008	25 / 23 Old Surgery	21 *Market Tavern*	19 Beech House	17 Shortland	15 Howkins	13/11 Works
1786 Map	F33 Freehold	C103 Copyhold	C102 Copyhold	Copyhold	C 101 Copyhold	C100 Copyhold
1912	Alfred Sale	Edward Wood *Cricketers Arms*		Alfred W.H. Jarvis *Fried Fish Dealer*	Sam Henry Rowley *Hairdresser*	Herbert James Hatton *Confectioner*
1901		William Whitehead *Licensed Victualler*	Robert Mears *Medical Practitioner*	George Eaton *Drapers' Assistant*	Samuel Rowley *Hairdresser*	
1891	Henry Holyfield *Hairdresser*	Ralph Crisp *Licensed Victualler*		Henry Albrighton		
1881	William Roberts *Victualler*			G. Hastelow *Ironmonger*		
1871	Stephen Arthrell *Retired Farmer*					
1861	Thomas Bates *Seedsman & Gardener*		George Sale	James Haddon *Grocer*		
1851		Francis Sanders *Wine Merchant*		George Sander *Watch Maker*		
1841					William Dutton *Bricklayer*	
1800		1811 John Sanders	1811 Sarah Hanson			
1786 Owner Occupier	Abraham Bracebridge Nicholas Smith *Surgeon*	Thomas Grew Richard Leigh *Stationer*	Nicholas Smith		Thomas Williams Thomas Mason Benjamin Pullen	John Underwood Chris Preston
1768 Poor Relief		Mr Grew 1756 Thomas Draper	1756 Nicholas Smith *Surgeon*			
1750			1738 Edward Farmer		1723 John Killingworth	1738 Francis Fitzgerald *Apothecary*
1700						
	1684 John Chamberlain	1684 Anne Draper	1684 Thomas Inge *Gent* 1671 John Vincent *Mercer*		1670 Widow Oadhams & Mary Smith	1671 William Symonds *Gent*
1663 Hearth Tax	John Hall *Gent*	Thomas Draper *Butcher*	John Vincent *Mercer*			
1650	1659 John Hall		1653 Eliz Power	1646 John Sutton *Barber*		

Market Street East Side (South End)

2008	9	7	5	3	1
	Ex-Servicemen's Club	Restaurant	Restaurant Estate Agent	William Hill	

1786 Map	C99	C98	C97 Copyhold	C96
1912		Robt Farmer Sheavyn *House Furnisher*	Maria Stanton *Grocer*	Baxter & Sons *Printers & Stationers*
1901	Emily Seymour			Frederick Baxter *Printer*
1891		James Minoult *Watchmaker*		
1881	Isabella Morris	George Martin *Clock & Watch Maker*	Thomas Stanton *Sadler*	John Baxter *Printer*
1871				Frederick Coates *Printer*
1861	Joseph Morris *House Proprietor*		Hugh Stanton *Sadler*	William Holland *Stationer*
1851				
1841			1834 John Payne *Butcher*	Unoccupied
1800			1817 William Payne *Butcher*	William Hanson *Draper and mercer*
1786 Owner Occupier	John Morris 1777 John Morris *Timber Merchant*	Samuel Hobley	John Payne	Samuel Stratton
1768 Poor Relief				
		1754 James Nightingale		
1750	1750 George Paul		1742 John Payne	1752 Samuel Stratton
1700	1709 Edward Latimore			1705 Thomas Collett & Hugh Adcock *Mercers*
		1671 Michael Orton		
1663 Hearth Tax	John Shellard *Blacksmith*	Edward Power	George Sadler	Robert Parker
			1658 George Sadler	1657 Robert Parker

Market Street West Side

Derby Lane — Market Place

2008		2 Paul & Company	6 Bates	8 S57	10 Fishing	12 SEL	*Royal Oak*
1786 Map	C105 Copyhold (*see* p.76)	F34	Freehold			F35	
1912		(No Information)	1912 William Cadman *Fishmonger*		1912 Louis Myatt *Greengrocer*		
1901				William Tilson *Brewer's Porter*	Alexander Simkins *Fruiterer & Fishmonger*	Thomas Hollo? *Beer Dealer's Porter*	Harry Green *Licenced Victualler*
1891			Emma Beck *Fishmonger*		Joseph Bray *Hatter* *Liberal Club*	Samuel Moreton *Shoe Maker*	Ann Meller *Publican*
1881			Emma Beck *Fishmonger*	Thomas Greeves *Master Machinist*		William Lazarus *Hat Shaper*	John Roadknight *Licenced Victualler*
1871			Thomas Gisbourne *Confectioner*			William Copson *Tailor*	
1861			Thomas Thompson *Confectioner*	Unoccupied	Elizabeth Bailey *Charwoman*	William Boswell *Coal Miner*	James Ball *Shoe Maker & Publican*
1851			William Bishop *Grocer*	Thomas Bailey *Basket Maker*		Maria Harrison *Dress-maker*	Joseph Choyce *Victualler*
1841			William Bishop *Shop Keeper*				Elizabeth Brackley *Publican*
			1832 Henry Radford *Butcher*				
			1793 Thomas Grew				
1786 Owners				Town Hall			Sarah Choyce
1650			1721 William Spencer 1648 Common butchery	1648 Town Hall			1675 William Lamkyn & Robert Browne

Market Place South Side

Church Street East Side

	Market Place South Side				Church Street East Side
2008	Atherstone Electrical	16 Throck-mortons	16a Arragon	The Wine Bar	The Wine Bar
1786 Map	F35 — Freehold		F36	F37	F37 Freehold
1912	Alfred Mercer *Tailor*	London Central Meat Co *Butchers*	Stephen Hilton & Sons *Boot & Shoe Makers*		George Cheshire *Shoemaker*
1901	Unoccupied	Unoccupied	Unoccupied		George Cheshire *Shoemaker*
1891	Unoccupied	Joseph Shevens *Manager Boot Stores*	Unoccupied		John Pickering *Grocer*
1881	Joseph Palfreyman *Provision Dealer*				Mathew Robinson *Fishmonger*
1871	Jane Ball *Shoemaker*	Unoccupied			Mathew Robinson *Fishmonger*
1861	Sarah Makepeace *Confectioner*				Charles Cooper *Brazier Journeyman*
1854		John Makepeace *Ag Lab*			Caroline Brown *Milliner*
1841	Lydia Makepeace *Shopkeeper*	John Makepeace			
					1790 Samuel Boonham
1786 Owners		Omitted from map			Omitted from map
	1777 Sarah Choyce				
1700	1701 Richard Haddon				
1650	1675 William Lamkyn & Robert Browne				

Church Street East Side

Long Street North Side

2008	*New Swan*	Derby Lane		82 Tags	84	86 Scope
1786 Map	F38 Freehold		C107 Copyhold	C107	C106 Copyhold	C105
1912	Arthur James Lock			F Parkinson *Chemist*	Mary Ann Peckover *The Board*	Goodwin, Poser & Brown *Grocers*
1901	Harry Green *Licenced Victualler*			Frederick Parkinson *Chemist*	Frank Peckover *Licenced Victualler The Board*	
1891	Ann Meller *Licenced Victualler*			Arthur Windridge *Manager Coffee Tavern*	William Jones *Publican*	Thomas Newcombe *Grocer*
1881	Charlotte Harrison *Licenced Victualler*			Philip Hall *Manager Coffee Tavern*	William Jones *Publican*	Sarah Morris *Housekeeper*
1871	Mary Parker *Licenced Victualler*			John Wheeler *Draper*	Charles Weetman *Licenced Victualler*	Thomas Cox *Ironmonger*
1861	John Cooke *Licenced Victualler*			Joseph Bacon *Draper*	William Oarden *Wine Merchant*	Unoccupied
1851	John Cooke *Innkeeper*			William Nosworthy *Chemist & Druggist*	William Oakden *Wine Merchant*	Unoccupied
1841	John Orton *Publican*			Joseph Carter *Chemist*	John Pears *Wine Merchant*	Thomas Green *Printer Bookseller*
1830						
1800	1790 James Badcock *Victualler*			1830 Geo Haddon *Builder & Stone Mason*	1830 Catherine Mousley *Wine & Spirit Merchant*	1800 Thomas Carver *Perukemaker*
1786 Owners				George Haddon	Elizabeth Mousely	Margaret Carver
				1757 Elizabeth Harrison	1752 Sara Carver	1761 Thomas Carver
					1704 Richard Carver	1720 John Roper
				1672 Richard Goodwin		
1663 Hearth Tax	Thomas Chalton			William Goodwin *Butcher*	Samuel Leet *Gent*	William Roper

Building Histories

Bob Meeson and Judy Vero

Building History One: The *Angel Inn*

This property is C108 on Fig. 7. *See* Figs. 21-4 and 53.

An angel has been universally recognised as a symbol of reliable aid and comfort at the roadside. This connection derives from the Biblical story of the guardian angel who guides and protects the lone traveller, Tobias. Hence, the 'Sign of the Angel' is usually found close to the entrance to a town and often near to the church.[1]

From early times Atherstone stood at the crossing of two major roads, the Roman Watling Street, from south-east to north-west, and the packhorse route to Derby, running to the north-east. The field plan of 1716 (Fig. 8) shows a faint line, indicating a track, from Fieldon Bridge (on the road to Derby).[2] By this date the road came into the town from the north, entering the Market Place at the north-east corner (where Friars Gate stands today). However, if the line of the track from Fieldon Bridge is continued into Atherstone it comes out at the north side of the *Angel Inn*. It thus seems likely that the original course of the track in medieval times brought it into the town at that point. In 1794,[3] the early layout was restored when the building to the north of the *Angel* was pulled down by Abraham Bracebridge to make way for the re-routed road to Derby. It is therefore very likely that the *Angel* is one of the town's oldest buildings, and has served as an inn for most of its history.

The Building

The chequered history of Atherstone's buildings is amply illustrated by the *Angel Inn*, where it is quite remarkable that any pre-Georgian building fabric survived. Now, standing detached, at the north-west corner of the Market Place, the *Angel Inn* was formerly attached to the north end of the buildings in Church Street. In 1900 the *Angel Inn* had a three-bay stuccoed façade containing Regency/Victorian tripartite windows on the first and attic floors.

The left-hand bay, originally timber-framed, has been demolished, and the stuccoed brick façade was replaced around 1920-30 by two gabled bays, with applied planks imitating timber-framing, in a style redolent of the 1920s. Despite the major alterations, in-situ fragments of the original timber-framing can be seen inside the building. The ceiling of the ground-floor

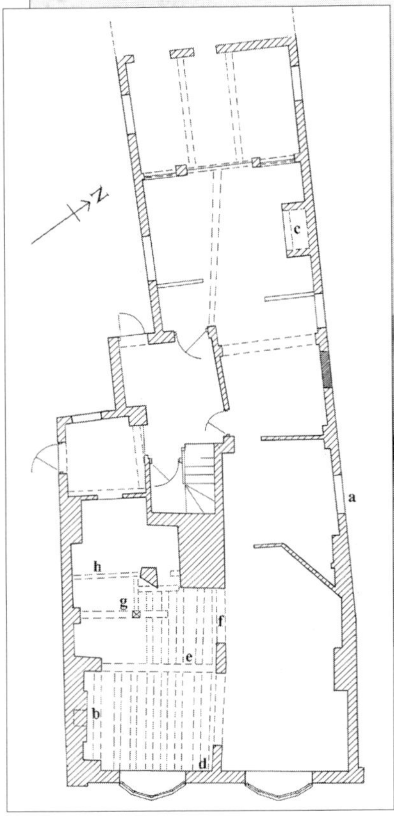

21 *Ground-floor plan of the* Angel Inn.

22 *The* Angel Inn, c.*1900*.

23 *The* Angel Inn, c.*1960*.

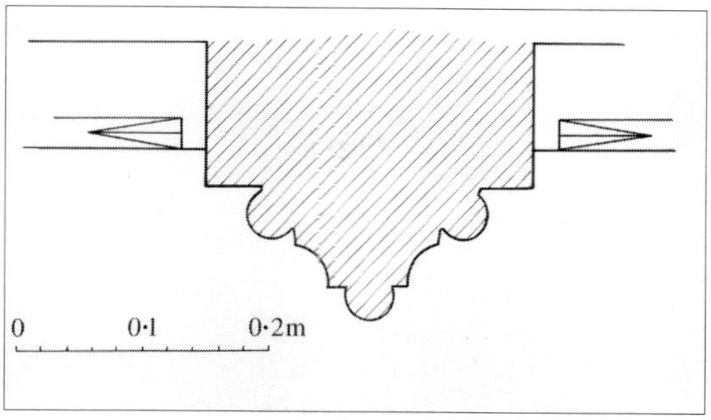

24 *Ceiling beam moulding; [e] in Fig. 21.*

25 *Marks on the fireplace bressumer at [c] in Fig. 21. The stippled circle is the end of a peg, and the shaded areas are taper-burns, but the scratch-marks might be apotropaic.*

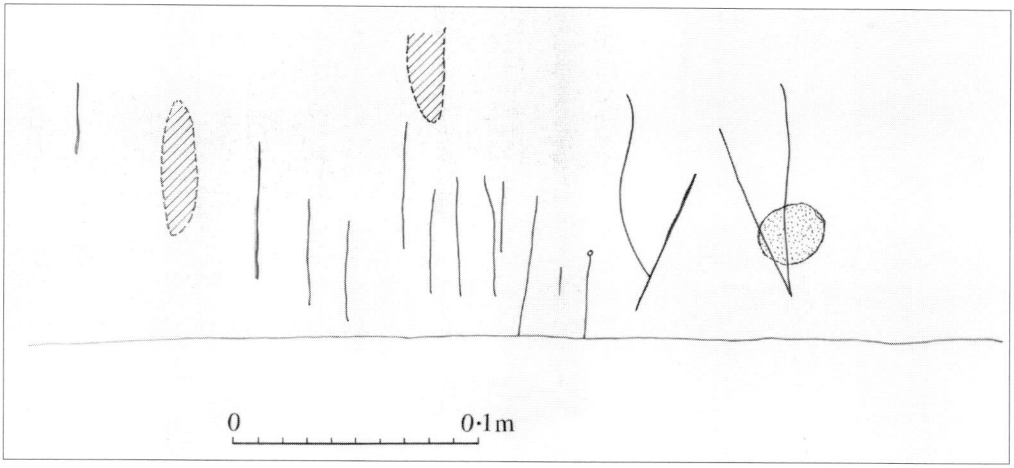

south-east room is substantially older than anything visible outside. Near the east (front) wall of this room, paired pyramid stops indicate the line of a former jetty-plate, and the shape of this plate can still be seen (at 'd' on Fig. 21). Accordingly, at least part of the front wall was originally jettied; that is to say, the upper floor was stepped forward of the ground floor wall. The aperture ('f') between the two front rooms is spanned by a re-used beam which is heavily-weathered on one face; it has a moulded arris and numerous mortices belonging to a close-studded wall, and this seems to imply that the north side of the building is a post-medieval addition.

The roof of the front range retains a truss with two struts rising to a single collar and carrying trenched purlins. An elaborately-moulded ceiling-beam ('e') and a matching half-beam are in a style that was current *c.*1500-20, and for the present, this is the best dating evidence available for the building.[4] The ceiling joists are laid in flat rectangular section, and their chamfers have pyramid stops. At 'g' there is a possible trimmer for a staircase inside the back wall at 'h'. Taken together, the limited surviving evidence suggests that the oldest parts of the *Angel Inn* could have been built within the couple of decades either side of 1500.

THE HISTORY

The first firmly identifiable innholder is Richard Robinson – the occupant in 1652.[5] By trade a butcher, he was the son-in-law of one of the town's leading men, Hugh Drayton. However, the Robinsons had lived in Atherstone for at least a hundred years before this and owned property in the Market Place from the late 1500s which may well have included the *Angel*.

In 1652, Richard Robinson sold the *Angel* to John Walmsley and his wife, Sarah. To purchase it they raised a loan of £106 from John Farmer, a yeoman from nearby Ratcliffe [Culey], using the building as security.[6] Over the following years the loan was repaid, and when John Walmsley was too old to run the inn himself he passed it over to his son John, with the condition that John junior paid him an income of £5 a year.[7]

The Walmsleys prospered. By the time that John junior died in 1712 he styled himself as a 'gentleman'. His property holding was now considerable and included the now lost the *Bear Inn* (near the west corner of Long Street and Dog Lane), a shop under the town hall, a 'messuage' he had bought from Samuel Bracebridge, and a number of parcels of land in the open fields. John junior had also served as a manor bailiff and become embroiled in one of the most controversial events of the day when he used devious means to claim as a heriot (a kind of death duty) a silver tankard from the recently-dead Samuel Bracebridge.[8] The lord of the manor, Seabright Repington, had a reputation for being heavy-handed and was forced to review his policy after this high-profile incident; nor would the event have endeared John Walmsley to his fellow townsmen. Accusations that he had misappropriated the tankard may well be substantiated by the fact that he willed to his granddaughters, Sarah and Isabella Cotterell, 'my silver tankard'.[9]

On his death, John junior was living at the *Angel*, though he had let out 'premises and appurtenances' to Christopher Broadgate.[10] The inventory of John's belongings lists the rooms as follows:[11]

Room	*Contents (notes)*
House Place	
Lower Parlour	(feather bed)
Chamber over the Stable	(bedsteds)
Brew house	
Little Parlous	(feather bed)
Buttery	
Parlour by the Kitchen	(beds)
Kitchen	
Parlour next the Street	(bed)
Little Chamber	(bed)
Shovel Board Chamber	(one bed)
Matted Chamber	(two feather beds)
Stare Head Chamber	(2 beds, one with 2 featherbeds upon it)
Closset	
Cockloft s	(2 beds)

Table 5 *Rooms in the inventory of John Walmsley junior, 1721.*

This being an inn, there were some 15 beds. No doubt the rooms with featherbeds would command a higher price, and those in the cocklofts would probably have housed servants. Privacy could not be taken for granted: strangers often shared bedrooms and sometimes even beds. The main living room ('House place') had a clock, a grate and cooking equipment. The 'matted chamber' may have been the only one with a carpet. It also contained 22 chairs, two tables, a looking glass and chest of drawers. This suggests that it also served as the meeting place of the manor court, which certainly met at the *Angel* later in the century.

The service area of the inn was similarly extensive, with a kitchen equipped with '38 pewter dishes.' A 'closet' contained '2 dozen of Plate and other things' valued at 16 shillings. By far the most valuable items were the 'quick and dead goods' – hay, wheat, barley, sheep, cattle, pigs and horses, which accounted for some £291 of Walmsley's total wealth of £397.

John junior bequeathed the *Angel* to his wife, Sarah, for her life, and then her heirs, though he also added, 'she to sell the same to raise mony to pay my debts'. He also bequeathed *'the Bare Inn'*,[12] and the messuage which he had 'lately purchased off one Samuell Bracebridge Esq',[13] after his wife's death, to his granddaughters, Sara and Isabelle Cotterell. But for these bequests they were obliged to pay £40 within six months of his wife Sarah's death. She was to be his 'sole executrix', helped by his two sons-in-law, Joseph Cotterell, of Bacons End near Coleshill (whose wife had died), and Henry Baddeley, wife of John's daughter, Elizabeth. Surprisingly, John junior's son, also John, was left only two acres of arable land.

The will was not proved until 1721, by which date Sarah Walmsley and the Baddeleys must have died, for Joseph Cotterell, alone, was admitted tenant to the *Angel*.[14] Since it had been left to Sarah Walmsley's heirs, one wonders why John Walmsley or, indeed, Elizabeth Baddeley's son, Henry, had no part of this inheritance. By 1726, Joseph had died and his two eldest daughters were admitted as his executors. Sara was now the wife of William Lowe of Coleshill, a mercer, and Isabelle remained unmarried.[15]

By 1755, Isabelle had married Francis Blakeman, and Sara Lowe was dead. The Blakemans and William Lowe sold the *Angel* to William Adams.[16] William took out a mortgage of £204 from William Norris, a dyer in Atherstone. It seems that Adams struggled to repay the debt, and in 1758 had to raise a further loan from Frances Burges, a gentleman heavily involved in town affairs.[17] On his death, though, the debt was paid off and the inn was inherited by his three sons, John, Samuel and Benjamin, who each received a one-third share in the property.[18] John sold his share to his two brothers who continued to occupy separate parts of the buildings.[19] The insurance book for 1785 gives some idea of the split:

> Mr Benjamin Addams Victuler in Ath Removes from the Sun Fire Office. Insuars his now dwelling House and Backbuildings all adjoining each other Built with Brick and Tiles at £150 allso a House lett to Samuel Addams and back building all adjoining to his now dwelling House Built with Brick and Tiles.[20]

In 1794, Samuel, a baker, raised a mortgage of £150 on his half. He may have been financing some building work, perhaps erecting a bakehouse on the site, for this was a year of change for the *Angel*.[21] Abraham Bracebridge had bought the neighbouring property and pulled it down in order to re-route the road to Fieldon Bridge (to what may have been its original course).[22] The *Angel* was thus restored to its traditional position on a major thoroughfare into the town. (For more on Bracebridge's changes to the town's roads, *see* 'Building History Two', p.89.)

Benjamin continued as innkeeper until his death in 1826. He died intestate and his eldest son, Thomas, inherited his half share. Thomas died three years later, leaving his estate to his brothers, Michael and George, though Benjamin's widow, Elizabeth, continued as innkeeper.[23] Michael Adams was a silk hat maker.[24] At Christmas 1828, he insured his part of the premises:

> Household goods, printed books, plate, linen, &c. in his dwlg ho & offices. Stock & implements in trade therein. Stock & implements in trade in a hatters finishing shop, lining & binding etc. Warranted not to have stove for drying hats in the above premises.[25]

Elizabeth died in 1839 and her son, George, took over as innkeeper. At this point, George and Michael decided to sell the inn – they put it up for auction the following May. But there were no bidders and it was not until December that a buyer was found – John Tavener, a linen draper from Nuneaton.[26] He presumably bought the *Angel* as an investment property, leasing it out to a series of tenants.

In 1845, Thomas Drackley was the innkeeper; by the 1851 Census it had changed to John Ball, a journeyman carpenter, who had come to Atherstone from Thorpe in Staffordshire. He and his Birmingham-born wife, Emma, had six children, of whom the eldest, Mary, aged 15, worked as a barmaid. The time when an innkeeper would stay a lifetime had gone, and possibly with it, any notion of this being a high-status hostelry. By the time of the 1861 Census, Mary Bucknall was innkeeper, and she stayed at least until 1881 when she is again recorded in the Census. By 1891, Charles Jackson was the publican, and by 1901,[27] Harry Howe, described as a 'licensed victualler.'

Today, the *Angel Inn's* main claim to importance is as the host of the Ball Game celebrations on Shrove Tuesday, when local 'heavies' repair to celebrate their victory or commiserate their loss. It is no better or no worse than any other hostelry in the town. Few customers notice the carved beam (*see* Fig. 24, above), even less the marks on the re-sited beam over the back fireplace (Fig. 25) intended by former occupants to ward off the devil. Besides that, the only other testament to the inn's antiquity is its name.

Building History Two:
Swan House, 23/25 Market Street

This property is F33 on Fig. 7. *See* Fig. 54.

The Building

Directly opposite the *Angel* across the Market Square is an imposing three-storey building standing on the site known in 1625, and possibly much earlier, as 'The Swanne House.'[1] Both buildings share the honour of flanking St Mary's Chapel, and remain among the most important buildings in the town. Remarkably, in around 1795, a road was driven through the centre of the house (*see* p.89, below).

The main range along the street is made up of three sections: one house to the north (No. 25, Market Street), the inserted road or enlarged carriageway, and what has become a separate portion to the south – No. 23. Features are lacking to indicate a precise date for the original building, but it probably dates from the later 18th century, rebuilt by the Bracebridge family as a large three-storey brick house. It was then an inn, with a central carriageway through which horses and coaches could reach the stables in the yard at the rear.[2] The principal entrance doorway led off this carriageway. When the public road was created along the line of this carriageway, the building was split into two separate houses (though it remained in one ownership). The extensive alterations at this date included a two-storeyed addition to the north side, the re-planning of the interior, and new doors and windows on the front elevation, which was then stuccoed.

The two-storeyed addition on the north side of No. 25 was probably built following the construction of North Street through the building, providing an entrance for the left-hand (north) portion. Most of its front elevation is taken up by double doors, part-glazed, part-panelled, set between side-lights, all within a chamfered surround below top-lights and a moulded cornice. Above, there is a 6-over-6 sash window with stone sill and stuccoed reveals, then a low parapet. What remains of the north side of the original elevation has a 6-over-6 sash window on each of the ground- and first floors. Curiously, on the first floor, the sash now in the bottom of the window has the horns on top; it appears to have been turned upside down. Above the road arch, a 3-over-3 sash window is tucked under the eaves of the blue-tiled roof. Adjacent to North Street, at the side of the road under the arch, there is a blocked window and doorway.

Inside No. 25, the entrance and staircase lobby has a late-Victorian or Edwardian tiled floor. The fireplace in the south wall has corner-blocks and a painted stone shelf – about 1800. The staircase has both a closed string and big end-balusters with fielded panels, Georgian turned balusters and a toad's-back hand-rail.

On the first floor, the walk-in cupboard east of the staircase has a black and red chequer-board tiled floor; it contains a shelf pierced by small holes – perhaps for draining bottles or decanters. The doorway to this room has moulded architraves, the door with four flat panels with flush-moulded edges. The very large front room has been subdivided by a late partition, which cuts across the fireplace; this has a stone surround and mantle shelf, and there is a servants' bell-pull to one side. The doorway in the south-east corner of this room connects with the first of two small lobbies, paved with more black and red chequer-board tiles, and has four-panel doors with flush-moulded edges. The door to the little cupboard in the lobby has four flat panels with flush-moulded edges. From here, service stairs with thin square-section balusters and a moulded hand-rail rise to the rear range attic (*see* below). The second lobby has vertical boards and a window seat on its south wall, and folding shutters, each leaf having four panels. The stone fireplace contains a late Victorian cast iron grate. There is an 8-over-8 sash window in north wall. This room, and the next two to the east, were originally all one – a big function- or dining-room. Two large windows in the south wall retain their tall folding shutters.

At the same time as the road was cut through the building, No. 25 was further extended by the addition of a five-bay, three-storeyed brick back range alongside North Street. The first bay beyond the arch contains a doorway under the shadow of a pentice, and a brick bearing the inscription 'RB 1795'. The ground- and first-floor windows are 6-over-6 sashes under splayed brick heads. The 3-over-3 sash windows on the second floor are tucked under dentilated eaves. The roof of this range is now covered with modern concrete tiles. Inside the back range, the attic contains a fixture including a one-and-a-quarter-feet-wide bench, around two and a half feet above the floor, which was pierced by four holes, each three-quarters of a foot diameter. The slender legs at the front are stiffened by a rail four inches below the bench. This is interpreted as a stand for washing-bowls. Two of the panelled doors in the attic (one flat, one fielded), have spring-loaded catches, and one room contains a late-Victorian or Edwardian stone fire surround.

The right-hand house, No. 23, was clearly much altered when it was cut off from the rest of the building by the new road. The lined stucco front elevation is of three bays and three storeys. On the ground floor, broad 8-over-8 sash windows with narrow glazing-bars flank a central doorway. The latter includes a rectangular over-door light, and is given extra height by a further panel above, then the casing is topped by a flat canopy. Both windows on the first-floor are 6-over-6 sashes with horns; those lighting the top floor are 3-over-3, tucked tight under plain wooden eaves. There was no internal access to this house at the time of the survey.

The final addition to the building is the range behind No. 23. This has not been examined internally; it is entered from North Street through a Regency style door frame with reeded surround.

THE HISTORY

The story of Swan House can be starting from the 1547 survey of the manor, in which it can be identified as a one and a quarter copyhold burgage belonging to Christopher Draiton (later Drayton). In 1555, Drayton, a butcher, wrote his will:

> Item I give and bequeath to Edward my fifte [5th] sonne my mansion house that I now dwell in, With my barne on the feilde side to hym and to his heirs forever. Provided allweys that my wife shall have hit with the thre quarterns of coppyholde lande during her naturall life.[3]

Edward mortgaged the property to Samuel Borrowe in 1582,[4] but soon afterwards he repaid the loan; in 1584 Samuel returned to the manor court and surrendered '¾ burgage between a tenement belonging to the school,[5] and one belonging to William Fox,[6] to the use of Edward Dreiton and Marie and their heirs, which Samuel had received in mortgage from them on 25 Oct 24 Eliz (1582).'[7]

The records are now silent until Edward's son, also Edward, died in 1625 at the age of 49, leaving two young daughters. This Edward Drayton was a vintner with extensive property in Tamworth, where he lived.[8] His wife, Joyce Goodall, whom he married in 1608, had been born in Atherstone in 1588. Edward left to 'daughter Elisabeth the Swann Howse at Atherston with all the household goods & furnituer belonging to it with the Tenter Croft & haulf a yard Land by the name of Pinchbackes Land within the Manor & Lordship of Atherston'. Mary, born in 1610, and her sister, Elizabeth, were minors, and the probate court decreed that their education should be the responsibility of their mother, Joyce Drayton.

The inventory of his goods at Swan House gives a glimpse of the house and its use at the time:[9]

Room	*Contents (notes)*
Hall	
Greate Parlor	*(amongst the furniture)* 1 bedsted, 1 truckle bed
Lodging Parlor	1 bedsted
Hie Buildinge in the Uper Chamber	1 bedsted, 1 truckle bed
Midle Chamber	1 bedsted, 1 standing bed, 1 truckle bed
Little Parlor	1 bedsted 1 bedsted
Yelow Chamber	1 bedsted, 1 truckle bed
Cheese Chamber	1 trucklebed
Chamber over the Hall	2 bedsteds
Butrey	
Yelding [brew] house	
Brewhouse	mashing vat *(used in the first stage of brewing)*

Room	*Contents (notes)*
Kitchin	
Item in the cellar at Aderston	2 hogsheads of lees
	10 gallons of wine
	11 caske brokage wine
	Half a tearce *(firkin or runlet containing nine gallons)*
	7 quart pots fine wine with botle
	5 pints with bottles and other implements
Item	debts owing for wine and other things at Aderstone £3 11s. 0d.
Item	money in the house at Aderston for wine £2 0s. 0d.

Table 6 *Rooms in the inventory of Edward Drayton, 1625.*

From this number of beds (14) and this well-filled cellar, it appears that Swan House was being used as a hostelry in 1625. The reference to the 'Hie Buildinge in the Uper Chamber' suggests that the building was three storeys in height. With Edward Drayton often absent in Tamworth, an innkeeper probably had day-to-day responsibility for the clientele. Drayton's inventory includes, 'his licence to sell wine att Tamworth yet continuing [for] the naturall life of Joyce his wife.'[10]

After Edward's death, Joyce seems to have married a Thomas Goare of Tamworth,[11] and also acquired a life interest in the *Swan*. In 1647 Joyce Goare obtained a license to let 'The Swanne House and the Taynter Croft' to Edward White, of Tamworth, a mercer.[12] Joyce is likely to have been well established in Tamworth, and White would have been one of her merchant contacts there.

It appears that during Joyce's 35-year absentee tenure the Swan House had a number of innkeepers. One of them, Jonathan Griffin, died in 1649 and his inventory, compiled more than two decades on from that of 1625, shows that there had been some adjustments to the accommodation since Edward Drayton's death.[13]

Room	*Contents (notes)*
Rome wheare he deceased	1 Bead and Blanket and 1 Bedstid
Little Back Parlor	1 halph *(half)* headed Beadstid
Dyning Parlor	
Rome called the Nether Parlor	1 Bead
Chamber called the Middle Building	1 Bead
Rome called the High Building	1 Bead stid … 1 trundell Bead*
Rome called the Tow Bead Chamber	2 Beads … 1 Beadstid

Room	*Contents (notes)*
Yellow Chamber	1 halph *(half)* headed Beadstid
Stare Head Chamber	
Cheise Chamber	
Rome called the Hall	
Kitchen	
The Brewhouse	
Buttery	
Wine sellers *(cellars)*	

* A trundell, or truckle, bed was a low bed on wheels that could be pushed under a high or standing bed when not in use.

Table 7 *Rooms in the inventory of Jonathan Griffin, 1649.*

Whereas the 'Middle Building,' 'High Building' and 'Hall' remain the same and may even have the same furniture, there was at least one new chamber and the inn now had a 'Dyning Parlor', too. There are 11 beds altogether, three less than in 1625, although a further indication of the number of overnight guests can be discerned from the fact that the 'Middle Building' contained a close stool, and there were six chamber pots in the kitchen. Dining was communal at the 'longe table' in the 'Dyning Parlor.' Another of the larger rooms was the 'Hall' which was furnished with 'three tables, three forms and stools and one cheare'. However, those requiring privacy, could use the 'Yellow Chamber' with 'one litel table and one forme one coffer one cheare'. As in other northern Warwickshire houses, upstairs was a 'Cheise Chamber,' from which the bed of 1625 had disappeared to make room for malt and oats, but still no cheese. The work of the inn went on in the kitchen, the brewhouse, and the buttery with 'the beere vesels and flagons.' In Edward's day, there had been two rooms dedicated to brewing, but now there was only one. Downstairs 'in the wine sellers [were] one hoggshead of sack, tow halphe hoggshead of sacke and 20 of French wine wrated at £30.00.00', 'one peece of a runlit of muskdine (a sweet white wine) at 10s. 00, wine pots and Botles.' The 'hogg one sow six piges' were no doubt kept in the yard and the 'three Cowes' may have had the run of the adjoining 'Taynter Croft.'

Following Joyce's death (apparently in 1660, at the considerable age of 72) it was sold by Edward Drayton's descendants to Richard Bauldwyn, a gentlemen from Chigwell in Essex, and his wife, Elizabeth.[14] Elizabeth was the step-daughter of the previous innkeeper Jonathan Griffin.[15] Her daughter, Mary, married William Nutte, whose family were Atherstone shoemakers. (Marion Alexander refers to Thomas Nutt, in Chapter Six, p.128.) The Bauldwins were people of substance and did not, as was usual, travel to Atherstone to be admitted tenants at the manor court, but carried out the transaction by attorney at the 'house of the Ladie Marie Ingram in East Barnett, Hertfordshire.'[16]

In the Hearth Tax of 1663, John Hall was the occupant of Swan House. At that time it had nine hearths, but the following year, when William Crispe was recorded as tenant, this had apparently grown to 11, though the number may have been disputed, because William refused to pay the tax.[17]

After Hall died in 1669, Robert Bickley became the tenant. He was a husbandman, with a large holding in the open fields. In 1677, while Bickley was still in residence, the Bauldwyns and Nutts surrendered the property to the use of Thomas Inge and his wife, Elizabeth, on condition that the Inges paid them £100 – this had to be paid at the 'great Dyneing Hall' at Grays Inn, Middlesex.[18] This may well be a sale rather than a loan, as no interest rate is recorded and the Inges actually moved into the Swan House. But Thomas and Elizabeth appear to have been in need of money because in 1683 they raised a further loan of £100 from Phillip Launder, a gentleman from nearby Upton in Leicestershire.[19] It was not enough to satisfy their needs and the following year they increased their loan to £170 10s.[20]

In 1702 Inge's wife, Elizabeth, living in Westminster, died, leaving, 'all the rents and profits of my Lands in Ireland or at Atherstone in the County of Warwick which shall be due to me at the time of my decease',[21] to her 'good friend Mary Meires of London, spinster'. She made no mention of her husband, and he appears still to be having financial difficulties. In 1703 he surrendered his life interest in Swan House to the use of Anne Wood, widow, its tenant and innkeeper.[22] He, too, moved to Westminster, but five years later passed the Swan House to William Salisbury, a gentleman of Stoke Golding. He left a will in which he entreated his executors 'with all convenient speed to raise by Sale of the premises so much money as will pay my debts'.[23] If there was a residue, £300 of it was to be spent on a commission in the army for his son, Richard, and the rest to be divided between his three children, Richard, Edward and Dorothy.

The buyer appears to have been Henry Warden of Atherstone.[24] But he held it for only two years, as in 1724, Abraham Bracebridge was admitted tenant.[25] Thereafter, the property disappears from the manor court records because, as with many others he owned, Abraham Bracebridge enfranchised this property (*see* p.34).

The further history of the house now has to be gleaned from other sources. In 1768 it was in the tenancy of a 'Mr Jee',[26] and in 1784, Richard Leigh was the occupant of the *Swan Inn*. He insured:

> His Household Goods in his Dwelling House consisting of Plate Beding and Chaire and his Stock of Liquors and oather Furniture his Utensiles and Stock in his Stables and Chaire House for £500.[27]

At the same time, Abraham Bracebridge insured the 'House, outbuildings and Stables' for £300. By 1786, Leigh had been replaced by John Rogers, who was perhaps the 'little odd landlord' referred to in 1789 by the Hon. John Byng, when he visited Atherstone:[28]

> Hence we journey'd in a pleasant evening, without any occurrence, till our crossing of the little River Anker, (which divides the counties of Leicester and Warwick) now so swelled by the late rains, as to make my passage unsafe, even by the help of a bridge; for my boots were well soaked. – T.B. was sent forward to the *Swan Inn* at Atherstone, a neat clean house, in this pleasantly placed town. – The old parlour was of my sort, with clean wainscoting; and our little, odd landlord, made us smile by the particularity of his manners; and he wou'd drag us about to show us the bowling green, and to hear all his stories about his being in Cambridge, and elsewhere; and when I began to speak to him about supper, he said 'Let me alone, don't speak, I will give you a pretty little supper.' We next took a tour about the town,and to the navigation canal and afterwards by the pleasantest walk possible to the village of Mancetter …

Whoever was inn-holder at that time did not find life easy, as is demonstrated by the rapid turn-over. John Rogers gave up his tenancy of the *Swan Inn* by 1790,[29] and became an agent for the Phoenix Insurance Company in an office in the Market Place. His place at the inn was taken by William Fletcher who also ran the post office there,[30] but was soon succeeded by William Carter.[31]

THE NEW ROADS

Abraham Bracebridge had a good reason for buying the *Swan Inn*. The road from Atherstone to Sheepy Magna (which went on to Derby) ran directly in front of Atherstone Hall, where he lived (*see* p.25 and Fig. 54). Furthermore, the Horse Fair and the cattle market (the Bullring) were held on the open ground between the road and the chapel. It is clear that he wished to remove what must have been a considerable nuisance. In about 1771, he put forward a plan for moving the road from the north to the south side of the chapel and connecting it to through the yard of the 'Sign of the Swan' to the eastern end of the back lane.[32] However, he met with unexpected objections and all that was approved by the magistrates in 1779 was for it to be moved a short distance south, so that it ran along the north side of the chapel.

He revived the proposal in 1796, completing the road at his own expense; this was possible since all the new parts ran across his own land. The new alignment ran south of the chapel (requiring the demolition of the house north of the *Angel Inn*), across the north of the Market Place, through the Swan yard and along the back of the Long Street burgages (*see* Figs. 3-5).

Although most of the townspeople supported the proposal, objections were put forward, not the least being that the yard was too narrow to allow passing traffic, and an appeal against the order allowing the diversion was held. In his case, Bracebridge's advocates made the following claim:

> … previous to the Making of the order, Obstructions Arose in the Swan Yard and Gateway by Chaises Drawing up to the Inn Gateway and Door and by the Dressing of Horses in the Yard – But Mr Bracebridge has built Conveniences in a Back Yard for Receiving Carriages and for the Dressing of Horses which

> will prevent Obstructions Remaining in the Inn Yard when converted into a Road The Rings and Hooks in the Yard to which Horses were tied and the Chaise Yard Gates have by the Consent of the Tenant been Removed and taken away in Order to make the Inn Yard as Free from Obstructions as Possible – It is here Observable That if any Nuisance shall be Permitted to Remain after the Confirmation of the Order the Tenant Will be Liable to an Indictment from such Nuisance.

Added in a different hand is the following (probably a verbatim remark):

> And it is at the pleasure of Mr Brac[ebridge] to subject his Tenant to such inconvenience if any sho[ul]d arise from the road.

The landlord, William Carter, was called on to express his view, but, no doubt with Abraham Bracebridge watching him keenly, Carter was not going to voice his true feelings and merely replied when asked about the traffic:

> I think a chaise might go by. There would be room to pass. The new dining Room in some little [way] has contracted the yard. If unloading into hay loft cd not … Some parts of new road [are] better.

Despite the opposition, Bracebridge won his case, and the necessary order was made in 1797. However, very soon it became apparent that the road had so disrupted the business of the inn that it became impossible to continue. By 1801 the *New Swan* had opened on the corner of Church Street and Derby Lane,[33] and by 1829 the *Swan Inn* had been converted to a dwelling.[34] By the 1851 census, it was one of the many sub-divided dwellings in the town. The two outside bays were completely separate with the rooms over the archway (the central bay) having become part of the north side. The whole building was still in the ownership of the Bracebridges, but in 1872 was sold to Thomas Handford, a surgeon, who set up in practice with John Lycett, occupying the northern wing as a surgery.[35] The southern wing was occupied at the front by Thomas Bates and at the back by the cottages of William Jennings and John Orton. In 1866, Bates's dwelling had been described as 'apartments.' After Thomas Handford's death in 1896, his children continued to hold the property in trust.

In the 20th century the southern section served as the town's doctors' surgery and more recently as a heritage centre, while solicitors' offices – Sale, Hill and Davenport – occupied the northern part. Today, the road through the archway is a curious anomaly, unsuited to modern traffic, but part of the character of the town.

Building History Three: *Market Tavern*, 21 Market Street

This property is C103 on Fig. 7. *See* Fig. 26.

The Building

Although today it has been upstaged by Beech House, *Market Tavern* has evidence of being a fine building in earlier times. Situated on the opposite side of the Market Place from the *Angel Inn*, it is, at first sight, more evidently Georgian, and that is how it is described in the statutory Listed Building Description: '... late C18, with late C19/early C20 ground floor ...' But one has only to step off the street into the bar to find that this was originally two rooms, divided by a close-studded timber-framed wall; the evidence is in the main ceiling beam, deeply chamfered on both sides, but also with closely-spaced double-pegged empty mortices. On each side of this former wall, the ceilings are divided by more deeply-chamfered beams. A large but impenetrable block behind the bar is probably the base of an interesting old chimney, which might contain a large fireplace, but at present is entirely hidden. Return outside, and even more interestingly, there is the tell-tale evidence of a former jetty (just inside the entry to the right) – a straight joint in the brickwork. Part of the original jetty plate appears to remain in situ. The upper floors have not been inspected, but portions of the late medieval timber-framed partition walls and roof trusses might have escaped the Georgian rebuild.

The History

No. 21 Market Street was a copyhold property, recorded as either a quarter- or a half-burgage in size, lying between Swan House and Beech House.[1] The first known occupant of the house is William Fox in 1593.[2] The next family to live there appears to have been the Drapers. Thomas Draper is unusual, in that, although described as a 'labourer', his will of 1635 was proved at the Prerogative Court of Canterbury – a privilege normally reserved for those with property in more than one county.[3] Thomas left a young family, with legacies to be paid on their 15th birthdays; £20 to his eldest son Thomas, and £10 to each of his two daughters, Mary and Elizabeth. Thomas's wife, Elizabeth, was to have the residue of his estate. There is a suggestion in the records that Elizabeth remarried five years later. Unfortunately, the parish register for this period is in a very poor state and only her name is legible. However, the next recorded occupant of 21 Market Street is Elizabeth Power, a widow.

Elizabeth's son, Thomas Draper, married Anne Parker in 1657 and was admitted tenant to the house (as a quarter burgage) in 1659, after his mother's death. Thomas was a butcher, and between 1659 and his death in 1683, he and Anne had nine children, the first five of whom were girls. His copyhold property was to be sold to pay legacies to the children, but Ann was to receive all his lands in the open fields, and his brick kiln. The house had three hearths in 1674,[4] and when Thomas Draper died in 1684, his inventory lists the names of twelve rooms:[5]

First Roome	Seller
Parlor	Chamber at Stairehead
Space *(occasionally found as a room name, here containing only a cupboard)*	Chamber over the House
Kitchen	Greate Chamber
Brewhouse	Cockloft
Chamber over the Kitchin	Shop

Table 8 *Rooms in the* Market Tavern *from the inventory of Thomas Draper, 1684.*

The house had six beds, so the younger children must have shared; probably the smaller ones slept at either end of the bed, their feet meeting in the middle. The 'First Roome' was effectively the kitchen, containing the cooking equipment: 'three spits one driping pann ... one Jack'. Beer brewed in the brewhouse was stored in the cellar, and 'three stone of wool,' was kept in the 'Cockloft.' Out in the fields, Draper had 35 sheep, four 'beasts', two horses, an old Mare (valued at 10s.), a sowe and pigs. Corn, both threshed and unthreshed, was valued at £12 0s., and a stock of brick and tile at £8 5s. Considering that Draper was primarily a butcher, it is surprising that his shop contained only a 'Cleaver & Rope & other Materialls.'

In 1703, Thomas's widow, Anne Draper, and her brother, Robert Parker (an overseer of Thomas's will), went to the manor court and surrendered 21 Market Street to the use of her younger son, William, then in his mid twenties.[6] William and his wife, Mary, continued to hold the property until 1738 when they passed it to their son, Thomas, and his wife, Mary.[7] The couple evidently had no children, and on Thomas's death in 1760, 21 Market Street was inherited by his sister, Ann. She was married to Joseph Grew, a butcher from a long-established local family.[8] At the same sitting of the manor court, Joseph and Ann passed the property to their son Thomas and his wife, another Ann. The Grew family appear to have lived elsewhere, as it was rented out to Walter Hunt, a schoolmaster.

The next owner of 21 Market Street was a stationer by the name of Richard Leigh, who was living there as a tenant by 1787, but had bought it by 1793.[9] Leigh moved to Cheltenham in 1811, having sold the property for £650 to John Sanders, a liquor merchant. Sanders raised a mortgage of £300 from John Baker, a gentleman of Mancetter.[10]

He also took the precaution of insuring the property:[11]

His now dwelling house, warehouse and outbldgs all adj	£200
Household goods & utensils therein	£50
Stock in trade therein (not including glass)	£240
Stock of glass therein	£10

It is interesting to note that his stock, which would have been mostly liquors, was more valuable than his house. When he renewed the policy 13 years later, the value of the stock had risen to £490, whereas the house remained at £200.[12] With such a high outlay on stock it is not surprising that Sanders then took out a further mortgage, by surrendering the 'equity of redemption' as security to the use of William Brown, a blacksmith.[13] The loan to John Baker was repaid in 1821, but by 1829 Sanders was bankrupt and his property was put into the hands of three trustees, who were to sell it; in the meantime Sanders was allowed to remain as tenant.[14] An indenture of appointment and release was drawn up between John Sanders, and the three trustees, who were all men of standing in the community: William Tompson Allen, a gentleman, the Reverend Henry Hutchins, vicar of Mancetter, and Charles Weetman of Mancetter, a farmer.

John Sanders went to the manor court and surrendered 21 Market Street to these trustees, who put it up for auction at the *Red Lion*, in three lots. How it was split is not recorded, but Lot 1 was sold for £760 to the hatter and banker, Joseph Willday. Sanders handed over the purchase money to the trustees, and remained in the house. It would appear that he actually managed to buy it back over the next few years, as his will written in 1834 devised the property to his wife, Frances Maria Sanders, who was co-executor with his nephew, Samuel Sandford.[15] Sanders lived on until 1840, but his executors were not admitted tenants to the property until 1849.[16] By then they were trading as 'Sanders and Sandford, wine & spirit merchants.'[17]

At the 1851 census, Frances, then aged 65, was still running the wine and spirit business with three men to help her. The premises appear to be operating as an inn, because among the occupants was Robert Breeden, described as a 'servant' and a 'barman.'

26 *Front elevation of the* Market Tavern.

Frances also had a house servant, Eliza Everitt, and a 'servant groom,' Charles Wykes. She was clearly well set up and the difficulties of the past were far behind her.

Frances died and by 1866 Ralph Crisp had taken over, combining his job as an auctioneer with that of wine and spirit merchant.[18] By 1896, 21 Market Street had become a public house, the *Cricketers' Arms*, run by William Whitehead.[19] The choice of name may have been prompted by a comment at the 1896 Annual General Meeting of the Atherstone Cricket Club, that 'Cricket was declining in Atherstone and the taste now seemed to be in the direction of football and golf.'[20] Cricket had been popular in Atherstone since the early 19th century. James Roper, a young printer, recorded in his diary for 8 May 1848, 'We got up at 4 o'clock this morning and had a famous game of cricket on the Outwoods with Sales young men, spice with Ginger Beer bottles, etc.' Two days later he mentions a 'New Cricket Club.'[21] William Harding, boot and shoemaker in the Market Place, was also a renowned bowler. He was described in 1845 as 'a capital player like a steam carriage.'[22] By 1912 Whitehead had been replaced at the *Cricketers' Arms* by Edward Wood.[23] The inn kept its name until the end of the 20th century, when it was re-branded as the *Market Tavern*.

Building History Four: Beech House, 19 Market Street

This property is C102 on Fig. 7. *See* Figs. 27 and 55.

William Eyre, gentleman, spent lavishly on the re-building of Beech House in 1708, so that to this day it remains the most prestigious house standing in Atherstone, and indeed is considered to be one of the best town houses in Warwickshire.[1] The name is thought to derive from the magnificent copper beech tree that stands in the garden and is reputed to have been planted for Queen Victoria's Diamond Jubilee.[2]

The Building

Beech House is the oldest remaining brick house overlooking the Market Place, and it remains the best, even if it has vernacular undertones. The Listed Building Description records the date, 1708, on a 'later stone above the basement', and the same date is found on a gutter hopper head at the back of the building. Its context within the Market Place is crucial to the general character of the core of Atherstone's conservation area, but it is equally important as one of a very small number of buildings that still retain a high proportion of their early internal fixtures and fittings. Many of the rooms are of outstanding quality, and deserve careful conservation.

Beech House stands behind iron railings, which form an edge to the basement well; and the front elevation is of five bays with a basement, two full storeys and an attic. The stone basement, rusticated quoins, moulded string, and the moulded and dentilated eaves cornice, all frame Flemish-bond red brickwork. The cellar is lit by wood and metal casement windows. On the ground floor, the main entrance is up five stone steps in the left-hand bay, where the doorway is framed by half-columns in Tuscan style, which support an open pediment over a radial fanlight. The six-panel door is set back between panelled reveals. The right-hand bay has a secondary doorway containing a six-panel door below a rectangular blind panel and a flat head with keystone. The windows in the other bays have broad, exposed frames and 9-over-9 sashes with thick glazing bars under flat heads with moulded keystones. The first-floor windows are similar, with the keystones rising to meet the cornice. Two flat-topped dormers have 3 x 4 pane casement windows. At the rear, the first floor has one large tripartite window with a narrow elliptical arched head, and a Diocletian window lights the attic. Refined though it is, the front elevation has vernacular touches, as it was not designed to the very best proportions that could be achieved at this time. Both doorways, and the windows at each end of the first floor, are sited disproportionately close to the giant corner pilasters – a foible that the contemporary architectural practice run by the Smiths of Warwick would not have condoned, but one which presumably did not offend the owner, William Eyre.

The imposing entrance hall has a fireplace set at 45 degrees in the south-east corner, with bolection mouldings, complete with fender. The dado rail is broken in the south wall by the door to the front reception room; this has six fielded panels and bolection mouldings. The hall is divided from the staircase lobby by an archway with panelled reveals and capitals, which support a semi-circular arch with key-block.

The main reception room at the front of the house has large bolection-moulded panels above and below the dado on all walls, and a moulded cornice. The fireplace looks early 19th-century, but the panelling on the chimney breast belongs to the period of construction of the house as, probably, do the alcoves with moulded reveals to left and right – the latter probably once contained shelves. The south wall between the dining room and the entry is a late example of square-panel timber framing.

The fine dogleg staircase has a continuous moulded string, a heavy moulded handrail, and turned balusters. Between the ring at the top and the vase below, each baluster spindle has straight converging sides, making it typical of the period, *c.*1700-20.[3] It is possible that the cloakroom under the stairs was installed over the original access to the cellars. Access to the kitchen is by way of a passage to the right of the staircase.

The upper floors have numerous fixtures and fittings of architectural importance. These include the staircase and balustrade, floorboards, the bolection-moulded panelling in the main front bedroom, panelled doors with such early fittings as lock-boxes, drop-latches and H-hinges. The basement also contains numerous period fixtures and fittings, including storage alcoves and compartments for wine, a fireplace with a simple

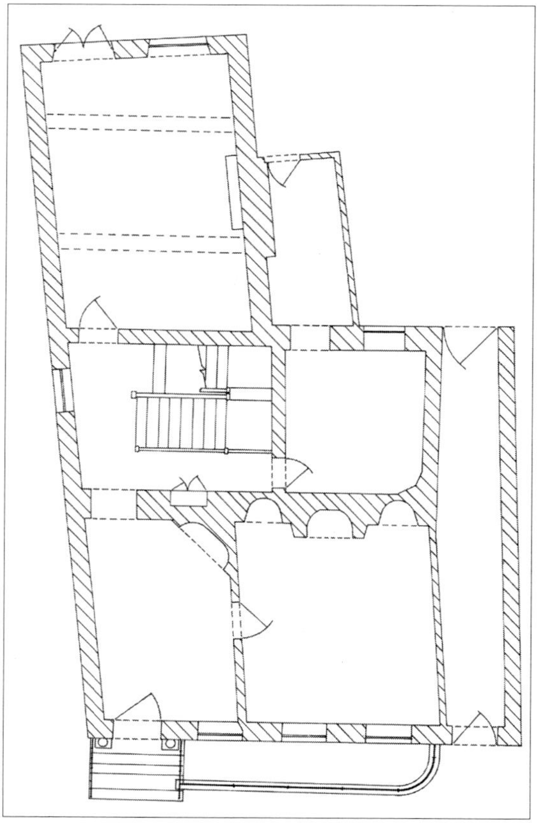

27 *Ground-floor plan of Beech House.*

surround, lath and plaster partitions, and various window apertures – significant socio-historical evidence of the service arrangements.

On the rear elevation, a lean-to roof now covers a short extension to the ground floor; the glazed door to the dining room is perhaps 19th-century.

THE HISTORY

Beech House was a half-burgage copyholding, and thus is recorded regularly in the manor court rolls (*see* Appendix to Chapter Three), through which it is possible to trace the site's history. Probate documents also give some indication of the interior of the building which preceded it. The first likely reference to the house appears in the will of William Alsoppe in 1551. He bequeathed 'unto Robt Aulsope my eldest sone the house that I purchased of the gyld ground'.[4] However, the interpretation is not entirely straightforward, since William's second son, John, was bequeathed 'the house that my mother now dwelleth in.' One of these two is 19 Market Street – later documents suggest the second of them.

In 1582 when John made his will,[5] he referred to the 'house in Atherstone wherein I nowe dwell', which he and his wife, Elizabeth, had:

> joyntlie together at this present delivered up a surrender of the house into the handes of two of the Lordes tenants, that is to witt John Hampton and Thomas Wrighte to the same end and effecte accordinge to the custom of the Manor of Atherston.

John Hampton and Thomas Wright are described as 'neighbours' and they also drew up an inventory of John's goods.[6] In addition, they were to be trustees of the property until Alsoppe's young son, Edward, then aged five, was of age. Thomas Wright was also an overseer of the will. He appears to have taken his duties very seriously, as he and his wife, Alice, actually moved into John's house. Thomas died around 1591, but Alice stayed on, paying rent for the house.[7] On Alice's death in 1594, when Edward would have been 17, his elder brother William was admitted tenant.[8] By then William would have been old enough to conduct his own affairs and possibly look after those of his younger brother, though the records do not reveal the position clearly.

William Allsoppe appears to have lived at the property until his death in December 1634. He left an inventory which gives us an idea of the accommodation on the site at the time, listing the following rooms:[9]

Hall	Parlour
Best chamber	Chamber over the parlour
Highe buildinge	Kitchen
Chese chamber	Seller
Butterie	Stable and yard

Table 9 *Rooms in the inventory of William Allsoppe, 1634.*

His widow, Dorothy, was granted probate along with their 'neighbour', Jonathan Griffin. Dorothy did not stay a widow for long. Two years later she remarried by licence.[10] Her new husband was John Roper, a blacksmith and citizen of London, from a local family who had been butchers in the town, but had moved to London, though they retained a considerable amount of property in Atherstone. It is likely that Dorothy took her family with her to London, as her son, John Alsopp, became a 'citizen and scrivener' of London. In 1653, after Dorothy's death, he came to Atherstone to be admitted tenant of the property, but soon leased it to Robert Bickley.[11] Perhaps they had lost interest in their home town, because in 1659 they sold the house to Thomas Loveday, a citizen and goldsmith of London.[12]

The house was rented out to John Vincent, a mercer,[13] and was still a relatively modest property with only three hearths. In 1671 Thomas Loveday and his wife, Lettice, sold the house to Robert Smith, a blacksmith from Nuneaton, who rented it to Prudence Chamberlaine.[14] She was the widow of John Chamberlaine, a mercer, who had left her and their children moderately well off.[15] When she died her son, John, took over the tenancy.[16] Although he did not own this house, he did have land at Pinwall Grange in Leicestershire, and left £250 in ready money in his will (1689).[17] After the death of his wife, Catherine, all the property was to be sold and the money equally divided between his five children.

One of the executors of John's will was Matthias Ward, the husband of John's sister, Prudence. Through her, he became the new owner of what must, by then, have been a crumbling timber-framed house with lath and plaster infill. When he died in 1699 he left to his eldest daughter, Prudence Ward:

> My house and all the building and backside thereto belonging in which I now live lying and being in Atherstone, She paying to my son Matthias Ward Fifteen pounds.[18]

His wife Prudence was to have a third of his personal estate, and the two remaining parts were to be equally divided between his three daughters, Prudence, Hannah and Abigail. Despite the fact that his son, Matthias, seems to have been left very little, he is named as an executor with his mother, Prudence. It appears that she stayed on in the house until her death in 1707. Her will divides the third portion which her husband left her between her four children, but her daughter Prudence was made 'sole executrix'.[19] Now that her mother was dead, Prudence no longer needed the house and sold it the following year to William Eyre.[20] He it was who, as noted, spent so lavishly on the re-building of Beech House in 1708.

William Eyre, gentleman, was married to Sarah Harcourt, the daughter of Elizabeth Harcourt of Tamworth. Elizabeth clearly had some concerns about her daughter's choice of husband because, in her will, she left property to Sarah and William's daughters, Sarah and Elizabeth, with the proviso that her 'friend' Francis Littleton should be the guardian of their inheritance, 'so that William Eyre shall have no part in their money'.[21]

Two years previously Eyre had purchased the *Bear Inn* (*see* p.80),[22] and over the next few years bought a number of properties in Atherstone, including the two houses in Market Street immediately to the south of Beech House.[23] Eyre's lavish spending on building Beech House stretched him beyond his means, as described in Building History Five.[24] He died bankrupt in the Fleet Prison in September 1723, and his household goods were sequestered by the Court of Chancery. His four copyhold properties were surrendered to the use of Jonah Cryness of Hackney, a gentleman, who was presumably his executor.[25] Elizabeth and Sarah inherited the houses as Eyre had intended, but in 1736 a half share of all four was acquired by Fisher Littleton, the 'friend' whom their grandmother had entrusted to look after their inheritance; it seems likely that he acquired this from Elizabeth.[26] Her sister, Sarah, married twice, first to Joseph Poole and then to Francis Soden of Coventry.[27] In his will, Littleton bequeathed his half share to his neice Dorothy Wolferstan.[28]

She married Samuel Pipe, a clergyman, and they had a son, Samuel. After her death, his father was admitted tenant to the copyhold property, as trustee for their son.[29] In 1772 Francis Soden sold his half of the house to John Underwood, a grocer. The tenant at the time was Nicholas Smith, a surgeon and apothecary, and within two years he had bought this half-share from Underwood. On the same day, Samuel Pipe jnr., now a young man and a lawyer in the Inner Temple, sold his share to Robert Lingard, a maltster. Why he did this is unclear, but it must have been a temporary arrangement because, by 1772, it was said that Nicholas Smith was the sole owner. Perhaps Lingard was acting for Smith?[30]

When Nicholas Smith died in 1787 he left his house to his daughter, Sarah, who married William Hanson, a banker and woolstapler. Sarah's eldest daughter, Mary, married George Sale, a mercer and draper from Swadlincote, Derbyshire. By 1827, it had been agreed that Mary and George should own the house, so her brother and sisters went to the manor court and surrendered the copyhold to their use. George Sale was a draper and mercer, with a business on the corner of Long Street and Butcher Row.[31] When he died in 1861, his sons, George and Hanson, as executors and under the terms of his will, offered to sell the property to their sister, Mary Ann Handford.[32] The asking price was £1000, but Handford wisely refused, buying the house five years later for £650.[33] More recently, Beech House has been owned by the proprietors of the shop which became Atherstone's first and only department store, C.H. Hiscox and Sons.[34]

Building History Five: 11/13 Market Street

This is C100 on Fig. 7. *See* Figs. 28-30 and 57.

Early in the 17th century this house would have been one of the most impressive buildings in Atherstone. It is not surprising to learn that this property was then owned by a family who had London connections and were generous benefactors to the town. However, Richard Warwick and his wife Hester did not actually live here, but in a 'great house' at the south east end of Long Street that, in the early 19th century, would make way for the town's new workhouse.[1]

The Building

The house now has a well-proportioned secondary brick façade, and appears from the front as an early 19th-century building.

In reality, it was once a spectacular timber-framed house, probably of late 16th- or early 17th-century origin, perhaps once the most imposing building overlooking the Market Place, prominently located on its east side. Each of the upper floors was strikingly jettied, at both the front and the back of the building. The adjoining houses, 15/17 Market Street, were built on very narrow plots (*see* p.54), but no such constraint applied to the builders of 11/13. It was not just its structure but also its plan-form that were new to Atherstone. Despite the size of the plot of land, instead of having a medieval plan-form comprising a main range one room deep, with a wing or back range, it was two rooms deep across the entire width of its plot.

The front elevation of the building has been entirely replaced by brick, but evidence of its timber-framed origins can be seen from the street; behind the right-hand shop-window, the upper portion of a corner-post rises to a girding beam which formerly projected forward to carry the jettied first floor.

As often happened in the 18th century, the rebuilding of the front of a timber-framed town-house was in response to fashion rather than structural necessity. While the public façade was replaced in brick, the close-studded rear elevation remained, most tellingly asserting the true character of this remarkable building with jetties at both levels.

28 *11/13 Market Street, front elevation.*

29 *11/13 Market Street: detail of former jetty.*

At the south-east corner of the building, another jetty post and a girding beam can be seen at the side of a staircase; the socket which contained the former jetty plate marks the line of the original ground-floor back wall. The outside walls are all close-studded, but surviving internal partition walls are framed up in relatively large panels.

Within two or three generations of its construction, this imposing house would be eclipsed by the new fashion for brick. That is probably why its front wall was rebuilt early in the 19th century and given new shop windows. It has a door with over-door light and a narrow bow-window to the left, then, to the right, is a double bow window with central doorway, again with an over-door light, all made together. The left-hand bow is a 4 × 2-over-4 × 2 sash with reeded architraves; the other bow windows are 16-over-16, but with fixed frames. The door between them has two fielded panels with flush-moulded edges below, and four glass panes above. A decorated entablature unites the ensemble. Above, the brick front is laid in Flemish bond. On the first floor, three 6-over-6 sash windows stand on a sill-band; they have broad exposed frames set close to the face of the wall, and rusticated flat arches with big key-blocks. On the second floor, three smaller windows have wooden frames and stone or rendered sills, but that in the centre is blind. Above again are moulded eaves and an old tiled roof.

INTERNAL FEATURES

None of the remaining fixtures or fittings can be attributed to the 16th century, but several 17th-century features remain, including a balustrade with turned balusters. The two staircases formerly served two discrete units – although they are now all one, the interiors of the two units are described separately, below.

Number 11

On the ground floor, room two, behind the double-bowed window, has evidence for large-panel framing in one wall, and it retains an attractive fretted-wooden cornice. To the rear, one of the cupboards on the south wall of room three is tucked under the staircase which begins its ascent in room four. The stripped pine door at the foot of the stairs has six flat panels with flush-moulded edges, and there is an over-door light above. On the wall at the side of the stairs, another jetty post and a girding beam are exposed; the socket which contained the former jetty-plate marks the line of the original back wall. The first-floor landing retains a balustrade with widely-spaced 17th-century turned balusters. The front room, over room two, retains a moulded dado-rail and has a good curved cast iron fireplace complete with fire-basket within reeded wood surrounds with corner-blocks and mantel. In the open cupboards to the left and right of the fireplace, glass shelves have replaced the shaped originals. The room over room three has panelled walls, probably all 17th-century, but of various designs, no doubt brought together from elsewhere in the building, with lambs-tongue stops on the ceiling-beams. The small cast-iron fireplace in the corner is now set into modern panelling. Next to the fireplace, an old door has been re-hung upside down. The

30 *11/13 Market Street: rear elevation showing jetties.*

window is a two-light casement, each of six panes – probably late Victorian. The flight of stairs up to the attic retains one flat baluster.

The attic gable at the back of No. 11 is one of a pair, including a tiebeam with a cambered top, two raked struts, a collar, and principals carrying trenched purlins. The space has been subdivided by a studded partition, employing re-used timbers, one of which is a weathered moulded cornice, probably originally applied to a close-studded wall.

Number 13

The door in the front elevation gives access to a narrow entry along the north side of the building. In the front room (1) the walls are lined with vertical boards. The fireplace in the east wall has a wooden surround with corner-blocks, and the fire basket survives. The substantial chimney occupies a large proportion of each floor level. On the first floor, the main room is entered via a doorway with a six-panelled softwood door; the room retains a good cornice moulding and a small stone fireplace with a low four-centred arch – possibly 17th-century. The other room on this floor is entered via a doorway with a plank door on four ledges, hung on strap hinges over pintles; it has an offset over-door light above.

On the attic floor, the front of the building is divided into two small rooms by a stud partition. The flat-panelled door in the partition has been made up to match the aperture; it is hung on strap-hinges over pintles. To the north east is the head of a turning stair, with a window for borrowed light, originally with two mullions. The room over room five, at the rear, has close-studded outer walls, but square-panelled framing for the internal work. The room has a tiny cast-iron fireplace with a basket and a cast iron shelf – probably Regency.

The History

Richard Warwick, a merchant tailor and 'sometime' citizen of London, died in 1633. He was not allowed enough time to write his last will and only a memorandum made on his death bed survives.[2] It is revealing of his philanthropic nature that his thoughts at that time were for those who had served him, 'Item hee did give unto Elizabeth Musson his mayd servant her lyfe in the house which he had off William Campion,' (i.e. left to her to occupy for life).[3] Another bequest was a silver gilt cup to Mancetter Church for 'the Administration of the blessed Sacrament of the Lords supper.' All the rest of his property was bequeathed to his wife, Hester, who, by the time of her death in 1646, owned five copyhold houses, a garden and orchard. Shortly before his death, two of these houses had been surrendered at the manor court by Richard and Hester, to the trustees of his charity.[4] The rent from letting them was intended to finance his charity, the details of which were contained in the surrender:

> To the use of Richard & Hester for their lives, then to the use of the poore of Atherston to buy yearelie for twentie poore men of the said towne coates and hatts, if the rent of the said howse will extend unto soe many or otherwise to buy soe many as the yearelie rent will extend, at the sight of Mr Richard Grey, Mr John Grey, Richard Abell of Manceter, clarke, Samuell Drayton, Mr William Buckley, Henrie Shepie of the said towne, whome I make feoffees

> for the said business, and in case anie of them decease, then the survivors to choose another to them, & dispose them accordinglie to the honestest poore of the said towne such as are not knowne guiltie of anie grosse sinnes as drunkennes, swearers, sabbath breakers etc, the which men soe elected are to come everie yeare on the feast daie of St Michael tharchangell to the said howse to fetch them the said coats and hatts, provided that is in the power of the said Richard to revoke if he will at any time within the yeare, the coates are to be lyned with cotton and a paire of tailers sheares made with redd cloth and stitched about with greene silke and sett upon the lefte sleeve and a yard of ribboning of carnation coulour and white about their hattes.[5]

In 1671, the two houses were sold by the trustees to Edward Hinton for £310 and the money invested in land in Leicestershire.[6] In 1811 the annual rent amounted to £45, though the costs of administering the charity were so high that only £20 of this was spent on coats and hats. By then, too, a die had been made of the 'tailers sheares' and this was imprinted on the buttons instead of being appliquéd in red cloth, as Warwick had intended.

Richard Warwick's tomb stands in Mancetter churchyard and is inscribed with the epitaph:

> Who, out of his great affection to his native town, Atherstone, gave a charitable gift of fifteen pounds per annum for ever to buy Gray Coats and Hatts for so many honest poor Housekeepers of the said Town as 'twill purchase yearly.[7]

Hester was similarly philanthropic on her death in 1646, leaving £5 to the poor of Atherstone, 'desiring that the Lame and aged and [newly] poore Christians may bee the best remembered.'[8]

Hester left the remainder of her real estate, two houses and a piece of land,[9] to her brother, Charles Careswell, a merchant tailor and citizen of London, and his wife, Zippora, who were also her executors. They continued to lease the house to Hester's friend, William Symonds, the existing tenant.[10] He was a mercer, who had been born in Nuneaton, and was also the overseer of Hester's will.[11] After Charles's death the house passed to his and Zippora's grandson, Charles Wells, son of their daughter, Hester Wells. As Charles was a minor, his grandmother Zippora was appointed his guardian.[12] However, she died before he reached the age of 21 and, in 1665, the year of London's great plague, Robert Hill, a long-bow string-maker, was appointed Charles's guardian.[13] He obviously had a strong influence on the boy's choice of career, as by 1672 Charles was a long-bowstring maker in London.

In that year, which was soon after he achieved his majority, Charles borrowed £30 from his great-aunt's friend, the occupant of 11/13 Market Street, William Symonds.[14] One can speculate on the reasons for this, but it would not be unusual for a young man who had just come into a substantial inheritance, to over-reach himself financially, and natural for a long-standing family friend to help him out. Charles agreed to repay the loan 'at the sign of the *Black Bull* in Cheapside.'

Whether this loan was ever repaid we do not know, though William Symonds's will, in 1686, acknowledged that he actually purchased the three properties: 'Item I doe give unto Mr Charles Wells of London of whom I bought the houses in Atherston the sume of twenty shillings.'[15]

No inventory has been located for 11/13 Market Street;[16] it is therefore difficult to form a picture of it in the 17th century. The Hearth Tax records six hearths between 1665 and 1670 and an extra one by 1674.[17] Its internal layout has to be gleaned from a few references in William Symonds's will. His cousin, Priscilla, is given 'one case of boxes that were my dear Daughters which are in my wife's Chamber.' His daughter, Mary, is given 'one case of Drawers that are in the chamber over the Kitchen.' There is reference to:

> the halfe headed Bedd in the flore Chamber and one paire of overworne Curtains there with those goods that I had of Mr Gramar for Mrs Birch her Debt that are in the corne chamber.

William Symonds also had a large number of books mostly on a religious theme, which he distributed around the beneficiaries.[18] He was strongly Protestant, leaving money to Nonconformist ministers and a copy of Foxes Book of Martyrs[19] to Nuneaton Church. (*See* Chapter Six, Table 12)

William was succeeded by his son, Joshua, whose own will bequeathed the property as follows:

> Item I give this house in which I now live with appurtenances and the house next thereunto adjoining cum [appurtenances] now in the tenure of [first name omitted] Geary to my wife during her life and from [ ] to my Cos: Jos Symonds sonn of Coz Jon. [ ] and his Heires for ever.[20]

The square boxes indicate some illegible ciphers and it is not surprising to learn that there was some questioning of this bequest because, attached to the will, a declaration under oath survives, made by John Stratford of the Middle Temple. In it he describes the events on the afternoon of Joshua's death in 1698.

It appears that Stratford's father, John Stratford of Merevale, had arrived at the house and found Symonds 'in his Parlour' in the process of writing his will. Stratford reported to his son that he had read back the details of the bequest of the houses in Atherstone. He had confirmed that the will was worded according to his intention. He was reported to be in 'perfect memory and had none other distemper upon him that appeared to this deponent but shortage of breath … Doctor Stephens comeing in ordered a Chirugeon to be sent for, who comeing let him the said Testator's blood and that the said Testator dyed within half and hour or thereabouts after.'

Although Joshua Symonds was married, he had no children, and the property is thus likely to have passed to his cousin's son, as he wished. However, it is not known who inherited after this Joshua, except to say that the next known owner was also a 'Symonds' though spelt differently. In 1710, the manor court rolls record the surrender by a Charles Simmons to the use of William Eyre.[21] Simmons himself was now living in 15/17 Market Street, while a Richard Geary was recorded as tenant of 11/13.

William Eyre was a gentleman, probably from Coventry, who built a new house in Market Street in 1708 that eclipsed 11/13 in grandeur and modernity.[22] (*See* Building History Four, Beech House.) Two years later, he had purchased a number of other prime properties in the town, including 11/13 Market Street, and the *Bear Inn*.[23]

Eyre was married to Sarah Harcourt, the daughter of Elizabeth Harcourt of Atherstone,[24] widow. Elizabeth appears initially to have welcomed the marriage, for in 1706/7 she settled on her son, Thomas, and on William and Sarah Eyre, the rents of extensive property in and around Birmingham that she had inherited from her father, Thomas Shelton of Tamworth.[25]

It was fortunate that Elizabeth Harcourt had retained the right to invalidate the deed: William appeared to be overstretching himself financially. She wrote her will in 1720, understandably dismayed at her son-in-law's mounting debts and fearful of losing her family's inheritance. The half of the estate which was intended for her daughter she now bequeathed to her 'friend,' Fisher Littleton, to be held in trust until her granddaughters, Elizabeth and Sarah Eyre reached the age of 21, or were married, in which case the granddaughters were free to settle any part of their premises upon their husbands. Fisher Littleton was to be the grand-daughters' guardian, 'so that William Eyre shall have no part in their money'.[26]

It appears that Elizabeth Harcourt's fears were well founded. William Eyre had gained a reputation as 'a proper person' in placing out money on interest, and had done this for two prominent local men, Edward Stratford and Francis Gramer. In 1704, he became acquainted with an unmarried woman to whom he had been recommended. Having 'conceived a good opinion of him,' this woman, Mary, went away to Salisbury leaving Eyre to look after her money.[27] In her absence he took it upon himself to manage the money without telling her. Eventually she became uneasy and sought an account from him. By this time Mary had married Edward Moyle of Nuneaton, who took an interest in his wife's affairs, taking a suit against Eyre in 1718 at the Court of Chancery. William Eyre was found guilty of misappropriating funds and committed to the Fleet debtors' prison in London, having had his goods sequestrated. The amount the Moyles were claiming was only £38 2s. 9d. One wonders how such a small amount could have led to Eyre's downfall. We know from other records that he had been involved in property deals in Coventry and Nether Whitacre,[28] and presumably he was already deeply in debt. His wife Sarah had died, and Elizabeth Harcourt was appointed guardian of his daughters, who were under 21. William died in prison on 18 September 1723.

After he died it was left to Jonah Cryness of Hackney to sort out his affairs. Jonah appears to have been the son of a former mayor of Coventry, who may well have known William from their childhood in the city. Four months later, William's four copyhold properties were surrendered to Jonah's use.[29] However, they were not sold off, but were passed to William's daughters, Elizabeth and Sarah, presumably as their father would have wished. One wonders how great the resentment must have been towards William when there was clearly plenty of family money to pay off his debts.

In 1731, Elizabeth Eyre, William's elder daughter, surrendered her half-share in the four houses to the uses of her will.[30] Unfortunately, the will does not appear to have survived and thus we do not know the names of the beneficiaries, though we would have expected her sister, Sarah, to have been her heir. Elizabeth died soon afterwards, hardly out of her twenties, and in 1736 her half-share of the four houses passed to Fisher Littleton, the 'friend', as remarked on p.98, whom her grandmother had entrusted to look after her inheritance. Sarah was married twice, firstly to Joseph Poole, and after his death to Francis Soden of Coventry. When Littleton died there is evidence that she and her husband, Francis, disputed his will.[31]

In October 1748, Dorothy Wolferstan, Littleton's niece, went to the manor court with his will and asked to be admitted tenant of her half-share of the four copyhold messuages. In the will, Littleton had written:[32]

> Whereas I am seized according to the custom of the manor in common with Mr Soden and his wife of several copyhold Burgages or Tenements in Atherston in the county of Warwick all which I some time since surrendered to the use of my last Will Now I do hereby declare this use to be and I do give and devise the same together with all my part of a freehold house or tenement in Atherston[33] aforesaid in the possession of Thomas Smith with all my Estate Right and title to the same premises together with all and singular the Appurtenances thereunto belonging to Dorothy Wolferstan eldest daughter of my brother and sister Stanford Wolferstan and Sarah his wife

Dorothy Wolferstan married Samuel Pipe, a clergyman, and they had a son, Samuel (*see* Building History Four), but she did not live to see him reach his majority. After her death, the elder Samuel was admitted tenant to the copyhold property, as trustee for his son.[34] The house had only one tenant, Francis Fitzgerald, an apothecary, from at least 1723, probably until Fitzgerald's death in 1760.[35] He, no doubt, had a shop on the premises.

In 1772, Francis Soden sold his half-share in 11/13 Market Street to John Underwood, a grocer.[36] Two years later, Dorothy Pipe's son Samuel, now a young man and a lawyer in the Inner Temple sold his half-share to Robert Lingard, a maltster.[37] That year, too, Underwood acquired the other half of the property, so that now it was returned to single ownership.[38] However, although it was owned by one individual, it was physically divided to allow two sets of tenants to live there. To Underwood, it was probably just an investment property. He did not live there; his home and grocery shop were around the corner on Long Street.[39]

In 1775 he leased, 'part of a messuage together with brewhouse, scullery, stable and the loft or chamber over it, garden, necessary house & other appurtenances,'[40] to the Reverend Christopher Preston. The north side of the property was occupied by Elizabeth Vincent.

After John Underwood's death in 1789, his widow Cicely inherited 11/13 Market Street for life, after which it was to go to his 'dear Sister Sarah Reynolds.'[41] Sarah Reynolds was the mother of the Reverend Edward Reynolds,[42] who was heavily in debt when he inherited the property on his mother's death. After his death in 1797, it had to be sold. The purchaser was William Hanson, described as a 'banker,' but also a mercer.[43] His wife, Sarah, was the daughter of his neighbour in Beech House, Nicholas Smith. By the time that Nicholas Smith died in 1806, Hanson, too, was dead, and Sarah inherited Beech House.[44] This meant that the three neighbouring properties, 11/13 and 15/17 Market Street, and Beech House were all in the same ownership. This led to what must have been highly inconvenient arrangements for their tenants.

The occupant of 15 Market Street had also been given part of 11/13 Market Street on lease – he was entitled to use the pump in the yard behind

15 Market Street, accessed through its entry, but had to pay three-fifths of the cost of the pump's maintenance.

On the day she took over ownership of Beech House, Sarah Hanson sold 11/13 Market Street to John Morris, a shopkeeper.[45] But the copyhold tenancy he received gave him rights over part of the neighbouring 15/17 and took away part of 11/13:

> Also a Right of Road up the entry in the Occupation of Benjamin Pullin[46] as the same is now used for Horses, Wheelbarrows or otherwise of the like breadth as the same now is And also the use of the Pump[47] standing in the yard belonging to the said Messuage in the Occupation of Benjamin Pullin the Owners Tenants or Occupiers for the time being of the premises hereby Surrendered contributing three parts in five of the charges of Keeping the said Pump in repair with the Owners or Occupiers of the Houses in the Occupation of Benjamin Pullin and William Pullin (Except out of the Surrender hereby made the back Kitchen Pantry and Cellar in the Occupation of the said Christopher Morris).[48]

The entry is still visible today, separating the two sides of 15/17 Market Street. It is far too low and narrow to have allowed the passage of anything larger than a small pony. It also runs beside the base of the double chimney stack which rises above the building.[49] Occupants of 11/13 would have been frequent users of this entry to collect water, as their property had no pump (though in later years a gate was inserted into the dividing wall). But for the privilege of using the pump they had to pay three-fifths of the cost of its maintenance.

In 1812, John Morris sold 11/13 to Thomas Sands, a boot and shoe maker. He paid Morris £190, and then raised a mortage of £400 from James Baker, a gentleman, of nearby Glascote.[50] Over the next 15 years, Sands borrowed more from Baker, and on Baker's death in 1840, a debt of £660 including interest, was still outstanding. The mortgages were inherited by Baker's nephew, James Baker, and his great-nephew, William Baker (the nephew's son). They called in the loan, and as Sands was unable to pay, the property was put up for auction. It failed to find a bidder, so Sands released the equity of redemption[51] to the Bakers for only £20, upon which they took possession and were consequently admitted tenants at the manor court.[52] James Baker and his son William continued to hold 11/13 Market Street for the next eight years, then sold it for £500 in 1849 to John Burton, of Wigston, Leicestershire, a yeoman, who bought it for his son, James.[53] (James Burton, aged 24, was a bookseller and stationer. He lived in the one house with his wife, two children and a servant, whilst his tenant, Diana Rich, a widow, lived and worked alone as a druggist and grocer in the other house.[54]) The property was now described as 'two messuages,' but the arrangement of sharing next-door's pump continued; they also had to pay the cost of the repair of the entry and half the repair of gutter between this property and the house in the occupation Sam Rowley,' (15/17 Market Street).[55]

For over 60 years in the 20th century, 11 Market Street was occupied by Johnson, saddlers. Their account books chart the changes in local transport from harness for dray horses to upholstery for motor vehicles.[56] Number 13 was occupied in 1932 by Mrs Gilbert, the agent for Singer Sewing Machines.[57] Today 11/13 is back in single occupancy.

Building History Six:
The *Old Swan*, 175 Long Street

This property is F12 on Fig. 7. *See* Figs. 31-2.

The Building

The *Old Swan* is situated some distance east of the town centre, on the south side of Long Street. The remnants of a medieval cruck frame revealed by the HART survey (*see* p.155) makes this fragment of the *Old Swan* the earliest structure yet identified in the town. It is one of the few buildings in the town for which the standing fabric can tell us almost as much as the documents, since it has not been possible to identify it in the 16th-century records.

Another mystery is its name. Four buildings in Atherstone have included the word 'Swan' in their title. The most prominent '*Swan Inn*' in early times was what is now the Old Surgery and former offices of Sale, Hill and Davenport, in the north-east corner of the Market Place (*see* Building History Two). At the end of the 18th century the *New Swan* appeared on the corner of Church Street and Derby Lane,[1] and at this point the inn in the Market Place was re-named the '*Old Swan*', to differentiate it from the *New Swan*. Later, in the 19th century, this house ceased to be an inn, and the name was transferred to the present site.[2]

The wide frontage of the house reflects an extremely complex sequence of alterations. The only known fragment of a cruck-framed building left in the town can be seen on the first floor, at '1' in bay 'D' (see Fig. 32). No remnants of the cruck-truss have survived in the roof-space, but fragments of the cruck-frame and the adjoining wing might remain at '2', buried in the wall. Not enough is visible to be certain, but it is plausible that the cruck-truss was at the upper end of a medieval open hall, with a contemporary or secondary wing to the east. On the first floor this wing, which is still jettied, was originally one large undivided space – probably a solar over upper-end chambers – but it is now divided by a partition wall into two rooms ('B' and 'C' on Fig. 32). The roof truss incorporates curved braces rising to a cambered tiebeam, a central strut up to the collar, and clasped side purlins trapped under the principals. In the West Midlands such roof trusses are generally attributed to the 15th or early 16th century, but a clasped purlin roof at Polesworth was recently dated to *c.*1583.[3]

At first glance, the western half of the front elevation appears to have a continuous jetty, but closer inspection shows two separate structures here. In the middle of the façade, above the main entrance doorway, the jettied

31 *Front elevation of the* Old Swan, *Long Street.*

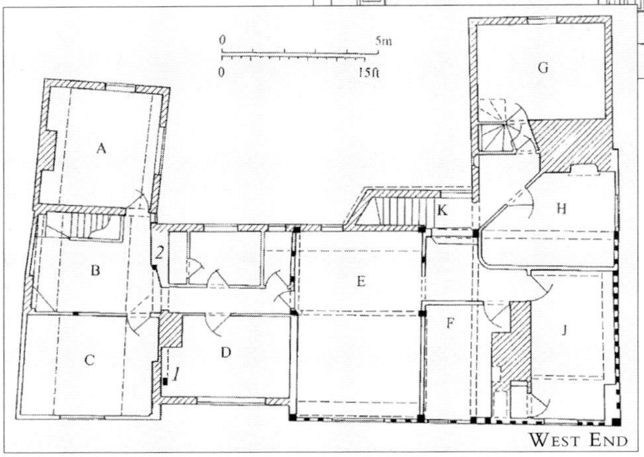

32 *Plan of the* Old Swan, *Long Street.*

first-floor framing is close-studded, with two curved down-braces. The upper ends of the braces are tenoned into storey-posts with splayed heads, and these carry a tiebeam rather than a wall-plate. Seen from inside room 'E', the same tiebeam retains at about 23½-inch intervals the redundant pegs that once secured the tenons at the feet of closely-spaced studs in the gable. The original roof over 'D' and 'E' has been replaced, and at lower levels much that might help us to understand the building is obscured by later finishes. The bay that now contains room 'D' might have been a single-bay hall, with jettied wings at each end, but equally, the wing at 'E' could have been a discrete unit.

The west end of the *Old Swan* adjacent to Welcome Street could be mistaken on the plan for a wing, separated from the structure so far described by a cross-passage at 'F'. However, two jettied wings have already been identified. The roof over 'J' and 'H' has trenched side-purlins, and the jettied front elevation employs a straight upward brace; both of these features are typologically later than the curved down-braces at the front of 'E'. In support of the stylistic evidence, on the front elevation there are two contiguous jetty-posts and storey-posts at the abutment of two discrete structures. Rather than a cross-passage within a single building, the narrow space at F might have begun as an entry at the side of a building on a narrow part-tenement, originally forming no part of the *Old Swan*. The existing close-studded west elevation is a mock-up added after Welcome Street had been laid out after 1855.

The History

Although the *Old Swan* is shown as a freehold on the 1786 Plan, it had formerly been a three-quarter burgage copyholding. It stands among a number of large properties, on the road to Mancetter, where the wealthy would have lived – and there is evidence of ownership in the 16th century by outsiders whose names do not appear in the Mancetter parish register. It is possible that in 1593 the *Old Swan* was acquired by William Roberts, gent, who also owned copyhold property to the east of the *Old Swan*.[4]

The first certain reference to the ownership of the property comes in 1646, when Robert Richardson, of Higham in Leicestershire, went to the manor court and surrendered it to the use of Henry Marshall. At the time Richard Pare was tenant. Thereafter, Henry appears to have lived in the property with his wife, Anne. However, it appears that one Edward Jackson of Weldon in Northamptonshire, and his wife, Katherine, had some rights to it, as in 1649 he surrendered it to the use of Henry Murhall (which seems to be a variant spelling of Marshall).[5]

In 1662 Henry Murrall (another variant spelling) is shown as the owner at the time of the Hearth Tax.[6] The house then had five hearths, though that number was to reduce over the next eight years. Hearths had been 'pulld up' and Murrall was in arrears. He seems to have been short of money, because in 1670 he mortgaged the house with 'all outhouses, gardens, orchards, etc.' for the sum of £70. The lender was William Scott of Twycross, a yeoman, and his wife, Elizabeth.

In 1672 the Scotts sold the building to Samuel Bracebridge, a haberdasher of hats, and his second wife, Elizabeth.[7] After this time, changes in its ownership disappear from the manor court rolls as Bracebridge 'enfranchised' the property, converting it into freehold.[8] However, his family continued to own it, at least until the mid-19th century (*see* the reference to Charles Holte Bracebridge, below).

The court rolls still tell us about the history of the *Old Swan*, but only through references to its occupants in descriptions of the adjoining properties ('abuttals'). Next door to the *Old Swan* on the east was a house belonging to William Mantle in 1659;[9] in 1678 John Power, baker, lived on the west side.[10] When the latter made his will in 1677, he bequeathed to his daughter, Mary, '… the high whole Tester Bedd with Furniture thereof being in the upper parlour next Mr Bracebridge his house'.[11] This may suggest that other buildings butted up to the *Old Swan*, even at that time.

The tenant of Bracebridge's freeholding in 1702 was Jeremiah Ford, a husbandman; he also rented land in the open fields from Samuel Bracebridge.[12] Soon afterwards, he must have sub-let the house, to one Richard Bancks, since Ford was one of the appraisers of Bancks's inventory in 1707.[13] This gives an insight into the house at the time, listing the following rooms:

Dwelling house	Best parlour
Seller	Kitchin
Little Parlour	Chamber
Little Chamber	Barne

Table 10 *Rooms in the* Old Swan, *from the inventory of Richard Bancks, 1707.*

As only three bedsteads are mentioned it is clear that the *Old Swan* was not then operating as an inn. Bancks had a considerable farming interest, with 69 sheep, four cows and a calf, a sow and four small pigs, five quarters of barley, three quarters of peas, hay and straw, with 20 strikes of peas stored in the chamber. He left no will, but among the probate documents is a condition or bond requiring his wife, Daringold, to 'well and sufficiently educate foster and bring up' their four children. In fact, she continued as tenant, and presumably went on running the farm.

Robert Seale (possibly pronounced 'Sale') was the next tenant, and he too seems to have concentrated on husbandry, especially as the property came to be known as 'Seal's Farm.' By 1754 William Clarke had taken over as tenant.

Later, we see the beginnings of the phasing-out of husbandry as the prime use of the premises. William Hanson, a mercer and wool merchant who lived and had his warehouse on the corner of Long Street and Market Street,[14] was clearly short of storage space, and rented a building and yard to the rear of the *Old Swan*. In 1786 Hanson insured 'his Wool in a Barn built with Brick and Tiles which he rent(ed) of Abraham Bracebridge Esq; in the first class £600.' He also insured 'his ricks in a rick yard adjoining the before mentioned barn £75'.[15] His premium was £1 14s. 4½d. Thus, as the town became industrialised, we see agricultural buildings converted to commercial use.

In 1793 the Atherstone Parish Rate detailed the occupation of the *Old Swan*.[16] Thomas Fletcher, Henry Hull and James Congreve lived in the front; Thomas Ward and William Hanson occupied the rear. The premises included barn, croft and large garden, and were rated at £35.

As mentioned above, the name 'Old Swan' seems to have been transferred from the Market Place to this building in the 1820s. William Alcock was probably its first inn-keeper; he took out a victualler's bond for the *'Old Swan Inn'* in both 1824 and 1827.[17] He stayed on until at least 1828, when he is recorded as the innkeeper of the 'Old Swan'.[18]

In 1825 William Broadbent occupied 'House Stables Outbuildings Croft Garden.'[19] He remained there until at least 1833, when another rent assessment showed him as occupier of '*Swan Inn*, and Croft', valued at £18 14s. 0d.[20] An adjacent piece of land of seven acres is also listed in the assessment, at a value of £15 13s. 5½d., showing the high value of land in comparison with buildings at the time.

The site of the *Old Swan* underwent one further development before it reached its present form. In 1855, Charles Holte Bracebridge, then the owner, and his wife, Selina, travelled to the Crimea with Florence Nightingale, Selina's friend. Although the expedition was not a success, the Bracebridges were feted as heroes on their return, and to mark the event Bracebridge decided to create a new road. It ran along the side of the *Old Swan*, linking Long Street to South Street, and was named 'Welcome Street', as a reminder of the tumultuous reception which Charles and Selina (and Florence's sister, Parthenope) had received.[21] Unlike the road through the yard of the *Swan Inn* in the Market Square (*see* Building History Two: The New Roads), this was not a controversial development. It is evident from the Ordnance Survey map of 1887 that the road was created at the expense of part of the *Old Swan*'s curtilage, as there is a decided 'pinching' of the land to the rear.

6 'Goods, Cattel and Chattels': Atherstone in the Sixteenth and Seventeenth Centuries

Marion Alexander

Introduction

When Henry, Marquis of Dorset, received from King Henry VIII the grant of a market town nine miles from Coventry – the manor of Atherstone – he sent George Medley, Robert Burdett, and Pyerce Ithell to survey his new property.[1]

In 1547, they recorded that the town 'standeth in the great hye way called Wattling Strete, on the border of the Felden countrey joyninge to the Woodlande', writing:

> This towne hath the market on the Tewesday and the ffayre on the Natyvytie of the Vyrgyne Mary [8 September]. Hit hath at this day no capytall mancyone or manor place as farreforthe as we can perceive.

They listed the lands held by indenture, and named their tenants; they also listed the 66 burgages held by manorial copyhold, each with its tenant and its neighbours.

Expressing the contemporary national concern about enclosure of the open, communally-worked fields such as those in Atherstone,[2] they noted that some of the demesne lands were sub-let and were:

> in the occupacons of diverse pore men as well husbandmen as artyfycers of the town and when so ever they come to the lordes handes to be lette or sette, yt shall not be mete to demise theym all to one man but to many and the mo[re] the better for the upholding of the towne.

This arable land was 'sparpled' among other lands, that is, in strips in the open field.[3] If enclosure were to take place they said:

> Yt will be an undoing to the town, not only for lacke of tillage whereof they have lytle … but also for lacke of comens whereof they have none but only the outwoods which is in maner nothing worth.

The copyholders of the burgage plots set out by the Monks of Bec along Watling Street and round the Market Place had 'rights' in the town fields (*see* Chapter Four: 'Obligations and Rights of Manorial Tenants). Some also owned land in the fields – perhaps one or two yardlands (30-60 acres) – and by the 16th century many of the will-making class were both copyholders and freeholders (For more on copyhold, *see* p.31).

The Outwoods on the ridge to the south of the parish were a community asset, used as a foraging ground for the many pigs and poultry. They also supplied the large amount of bark needed for Atherstone's leather trade, despite the fact that the surveyors for the Marquis described them as 'nothing worth'.

We may think that at this time, in 1547, people would have been aware and fearful of changes that might disrupt their familiar routines. Possibly some of the very oldest inhabitants could recall the momentous events in their region, when Henry Tudor confronted Richard III at the battle of Bosworth, across the border in neighbouring Leicestershire.[4]

The inhabitants of Atherstone in 1547 would have seen, too, that the church as an institution was changing; over many centuries it had become very wealthy and very powerful, and Henry VIII had decided this had to be dealt with. He dissolved the monasteries, bringing much of their wealth under his own control. The Pope had declared Henry 'Defender of the Faith' in the 1520s – Henry later went one step further by declaring himself Head of the Church of England.

Again, in 1547 many people in Atherstone would still remember the departure of the friars from their home in the Market Place, after its closure a little over ten years earlier. They would also recall the closure of the great Cistercian abbey of Merevale on their western border.[5] Henry VIII had pensioned off the friars and monks and sold on the lands to his favourites, such as the above-mentioned Henry, Marquis of Dorset. Despite these changes, Henry himself remained an orthodox worshipper. However, he appointed a Protestant reformer as his son's tutor, and after Edward VI came to the throne in 1547 the Act of Uniformity was passed, altering much of the previous tradition.[6] The people were also to see, under his son, all their statues and icons removed from their church and the mass said in English instead of the Latin to which they had been accustomed. Even worse for them, at a time when few could read, would be the painting over of the bible stories decorating the walls of their church.

How did all these changes impact on Atherstone? To what extent were the populace affected?

This chapter offers a glimpse into the religious beliefs, the homes and lives of the people who lived in the town during these changing times, a people already concerned about the threat posed by enclosure (though this, as noted in Chapter Seven, only finally took place in 1765). It will also show the communal working patterns of those labouring in the fields, which had remained similar for centuries but which were gradually to change over the next 200 years.

Sources

The chapter draws on the wealth of surviving documents from which Atherstone benefits:[7]

the parish register
probate documents
manorial records

The 16th and 17th centuries are a rewarding period for historians. Compared with the medieval period, records are improved in three ways: they are easier to read, refer to a wider range of the population, and are more numerous. First, improved readability came with the change of language: medieval documents were mainly in Latin, but during the 16th century it gradually became more common to use English (albeit occasionally adding a Latin ending to a word). Second, the wider range: medieval documents usually dealt with the affairs of the aristocracy, but during the 16th century probate documents in particular mention people further down the social scale. Third, the increase in the quantity of documentation is due to several factors, one arising from the determination of Henry VIII to consolidate his position and increase his control. Towards that end, on Henry's behalf Thomas Cromwell issued a mandate in 1538, instructing every parish to purchase a 'sure coffer'.[8] The coffer (a locked chest) was to hold the book into which the minister had to enter every marriage, baptism and burial at which he officiated. Fortunately, those for Mancetter Parish, which included Atherstone, have survived. Beginning in 1576, these parish records are an outstanding asset for the history of the town.

Some of the most important and interesting evidence for living standards is available in the probate documents: wills, inventories and bonds. Wills give details of land-holding, property and family relationships. Inventories describe 'goods, cattel and chattels'[9] – the personal possessions of the deceased. Bonds detail arrangements made for under-age children when a deceased person had left no will: when Mary Tomlinson died in poverty in 1673 the overseers of the poor, Richard Goodwin and John Abell, were bound by a signed bond to administer the goods and provide for the children of Mary during their minority.

An inventory of goods was required before probate was granted by the church court, and those for the period 1520-1750 are the most valuable for social historians, implying, through their material possessions, the lifestyles of the lesser gentry and tradesmen. As illustrations of their character, a representative selection of inventory texts is included in the Appendix to this chapter.

The appraisers from Atherstone would go to Lichfield or Coventry (or to the Prerogative Court in London if land was held in more than one area) with a document which provided:

> A true and perfect inventory of all and singular the goods cattel and chattels of … (deceased name and occupation) taken and appraised … (date) by us … (appraisers names and often occupations) as followeth:

The inventories were invariably taken soon after the death, when three or four neighbours, friends, or people of standing in the community were called in to assess the value of the goods left by the deceased. The appraisers would go from room to room, usually naming them, listing the items there and estimating their value. They would usually enter the house through the hall – the main living area – and would then visit the further ground-floor rooms, which might well include a chamber or a parlour. The kitchen, buttery, brew and/or bake houses would come next, possibly separate from the main house because of fire risk. Upper rooms would be listed, such as a chamber which might be over the hall, the parlour or the entry. Goods at other locations might also be included: Peter Eckersall's appraisers in 1604 gave a valuation 'as nere as they could guess', as the goods were lying in a house that 'hath bene enfected'.

Wills were often made some time before a person's death, but occasionally, when the sick person was unable to write but of sound mind, a nuncupative will was made. The will of John Greatalder was such a one (*see* p.134 for full text):

> Memorandum that on Sundaie at night beinge the Eighte Daie of the month of December in the year of our Lord god 1622 John Greatalder of Atherstone in the countie of Warr' Mylner deceased being of sound & perfect mynd and memory did utter and declare his nuncupative will in manner and forme following …

He was a bachelor and his will shows that he left all to his brother, Richard, who has obviously been looking after him during a long illness. It would be interesting to see what was in his locked coffer where his bonds and writings lay.

Sometimes documents seem to offer tantalising puzzles: George Lander, in his will dated 1667–8, left a close to his sister Alice Sadler, from which, he instructed, neither she nor her assigns should:

> … sell cut down or anyways destroy at any time any manner of timber or any other manner of trees whatsoever standing, growing remaining or being in or upon the said given and devised and bequeathed close or parcel of land.

Present-day sensibilities might lead us to question whether George's awareness of the danger of over-felling arose purely from reasons of conservation. (George's father, Thomas, had been a brazier and probably used wood as his fuel.) However, a much more likely explanation emerges from the fact that Alice was to have the land for life, after which it was to go to her son George. Because the land was not left outright to her, George (her brother the testator) could place a restriction on it. The real implication of this is his knowledge of the value of trees – when cash was needed, trees could be felled.

Occasionally, other documents give us additional information. When baker Richard Biddle died in 1681, an account listed the expenses incurred after his death. The funeral expenses were £3 12s. 0d. The attorney, Richard

Drayton of Atherstone, charged £3 10s. 0d. for his services, and £4 was paid to the officers of the year for the poor of Atherstone. Further expenses arose because Richard's children (son Richard and daughters Susanna Biddle and Anne Mason) renounced the will in favour of their uncle Jonathan Biddle. £1 19s. 4d. was charged for drawing the renunciation document and other expenses at Lichfield, also for attorney Drayton's costs:

> Spent in travel to Lichfield twice before he could obtayne the Administration and for his owne horse 0. 10. 0

However, by 1750 the golden period for inventories in Atherstone was over. After then, although inventories were still being drawn up, they generally listed the rooms only, and not the goods, while the accompanying probate grants simply recorded the total value as 'not over' so many pounds. But even from the 'golden period', in practice probate documents have survived for only a small proportion of the community, and these are usually for people who were either members of the local élite or who had acquired wealth during their lifetime, possibly through trade. A comparison with the Parish Register for the 1590s shows that only about eight per cent of deceased household heads have surviving probate documents. This figure rises to about fourteen per cent by the mid-17th century and possibly as high as thirty per cent by the mid-18th century.

For Atherstone, despite these limitations, they do provide a glimpse of the personal lives of the better-off inhabitants during the period 1520-1750. Not surprisingly, the documents demonstrate that their subjects enjoyed an atmosphere of relative comfort, prosperity and independence.

Another valuable source complementing the probate information is the manorial evidence found in the court rolls for Atherstone Manor.[10] The town is unusual – and fortunate – in having retained records of copyhold transactions in the manor court rolls from the 16th to the 19th centuries. Each time a property changed hands the contemporary manor court roll recorded the transaction: from whom, to whom. What is more, the owners and/or occupiers of the abutting properties were also named. Very often occupations were given, sometimes with family connections and incidental detail. (For more on the copyhold system, see the section in the Appendix to Chapter Three.) These manorial records have been drawn upon for other chapters in the book (extensively through Chapters Seven to Nine).

POPULATION

Our earliest estimate of the population of the town in this period can be drawn from the Lay Subsidy listing of 1524, which shows 100 tax payers. A third to a half of the remaining population would have been too poor to pay tax; thus, estimating an average of five persons per household, the population would have been about 650-750.[11] Some twenty years later, when the 1547 survey was taken for the Marquis of Dorset, there seem to have been about 160 occupiers of properties in the town (*see* Table 4 in Appendix to Chapter Three), suggesting a population of 800. A little later, the Diocesan Returns of

1563 record some 104 households in Atherstone, suggestive of a population of several hundred. This figure, lower than in 1547, may reflect the troubles of the town in the epidemic of 1558-9.[12]

During the second half of the 16th century, Atherstone experienced high inflation and considerable population increase, like many other towns (and as in most towns the population increase was to continue during the following century).[13] Nevertheless, there were some set backs. For instance, the epidemic of influenza which ravaged all England during the years 1557-9 certainly affected the town.[14] In the early part of the 16th century, surviving probate documents averaged one a year. They were well formulated, usually giving the occupation of the deceased, the names and occupations of the appraisers and the names of all the rooms. By contrast, in the two years 1558-9, no fewer than 12 wills were proved at Lichfield, with a further four in the Prerogative Court of Canterbury – and a sudden and unusual rise in the death rate seems a more likely explanation than an improvement in administration. After this peak in 1558-9, there follow almost two decades for which no Atherstone inventories survive.[15] Only in the 1580s do inventories begin again for Atherstone and these were of much poorer quality than the earlier ones, with occupations and room names omitted and appraisers rarely named. By the next decade, the administrative skills of the town had revived, with the documents more adequately compiled. Perhaps the local Free Grammar School which was founded in 1576 helped in this respect.

Periodic ravages of epidemic disease continued into the 17th century. Even as the century opened, 1604 saw a major epidemic, probably plague; the burial rate increased fourfold from the normal yearly average of 30 burials. This figure was exceeded in one month alone in May 1604, with 31 burials. A further 92 people were buried in the next five months, 28 of them during August. The total for the year was 145 burials, affecting many families very badly. Other difficult years during the 17th century were 1625 and 1641. Nevertheless, the baptism rate stayed stable; indeed, it often rose soon after the crisis years. Furthermore, it is likely that people were moving into the town. The series of Hearth Tax assessments from 1662 to 1674 list a maximum of 257 properties, indicating a population of about 1,300.[16]

Religious Belief

Nationally, in the 10 years following the death of Henry VIII in 1547, the Church, which under Henry had gone from Catholicism to Anglicanism, went on to radical Protestantism as Edward VI succeeded him, to Catholicism again on the accession of Mary, then back to Protestantism under Elizabeth. It was a time for great caution – a caution not exercised by Robert Glover of Mancetter and his neighbour Joyce Lewis. They were both burnt as martyrs in 1557.[17]

Their neighbour Sir Robert Barefoote,[18] the vicar of the church of St Peter's at Mancetter (parish church of the area that included Atherstone) was probably fortunate to die in 1538, before the radical reforms of Edward VI, whose Act of Uniformity banned all religious icons and relics. Sir Robert's 'Saynte Jhons hed of Alabaster' in a tabernacle, mentioned in his inventory, would certainly have been frowned upon.

His books were listed but not valued, as his appraisers would not have been familiar with such unusual items; in other inventories of the period, even bibles are unknown. Sir Robert's remarkable list of 'Bookys' comprises:

Item as given in the inventory	*Comments*
The bible in iiii bookys cum glossinterliniatt	A bible with interlined glossary
Constitucion Lynwood	William Lyndewode, *Constitutiones provinciales ecclesiae Anglicanae* (Constitution of the English Church, first published at Oxford in 1483)
Ortus vocabulorum	The first Latin/English dictionary to be published in England, printed at Westminster in 1500
Formulare instrumentorum	*Formularium instrumentorum ad usum Curiae Romanae* (A formulary, listing the forms of 'instruments' – deeds, writs, etc. used in the Curia in Rome, first published there in 1474)
Summa Angelica	One of the most popular books of the 15th century, a dictionary of moral theology by Angelo Carletti de Chivasso
Postilla	Probably Guillermus, *Postilla super epistolas et evangelia* (A commentary on the Epistles and Evangelists, of which an enormous number of editions was produced before 1500)
Sextus decretalium	Pope Boniface VIII, *Liber sextus Decretalium* (Book of the Sixth Decretal [Papal Decree])
Salustius cum comentar	Almost certainly a volume of letters by Sallust with a commentary, printed in Venice in 1500
Other olde books writton nothing worth	'writton' presumably indicates manuscripts rather than printed books

Table 11 *Books owned by Sir Robert Barefoot, 1538.*

Some of these titles suggest that Sir Robert was knowledgeable in church law and perhaps held a post in the Diocesan courts at Lichfield. Like many village priests, he may well also have taught school-children, in his case in Mancetter or Atherstone,[19] perhaps using these 'olde books worth nothing'.

By the mid-17th century, conditions had changed both locally and nationally. The Civil War had been fought between king and parliament, and the country had experienced 10 years as a commonwealth. The king had been restored to his throne and all appeared to be as it had been. However, the ideas generated during the period had influenced the way of life: while it does seem that Atherstone people were not deeply involved in the Civil War, locally the Parliamentary cause had seemed more acceptable than the alternative; and here, as elsewhere, the hierarchical society was now no longer as secure as it had been.

Before the Reformation, the wills of the people of Atherstone start with fervent religious declarations of which the following is a typical example:

> I give and bequeath my soul to Almighty God, our Blessed Lady and all the company of Heaven
>
> (John Skarborow, 1522)

William Altofte, Sergeant to the King, also made this request, in 1521:

> In the name of my mortuary that all right and custom doth require in the day of my burial in wax bread and ale and all other necessaries

Even 30 years later, despite their time under Henry VIII and Edward VI, during the reign of Catholic Queen Mary some people continued to use the old format (but now maybe out of wariness, not belief):

> I give and bequeath my soule to almighty god my maker and redeemer and to the blessed virgins son, Mary his mother and to all the holy company in heaven
>
> (Amias Hill, gentleman, 1558)

However, in most cases after the Reformation, wills quickly changed from Catholic to Protestant forms, and it is clear that in their religious life the townspeople's inclination was towards Protestantism. Thus, Jonathan Abell in his will of 1656 bequeaths his soul simply to:

> Almighty God my creator and redeemer, believing that I shall receive full pardon and remission of all my sins and be saved by the precious death and merits of my blessed saviour and redeemer Christ Jesus

Symon Preston, a weaver who died in 1558/9, bequeathed his soul to:

> Almighty God my maker and Redeemer In whose merits and passion I put my whole trust and confidence there in to be saved and Redeemed

In 1612, Thomas Barfoot a husbandman, a relative of the former Vicar Sir Robert Barefoote, had a long, puritanical declaration:

> First and Cheefely as Christianitie requireth constantlie craving pardon with sorrowfull hart for my great and manifolde sins which I have committed throughout the Course of my whole life I do commend and leave my soule to the great memorie of Jesus Christ our only Saviour and Redeemer by the blessed merritts of whose death and bloodsheddinge I remaine stedfastlie assured to be partaker of his everlasting kingdom not doubting but that his

> mercy doth far exceed my manifold offences and therefore bylding my faith Firmely upon his assured promise unto ... I doe make true accompte to be of the number of his elect

Some of these may have been worded by the people who actually wrote the wills, but their proposals were obviously acceptable.

Furthermore, after the dissolution of the chantries in 1547 (the chantry is discussed in Chapter Four: The Church), people no longer left bequests to the chantry priests to pray for their soul and intercede for them through the Blessed Virgin Mary. Thereafter, testators with charitable inclinations left their money to the churchwardens, to administer it for the benefit of the poor. Thus, in 1634-5 John Pennyfeather, a tanner, left 10s. to the poor of Mancetter and 10s. to the poor of Witherley. He also left 9s. for a pewter flagon for the church at Mancetter and 6s. 8d. for the minister, Richard Abell.

Unlike his predecessor, Sir Robert Barefoot, who had died at a moment opportune for his religious views, Richard Abell was vicar of Mancetter during a particularly volatile period in the religious life of the community, from 1622-61, seeing the Civil War, the Commonwealth period and the development of Puritan ideas. He was a descendant of the Abell family, who were 16th-century blacksmiths, and an ageing man of around eighty by the time of the Restoration and his death. He seems to have conformed to all the changing requirements and kept his living. Atherstone-born Obadiah Grew – baptised in Mancetter Church in 1607 – was less compliant; he was ejected from his living in Coventry. Obadiah was the son of Francis, and he and his siblings were all given good Protestant names, including Israel and Abigail. Among his cousins were Patience, Obedience, Humility, and Content. When William Grew, their father, died in 1619, he specified in his will that his 10 children should all be educated in good Christian ways. It is likely that Richard Abell took on this task; it would have included familiarity with the bible, which Catholics had always been discouraged from reading. Many of Obadiah's family continued to live in Atherstone, but they were not known to be active dissenters. However, baptismal names used by the Grews and other families do suggest a dissenting inclination.

In the 1670s, a dissenters' meeting house was established by a local mercer, William Symmonds, who died in 1685.[20] He had a remarkable number of books, mostly Christian, which were named in his will. He bequeathed these to various friends, relatives and servants, sometimes with instructions or comments (as listed in Table 12, p.122).

Despite being listed as a Presbyterian minister, he was asking that the Book of Martyrs be set up in one of the neighbouring parish churches, and he still wanted his body to be 'decently interred in Mancetter Churchyard as neare unto my deceased children as may be at the discretion of my executors'. He did, however, bequeath 20s. each to 20 nonconformist ministers.

Beneficiary and testator's comments	*Books*
Brother Mr Richard Symmonds 'promised to him'	One physicke book
Nephew Mr Samuel Symmonds 'bookes I formerly lent him and still in his possession'	Five volumes of Mr Pooles Sinopsis (Matthew Poole, *Synopsis Criticorum*, 1666-76, a work of Biblical interpretation)
Sister – Symmonds	One book of Mr Baxters called his everlasting rest (Richard Baxter, *The Saint's everlasting Rest*, 1650)
Daughter Mary Simmonds *'formerly intended for her'*	Mr Gornalls xtian armour the first second and third bound up in two Volumes (William Gurnall, *The Christian in compleat armour*, 1655, etc.) Also one Book called the Queens Delight (M.W. [only the author's initials are known], *The Queens Closet opened … A Queens Delight, or, The Art of preserving, etc.-The Compleat Cook: expertly prescribing the most ready wayes … for dressing of flesh and fish, etc.*, 1655, etc. [Clearly a very useful cookery book]
Cozen Edward Symmonds	One Booke called Calvins Institutions
Wife of Cozen Edward 'if married'	One Booke of Mr Howes blessednesse of the righteous (John Howe, *The blessedness of the Righteous opened*, 1673)
Cozen Jonathan Symmonds	One booke of the Bishop of Armagh his body of Divinity (James Usher, *A body of divinity*, 1648)
Sister – Symmonds	One booke of Mr Baxters called his everlasting rest (as above)
Cozen Josuah Symmonds	One book of Bishop Andrews his body of Divinity (probably as above)
Wife of Josuah Symmonds	One booke called the whole duty of man (Richard Allestree, *The whole duty of man*, 1674)
Cozen Priscilla Symmonds	One bible which I bought of the book binder in the horsefair together with one booke called the Gospel Glasse (Lewis Stuckley, *A Gospel-Glass*, 1670)

Cozen Thomas Inge	One booke called by the name of Mr Baxters poore mans family book (Richard Baxter, *The Poor Man's Family Book*, 1674)
Cozen Elizabeth Inge	One booke called by the name of Ambrose his Media (Isaac Ambrose, *Prima, Media, & Ultima, the first, middle, and last things; in three treatises*, 1650 – obviously only one of the volumes)
Friend John Stratford	One Booke called the history of the Venetians (perhaps Giovanni Francesco Busenello, translated by Sir Thomas Higgons, *A Prospective of the Naval Triumph of the Venetians over the Turk, etc.* 1658)
Cozen John Prime	One booke being the first volume of Mr Perkins his workes (probably William Perkins, *The Works of that famous and worthie Minister of Christ … M.W. Perkins*, 1608, in three volumes)
Wife of John Prime	One booke called the souls preparation for Christ (perhaps Thomas Robins, *The Afflicted Souls preparation for death*, 1668)
Maidservant	Fenners Alarum to drowsey saints (William Fenner, *Christ's Alarm to drowsie Saints*, 1646)
2nd Maidservant 'if any'	Mr Fenners Divine Message (William Fenner, *A Divine Message to the Elect Soul*, 4th ed. 1657)
To the use of the Townes men of the Towne and parish of Nuneaton, if they have them not already. If they have them I give them to the Townesmen of Tamworth. Whichever of the said townes have them shall provide one deske and two chaires to fix the bookes thereto which shall be provided by the churchwardens and fixed in some convenient place in the parish church that all may have the use of the reading of them before or after sermon or service	Booke of Martyrs bound up in two volumes and claspt and with bosses and buste leather (John Foxe, *Actes and monuments of these latter and perillous dayes*, generally called Foxe's *Book of Martyrs*, first published in 1563)

Table 12 *Books bequeathed by William Symonds, 1685.*

Sixteenth-Century Lifestyles

One person who lived in considerable and much better style than others locally at this period was Sir Robert Barefoot (as noted, the vicar of the church of St Peter's at Mancetter). In addition to his books already mentioned, his inventory listed his clothing:

a Tawney gowne furred with fox
an fur gowne lyned with black saye
a gowne of pewke lyned with Tawney saye
a gowne of Tawney medley furred with blacke lambe
a shorte gowne of Tawney medley lyned with blacke cotton
an olde blacke gowne lined with blacke cotton
an olde Jakett of Tawney chamlett
ii Jacketts of tawney cloth
a Jakett of blacke cloth
a dowblett
a Jerkin of Tawneye chamlett
a clothe dowblett
a peticote
a lether dowblett
iii paire of little medley shoose

These items were all in a chamber at the vicarage; most inventories simply valued 'apparel' without giving any details.

In The Yelde House (probably 'Old House') he had:

iii curtins of lined cloth
an olde counterpayne of Tapstrye work
a coffer with lock and key
a quiver for boe & shafts

He also had a bed, bedding and a board and trestles in this chamber. The Inventory also includes:

In redy money & other Juells

in golde & silver in his chamber & in his purse	£iiii		xvid
v tacklehooks and ii buttons of silver			xxd
v aglets & a butters clawe of silver			xxd
a notarie signe of silver			xiid
ii silver spoons		iiis	iiiid

He has linen curtains and painted coffers with locks and keys, presumably to secure gold and silver items such as his silver spoons, 'butters (bittern's) claw' and 'notarie signe'.[21] His cupboards were carved and his chairs 'thrown' (made on a lathe). His tacklehooks, silver buttons and five aglets (metal tags of laces) would have been part of his apparel.

John Abell typifies the opportunities available at that time for those with sufficient foresight to make the right moves. Members of the family first appear as tax payers in the 1525 Lay Subsidy. They were not listed the year before; either their wealth was not sufficient, or they came to the town in 1525. When blacksmith John Abell died in 1558 (possibly from the influenza epidemic mentioned above (*see* p.118) his 'goods, cattel and chattels' were valued at £81, mostly in agricultural produce – barley, peas, calves, sheep – rather than the items in his smithy. His appraisers were his son-in-law John Repington (the Repingtons were later to be lords of the manor), Anthony Green (whose family were bailiffs), and William Beck. Yet despite these connections, John's home appears to have been modest. No rooms are named and his household items are very basic, listed after all his farming stock, as was often the case in early 16th-century inventories. His will mentions a wife and two under-age children, so he was probably in his early thirties. He does, though, seem to have had an eye to the future. He had a stone of wool and a barrel of soap, also flax and yarn, suggesting he was interested in the cloth trade.

Although John Abell was in the top five per cent in terms of wealth in the 16th century, the wealthiest in the period before 1600 was shoemaker Thomas Nutt, who died in 1585 – the shoemakers generally tended to have above average wealth; they were not the poor cobblers of folk tradition. He left £120, at a time when the average value of inventories was about £30, while some – mainly widows – left as little as £6 in total goods and chattels.

Few testators left large amounts in goods and chattels; the wills show that much of their wealth was invested in land, both in Atherstone and the surrounding area. In the early 16th century, many had taken advantage of the long leases being offered on land held by the monks of the Cistercian abbey of Mount Grace in Yorkshire. Margaret Green and her husband Robert are named in 1547, holding Hall Closes and, when she died, a widow, in 1586, her inventory listed:

> One lease of a house and certaine ground being in Atherstone and Merevale
> of the yearly rent by the lesser xiiiis id. £x.[22]

One husbandman who died in 1707 held a 1,000-year lease on three cottages in Atherstone, due to expire in 2689, making it effectively a freeholding. They seem to have had a great confidence in the future.

Nevertheless, the growing population was still reliant on the same area of land within Atherstone. Some supplemented their agricultural income with trade income, much of which was from leather and hides. The butchers and tanners tended to be wealthy, the latter with capital locked up in their stock of hides, which they had to keep for six months. Both were deeply involved in agriculture as well as trade, and belonged to the wealthiest and most socially influential tier of families in the area. They tended to call themselves gentlemen or yeomen in their wills, but appraisers often called them husbandmen, or referred to their trade rather than their status. Yeomen, husbandmen and gentlemen are named frequently, not only as testators but also as appraisers, overseers and witnesses.

A common bequest in a will was 'one ewe and a lamb' (often to godchildren or relatives), and the inventories show that a higher proportion of the agricultural wealth was in animals rather than crops. Most had only a few cattle or sheep, as they were limited by their 'stint' in the open fields and by the fact that the low-lying land near to the river was damp and less healthy, particularly for sheep.

That same John Abell, the blacksmith who died in 1558, had a flock of 50 sheep, but because lack of space made it impossible to rear them in Atherstone, he kept them on a close in Mancetter, mentioned in his will. John also had cattle, like most of his neighbours, but could only keep two or three in Atherstone. The bigger herds, often owned by the town butchers, were kept in closes in Mancetter and Hartshill, where the bulls also were kept. Oxen were still used in the fields until the 1580s, but were gradually being replaced by horses. John left a bay mare to his daughter in his will, but this was not valued in his inventory. He had pigs, but unlike many others, he had no poultry listed; nor did he have hives of bees, as did three other 16th-century families.

The arable strips in the three open communal fields of Atherstone were used mainly to grow rye, oats and barley; useful crops for feeding stock and for the malting and brewing found in most households. Many of the inventories mention 'corn on the ground' without specifying the crop, but wheat is rarely mentioned. In the Autumn, after the harvest had been cut, strip holders were allowed to graze their animals on the fields, which were used on a rotation system.[23]

The cloth trade was also attractive. Linen cloth is much in evidence in the inventories, with many yards of flax, yarn, hemp and canvas mentioned; indeed, evidence for a cloth trade is available from as far back as the 14th-century Lay Subsidy. The presence of the 'Tenter Flatt' on the early 18th-century map of the town may well imply usage in the preceding centuries, and demonstrates that this was an area used for stretching and drying the cloth.[24] Wills and inventories both mention considerable quantities of wool and felt, along with the shears used by fullers to process the cloth. In Joseph Robinson's case, when he died in 1675 administration was granted to Michael Wilson, a clothier of York, his principal creditor. A letter signed by Joseph's wife, Mary Robinson, of Elland in the county of York, declared:

> I doe wholly and freely renounce the administration over unto the said Michael Wilson ... for him to administer the goods ... in any place whatsoever sayd goods shall be found. Goods lying in Elland Coventry Nuneaton Atherstone ... he being chief and principle creditor above all the rest.

No trade is given for Joseph Robinson, but he was most likely selling cloth in the area when he died, although actually living in Elland. Robert Bickley valued his goods in Atherstone at £3 16s. 3d., all cloth. The goods in Nuneaton were also cloth, valued at £3 15s. 0d.

As the following chapters show, by the 19th century, many Atherstone people relied on the hat trade for work. However, its origins are much earlier – John Abell's barrel of soap (*see* p.125, above) could possibly have been for this trade. By the early 17th century, as the Victoria County History notes, Atherstone was benefiting from the decline in the cap trade in Coventry. So although two feltmakers, Thomas Wildey and Joseph Hatton, were quite poor when they died in the 1690s, they were at least in the right trade. Thomas's forebear, John Wildey, had been a carpenter when he died in 1604; a century later, the Wildey's were to establish a thriving hat factory, as did the Hattons. (Judy Vero tells the story of the Willday hatting business in Chapter Eight.)

Housing in the Sixteenth and Seventeenth Centuries

The comparison between the early and the late 16th-century inventories substantiates the view of W.G. Hoskins that considerable rebuilding took place at this period.[25] Thus, there would have been work for those in the town who were unable to get their main livelihood through agriculture. An example is the carpenter John Weston, who died in 1589 and clearly relied mainly on his trade – although he did have one cow, pigs and poultry. Many others, too, turned to building for their living, with the probate documents revealing a plumber, a nailer, a glazier and a tiler.

These last two occupations evidence the new fashion for window-glass and roof tiles, both changes which made night work much safer in a time when lighting was provided by candles. A 'paine' (a manor court bylaw) of 1746 ruled that no one without a tiled roof could work after dark because of the fire risk (*see* Chapter Three, p.23; Chapter Seven, p.139).[26] Thomas Roper's tile-making trade must have thrived. His will was proved in the Prerogative Court of Canterbury in 1593, but there is no surviving inventory. However, his will mentions extensive bequests, an indication of his prosperity. He had a tile house on a close, which was held by lease from Richard Preston, left for his two sons John and William to occupy together. They were also bequeathed £13 6s. 6d. each. His son Ralph, born in 1580 and probably the youngest son of the family, inherited £10 and all the leases held in the lordship of Mancetter, together with

> all my tenement nowe in the occupation of Richard Wright and on close belonging to the same in the tenancy of me the said Thomas and being beholden of my Ladye Deverex.[27]

When, in 1558, the above-named John Abell ended his day at his smithy, he went home to a house that, despite his being a wealthy man in 16th-century terms, was probably much the same as he and his family had occupied for many decades. His hall – the centre of all his family activities – would have been a strictly utilitarian place, with very basic contents compared with those of his neighbours. He had a 'bord'-and-trestle, which was flexible and easily moved. He had not decorated his walls with painted cloths for extra warmth, as others had, nor did he have cushions and carpets. Carpets were usually for covering cupboards, but John's inventory mentioned neither cupboards nor even shelves on which to store any pots and pans. However, it is likely that John had a kitchen to house his cooking utensils, spits and fire irons.

During the 16th century most people increased the size of their house by providing separate kitchens and butteries, giving more space for cupboards and shelves to store cooking utensils and pots. Brew and kiln houses were also introduced, holding, respectively, the troughs and brewing vessels and the kiln for drying grain. Houses were also enlarged by the addition of separate sleeping chambers, often called parlours (*see* below, p.131).

Joined tables, of a more permanent type than the former trestle tables, were used, and the bedding put on bedsteads (of joinery work). The upper parts of the house were boarded over and used for storage. Apples, corn and malt were often found in these upper chambers; they were rarely used as the principal sleeping chambers until the end of the 17th century.

By the end of the 16th century, another John Abell, likewise a blacksmith, was not prepared to live in as spartan a manner as his forbear (possibly his grandfather). This John died in 1598. He had an 11-roomed 'mansion' house with 'the parlour that was the old house'. Round the house of the previous John he had built a hall, buttery, kitchen, nether parlour, shop, kiln house and malt house. Most of these rooms had chambers over them. Yet the value of his goods was only £15 3s. 10d., with £43 4s. 0d. owed to him in debts. The emphasis in the balance of his wealth differs from that of his ancestor (grandfather?), for by comparison, when the earlier John died in 1558, his goods were valued at £81 3s. 4d.

Similarly, when Thomas Nutt died in 1585 his appraisers mentioned no rooms – he could have been living in a one-roomed house – but he had goods worth £120. When his son Edward died eight years later, he left a house with five rooms, including two parlours, a shop and chambers over. It is not clear whether he built round the old house as the Abells had done or built a new one. Yet his goods were valued at only £53 5s. 8d. It is interesting to note that most of these goods, like his father's, were still farm stock and textiles; only £5-worth was in goods of his stated trade of shoemaker.

Seventeenth-Century Lifestyles

During the 17th century, the inventories increased not only in number but also in length, listing far more material possessions than earlier. Their evidence shows the pressures driving change within the community, revealing the gradual shift from dependence on agriculture into an expanding range of trades.

During the previous century, particularly in the early period, all the inventories had been for people whose main income derived from agriculture. But, as noted, some had started to supplement their income by following other trades while still keeping their stake in the communal fields, where they could grow crops for animal feed and could graze their stock. The trend accelerated in the 17th century. William Abell provides us with one instance. William, who died in 1660, was another blacksmith descendant of John, and blacksmiths, wheelwrights and braziers continued to be some of the more prosperous members of society. So, although he had just the one cow – hardly great agricultural wealth – his status as blacksmith allowed him to keep his position in society: witnessing wills, appraising inventories and serving on the manor court.

By the end of the 17th century, this pattern had altered considerably. The growing population now left many of the will-making class (as had long been the case for the rest of the populace), totally dependent on their trade or forced to labour for a living. Thus, John Goodman, when he died in 1679, in his will still called himself a husbandman. But to his neighbours he was a labourer, dependent on others for his work. Richard Biett died a day-labourer in 1685, with few possessions; even his clothes were 'a gift of the parish'. Yet his family had been copyholders of the manor for over 150 years. Richard had fallen on hard times (*see* Appendix to this chapter).

In the 17th century, as in the 16th, the most important and lucrative industry continued to be tanning, a trade monopolised by the Drayton family, who had started as butchers. They seem to have taken advantage of their position by abusing their grazing rights in the open fields. In 1699, the manor court felt compelled to pass a bylaw stating that a married butcher should be limited to 10 sheep in the fields, while a bachelor should only have five. The fine for exceeding these limits was 6s. 8d., one of the highest listed, reflecting the seriousness of the offence. By the 18th century, the Draytons were 'gentlemen' and were living in Mancetter, which provided more space than the crowded Atherstone Market Place where they had previously lived and made their money.

Malting was another very lucrative trade.[28] The Abell family, while continuing as blacksmiths, moved into malting, also. Maltster John Abell left £288 when he died in 1696. He had £52-worth of goods in his malting chamber and £100 owing to him in good debts. Barley was grown in the fields and ale was sold in the market; many women were brought before the court for breaching the assize of ale (a tradition continuing from medieval times, as Watkins chronicles on p.44). Although the local consumption of domestic ale must have helped the maltsters, the number of inns undoubtedly also fuelled the trade. The twice-weekly market and the position of the town on the Watling Street – the major road from London – brought in many travellers. A cheese market at Atherstone also attracted many visitors, leading Daniel Defoe, writing of his travels throughout England, to comment on the market's size.[29] (In addition to his footwear, shoemaker Richard Abell in 1620 had 25 cheeses ready for market.)

In the 17th century, 32 inns were listed in the mile-long street.[30] So the growing population and the number of visitors gave employment for the many victuallers, bakers and millers mentioned in the inventories. Indeed, the late 17th century and early 18th century saw an increase in the range of service trades and the number of their providers. Apothecaries and barber-surgeons took care of the health and appearance of the community, while glovers and shoemakers still continued to find employment.

The inventory of an ironmonger, Edward Healey, who died in 1694, gives us a fascinating insight into the range of goods used in the town. He not only supplied all the normal items such as pans, brushes, kettles, knives, candles and candlesticks, wire, glue, oil, hammers and nails, and tar but also:

Raisins 110 pound weight	£1	9s.	10d.
A parcel of alum 44 pound weight		18s.	1d.
14 pound of treacle and runlet		4s.	0d.
a parcel of aniseeds		1s.	8d.
a parcel of cement one pound		6s.	0d.

2 pound of gunpowder	1s.	4s.
4 pounds of beeswax	3s.	4d.
a pound and a half of caraway seeds	2s.	1d.
brimston 3 pound weight	1s.	0d.

He also sold in his shop clove-water, pepper, mace, sugar, nutmeg and herrings. His stock ran further to knitting pins, buttons, buckles, lace, clogs, smoothing irons and house locks for safety; in fact, more or less any requirement people may have had … tools for the garden and fields, lettuces and frames, cabbage nets and:

> 3 firkins of the best sope and 3 small parcels of sope £3 15s. 8d.

One item was obviously enjoyed by Edward himself; in the chamber over his shop he had a tobacco knife with some tobacco. The rest of his stock, 114lbs of tobacco stems, he kept in his shop, while 'leafe tobacco in the hogsheads' was in his warehouse. However, this was not a new product, as Atherstone people had been supplied 60 years earlier by John Loveday; he was described as 'a Tobacco man' in 1635 (*see* Appendix to this chapter). Thomas Hunt, another ironmonger, one who died in 1712, likewise supplied Spanish tobacco, also clogs and coffin handles. In addition, Thomas listed arsenic and ginger. It would be interesting to know who were the customers of these ironmongers. The pots and pans, knives and kettles and clogs would almost certainly have been bought by that 92 per cent of the population who did not make wills, but what about the tobacco, spices and coffin handles? It is also unlikely that this less well-off majority visited the apothecary or the barber-surgeon. These practitioners, in their turn, probably obtained some of their supplies from the said Edward Healey. Unfortunately, the inventory of William Loader, a barber-surgeon who died in 1689, reveals little of these. His shop contained:

> Basons and linens, chests, phisick, salves, a pestel and mortar, 2 basons, 1 leaden Cistern, 1 looking glass, 3 chairs, 1 dozen combs and a chirurgeons box of instruments.

The Development of Material Wealth over the Sixteenth and Seventeenth Centuries

Material wealth changed over the 250 years between 1500 and 1750, as would be expected, with the inventories revealing that change. In the 16th century, only Thomas Nutt the shoemaker left more than £100. By the 17th century, 26 people were able to leave over £100 in goods and a further nine people left even more, the richest of these being Edward Preston, a yeoman who died in 1626, leaving £366 19s. 6d. In the first half of the 18th century, the bequests of 18 people exceeded £100, while George Freer, a tanner, left almost £1,000.

Although, as noted above (*see* p.128), the size of houses increased over the period, the individual room-use changed little. The norm during the 16th century was to have a hall, which was the main living area, plus a parlour and/or a ground floor chamber, with the name 'parlour' gradually superseding the name 'chamber'. John Wyttington's appraisers in 1537 referred to his 'chamber alias parlour', suggesting the then strangeness of that latter description. But by the end of the century the chamber was normally an upper room used for storage of malt, corn or apples, also items of lesser quality bedding, such as canvas sheets. 'Parlour' had become the standard term for the principal sleeping room, which, again as noted above (*see* p.128), were often by this time on the ground floor. Additional rooms such as brew houses, malt houses and bake houses were added to the house for the purposes of extra comfort and room for the increasing number of goods.

The rudimentary and minimal items of the 16th century gave way to higher quality goods as time passed. So although the hall remained the main room well into the 18th century, the quality of the furniture changed. Joined and carved tables, chairs and cupboards became more common, and leather and twiggin (wicker work) chairs were added later, with cushions – some silk or tapestry – for extra comfort. As early as 1557, a miller had 13 chairs, and to make them more comfortable, two needle-work cushions, three of green silk and three of green cloth (*see* Appendix to this chapter). Most of the domestic cooking remained in the hall until the 18th century, and even then only a few householders used the kitchen for this purpose. Rather, the kitchens were for brewing and storage. Copper and brass utensils were used for cooking, while pewter dishes and tankards were for eating and drinking. The early 16th-century meal had been eaten from wooden trenchers, but for the town's élite these were superseded by pewter, which in turn in the 18th century gave way to earthenware, much of it described as Ticknall ware, from Ticknall in Derbyshire.[31]

The plain bedsteads of the 16th century became more elaborate, with tester beds, canopies and valances, and truckle beds. Feather mattresses, flaxen sheets, pillows, blankets and coverlets were listed, also lesser quality bedding, such as canvas sheets and flock mattresses. Warming pans, candlesticks and even lanterns were additional comforts. A lantern maker, Thomas Bayton, was supplying the town before his death in June 1618 (although his main income was from agriculture).[32]

The typical parlour would also contain the linen and apparel stored in the many coffers, chests and cupboards. These items were often family heirlooms and were regular bequests in wills. In 1634, John Pennifeather, a tanner, left a pair of flaxen sheets and a pair of canvas sheets to his servant, Alice Kisse. This was a generous gift for a valued employee. In 1558, Hugh Middleton, a draper, had in his stock flaxen sheets at 3s. 4d. each and canvas sheets at £3 for 40. He also carried table cloths at 1s. each, and napkins at 15s. for sixty. A towel was valued at 1s. 4d., while a pillowbear (pillow-case) was worth six pence. He did not stock sheets of *hurden* (course hempen cloth), which were regularly listed in others' inventories.

Luxury or unusual items were confined mainly to the wealthier families. John Rampton, the miller mentioned above, had glasses for his spirits; otherwise, drinking glasses were rarely mentioned until the 18th century. John Eyton had 'glasses with drogges' (presumably drugs) in 1535. His occupation was not listed, but he could have been an early apothecary, particularly since he also had a 'styllytory' (for distilling). Chamber pots were sometimes mentioned, also ewers and basins. Silver spoons and tankards were listed fairly often and, with gold rings, often featured as bequests in wills. Clocks became more common by the 18th century; also found were looking glasses, pictures and even flower pots. Bird cages were listed in a number of 17th-century inventories. Appropriately on the doorstep of Bosworth Field, some items of battle were named during the 16th century: two suits of armour and bows, arrows and quivers – while one inventory (perhaps that of an arrow maker) includes a 'frame to set in bows and arrows'.

The best quality possessions were the preserve of a few élite families. By contrast, many seem to have had a declining standard of living, and their quality of goods was poor, with items often described as 'old' or 'sorry.' When Anthony Middleton died in 1685, his only bedding was two chaff beds and two canvas sheets – this for a descendant of a family which had held an influential role in the town for over 100 years. In 1647, Edward Chamberlayne's appraisers listed a moth-eaten carpet and 'overworn' sheets. Straw and chaff beds were mentioned on a number of occasions in the late 17th century; they had been rare during the 16th century.

Conclusion

This chapter has made an assessment from surviving probate documents of the standard of living and life style of that proportion of the population of Atherstone whose wills and inventories have survived. By the end of the period 1522-1750, it is clear that the standard of living of a few wealthy families was increasing. However, for the majority, even those who had previously enjoyed better times, life was becoming more difficult. The population was rising and the pressure for building space, exacerbated by the restriction of the surrounding open fields, was increasing. Some families (for instance, the Draytons) had moved to Mancetter and Hartshill, and others to further afield. Some apprenticed their sons outside the town. As an example, Abel Roper son of John, a husbandman, was apprenticed in 1629 to a London bookseller, Henry Seile. Abel's nephew, another Abel (son of Isaac Roper, an Atherstone butcher) was later adopted by his uncle and apprenticed to him. The younger Abel later became a Tory journalist and started *Post Boy* in 1695. (Chapter Seven makes further reference to Abel Roper, p.140-2.)[33]

As the next chapters will show, the enclosure in 1765 brought in new families to fill the vacancies left by the emigrants in the houses along the mile-long section of Watling Street and the Market Place. The former fruit and vegetables on the backs of the burgage plots were swept away by the bricks and mortar of the newly-built tenements.

Chapter 6 Appendix: Texts of Inventories

Marion Alexander

The full texts are given of a sequence of characteristic Atherstone inventories ranging in date from 1557 to 1705, together with the nuncupative will of John Greatalder, particularly remarkable because of the additional notes about the history of the family. The inventories have been chosen in part because they are comparatively short, so they do not include any examples for the largest houses in the town.

In the transcripts, the following conventions have been used: capitalisation and punctuation, but not spelling, have been modernised. For values, Roman numerals are modernised, but they are retained for numbers of inventoried items.

John Rampton, Miller [Probate date 1557]

An Inventarie of the goodes cattells of John Rampton deceased praysed by Robert Hylleye, Randell Power, Richard Nueton, Robert Sykes of Atherston accordinge to theyr consciences

Witnessinge the same with theyr hands

In the Hall

Fyrste iij table bards [*boards*], ij formes, a carpett for the grete Borde, xv platters, ij peuter potts,

iiij Basons over the chymneye [*no values for this or next entry*]

In the Nether Parlor

Item one longe forme, an aumbrye wth a tynning cover, a bownde cobert withe a grene carpett

In the Butterye & a brode [*abroad, i.e. around the house*]

Item xxiij platters, viij puter dyshes, vi poteinger dishes, iiij counterfettes & sawcers,

iij basons & a ure [*ewer*] a pote of tyne, viij puter potts,

ij saltes, xi sponns of pewter 20 0

In the Kichin

Item v candlestickes, ij chafingdishes iij Latyn ars [*ewers?*], one bason at the hall dore, ij smale potes of brasse, ij chaferns of brasse, xv brass panes & catherns [*cauldrons*] grete and smalle, iij skellyttes of brasse, iiij cresettes of iron, v spytts, ij payre of cobburnes [*cobirons, spit supports*], iij brandyrons, xij brasse potts grete and small and a

posnett, ij fryinge pannes, an olde skellett of brasse, one skimmer and a brason ladyll	5	0	0
Item xi glasses, ix redd stone potts for beare, xiij cheares, vi cosshyns of the best sorte, ij of nylde [*needle*] worke with cruell [*crewel*], iij of greene sylke, ij of greene clothe, xij of an oder sorte, iij featherbeds, vij mattresses, iiij carpettes, xiiij blankettes, ix coverings & coverlettes iiij good tedsters [*testers?*] & iij bad, xij pelowes good & bad, iiij wendowe sheetes for beddes, vi windoshetes to occupye abrode, vi saxes, ij bages, viij cofers grete & smale	6	0	0
Lenons [*linens*] smale & greate		20	0
Bestes & horses			
Item ij oxen	5	0	0
Item v kye	6	13	4
Item iij geldings		40	0
Item ij mares	3	0	0
(C?) rolinge cauves & swine		40	0
Item one iron bond wayne with yoke and tewes [*tows*], tobes & fatts [*vats*], lomes, pales with such other woden stoffe praised at	3	0	0
Item corne	20	0	0
Item haye	3	6	8

[*no total given*]

NUNCUPATIVE WILL OF JOHN GREATALDER, MILLER, 1622

Memorandum that on Sundaie at night beinge the Eighte Daie of the month of December in the yeare of our Lord god 1622 John Greatalder of Atherstone in the countie of Warr', Mylner deceased beinge of sound & perfect mynd and memory did utter and declare his nuncupative will in manner and forme followinge viz: he beinge asked who should have his keyes which did open his chest and the little coffer within it where his bonds and writings laye, he answered and said his brother Richard, meaninge Richard Greatalder of Atherstone and beinge further asked what he would do with all That which he had, whether he would give it to his brother Richard and unto his children, he answered yea, so that he meaning the said Richard Greatalder should give his younger brother, meaning Thomas Greatalder, Some thinge. And presentlie after that he the said testator had uttered the aforesaid words was asked againe whether he was Contented that his said brother Richard should have all gevinge his said younger brother some thinge, he replied yea. Whereupon the said keyes were delivered unto the said Richard in the presence of the said testator & with his consent.

Theis beinge witnesses: Mary Grewe the wife of Francis Grewe, Mary Daiton widow, the elder Christopher Everard and Edward Drayton the younger, Thomas Taylor and Francis Grew

[Note in Latin of grant of probate to Richard Greatalder, 1623]

A second sheet carries notes about the deceased and his family
First the testator was a batcheser [*bachelor*] and a milner
Richard Greatalder was his eldest brother in whose [*house*] hee died, he had most of his diet and victuals from Richard and he had most of his helpes from his said brother Richard
Richard was the milner of the mill before and taught him his trade and so left him in the place and at his owne costs and charge did apparel him double at his first coming thither.
The said Richard dwellinge at the Chrywall Mills was importuned by the testator to come from there and to take a house with him in Atherstone so then they might live together, and so for a yeare and a halfe lyved loveingly together until the said testator did go unto a water Mill beinge persuaded that it was more helthfull for his body.
The said testator in his life tyme did Conceave much unkyndness against his brother Thomas and did not regard him for sundry respectes, namely for that hee tooke an administration of the testators fathers goods and so defeated the testator and the said Richard. Besides, he tooke a house over the head of the said Richard which did much discontent the testator.
Besides he was indebted unto the [*deceased?*] bascave and the testator did take this hard use of the said Thomas against the said Richard so unkindly, that he assigned over 2 bills to the said Richard with bond of attorney to recover the same by Court of law.
Besides the said deceased did lende unto the said Thomas other sums of money which he could not get of him.
The said Richard hath 2 small children and Thomas hath none and his holding very good
The said Richard [*for John?*] did leave 16 oxen 2 yron bound waynes and divers other thinges which Thomas hath.

JOHN LOVEDAY, TOBACCO MAN, 1635

An inventarie of the goods and chattelles of John Loveday late of Atherston in the Countie of Warr' Tobacco man deceased, vewed & prized the second day of December Anno domini 1635 by those whose names be underwritten

Item his apparel and monies in purse	00	13	00
Item in the *Upper Roomes* three bedsteeds	00	12	00
Item all the beddinge and bedclothes thereunto belonginge	00	10	00
Item heay and a pannell [*pack-horse pannier*]	00	10	00
Item in the *Cellar* old trumperie [*probably the Hall or Kitchen*]	00	02	00
Item two little brase pottes, three little kettles, a little pan	00	10	00

Item six puter dishes, two salts, one bason, two brase candlestickes, a pestell & morter, a skimmer	00	06	00
Item two cheires, one little table, two buffet stooles, six cushins	00	03	04
Item the *Iron*: one landiron, two paire of tonges, pot hangles, two spitts, one paire of cobberds, a paire of bellowes	00	03	00
Item one cubberd, a dishboard, two peales with other implements in house not worth the nameinge	00	09	00
Item in the Shoppe Tobacco and all the boxes	00	13	04
Item two old chests and one Coffer, two paires of scales	00	04	00
Item one puter pint pott and the weightes	00	01	04
Item tobacco pipes, pines [*pins*], buttons, lace and all other implements of smale valew *in the Shoppe* with one little cofer, two loomes & a little table and forme	00	08	00
Item two jugges with some sollit oyle in one of their glasses, a pented cloth and all other implements not worth the nameinge	00	02	06
Item two slippinges of yarne with a little tooe [*tow*]	00	01	04
Item two pare horses and one old cow, a packsaddle	03	00	00
Item in the yard furrs, wood and all other implements	00	04	00
Item one pigg	00	05	00
Summa totalis	09	08	06

Anthonie Smith, Thomas Neadon, John Turner } prizers

Richard Biet, Day Labourer, 1685

23rd March 1685

This is a true and just inventory of the goods and Chattells of Richard Biet day labourer in the parish of Mancitter lately desesed

Imprimis As for his clothes, they were as a gift from the parish

Item A chaffe bed with 2 Blanketts	0	4	0
3 small pewter dishes with a salt, 4 spoones & 3 porrengers	0	5	0
3 old Brasse Kettles, 1 brasse pott	0	10	0
1 old hachet, 1 Brome hocke [*hook*], fyer shovel and tongues, 1 grate	0	4	0
1 Chayre and 1 stoole	0	0	9
2 olde small tables and a old coffer and a box	0	6	0
In one old coffer more 3 payer of course sheetes with a table cloth, 2 pillow bears [*cases*], 2 towells and some old napkins with old Trumpery	0	6	8
2 old wheeles and a hayer sife and a Reele, 1 paye of woollen cards	0	1	6
1 old Barren Cow	0	13	4

1 yeare old and vantage but since dead & valued then at	0	13	4
1 calfe at	0	6	0
Halfe a day worke for winter corne	0	13	0
Hay at	0	6	8
[Total]	4	1	1

This is a true and just apraysment by us whose names are here subscribed William Mason
The mark [**K**] of William Key

Richard Bull, Shoemaker, 1705

A true Inventory taken of the goods & Chattells of Richard Bull Shoemaker of Atherstone in the parish of Mancetter in the Couunty of Warwick Batchellor lately deceased & taken December ye 5th 1705 by us whose names are under subscribed

	£	s.	d.
Imprimis his purse & Apparrell	1	1	6
Item in the *Dwelling Houses* landiron, 1 paire of tonges, 1 fire shovell, 2 spittes, 1 cleiver, 1 frying pan, 4 iron candlestickes, & other irones in the chimney	0	13	2
1 jack, 1 candle box	0	5	1
2 tables, 9 joyned stooles, 3 lowstooles	0	17	4
7 old chaires	0	4	4
One great cubberd, 1 livery cubberd	0	10	6
1 parcell of old bookes	0	13	6
1 warming pan, 1 birdcage & a looking glass	0	6	3
9 puter dishes, 3 plates, 1 chamber pott, 2 flaggons, 1 puter pinte, 1 dussen of puter spoones 1 parringer, 2 saltes	1	9	6
Item in the *Parlour* one feather bed, 2 pillows, 1 boulster, 2 blankitts and 1 rugg, 1 joyn beddsteads & curtains & vallens, matt & cord	3	12	6
One other feather bed, 3 boulsters, two blankettes, 2 coverliddes, 1 joyn bedd, curtains vallens, matt, cord & rods	03	9	10
One hanging press, 1 leaverry cubberd, 2 coffers, 4 boxes	00	19	0
1 table, 1 joyn forme, 4 cheares	00	10	0
5 paire of fine sheetes	01	10	0
2 paire of course sheetes	00	12	0
1 dozen of napkins	00	06	4
1 sheet & some course linnen and window curtaines	00	07	0
1 table cloth	00	01	3
Item in the *Buttery* 5 barrells, 1 dusson & halfe of trensheres, 1 lanthorn 1 old chaire & some Ticknell Waire	00	12	6
2 dussen of glass bottles	00	02	6
1 Iron voice [*vice*], 1 paire of garden sheers	00	06	0
1 ax, 1 lanthorn, 1 mousetrap, 1 paire of wooden scales & some other odd things	00	02	6

2 brass pottes, 4 small kettles	01	10	0
Item in the *Brewhouse* 1 furnice	01	03	4
3 tubbs, 1 lading gallen	00	08	0
1 mault mill	00	17	6
2 wheeles, 1 reell	00	01	8
2 leathern buckets	00	03	4
1 heirecloth	00	06	8
2 shovells, 1 fork & a mucke rake	00	02	00
1 paile	00	00	06
Item in the *Maulting Chamber* 1 trey, 1 strike & peck, 4 hives	00	09	6
Item in the *Chamber over ye Buttery* one paire of truckle bedsteads	00	02	00
Item in the shop 5 paire of shoes and a small parcel of leather	00	12	06
3 hammers 3 paire of pinsoins & other implements belonging to a shoemaker	00	09	06
1 screen 1 table 1 coper [*copper?*]	00	04	02
& severall other odd things	00	03	04
Total is	25	07	05

Praisers John Walmsley
Sam Shellard

7 A Time of Change: Eighteenth-Century Atherstone

Judy Vero

Introduction

In 1708 when William Eyre built himself a new home in Atherstone's Market Place, he could hardly have imagined that 300 years later it would remain the finest house in the town.[1] With a carved oak staircase, panelled rooms, basement kitchen and a Dutch gabled roof with dormers, it epitomised the new Queen Anne style, flaunting its Protestantism and merchant wealth. Yet by the end of the 18th century, the living conditions of the average resident were far removed from this luxury, and were to deteriorate more as the town moved towards industrialisation in the 19th century. An increasing population, attracted to Atherstone by the growth of the hat industry, resulted in intensive development of the gardens and burgage plots behind the houses. This marked the beginning of Atherstone's 'yards', which were to become notorious for their poor housing standards.

Causes of the changing character of the town include the enclosure of the commons and the arrival of a wider range of opportunities for the financing of development. They are described and evaluated below. The remainder of the chapter explores the origins and development of the yards in Atherstone.

Buildings and People

Some rebuilding is recorded at the end of the 17th century, as happened elsewhere in Warwickshire when awareness of the risk of fire encouraged the replacement of combustible building fabric with brick, tile and slate. The dormer windows of the cottages on the west side of Church Street and the *White Horse* in Long Street (formerly known as the *Kings Arms*) are of this period.[2] These brick dwellings, which still retained some timber-framing on the inside, would have replaced the lath and plaster thatched houses which by this period were outdated and crumbling. Added to this, the risk of fire caused these buildings to be singled out in the town's bylaws:

> A Paine made that no Person shall have any Fireplace in any such building as is thacked appearing dangeruos and not parged nor in any Working Shop nor work by Candlelight in any such Room on pain of ... £1:19s. 4d. (Paines of Atherstone, October 1746).[3]

At the beginning of the 18th century, Atherstone had a population of a little over 2,000, spread over its 180 burgage plots. The town displayed the characteristics of an 'open' settlement,[4] with many property owners and a large number of trades supplementing agricultural activity. The absentee lord of the manor from 1693 to 1758, Edward Repington, did not interfere in the activities of the townsfolk. Indeed, his position had been usurped by the Bracebridges, who, though of gentry stock, had become the leading merchant family. Chapter Eight will chronicle how, as haberdashers of hats, they organised the cottage hat industry, until they sold out to the Willdays at the end of the 18th century.[5] Under new ownership the industry expanded, attracting an influx of migrant hatters, increasing the population and transforming the town's economy from agricultural to industrial.

In addition to William Eyre's house in the Market Place, there were a number of other imposing residences, though unlike his, most have been greatly altered. These houses were generally built by wealthy merchants on full burgage plots. They are to be found around the Market Place and scattered along Long Street. The largest is Atherstone House,[6] in the Hollow (the lowest part of Long Street). Built in the late 17th or early 18th century, in 1782 the property comprised 'gardens, orchards, backsides, barns, stables, hovels, dovehouses',[7] and was occupied by the Baxter family – lawyers and stewards of the manor.[8] But despite the generous proportions of the house and the pleasant ambience of the grounds, it had an unpleasant neighbour in the form of a tannery which took advantage of the stream that ran across Long Street at this point.

The town plan of 1786 shows two other copyhold houses on full burgage plots at the south-eastern end of Long Street,[9] and the late 16th-century manor court rolls give further evidence for them.[10] One, to the west of 'le Marlpoole', was occupied by Thomas Roper, a tile maker, who died in 1593, bequeathing it to his son John.[11] No doubt the Ropers took their clay from this pool, which later functioned as a watering place, until it became a boating lake and ornamental pool in the 19th century.[12] Next door, Richard Preston had a 1¾ burgage plot.[13] This property would become the site of the new workhouse in 1836, replacing the workhouse that had been established by 1786 at the north-east end of Long Street.[14]

The 18th century, as noted, was a time of change for the local community. Old families who had dominated trade and town life since the 16th century (if not earlier), gradually severed their connections with Atherstone, moving to London and elsewhere. Among them were the Draytons, one branch of whom became plantation owners in South Carolina, building one of its most important historic houses, Drayton Hall.[15] Others, such as the Goodalls, disappear from local records. The Abells and Ropers became more strongly London-based. Abel Roper, whose family owned a house on a full burgage on the south side of Long Street,[16] was sent to London to be apprenticed to a bookseller. Later he was credited with distributing pamphlets intended to lead to the deposition of James II and 'pave the way for the Revolution'.[17] Other families also switched occupations; for instance, the Powers gave up the bakery trade to become hatting entrepreneurs, clergymen and schoolmasters in the 19th century.

33 *Abel Roper.*

From note on obverse of the Aylesford collection portrait:

Abel Roper was a native of Atherstone, and his parents having many children to provide for, an uncle who was a bookseller in London adopted him at the age of 12 years and sent him to school. He made considerable progress in learning and is said to have spoke Greek by rote, when he did not understand Latin.

At 14 he was bound apprentice to his uncle upon whose death he was turned over to another bookseller C Wilkinson and having attained the age of 21 he received 100£ left him by his uncle with various valuable copyrights, and soon afterwards marrying his master's daughter, he commenced business for himself. The party who were endeavouring to expel James 2 from the throne, fixed upon Roper as the distributor of pamphlets written to pave the way for the revolution, in which he was indefatigable; and was the original printer of the famous ballad of 'Lilli-bulero'.

At length he sold works that were equally subversive of religion, morals or government, looking only at what he gained; and his unequalled impudence

> and unmoved countenance carried him through many difficulties with impunity.
>
> In *The Postboy* which he published, he attacked the Tories and the Whigs just as he was hired. Swift threatened to be revenged for his abuse. He published the ribaldry of Tom Brown, and libelled Louis 14, beside compromising the celebrated women of his day, in *The Question of Ladies*. His *Newsletters into the Country* procured him a severe reprimand from the earl of Nottingham, secretary of state. Among other misdemeanours he was summoned before the Lord Mayor for reflecting upon the *Society for the Reformation of Manners* and was prosecuted but a bribe saved him from the severity of the law: though it fell upon him for publishing Dr. Drake's work, who disowning it, Roper was for a short time in the custody of a messenger. Tom Brown attempted to cane him, for publishing Dr. Kingston's attack upon him: but it ended in a boxing match, when Abel beat Tom, and from enemies they became friends, Brown assisting him in his *Auction of Ladies*.
>
> Roper died in 1716 and it has been remarked of him that like many others of his brethren of the quill, he had 'an excellent talent at a specious lie, and knew how to make vice of virtue, or virtue of vice, according as they clashed or coincided with his party'.

As the old families moved away, new ones came to take their place. William Underwood brought his family from Hinckley and obtained settlement in 1715.[18] He established himself first as a tailor, then, in 1730, as an innholder, when he bought the *King's Head* on the north side of Long Street, to the east of Butcher Row.[19] After his death, his wife Sarah married into the prominent Reynolds family. William's son John, who inherited £40 from his father at the age of 21, became a grocer, buying the neighbouring property in 1762,[20] and a house in the prestigious Market Place in 1772.[21] When he died in 1790, he was firmly described as a gentleman. Many others shared William's success, though some over-reached themselves and their bankruptcies remain in the records as sad epitaphs.[22]

The First Bid for Enclosure in 1735

William Underwood and his family, who were mentioned above, may well have been attracted to Atherstone by the generous rights of common which were available to all householders, whether they were freeholders, copyholders, or cottagers.[23] Atherstone had three open fields, Aldermill Field to the west, Middle Field, and Windmill Hill Field to the east (pp.18 and 46 make reference to these fields in earlier centuries). These fields were divided up into yardlands or virgates, which were each of some twenty-two to twenty-nine acres in area. Each of the yardlands (the conventional description used for an open-field land-holding) was divided into strips which varied in size; in the most part they were probably between half and one acre. The strips were privately owned both as freeholds and copyholds, but the cottagers had an ancient right to glean after harvest, turn their animals out on the stubble and, of course, graze them on the common land. The wooded areas to the south provided a source of wood and underbrush for fuel and beyond were coal outcrops (for instance, *see* Colepit Field, p.47). But in 1735 these benefits were under threat from enclosure.

Unusually, it was not the lord of the manor, Edward Repington, who was advocating the enclosure of the open fields; he owned only five acres and had little to gain. Instead it was Abraham Bracebridge, head of the town's leading merchant family, who submitted the bill to Parliament.[24] The strips in the open fields covered 700 acres, divided into 24 yardlands. By this date, Bracebridge owned 18 of these yardlands, amounting to approximately 525 acres; he would benefit from the increase in their value that would arise through enclosure. The map of 1716 labels no fewer than 1445 separate pieces of land.[25] Most of these were strips, though they varied greatly in size. Those in the fields south of Watling Street tended to be larger, which could indicate that, away from the alluvium of the river plain which skirted the fields to the north of Watling Street, the land was less fertile. Therefore, although the plan shows Bracebridge's six tenants holding 692, while the other 26 freeholders held the remaining 755 pieces of land, these figures do not account for the individual sizes of the strips.[26]

Bracebridge and his family had accumulated this land over three generations. The Bracebridges had been in Atherstone since the early 17th century, having settled at 'Duffcoate Shop' near the Market Place, where Richard Bracebridge carried on trade as a haberdasher.[27] By 1640, his son Samuel, described as 'a haberdasher of hats',[28] had begun to buy land. A purchase of three yardlands (around one hundred acres) was passed by Samuel to his son Abraham in 1672.[29] It was said later that he purchased them 'at low value.'[30] Abraham, also a haberdasher of hats, continued the acquisition of property in the next century, renting out his land to four major tenants: George Geery, a baker, Robert Bickley, an innholder, John Mason, a skinner, and Joseph Billington (trade unknown).[31] Bracebridge had the reputation of being 'a trader and no great farmer,' which explains why most of his land was rented out.[32]

So, with most of the town's land in his ownership, Bracebridge would have been fairly confident of success when he applied for an act of Parliament in 1735. However, he had not accounted for the feelings of local people. They had a champion in John Reynolds, who had local connections. He wrote to 'the leading men of the Town,' urging them to set up a fighting fund:[33] 'If you are in earnest to prevent the Inclosure tis time for you unanimously to exert yourselves and to come into proper measures to oppose it.' 'Twenty shillings a cottage' was suggested, a considerable amount for those whose family income might be as little as £20 a year. However, whether this was to be paid by the gentlemen or the cottagers themselves is unclear.

The battle raged for some years and is recorded in a bundle of documents at the Warwick Record Office. Collected by Bracebridge himself, they record the views of both sides, often in strong language.[34] In a paper of 'Grievances that will result from the Inclosure,' an anonymous writer points out that the generous rights of common had been good for the town's economy.

> The great Privileges and Advantages belonging to the Inhabitants of Atherstone have allur'd Numbers of People to settle there to the great benefit of the said Town and encrease of Trade in several Branches.[35]

More than a hundred of the inhabitants exercised their right to keep one or two horses and one or two cows on the commons. It was claimed that the proposal for a common plot of 80 acres, 'in the worst part of the Fields,' would be grazed out in 'a Month or Six Weeks'. Grazing land for horses was particularly important to 'Tradesmen of a lower Rank' who needed a horse for business purposes and also:

> To fetch Coals for their own use and to let out to hire to the great Advantage and more easie support of themselves and families more especially in a dull time of Trade which is the case now with reference to the Two most considerable Manufactures in the said Town Tammy-weaving and Felt-making.[36]

If the bid were successful all this would be lost.

> There will be no Teams kept in the Town whereby the Inhabitants Especially smiths Carpenters Coopers Masons Joyners Weelwrights and all who shall have occasion will be oblig'd to lose a great deal of their time in Seeking Carriages of which the Neighbouring Teams will be appris'd and consequently make all Carriages dearer even to Extortion.

Opponents of enclosure also claimed that the market, which at the time 'florish'd', would be 'greatly lessened if not totally ruined'. They foresaw 'Expensive and Vexatious Law-suits' over the allocations of land that would:

> lessen the value and lower rents of Houses diminish the Number of Inhabitants … straiten & incommode Tradesmen in their Circumstances Increase the Number of their Poor and the Burden of Poors Rates ruin the Market and give a fatal wound to Trade …'[37]

It was argued that enclosure would deprive the cottagers of the opportunity to supplement their incomes and to 'better' themselves. Perhaps more importantly it allowed them independence.

> For these useful and inferiour people can support and live without the people moving in a superior Sphere, better than the Superiour can without the Inferiour.

Those who prospered were able to buy stock and further better themselves.

> As the families grow up one under another here is employment for them in case no other work offers and hinders but little their Spinning and Carding at home which we do not account for as tis no part of their privileges Those who are able to buy stock as Horses Cows & c. without doubt find their account in it shou'd they not still have the conveniencys abovemention'd to have recourse to.[38]

The bundle includes a defence of the cottagers' way of life and an assessment of the rights of common of the town, which gave an opportunity to those without land to supplement their income:

> To compute the benefit of Fields kept open by means of these rights to the Labourer and family; by the Harvest work, the Men will get 6s per week – and beer the Women will get 2s till Corn Harvest then 3s per week the Boys [ ] per week The Gleaning of the Fields computed 15s a family – in a Season ... Besides their Harvest work they have the Privilege of fire Boot in a large extent call'd Outwoods, that is cutting and bringing Wood for the Use of others as well as themselves in wch are also employ'd Men Women and Children at the time they are not busied in other work. In this way it hath been known a Man will get 6 or 8s a week. Whilst he can follow it at all other workmen now get 4s per week and Beer and are mostly employ'd in the branches of good Husbandry such as Muck Cart Trenching, Threshing in winter &c Thus in a great measure they are constantly emply'd.[39]

The language then becomes highly vitriolic, prefiguring the class-struggle of a later century.

> In case of Inclosure the Inferiour will be made slaves and oblig'd for what little work will be found to work for what wages those Mercenaries who at present call them Thieves will please to give them for if they think much of their Living on their Privileges, they will grudge them every farthing which comes out of their Pockets shou'd they be reduced and apply for support.

However, a note of censure towards the 'inferior' creeps in. It seems clear that the writer is a representative of the privileged class, as he goes on to say, 'for the 20s will like the weekly pay be piss'd against the Wall & the Families no better'.

In his determination to win the war, Bracebridge was unscrupulous. With the aid of the lord of the manor, he 'caused a horse race that used to be annually run at this town, to be moved to another town five miles away' (Nuneaton).[40] He was also 'engaged in a law suit relating to the town', and was said to have taken possession of 'all the town books and writings, which he now refuses to deliver or show to the townsmen'.[41] An enclosure bill was drafted but the bid was abandoned after the opposition group employed two London attorneys to oppose it. This put an end to Bracebridge's hopes of for almost 30 years.

Enclosure: Success in 1765

In 1765 the Bracebridges finally won the day. Again, the cottagers fought the bill, but this time the general climate had changed and the economic advantages of better crop yields and selective breeding were more widely recognised. At enclosure, Bracebridge owned 19¾ yardlands and several 'Field Closes and other parcels of land Meadows and Grass Ground lying dispersed in the said Common Fields, all which were freehold of Inheritance'.[42] He was allocated 341 acres whilst the other 28 holders had 199 between them, with the lord of the manor being awarded only seven acres. He was forced into agreeing that 100 acres on the north-east side of Watling Street (at some distance from the town) would be allocated to the cottagers to compensate them for their loss of common rights.[43] He wrote, 'Neither my own opinion or advice of Friends will suffer me to comply with so unreasonable a demand as 100 acres', but his protest was to no avail.[44] More of his apparent deficit of some two hundred acres (compared to what he owned in 1716) is accounted for by the allocation of 65 acres to the lay impropriator of tithes, Thomas Clare, a mercer, in lieu of the tithe income he lost. Acre for acre, his ownership was reduced, but there was some compensation in the improved quality. However, both Bracebridge and the other owners now had land free of both tithe payments and grazing rights.

Enclosure of the Outwoods, Cow Pasture and Clay Pits: 1786

As we have seen, in 1765, 100 acres were designated common land for the use of the owners of the common rights; this area was later known as the Cottagers' Piece (part of Windmill Hill Field that bounded the River Anker). This no doubt boosted the value of common rights. In addition, common right holders, that is, 'Proprietors of ancient Messuages or Dwelling Houses, or Scites of ancient Messuages or Dwelling Houses,[45] had the use of 152 acres to the south of the town, beyond the cultivated fields. This land – the Outwoods, Cow Pasture and Clay Pits, – was wooded with 'Timber Trees, Spring Wood, Underwood, and Underbrush.' It was immensely important in providing a means of existence for a number of tradesmen. Not only did it provide grazing areas for horses and cattle, but also timber could be cut down and brought into the town for sale.

However, this was to change. Under a bill in 1786, for 'Dividing and Allotting certain Commonable Grounds, or Waste Woodlands in the Township of Atherstone', this land was to be enclosed. An area of 72 acres lying on the north-west side of the turnpike road to Coleshill was vested in Charles Edward Repington, as lord of the manor, and the rights of common were extinguished. The 80 acres comprising the Outwoods, on the south-east side of the turnpike road, plus the Cow Pasture and Clay Pits, which had been designated common land under the 1765 Act, were 'assigned and allotted to and absolutely vested in, the Proprietors of ancient Messuages'.

The common right holders did not enjoy full rights over this award of the Outwoods, Cow Pasture and Clay Pits. Repington was granted the right

> Within the Space of two years & a Quarter [inserted in ink] from the time of passing of this Act, to enter into and upon any Part of the said Outwoods, Cow Pasture, and Clay Pits hereinbefore assigned and allotted unto the said Proprietors of ancient Messuages ..., as aforesaid, and there to fell and cut

> down all the said Timber Trees, Saplings, and young Trees now standing, growing or being thereon, and with Carts and Carriages to take away the same, at his and their Wills and Pleasures, and to and for his and their Use and Benefit: Provided nevertheless that no such Timber Trees, Saplings, or young Trees be Axe-fallen, but grubbed up and fallen in the usual and customary Manner.

However, should the common right holders wish to retain any of the trees for shade or shelter of cattle, then they would have to pay Repington a, 'Sum not exceeding thirty pounds [figure entered in ink]', for them. The common right holders were, however, allowed to draw up their own rules for managing and regulating the use of the land.

Watts and Winyard have pointed out that the 'number of freeholders living in Atherstone declined from 60 in the 1730s to 36 in 1774 with just 29 of those actually resident in the town, showing that enclosure did have some social consequences'.[46] By 1790, the net value of Bracebridge's estate had increased by 64 per cent from the figure for 1748.[47]

COMMON RIGHTS – AFTER THE 1786 ENCLOSURE

Before the 18th century, all houses in Atherstone, whether copyhold or freehold, had a right to graze one mare, gelding or cow on the commons. But as the town industrialised and became less dependent on the land, the manor court rolls show a gradual separation of these common rights from the property to which the right was attached. Often common rights were bought as investments, to rent out for the income, and those who were buying them up tended to be the traders and entrepreneurs of the town, as is illustrated by the following examples.

In 1783, Elizabeth Cudd, the daughter of Joseph Orton, a local tailor, acquired the common right to a modest quarter burgage property at the south-east end of Long Street.[48] The common right would have been particularly important to this house because it is shown as having almost no land, or 'backside', behind it. In 1828 the common right was inherited by Elizabeth's stepdaughter, who sold it to Henry Radford for £50 in 1833.[49] Another common right was sold in 1789 by George Farmer, a tammy weaver, to Richard Harrison, a yeoman from Ansley.[50] He kept it for two years then sold it to William Rowley, a ribbon weaver. Rowley sold it in 1830 to Henry Radford for £50.[51] The house itself had sold for £140 the previous year, giving an idea of the comparatively high value of grazing land as compared with bricks and mortar.

When the Reverend Edward Reynolds sold his rental property in 1793, he kept back the common right.[52] When he ran into financial difficulties, Reynolds sold his common right to John Hinks, a woolcomber. Over the next few years it changed hands several times.

In the 19th century, the town's leaders accumulated common rights. Those sitting on the manor court would probably have had privileged information. Henry Radford, steward of the manor between 1816 and 1877, was not inhibited by modern-day notions of probity or conflict of interest.

In 1830 he bought five common rights from William Thorley, a former pawnbroker,[53] four from William Rowley and a further six over the next few years.[54] Stafford Squire Baxter bought six in 1845 from the banker John Hood Chapman's executors,[55] then five in 1849.[56] However, by this time the price had fallen to £38.[57]

It may seem a misnomer to continue to refer to 'common rights' after the commons were enclosed, and they had become not only the preserve of 'proprietors of ancient messuages,' but also of individuals who could afford to buy them. Today, the detachment of common rights from 'ancient messuages,' which began in the 18th century, is almost complete. Now they are highly prized and owned by a few individuals, mostly living away from Atherstone. The largest holding is that of the 'piecemaster' who lives in Surrey and calls occasional meetings of common right holders to discuss tenancies. The most significant of these is the lease to the Atherstone Golf Club, which has rented the Outwoods for over a century, leaving local people with little more than the right to follow the footpaths across the course. However, the Cow Pastures is now owned by Atherstone Town Council and is in use as a public playing field.

Investing in the Town

Alongside the changes brought about by enclosure came increased development within the town. The manor court rolls provide a fertile source of evidence for this, and enable us to see how some of this development was financed.

Records of mortgages in the court books are particularly important in tracing the development of the town at this period. When the mortgagee needed to raise capital on the security of his house, he used the procedure of a conditional surrender, as described in the section on copyholding in the Appendix to Chapter Three.

During the 18th century, Atherstone developers could usually depend on local farmers for finance. In 1760, agriculture accounted for one third of all investment and would not be eclipsed by industry until 1790.[58] Harvests were generally successful, with only six years showing serious crises before 1792. It is thus likely that farmers had considerable funds to lend. The alternative would have been to keep their cash in a strong box under the bed, a risky option in any age.

Other frequent lenders were maltsters, innholders and mercers. Some, such as John Cook of the neighbouring parish of Merevale, were not ostensibly wealthy. Though a mere labourer, he was able to advance £30 to the Frith family against their quarter burgage on the north side of Long Street.[59] Few widows were lenders, though gentlemen (which title often belied the fact that they had made their money in trade) appear frequently. Most lenders were relatively local but some came from a wider area of Warwickshire and the adjacent counties.

It has been said that 'eighteenth-century business flourished as a face-to-face society of friends, cousins and business associates.'[60] This was the first point of call for finance, but when personal contacts had been exhausted, there were opportunities further afield. Peter Mathias has suggested that a local attorney was often the key intermediary in such transactions. This would certainly explain how Joseph Harper, a gentleman of Kidderminster, came to lend George Smith of Atherstone, a tammy weaver, £100 against a messuage and a 'newly-erected barn' on the south side of Long Street.[61] At a time when the average purchaser was unable to read and newspapers were not widely available, it would have been essential to have a local 'enabler' of mortgages. In Atherstone such a role could have been fulfilled by the Baxter family, of whom three generations – Michael, Stafford Squire and Dudley – held the position of steward of the manor between 1746 and 1813. Stafford Squire Baxter was also lord of the manor between 1787 and 1811. As attorneys based in Furnivals Inn, London, the Baxters would have been in an excellent position to bring those with capital to invest into contact with house purchasers and businessmen. It is clear that there was a healthy local mortgage market, which helped towards the expansion of the town in the later 18th century.

Early Development of the Yards

The beginnings of developments in the yards are difficult to date with any precision. By 1700, approximately ten of the 180 plots are recorded as having back development. However, the Hearth Tax of the 1660s suggests that some of the burgage plots may have been in multi-occupancy at an earlier stage. Through rent rolls dating from the mid-17th century, and the manor court rolls with their abuttal information, it is possible to create with some accuracy a street sequence for all the properties in the town (*see* Chapter Five: Streetscapes). The Hearth Tax listings follow this sequence, and the year for which the most complete return survives, 1670, lists 187 names,[62] almost the same as the 180 burgage plots shown on the 1786 Plan. Some of the properties have more than one name as occupant, and it would appear that a second household sometimes occupied the same plot, either in part of the front house or in a separate building.

The second household was often a widow or aged parents who had been displaced by a younger generation. They appear to continue to live in part of the family home and indeed wills and surrenders show that when a house was passed to the younger generation, it was sometimes split to leave part of it to widowed or aged parents.[63] On the death of the parents the annex would revert to the children.

One such example occurs in 1655, when widow Ellen Petty stated the terms upon which she would surrender her home at the south-west end of Long Street to her son and daughter-in-law. She reserved the use of the 'House standing on the backside of messuage' to herself for life, 'with libertie of ingrees & egress, then to George Pettie her son & Suzan his wife'.[64] Another example is found in 1661, when Margaret Simondes, widow of Amyas, was in a similar position. She reserved for herself 'Part of building lying of the backside of the messuage in the occupation of Henry Barfeld, with free ingress & egress in & through a passage into the street & to well & garden, to the use of Margaret.'[65] This was a prenuptial surrender, as her son, William, was then admitted to the property with Anne Proudman, his 'intended wife'.

There is more evidence of extensive multi-occupancy of back yards before the 1765 Act. The most significant developer was Thomas Haddon, a joiner, who started buying up properties in the town in 1735 and held six copyhold,[66] and one freehold messuage by his death in 1759.[67] But he died in debt. In his will he left property in Atherstone and elsewhere to his widow, Mary, for life. He then left property to his heirs or, 'for want of such issue', after Mary's death to his brother, William Haddon, and his sister Ann, wife of John Dann. However, there is no mention of his daughters, Elizabeth and Mary, infants, his heirs at law, by Elizabeth Haddon, 'widow, their mother & guardian'. This leaves one to wonder if Haddon had married Mary whilst his first wife still lived. The daughters' cause was taken up by the executors, William Haddon, and Anne and John Dann. Mary pursued her case successfully through Chancery. In 1762, the will was declared to be 'well proved' and she was allowed to inherit the property. Some items were then sold off to meet the debts.[68] But Mary had little opportunity to enjoy what was left as she died soon afterwards, and the property passed to the executors. Thomas Haddon's debts were still unsettled 20 years later when more property was sold.

The impact of the markedly accelerated development of the yards meant that cottagers were forced to devote most, if not all, of their working day to trade, often as labourers. Many found a call for their labours in the felt hatting industry, for the late 18th century was also the time when that industry expanded. Much of this expansion was due to the young John Willday, who, as the next chapter recounts, inherited an extensive business in 1762. Feltmakers were drawn to Atherstone from other hatting centres. Property owners who had traditionally lived in the front houses, whether as copyholders or freeholders, now saw an opportunity for investment. With neither the Bracebridges nor the Repingtons apparently willing to give up any of the surrounding green land for building, the only spaces where development could take place was on the burgage plots behind the houses. As noted at the end of Chapter Six, these 'backsides' had previously been used to grow vegetables, or to complement the common rights by offering limited grazing for a cow, a couple of sheep, or a horse for use in trade.

Subdivision and Development of the Yards

In the 18th century, no one felt themselves too important to become a property speculator. Samuel Stratton was already wealthy through his trade as a mercer. He achieved the title of 'gentleman', and his daughter, and only child, married into the Baxter family. Stratton owned four properties on Long Street (*see* p.176) in addition to a freehold house in front of the church. In 1765, he bought a property on the south side of Long Street, which had been developed with 14 back tenements by Richard Davies.[69] Stratton insured these for a total value of £500.[70] When he died, all his property was inherited by Dudley Baxter, in the right of his wife, Elizabeth Mary, Stratton's daughter. The couple lived at Stoke Golding, Leicestershire, showing that as early as 1807, Atherstone was becoming a place where investment could be lucrative, but where the better-off might not wish to settle.

Some saw property investment as a less strenuous way of building up assets than trade. William Nurthall, a fellmonger, or skinner, was a minor freeholder who had been allotted a plot of just over an acre by the enclosure commissioners. But this would not be enough to support him and his family, especially if the cost of quick-setting, fencing and ditching was taken into account.[71] Nurthall had purchased one half burgage with three back dwellings at the south-west end of Long Street in 1758.[72] He raised a mortgage of £200 which enabled him to purchase the adjoining half burgage.[73] By 1851 it would become the over-crowded Avins Yard that Alcock describes in Chapter Nine.

Sometimes property was split permanently between a number of children through the bequest of a parent. When gardener Benjamin Mills died in 1771, his property,[74] on the south-east side of Long Street to the west of that building known today as the Conservative Club, was split between his grandchildren. A quarter burgage in size, it was already in multi-occupancy with three non-family tenants living in part of it.[75] He bequeathed the messuage and stable to one grandson, George Richardson, who had to compensate another grandson, Benjamin, with 30 shillings per year as a condition. A messuage on Long Street, and part of a back tenement, were left to one granddaughter, Hannah Moore, and to another granddaughter, Elizabeth Wilson, and her husband, John, he left the back tenement in which they lived. Benjamin obviously had a special fondness for this granddaughter who lived close by, as he also left her 'that little room at the end of the stable to enjoy it with the other part of the messuage for ever'. Benjamin's eldest son, Benjamin, and his wife, Elizabeth, were left 'that other back tenement which remains undisposd of'. In addition to this, all recipients were allowed the 'shared use of the grass ground and well'.

Such complicated bequests did not augur well for the future return of the property to single ownership. Within a few years it was part-mortgaged to William Chapman, a mercer, and part-owned by Richard Pipes, bargeman, and Dudley Baxter. Had it not been for the fact that the wealthy Dudley Baxter lived next door, this property would surely have developed into a crowded yard. By 1817, the property was described as 'site of a messuage for many years fallen down'.[76] Dudley Baxter was able to buy out part of the other ownership, though he was not successful in persuading all members of Benjamin's family to sell. One grandson, George Richardson, left a posthumous daughter, Elizabeth. His widow, Ann, married Thomas Kent, a gardener, who brought up Elizabeth. Elizabeth never married, but had an illegitimate child, Ann Richardson, by Samuel Rowley, a hairdresser. In 1842, this Ann Richardson inherited the part of the property still left in family ownership, and at last the Baxter family managed to get their hands on the whole property. As Ann was too young to surrender a copyhold property in court, Henry Radford, Dudley Baxter's executor, invested her share of £60 in 'public stocks' in his name and that of Charles Holte Bracebridge of Atherstone Hall. What benefit Ann had from this we do not know, but the land was later developed with two back tenements and by 1851 was known as Kents Yard.

The later development of the yards is complicated by cross-burgage purchases, often of small lots, which were then intensively developed. Much of the development was enabled by mortgage and sometimes, for the borrower, it was the beginning of a spiral into debt. Second and third mortgages are not unknown, often with an element of 'borrowing from Peter to repay Paul.' Though lenders often had their fingers burned, a steady stream of investors was willing to risk hard-earned capital for interest rates of four and five per cent. Some made a business of lending; for instance, the Willdays and the Chapmans, hatters and mercers respectively, who became the town's first bankers (*see* p.162). Bank House is so called because John Hood Chapman lived there.[77]

One Yard's Story: The Coach and Horses Yard

As we have seen, plenty of local men were looking for capital, among them Benjamin Harris, a mason and bricklayer. He was a prolific builder who, in 1775, purchased a ¾ burgage at the south-east end of Long Street. Over the next 20 years he developed the plot with 15 back dwellings and a chapel for Independent Dissenters.[78] The development appears to have been financed by a loan of £300 from the Atherstone grocer mentioned above (*see* p.142), John Underwood, which was taken out jointly by Harris and the previous owner, Thomas Turner.[79] In 1796, a further loan of £500 was necessary. He obtained this from Richard Weaver, a hat manufacturer, styled 'gentleman', of Atterton in Leicestershire, two miles from Atherstone, and as security had to surrender part of the premises amounting to ⅜ burgage, on which were built a 'new erected house behind the front messuage and several dwelling houses behind'.[80] A year later Harris sold off 'outbuildings, garden and two back tenaments' to William Minion of Atherstone, a victualler, who himself had to take out a mortgage to finance the purchase.[81] There were then 17 back dwellings on the site. The property was further sub-divided in 1802 on the death of Harris, then described as an 'architect'.

In his will, Benjamin Harris showed no generosity towards his sons, who had to purchase their existing homes.[82] His widow was left five copyhold messuages and the chapel remained vested in the trustees, but the mortgage had to be repaid. James, the eldest son, a printer, was living in a house on the site, but to remain he had to purchase it from the executors for £290. If he declined to purchase the house, the executors would refund the £9 he had spent on improvements. It appears that James did buy the house, though he had to raise a mortgage of £150. Another son, Charles, was offered three back tenements, the house he lived in on the site 'and the Garden he occupied there with as far as the second Apple Tree from the front of the House and the Hatter's Shop'. At the time, Charles refused the offer, but appears to have had second thoughts because he was admitted to it four years later.[83]

Other parts of the property passed into separate ownership. The trustees sold a 'newly erected tenement with yard' on ⅛ burgage for £150 to Joseph Freeman, a house painter of St Martin in the Fields, Middlesex.[84] Four tenements went to Thomas Burton, a farmer, from Netherseal, Leicestershire.[85]

These sub-divisions necessitated complicated conditions to retain rights to amenities on the site, such as the use of pump and 'necessary house'(privy), right of carriage, drift and foot road between Long Street and the Back Lane. There was also the obligation to share in the costs of the repair of the pump, necessary house and road.

The chapel was redundant by 1827, when a new Independent Chapel was built in North Street. From 1841 it was used by the Primitive Methodists, a sect which had considerable support from the hatting community. In 1844 a group, mainly hatters, purchased the building for £150 from James Harris, the last remaining trustee.[86] The Primitive Methodists were strong teetotallers and one wonders how they reacted to the proximity of the *Coach and Horses* public house on the same burgage plot. By 1850, there were 18 dwellings in Coach and Horses Yard.

Legacy of the Yards

By 1800, Atherstone had become a socially polarised town, the wealthy living in large houses with gardens and dovecotes, hard against the burgeoning yards. Some were beginning the exodus from the town which would continue into the 21st century. As land became available outside the medieval town envelope, larger properties could be built there, though some preferred to settle in neighbouring villages. Inside the town, the problems of poverty multiplied and the select vestry minutes of the early 19th century are full of tales of the suffering of yard dwellers.

As an example, in Binghams Row, of the 16 people living in the back tenements in 1832,[87] three are recorded as seeking relief.[88] In November 1826:

> Samo Bayard applies to have some rent paid this winter. To stand over.

He tried again in January 1827:

> Samo Boyard applies to have a part of his rent paid during the time he is not fully employed. It is ordered that he be paid 2 shillings per week until he is fully employed.

He applied again the following winter, but this time nothing was allowed. In April 1827:

> William Pinchback applies for relief not having any work. Postponed for Mr Bingham to enquire of Mr Willday as known and thus left to.

In December 1827:

> William Hall applies for work. Nothing allowed.

We cannot begin to imagine what the suffering was like for these people, where one's success at getting a handout from the vestry depended on who was sitting in judgment. In March 1827:

> James Brown applies for relief. Not allowed he having been drunk on Wednesday last and fighting.

For some the poverty was probably more than they could bear:

> Mary Cooke wife of Micho Cooke applies for relief her husband having run away a fortnight ago and left her with three small children.

She was allowed four shillings per week.[89]

8 Hatting in Atherstone: The Rise and Fall of an Industry

Judy Vero

Introduction

Today's Atherstone owes much of its character to its history as a centre of the felt hatting industry. This chapter recounts the industry's early development, showing how the growth of hatting depended on the topography of the area, particularly the water supply. As a case study, a detailed account is given of Willday's 19th-century factory. The chapter also provides a background to the population growth whose impact on the housing of the town is discussed in Chapter Nine.

Atherstone's hatting started as a cottage industry, and appears to have developed through the involvement of the Bracebridge family from the early 17th century. However, the number engaged in the trade could only be guessed at until the History of Atherstone Research Team (HART) began a study of the 20 volumes of Atherstone's post-medieval court rolls.[1] It then became possible to trace the ownership of the copyhold property which comprised two thirds of the buildings in the medieval town envelope.[2] The date of the 1851 census was chosen as a cut-off point for this study.

As outlined in the Appendix to Chapter Three (under 'Freeholds and copyholds'), each of the transactions at the manor court recorded the name of the person who surrendered the property and that of the person who was admitted tenant. In addition, the abuttals (the owners or occupiers of the properties on both sides) were entered. It was thus possible for HART to assemble a sequence of ownership for each of the 120 copyhold properties, associating almost all of the 3,604 copyhold property records from 1645 to 1851 with the individual copyholdings.[3] Some of these sequences are detailed in the building histories in Chapter Five. Furthermore, the history of many of the 61 freehold properties has also been traced, by using the abuttal information and through the generosity of property owners who lent their deeds to the project. Though painstaking, this was a satisfying exercise because it enabled the identification of many of the properties referred to in the extensive archive of probate material for Atherstone.[4]

No fewer than fifty of the town's 180 burgage plots show evidence of hatting at some time. We can now be reasonably certain of the locations of the major hatting concerns, also of many of the small workshops in which the pre-industrial cottage industry operated.

Another helpful source has been the day-to-day insurance records which begin in 1784. They contain descriptions of the properties insured, detailing areas of specific fire risk, such as thatched roofs and stoves for drying hats.[5]

The Importance of Water in Atherstone Hatting

Local tradition says that the presence of a copious supply of soft water turned out to be a great attraction to the abbot of Bec.[6] Later, this supply was one of the reasons hatting came to Atherstone: pure water is one of the requisites of the trade. It is not surprising, therefore, to discover clusters of hatting activity close to the four watercourses that flow into the town from the Arden hills to the south, and then cross Long Street. However, the hatters were preceded by another industry relying on water. Wills and/or inventories were left by five tanners in the period 1533-99 and a large number of cattle horns and bones came to light in 1994 during the laying of a new storm water drain under Long Street.[7] It is clear that tanning was a major industry, occupying the prime sites close to watercourses, which were later taken over by hatters and dyers.

Water from the brooks was highly prized, as a court case in 1857 demonstrates. William Stratford Dugdale, who owned the land to the south of the town, stopped up the Innage Brook with the intention of exacting an annual fee from the recipients of the water. A case was taken by Charles Holte Bracebridge against Dugdale because the supply of water to his 'moats' (formerly the fish ponds of the Augustinian Friary), had been cut off.[8] Witnesses described how the Innage Brook divided into two soon after it passed under the Coventry Canal. These streams were then divided further, to provide water to serve the tanneries and hat manufactories of this area of the town. The Innage Brook marks the parish boundary with Merevale to the south and Grendon to the north. As such, the main course ran along the South Backway and crossed Long Street between the *White Hart* and Grendon House. A tributary of this stream passed through the premises of Joseph Willday,[9] where water was siphoned off into a cistern for use in hatting. The brook crossed Long Street and supplied water to a second factory before running into Bracebridge's 'moats' on the north-west side of the town.[10]

In addition, according to Charles Hanson Sale writing in the early 20th century: 'A stream of considerable volume ran across Long Street in the Hollow, near the Tannery hatworks'.[11] (The area known as 'The Hollow' is the lowest point on Long Street.) This brook is also shown on the field plan of 1763,[12] but today has been culverted through the town. As hatting grew up close to this second brook, it is likely that it, too, was divided to serve two areas of Long Street.[13] Two other brooks are recorded, one running through the centre of the town close to the *Red Lion Hotel* and the other forming the parish boundary with Mancetter, some distance east of the centre of Atherstone.

The Early Development of Atherstone's Hatting

The earliest method of making felted headwear was to full (that is, to felt) a cap knitted in the round, and the improved technique of felting carded (rather than knitted) wool was imported from the Continent in the early 16th century.[14] Coventry was a centre for the capping trade in the medieval period, though there is no evidence to suggest that it spread from Coventry to Atherstone.[15] In time, feltmaking migrated from the cities (particularly from the City of London, where it was established by Royal Charter in 1604), its exodus impelled by the increasingly restrictive practices of city guilds. These practices were intended to regulate trade and maintain standards, but they soon became such a constraint that some hatters sought to escape them, a trend that has been established from studies of hatting in London, Lancaster, Chester and Coventry.[16] Hats could be made more cheaply in the country, where there was very little regulation of the trade. Local entrepreneurs, or 'haberdashers of hats', could weigh out wool for making up in a feltmaker's own home – a practice that was forbidden by the Worshipful Company of Feltmakers in the City of London.[17]

Unequivocal signs that Atherstone was to become a centre for hat-making appear in the 17th century,[18] when we first find wills and inventories of feltmakers. However, the few references to hatting in these documents are unlikely to give a true picture of the extent of the activity at the time. Hatters were not generally wealthy enough to leave wills or inventories, so it is possible that far more hatters lived in the town than have been recorded.

In early 17th-century Atherstone, the Bracebridge family began to organise the local 'putting-out' trade. The Bracebridges had warehouses within the curtilage of Atherstone Hall, where they weighed out materials for collection by the cottage feltmakers, who worked in small communal workshops, which had convenient supplies of water to fill the feltmaker's kettle and fuel to heat it. The 'putting-out' trade was clearly lucrative, for on his death in 1694 Abraham Bracebridge left over £1,000-worth of stock and was owed £4,000 in trading debts.[19]

Two related families of hatters, who lived close to each other near the brook which ran through the Hollow, were the Walmsleys, at what is now the *Black Horse*, and the Foxes a few doors to the west.[20] Two women from this family left both wills and inventories, their husbands having pre-deceased them. Kathrine Fox, who died in 1682, had a 'Hall' in which she kept 'nine & twenty hatts', and trimming materials:

> one dozen of hat linings one dozen of hatbands one looking glass 2 hatcases & other od bands appraised at £3 16s. 4d.[21]

Her 'Parlour' appeared to be free of hatting equipment, but the 'Chamber over the Hall' was used to store her stock of wool, which comprised:

> one Pack of Welsh Woole 3 Todd 22 & six and sixe pound more of Welsh Woole one Tod and twenty six pounds of Lambs woole and foure pound and a halfe of od woole', appraised at £12 17.6d.

In the 'Chamber over the Parlour' she had ten shillings worth of 'Alder barke', which implies some connection with tanning. Kathrine had 'Work houses', though they appear to have served a domestic as well as a hatting use. In addition to 'Three brass kettles' and 'coales', they held cooking utensils. When Kathrine wrote her will she left all her 'workinge tooles belonging to the trade of a hatter' to her son, Samuel. Her goods totalled £42 4s. 4d. in value, which made her relatively wealthy by 17th-century standards, while the large amount of stock suggests that she may have been putting out work to other hatters.

Kathrine's cousin, Thomas Walmsley, living where the *Black Horse* stands today,[23] does not appear to have been so affluent. In 1659 he had surrendered his house to the use of his daughter, Elizabeth, and her husband William Fallowes,[24] but continued to live nearby. He is recorded as having two hearths but 'very poore,' in the Hearth Tax for 1671. His wife, Anne, left only £6 14s. 10d.-worth of possessions when she died in 1690.[25] In her inventory, 'Dwelling house', 'Chamber' and 'Buttery' denote the main living accommodation. The 'Shopp' was clearly in use for feltmaking as it contained 'two old Working kettles & 2 basons of Iron Mettle.' These kettles were the vessels containing a mixture of hot water and wine lees or other alkali, around which the men would carry out the main felting process. In addition, Anne had '3 bowes & 3 hurdles' which were used in the preceding process of 'bowing' the wool. The feltmaker's bow was approximately seven feet long, made of ashwood and strung with cat gut, which was plucked over the pile of wool to encourage it to fly into the air and disperse into a flat layer, termed a *batt*, which could then be carried on a hurdle to the bason.[26] This was an iron plate over a low hearth on which the first stage of feltmaking was carried out. This was a very gentle working intended to begin the felting process without the batt breaking up.

Anne also had '2 duzen of old hatt blocks' on which the felted 'hood' could be stretched to the required shape. It would appear from Anne's inventory that trimming, which involved the addition of leathers and ribbons, may have been carried out elsewhere; possibly in Kathrine's house, especially as trimming was women's work. Anne's will is somewhat at odds with the disparaging description of the 'Two old Working kettles' of the inventory. She left the 'great Iron kettle,' to her son, William.

At the opposite end of the town, close to the *White Hart* and the main course of the Innage Brook, another cluster of hatters was in business, dominated in the records by the Ragdale family.[27] When feltmaker John Ragdale's inventory was drawn up in 1702, he left no hatting equipment in his four-roomed house (perhaps because his son was already using it).[28] His wife, Alice, was to live with his son, Asael, also a hatter, who was to 'maintain her with meat and drink and all things necessary to her content'. Independent of his father, Asael had bought a copyhold property in 1687 a few doors along the street, where *The White Bear* public house is today.[29] As the only son, Asael thus had two houses, the freehold one which he bequeathed to his son, Samuel, in 1728, and the copyhold house which went to his son, John.[30] Though the Ragdales had certainly prospered as hatters, neither their wills nor inventories mention any hatting equipment.

By the mid-18th century, this cottage industry was flourishing in the back yards of at least 38 of the town's properties and that number was to grow.[31]

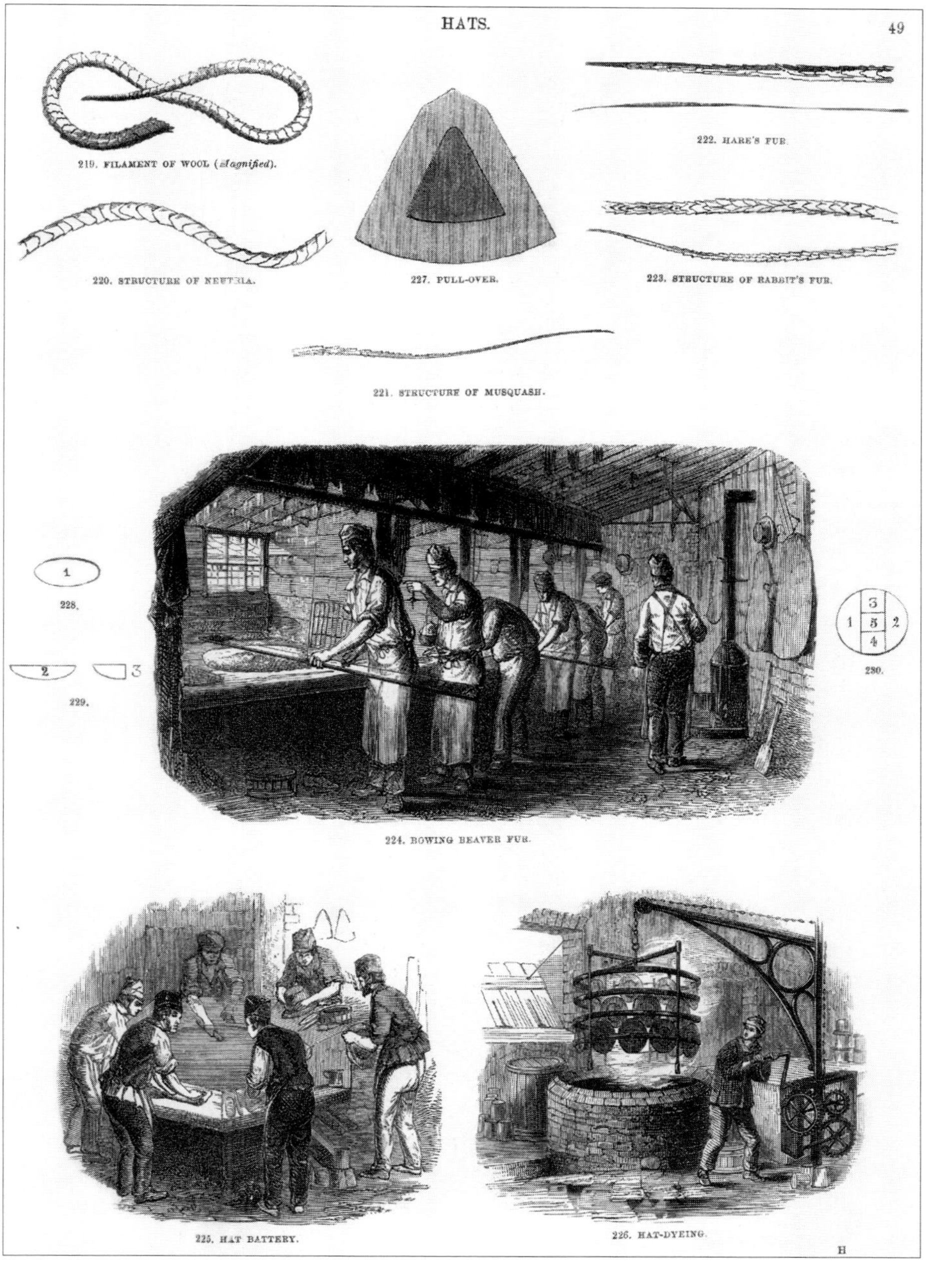

34 *The hat battery. The processes of felting wool and fur were similar, although fur hats were not made in Atherstone.*[32]

However, hatting was fighting for space against the need for homes to accommodate the young hatters who were flooding into the town in search of work. In some cases, a hatter had a single workshop, behind or attached to his cottage, which was likely to be one of a row of tenements lining a court where pigsties, privies, stables, workshops and homes were crowded together.

By the end of the 18th century, felt hat-making had become a major source of employment for Atherstone. It supplemented an agricultural economy which, as Chapter Seven relates, was jeopardised by the enclosure of the open fields in 1765, bringing the loss of the cottagers' rights to grazing, gleaning and the many other benefits of the open-field system.[33] By now, also, the hatting trade was beginning to industrialise, with a number of larger premises developing to use the emergent machinery. Thus, many who had subsisted on a mixed economy of hatting and agriculture had to find full-time employment in the nascent manufactories.

In 1784, William Power, a hatmaker, insured his recently acquired

> House and out Houses joining each other in the first class £100 also his Household Goods & Stock & c. in the second class £200.[34]

The premises, on a quarter of a burgage at the south-east end of the town,[35] contained his 'Stock in trade of hats, wool & his utensils.' By 1796, he had died and the insurance was renewed by his widow, Ann, and his son, John.[36] The premises had developed into what must have been almost a factory where all processes were carried out. It included:

> bason shop and warehouse over the same, dye hous & stiffeing shop, stove five finishing shops,

and stock inside them all. The stock was insured for £340 and the buildings for £210. By 1798, when the policy was renewed, fire had become a major risk against which insurance companies were on their guard, as the following clause shows: 'Warranted not to have any stove for drying hats in the above buildings'.[37] Expansion continued with the building of a 'Mill used for carding of wool' in 1802, and a steam engine in 1817. However, it appears that John Power had over-stretched himself, for he was unable to pay even the five per cent interest on the £1400 he had borrowed to finance the expansion.[38] In 1835, John and his son, also John, were declared bankrupt and the property was put up for sale at the *Red Lion* by the main creditor, a gentleman by the name of Thomas Tanner, from Biggin Hill, Surrey. Another hat manufacturer, Samuel Allen, acquired the premises for £376 19s., and this left Thomas Tanner over £1,000 out of pocket.[39]

On the west side of the Market Place,[40] by 1802 Edmund Simonds had installed a horse-powered carding machine for carding wool.[41] His factory contained 'bason & stiffening shops ... dy house & planking shop', finishing shops and stove. It appears that some of his employees lived in tenements on site. His son, Edmund Simonds, junior, was another hat manufacturer; though well-established, he was declared bankrupt in 1817, having become indebted for over £100 to William Muston, a woolstapler.[42] Simonds's premises at the north-east end of Long Street were sold off by the bankruptcy commissioners.[43]

However, even after the establishment of factories, many hatters still worked in small domestic shops adjacent to their cottages. Some property owners built tenements to accommodate the hatters who were flocking to the town. In many cases, the accommodation was poor and the enterprise was clearly no more than speculative. Other property owners, who saw that the presence of hatters might put off more fastidious tenants, dissuaded feltmakers from occupying their premises. As reported in the *Hatters' Gazette*:[44]

> The makers were a rough and ready set of men, sadly wanting in feelings of self respect and in regard for public opinion ... (They) worked in miserable sheds, subject to extremes of heat from their kettles and of cold from the damp draughts and clouds of vapour round their planks. It was natural that they should seek comfort in strong liquors which brought in their train a low standard of civilisation.

It does appear that hatting came to be considered a 'bad-neighbour.' In 1793, a condition on the copyhold surrender of a messuage at the north-east end of Long Street that had in the past been used for hatting, stated that

> no part of the premises be used as a Hatters Shop without the Consent in Writing of the said Edward Reynolds ...[45]

At some point in the late 18th century the Bracebridges lost their 150-year domination of the trade. This change appears to have coincided with a marriage into the Warwickshire gentry and perhaps a feeling that it was time to move on.[46] Their place was taken by the Willdays, who, having been cottage hatters in the 17th century, perfected their trade through a London apprenticeship and returned to work for the Bracebridges. Ultimately, after the Bracebridges finally achieved the Enclosure Act they had sought for 30 years, they sold out their hatting interest to Joseph Willday.

The Willdays

As noted above, the Willday family had been making hats in the town since the 17th century. In 1649, Richard Willday is recorded as tenant of a freehold property at the south-east of Long Street, which was described as a

> Cottage house ... (with) 2 roomes below stayers & twoe above, containing 43ft x 14ft with a little plot of ground containing 10 pole covered with tile. Abuts street (N) common field (S) in reasonable good repayre, it being lately repaired by the tenant'.[47]

No doubt Richard was already prospering. His son, Thomas, born in 1632, became a feltmaker and continued to live in the same house with his wife, Mary (Alexander makes reference to Thomas Wildey in Chapter Six, p.126).

Their son, Samuel, was bound apprentice to a feltmaker in London.[48] After his return, he was able to buy the family house, which was conveniently close to a watercourse, and had a workshop.[49] Samuel's elder brother, John, was fortunate to marry the daughter of John Smith, a skinner, who owned the neighbouring property. When Samuel Willday died in 1721, he left goods to the value of £369 7s. 10d., including, 'Stock in hatts and wooll Copperas & Logwood'.[50] These last two items were ingredients of black dye. Also, 'more hatts in ye Press, Tools in the Shop, Bow Strings'.[51]

Samuel's son, Joseph, was aged only nine when his father died. He also served a London apprenticeship, leaving his mother, Ellin, to carry on the trade in her son's absence. She had inherited a life interest in her husband's estate, which included money lent out on mortgage, an indication of the success of his hatting business. However, Ellin herself seems to have had a head for business. She lent money on mortgage against several properties in the town. Occasionally, money was outstanding for more than a generation. William Ball and his wife, Ann, borrowed from Ellin in 1722 (the year after Samuel died). Forty years later the money had still not been repaid, but the Willdays received the principal and its accrued interest, when the property was finally sold.[52] Around this time, Ellin lent two other sums on mortgage, one of which is recorded as £50.[53]

At the age of 21, Joseph married Anna Farmer, the daughter of a tallow chandler who had settled on her a messuage and half burgage, known as the 'Garretts House' at the corner of Long Street and Butcher Row.[54] On his marriage, Ellin leased to Joseph for 99 years the large copyhold house, of three-quarters of a burgage at the south-west end of Long Street, in which she was living.[55] It was here that Joseph now moved his business, letting his freehold house to William Bailey, who seems to have been a feltmaker. By 1736, Joseph had become so prosperous he was able to lend out money on mortgage.

Of Joseph and Anna's eight children, only three survived. The eldest, John, born in 1734, built on the proceeds of hatting, as we have seen, and was eventually able to formalise his father's investments in mortgages to become one of the town's earliest bankers. He may have worked for the Bracebridges, who were by then beginning to lose interest in hatting, preferring to concentrate on the acquisition of land, for it seems that by the 1770s John had purchased the Bracebridge business.[56] John was also investing in property himself, purchasing two further copyhold properties to the east of his house at the south-west of Long Street.[57] By 1771, John thus held one and a half burgages. Insurance records for Atherstone which begin in 1784 give an indication of the expansion of his hatting business. In 1797 John Willday insured a water mill, water wheel and cog wheel, with engines, a stable and two horses, in Hartshill, the hamlet some two miles from Atherstone and within the same parish.[58] In Atherstone there was no watercourse with sufficient power to drive a carding machine, so it was a case of either carding the wool elsewhere, or as Edmund Simonds did, of using horses to power the carding engine.[59]

We are fortunate to have the record of an interesting anecdote about John. In 1784, by which time he was operating a large business, he happened to board a stagecoach with James Boswell, biographer of Samuel Johnson, who recorded the event in his renowned diary.

> July 2nd 1784. Travelled from London to Coventry with Mr John Willday, an eminent hatter from Atherstone, Warwickshire. Has sold 13,000 in a year.[60]

He then goes on to add a little colour to the entry:

> Points of similarity which he (Willday) said a man might travel all his life and not find:- wife (maiden name) Montgomerie. Her family consumptive though she not. Five children. A governess Mrs Stevenson from London; well looking, fine bosom, elegant in dress, uses many perfumes, fond of admiration, writes

many letters, teaches French and Music, is a little harsh to the daughters. A pretty maid who opens the window shutters every morning.

As noted, John Willday had become one of Atherstone's first bankers, with an office on Long Street in front of his manufactory. He lent out money on mortgage to local hatters, such as John Smith in 1792, whose widow repaid the loan eight years later.[61] When John Willday died in 1808 he left a considerable estate, which included property in Pennsylvania.[62] John intended his eldest son, Thomas Montgomery Willday, to 'take possession of and enter upon the house and premises now occupied by me as a Manufactory for the Hatting Business', and to 'take to the Stock in Trade and all Materials not [worked] up and all other things relating to the hatting manufactory', and directed his executors to advance a sum of money not exceeding £3,000 on which Thomas was to pay interest at four and a half per cent.[63] He appears not to have taken up the offer as, in 1808 when probate was granted on his father's will, he borrowed £3,000 from his sister Eleanor (John and Susanna Willday had six children). However, Thomas Montgomery appears to have worked as a hatter until his untimely death in 1813, aged 36, presaged by his father's words to James Boswell, which recognised Thomas's mother's 'consumptive' family.

Willday's Hat Manufactory

Thomas's brother, Joseph, was by then 28 and described as a 'banker'. He quickly took over the hatting business and by 1814 a considerable manufactory had been erected on his three burgage plots, which also extended to parts of the adjoining plots.[64]

The insurance policy for 1814 describes the premises:[65]

One Coachhouse with chamber & Garratt over used as a Warehouse No. 1 in Plan

Stock of Hats & Utensils therein

His now dwelling house & Offices adjoining with Chambers & Garratts over Nos. 2, 3, 4, 5, 6

Household Goods plate Linen & Printed Books therein

China Glass & looking Glass plates therein

Stock in Trade therein

A Trimming Room Looking over room & White hat room, all adjoining with Chambers over same Nos. 7, 8, 9

Receiving Room 2 Finishing Shops & 3 Damping rooms all adjoining being Nos. 10, 11, 12, 13, 14, 15 with rooms over

Stock in Trade & Utensils therein

A Blocking Shop & Dying Shop adjoining being Nos. 16, 17

A Wash House Stable and Rooms over adjoining being Nos. 18, 19

Saddle House warehouses and clearing & stiffening Shops all adjoining being Nos. 23, 24, 25, 26, 27, 29, 30

Stock in trade & utensils therein
Pantry Larder & Rooms over adjoining Nos. 31, 32
Stock in Trade & Utensils therein
A Warehouse and Brewhouse adjoining with Rooms over being Nos. 33, 34
Stock in Trade & Utensils therein
A Dwelling house & Offices adjoining Separate from Bakehouse in Tenure [of] H Roe
A Brewhouse Pigstys & Privy all adjoining separate
Two Bakehouses with Rooms over separate near
Two Stables adjoining separate – Thatched
Two Dwelling houses adjoining in yard belonging in tenure of H Nixon & J Hewitt
Two hatters finishing Shops adjoining
Stock & Utensils therein
Two Hatters Finishing Shops adjoining having small Stoves therein
& Stock & Utensils therein
All Situated in Atherstone aforesaid & Except as aforesaid Brick & Tile Warrant not to have any Stove therein for Drying hats
Total Sum insured £5900. Total Annual Premium £18.14.6d

Table 13 *Insurance policy for Willday's Hat Manufactory, 1814.*

The following reminiscence of 1819 comes from the dispute between Charles Holte Bracebridge and William Stratford Dugdale, heard at the Warwickshire Assizes in 1859. As the witness stated, water for feltmaking at Willday's manufactory came from a tributary of the Innage Brook:[66]

> This watercourse was covered in by Joseph Willday in 1819 and converted into a subterraneous course. At the pond occupied by Wm Bishop which adjoins the South Backway or Station Street there was formerly a lading place and the water was used therefrom by the inhabitants of the town and also sold by many people until a recent period. At this time there was a fence of post and rails to guard passengers going along the street from the pond, but before his death Joseph Willday removed the post and rails and built up walls enclosing the garden and pond altogether from the South Backway and the lading place was from such time done away without any objection from the inhabitants. From the pond in the garden in the occupation of Wm Bishop after passing under the South Backway the stream formerly flowed into a large pond in the garden now occupied by Chas Phillips ... The said Joseph Willday in his lifetime from the pond in the garden then in his occupation had placed piping by means of which he could convey a supply of water from the pond across his garden into the premises used by him as a hat manufactory and adjoining his said garden and at the time when the pond was filled up the small space or tank was reserved for enabling the water to rise to a sufficiently high level to run down such piping into the said factory premises whenever it was required.[67]

Willday's manufactory in Atherstone represented the transitional stage between the cottage system and the industrialised process. It had a mixture of domestic and trade functions which recalls the earlier system, while yet benefiting from the advantages of mass production. The names of the manufactory's rooms enable us to see how the Atherstone hat industry was operating in 1814, as is shown by the following account of the processes involved. (There could be slight variations in the order of processes, according to the type of hat being produced.)

The feltmaker collected carefully weighed-out supplies of wool, which had already been carded in Hartshill (*see* above, p.162), from Willday's 'warehouse':

in his own domestic workshop the feltmaker would bow, bason and plank the wool to produce felt hoods;
the feltmaker brought his 'padding poke' of hoods back to the factory *looking over room*, where they were examined before payment;
the conical hoods were matured, stacked in tall piles, chalked with the size;
when it was needed the hood was sent to the *damping room* (probably no more than an outside area open to the elements) to increase moisture content and make it receptive to dye;
the hood was dyed in the *dying shop*;[68]
then brushed with proof in the *stiffening shop*;[69]
it was then dried in 'small stoves' within the *finishing shop* (the drying process presented a problem for insurers;[70] furthermore, some of the neighbouring outbuildings were still thatched – including brewhouse, pigsty, privy, bakehouses and stables behind what are today Nos. 45 and 47 Long Street);
the hood was shaped in the *blocking shop*, having first been damped to make it sufficiently pliable to withstand the stretching needed to pull it over the wooden block that gave it its shape and hat size;
back in the *finishing shop* the hat was polished using a variety of brushes and tools to give it a smooth surface;
finally the hat went to the *trimming room*, which would have been full of linings, leathers, ribbons, feathers and anything else that could be added to a hat according to its utility or fashion status (women usually came to the factory and took a bag of hats and trimmings to work at home);
the hats were brought back to the *receiving room*;
then to the *looking over room*, where they were examined;
they went next to the *packing room*, which was next to the *office*, where the paperwork to accompany the order was done;
then the hats went to the *warehouse*, where they were crated for despatch to London and beyond.

By 1827 the carding process had been brought in from Hartshill and more modern machinery had been installed with 'standing and going gears … clockmaker's work, carding and breaking engines mounted in use'.[71]

The raw material of Willday's trade was the hood, over which so much independent time and sweat was expended outside his factory walls. But although the feltmaker still worked in effect 'at home', both his shop and dwelling were often in Willday's ownership. This is particularly true after 1844 when, on Thomas Bingham's death, Joseph Willday purchased the 29 dwellings of Binghams Row.[72]

A significant event occurred in February 1834: Joseph Willday was involved in a dispute with his workers which culminated in a lockout.[73] Although the dispute was eventually settled, soon after there was a surprising development, recorded in the manor court rolls:

27 May 1834 Joseph Willday, Ath, banker, applies for licence to demise 'certain copyhold ... messuages ... factories, warehouses, buildings, yards, gardens,lands, etc ... with all outhouses, offices, stables, ways, waters, watercourses, fences, easements, etc ... for any term of years not exceeding 21 years.[74]

There can be little doubt that the lessees, though un-named, were Willday's brother-in-law, Charles Weaver, married to his sister, Susanna, and Weaver's partner, Richard Walsh. Described as 'hat manufacturers and bankers,' they already had a hat business in Rugeley, Staffordshire. Weaver and Walsh did much rearranging of the premises and modernised them with a 'stove & gas works cast iron & brick'.[75]

Willday was aged 49 when he leased his manufactory. There was no question of retirement at that age, and in any case he clearly derived great satisfaction from his work. However, the year 1833 began a period of hardship for the Atherstone hat industry, on account of the abolition of the slave trade.[76] A description of the town in 1845 records the following:

There is a manufacture of hats under Mr Willday, to a considerable extent in the fine hat trade which, within the last few years, has superseded the felt hat trade, which was principally devoted to the supply of hats to the slaves in the West Indies. Emancipation has given them more refined notions.[77]

Applications for poor relief graphically demonstrate the consequences of the abolition of slavery for Atherstone:[78]

22 December 1834	Jos Haddon a Hatter has no work applies for relief – 2/- as a loan Wm Baker a hatter a pensioner applies for an advance on his pension – allowed Jno Jee a Hatter no work when in work got 14/- a week 5 children – lend 5/- a week Wm Taylor a Hatter no work wife & 4 children – 4/- a week loan
5 January 1835	Wife of R Gretton Husband out of work a Hatter has 6/- for herself, her husband & 2 children can't allow more being 1/6d each Wm Masser a Hatter wife & 4 children 6/- Ambrose Houghton a Hatter a wife 4 child at Home getting nothing 6/- Wm Leedham a Hatter out of work a wife & son 25 yr age not allowed wait Jno Perkins wife Husband gone 4 children at home 4/- Wm Hattons wife Husband gone off 4 children all unwell 4/- Jno Lakin [H]atter Wife & 3 child 4/- Wm Shaw a Hatter a singlean has got 13/- when in work 1/- Wm Muston a Hatter no work wife & 3 children 4/- Jo Rowley a Hatter no work wife 6 children at home 7/- Wm Harding a hatter no work wife & 4 children 5/-

Table 14 *Selected entries from the* Select Vestry Minute Book, *1828-36.*

After only four years, Joseph Willday took back his business, and Weaver and Walsh moved to new premises beside the Coventry Canal, where in 1838 they insured a 'Wool and Carding Mill, called Pinchback Mill, & Warehouse'.[79] It would appear that they were now involved in wool preparation, and may have relocated the carding mill from Hartshill to Atherstone, where they now had a steam engine to power the machinery. They also had a stock of logwood, which would suggest that they were preparing it for use in hat dyeing. Their business could have complemented Willday's. However, we do not know this for certain. Joseph Willday was an irascible man who made enemies,[80] and could very easily have fallen out with his brother-in-law.

Not too long after Willday took back his business, the premises suffered the fire to which Willday's 'fire flyer' refers (*see* Fig. 35). We do not know how extensive this fire was, but it provided the opportunity for alterations to the premises later in 1841. The Insurance records of that year allow some identification of surviving features of the 'Considerable alteration' which Joseph Willday made in that year. Edward Neale, agent for the Phoenix Fire Office, wrote that

> the whole of the second floor is converted into Hatters finishing shops for the fine hats. There are two hearths for heating their Irons ... the hearths are Blue Brick laid upon Cast Iron and the Chimneys project on the outside the Walls.[81]

Fragments of this factory are still standing today (*see* Fig. 36) and provide a stark contrast to the impression of innovation and expansion which is left by the insurance records. The factory was fitted with a variety of ill-matched windows and doors. The iron-framed windows are of assorted sizes, inserted

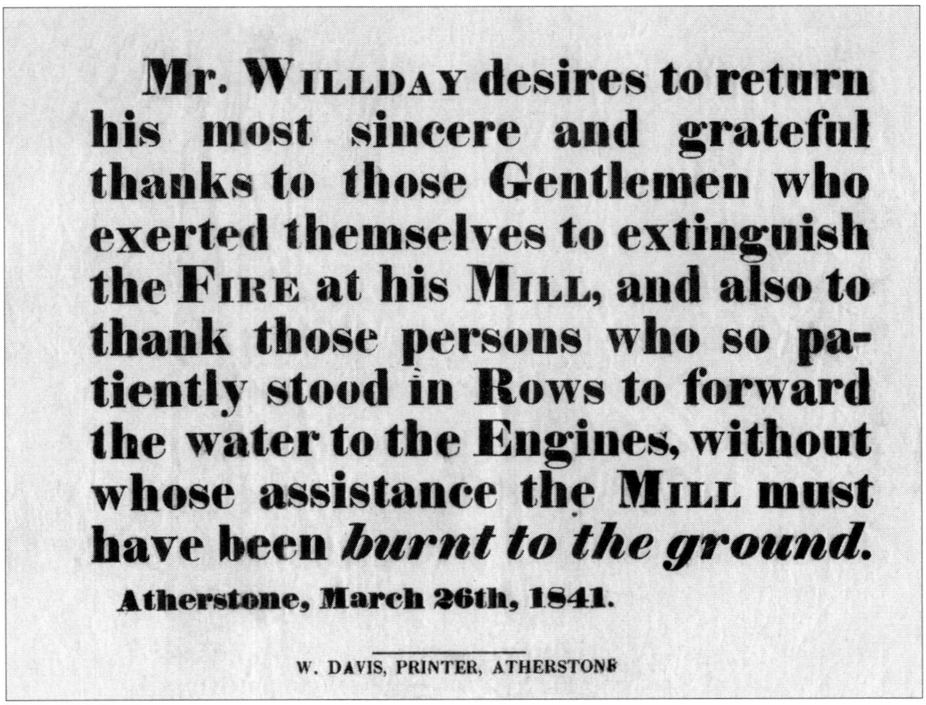

Mr. WILLDAY desires to return his most sincere and grateful thanks to those Gentlemen who exerted themselves to extinguish the FIRE at his MILL, and also to thank those persons who so patiently stood in Rows to forward the water to the Engines, without whose assistance the MILL must have been *burnt to the ground.*

Atherstone, March 26th, 1841.

W. DAVIS, PRINTER, ATHERSTONE

35 *Willday's fire flyer.*

at different levels, some necessitating a breach in the dentil course under the roof eaves to fit them. Doors are of mixed periods, some dating from the 17th century, probably taken from a high status house, presumably when they were no longer in fashion.

Oral recollections indicate that Joseph Willday was an ascetic character who could be very harsh with his workers.[83] He remained unmarried and was regarded with curiosity by local people for his practice of reading the bible to the inmates of the workhouse. In his factory, too, prayers were read every day before work. He encouraged his employees to keep the factory clean and to take pride in their own skills.

When Joseph died in 1852, aged 61, he left bequests of £1,000 to each of five charities in London, Liverpool and Birmingham.[84] The majority of his wealth was inherited by his niece, Catherine Whitby, the daughter of Joseph's sister, Anna, whose debt-ridden husband, Henry, had been carefully omitted from his father-in-law, John Willday's, will. Catherine, who had moved into her uncle Joseph's home, Rose Cottage, appears to have managed the hat manufactory after Joseph's death with the help of Charles Phillips, who, described as a 'mercer and a draper', was one of the executors of Willday's will. He lived in the large house on Long Street, which had previously been Joseph Willday's home.[85]

Hall and Phillips

In 1861 Phillips formed a partnership with William Hall, the younger, and they rented the former Willday's hat manufactory for seven years at a rent of £372 10s. 6d.[86] The agreement allowed Hall and Phillips to:

> Alter buildings used for trading purposes and to remove all or part of the said machinery, fixtures, utensils, implements to re-erect new and improved machinery, to put down and erect steam engines, boilers and furnaces, going gear and shafting, steam pipes, gas pipes and other fixtures and utensils, making good as payment in deficiency of value.

They were also entitled to 'take away for their own use such new and improved machines and all steam engines, boilers and furnaces, going gear and shafting articles'. The arrangement obviously worked well, as Hall and Phillips renewed the lease in 1868 for a further 21 years. By 1879, an advertisement in the *Umbrella and Portmanteau Trades Review* describes them as 'Makers of silk hats, hard and soft felts, framed hats, &c., &c. in all qualities'. They also made military and police helmets in cork and felt. As well as the premises in Atherstone, they had a large factory in Nuneaton, and offices in London and Paris.

A contemporary account of the factory in 1880 well describes the haphazard way in which hatting premises expanded:

> The old-fashioned white stuccoed building fronting the Long-street at Atherstone, which was Willday's warehouse for over 100 years, would mislead a passer-by as to the magnitude of the business there carried on by Messrs. Hall & Phillips. One must pass through the passage to the rear, and will there find a whole street of workshops and warerooms stretching through to South-street

> on either hand, and with intricate courts branching out to yet more shops. These Atherstone works have not been arranged on any regular plan, but their extent and their intricacy illustrates the growth of this ancient business. Block after block of buildings has been added on, where room could be obtained, because room must be had ...[87]

But it was claimed that they found it increasingly difficult, based in Atherstone, to serve their customers, on account of the poor train service to the capital which connected them to their markets abroad. So in 1887 Hall and Phillips closed their factory in Atherstone, taking 150 of the workforce with them to Nuneaton and its superior rail connections. Three years later, the property was put on the market, though it failed to sell for some time.[88]

It was 1892 before a speculator by the name of Ebenezer Brown, of Attleborough, bought the buildings. What he paid is not recorded, but in 1894 he sold the part that had formerly been the three-quarter burgage plot to Joseph Lester Vero,[89] a slipper manufacturer, who set up a manufactory using some of the storerooms, makers' shops and warehouses that the Willdays had erected, without extensive alteration. This business carried on until 1988. The premises to the east were sold to the Co-operative Society by 1896 and are still in use as a retail store.[90]

The rear part of the premises was sold for £400 in 1894 to Charles Vero, a cousin of Joseph Lester Vero.[91] He was a hat manufacturer who, with his partner and brother-in-law, James Everitt, had already established a large manufactory straddling Station Street to the west. The old buildings were described as a:

36 *Remains of Willday's factory, 2007.*

> Block of Factory premises Chimney Stack Boiler and Engine Houses with Yard and also a Cottage … having a frontage of sixty-one feet nine inches to Station Street … and containing 800 square yards … Together with the Engine and two Boilers Shafting large iron tank and other machinery and Plant.[92]

In these buildings Vero and Everitt diversified their hatting business by setting up a factory to manufacture skirts.

The three-storey building that stands on the site today was a replacement for one which burnt down in the early years of the 20th century.

Hatting in the Twentieth Century

By 1924, six hatting factories were still in business, providing the majority of the employment in the town. Following the Second World War, when men tired of headwear and car ownership spread, the demand for hats fell. Of these six factories, three survived into the 1980s: Austin Aspden (formerly Denham and Hargrave), Vero and Everitt, and Wilson and Stafford. Wilson and Stafford continued to make felt hats until 1999, when they went into liquidation. The machinery was taken from its premises, Britannia Works, and shipped to Russia.[93]

Conclusion

Atherstone now has very little visible evidence of the hatting industry which played such a major part in its history, apart from some remains of the buildings which the factories occupied. Over 20 years ago there began talks of a museum or display area, to exhibit the substantial collection of equipment and memorabilia which is held in the town by private individuals. If this initiative fails, there is a danger that, within a generation, the industry which shaped the town, for better or for worse, will have passed out of living memory.

9 Housing the Urban Poor: The Nineteenth-Century Development of Atherstone

Nat Alcock

Introduction[1]

Atherstone is a typical small north Warwickshire market town – apart from its striking topography. The earliest large-scale maps of the town (*see* Fig. 37) show how, in 1888, it still had its medieval layout with narrow burgage plots lining both sides of Watling Street (Long Street), but demonstrate also that many of these were packed with small houses – the notorious Atherstone yards.[2] This chapter examines the nature and development of these slum yards and their buildings, following on from the story of their origin discussed in Chapter Seven. The emphasis is placed particularly on the individual buildings, using a combination of sources to reveal their character.

The case studies (*see* below) and much other evidence indicate that the yards' development started in the later 18th century and was largely complete by the early 1800s. A schematic map of 1786 (*see* Fig. 7) identifies a total of 181 burgage plots within the town,[3] and by the mid-19th century some sixty of these plots had been developed as yards filled with tiny houses for the workers in the hatting factories (others had smaller groups of houses behind their frontages).[4]

As noted in previous chapters, for the two-thirds of the town held by copyhold (*see* Appendix to Chapter Three), ownership and occupancy of Atherstone property can readily be investigated from the manorial court books that survive continuously from 1645 to 1871.[5] This evidence for the copyholdings is supplemented by a parish rate assessment for 1793 that lists both owners and tenants, distinguishing the latter by the letters 'F' and 'B', for those living in the front houses (i.e. on the street) and the back houses (i.e. in the yards).[6] A further very unusual survival is a series of volumes listing insurance policies taken out with the New and the Phoenix Fire Offices starting in 1784, which provide detailed property descriptions.[7]

Other evidence comes from an evocative series of photographs taken in the 1910s, from reports of the Medical Officer of Health in the 1900s when slum clearance was being actively pursued,[8] from the evidence at Public Inquiries into Closure Orders, from the memories of the last occupants of the yards before they were demolished and from the yards' rediscovery through archaeological excavation.

Background

The growth of towns in the 18th and 19th centuries to house the workforce of expanding industries was an inevitable consequence of the Industrial Revolution that has previously been examined both generally and for specific towns.[9] A major distinction can be made between development within pre-existing burgage plots, as in Atherstone, and development on unconstricted new sites. For the former, the characteristic result was the creation of narrow yards (in many other areas known as 'courts')[10] filled with houses. On green-field sites, the back-to-back plan was found to be particularly convenient. These were not necessarily any less densely built-up than courts elsewhere, but had more options in house planning and especially in the overall layout of the development. In Atherstone's yards, as the following examples show, a very uniform pattern resulted. However, in both types, the developers shared the same objectives of maximising the rental achieved from their investment.[11]

The choice between newly-built back-to-backs, and development as courts or yards on burgage plots, was governed particularly by the accidents of ownership and of estate policy. Thus, in Leeds, where the fields surrounding the town had many different owners, building land was readily available and development was principally outwards from the historic centre (though the earliest growth took place within the burgage plots). Nottingham is the notorious example of court development, because the land outside the city proper did not become available for building until the later 19th century. Atherstone, although a small town, shared the same problem. In Atherstone, two major landowners, the Bracebridge and Repington (later Dugdale) families, were not prepared to make land available until the 1900s.[12] As a result, the population density in its most crowded areas exceeded that of central Birmingham.[13]

The increase in the provision of workers' housing is, of course, closely linked to increase in population, but must be seen as a consequence rather than a cause. Although the available evidence lacks precision, the logical sequence of events must have been:

(i) the growth of industry, whether factory-based, or as a demand for home-based production
(ii) the influx of workers to the new employment opportunities
(iii) their need for housing
(iv) the satisfaction of this need through development

For Atherstone, we have few reliable population figures preceding the census, but hatting began to dominate the town's economy in the later 18th century (*see* Chapter Eight). Industry-driven population growth was undoubtedly well under way by 1801 (*see* Table 15).

The Atherstone Yards

The Development of the Yards

The five yards marked on Figs. 37 and 38 have been selected because they provide particularly good evidence.

Date	*Estimated population*
1671–2	*c.*1300
1801	2,650
1851	3,819
1881	4,645
1901	5,248

Table 15 *Population figures for Atherstone from the 18th century onwards.*[14]

The first to consider is Binghams Row (later Willdays Terrace), 'C' in Figs. 37 and 38.[15] The quarter burgage plot was acquired by Thomas Haddon, a carpenter and joiner, in 1756, though, following his death the next year, ownership was disputed; the property was eventually sold in two halves to William Bingham, another joiner, in 1783–4.[16] He developed the yard soon after this, though unusually without taking out a mortgage. By 1790, when he was described as a grocer, he insured it as:

> Stock in Trade £50 and his Household Goods in his Dwelling House £50 Built with Brick and Tile Allso Insuars 3 Houses to the Street Front now lett to Elizth Jennings Elizth Gisbourn and Mary Hough and 13 Houses in his yard lett to diffrant People all Equal proportion £200 Built with Brick & Tile.[17]

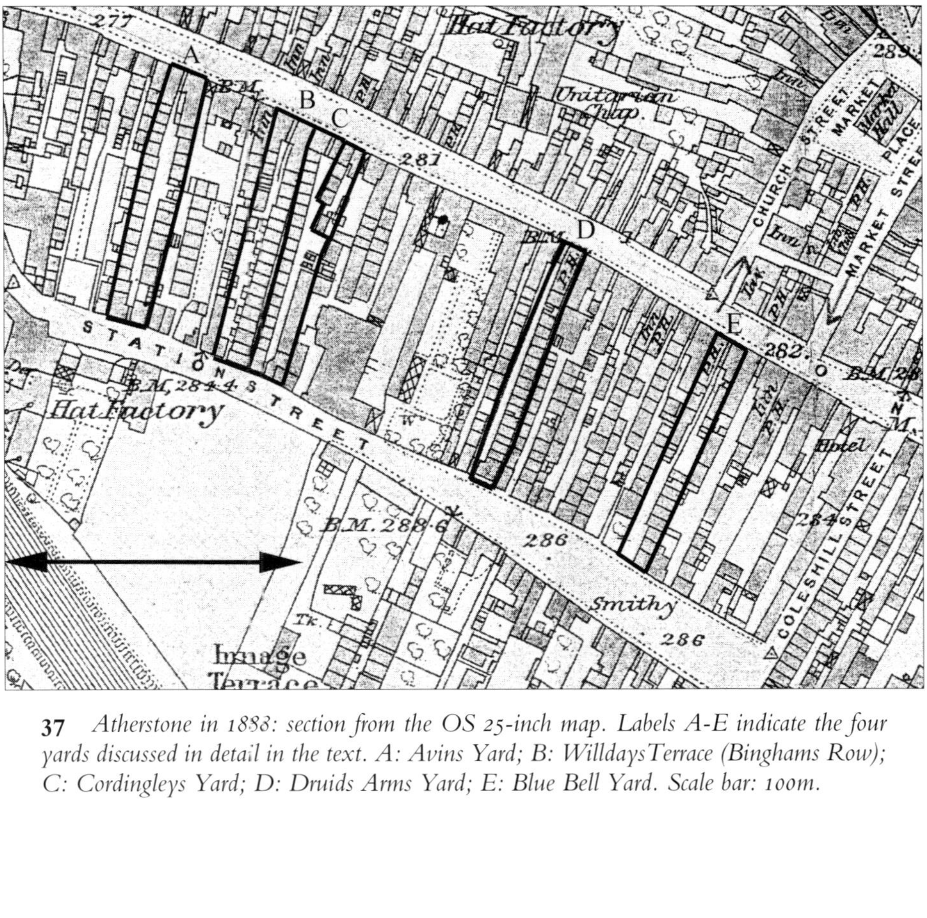

37 *Atherstone in 1888: section from the OS 25-inch map. Labels A–E indicate the four yards discussed in detail in the text. A: Avins Yard; B: WilldaysTerrace (Binghams Row); C: Cordingleys Yard; D: Druids Arms Yard; E: Blue Bell Yard. Scale bar: 100m.*

Correspondingly, the 1793 parish rate names three front and 13 back tenants.[18] William's son Thomas inherited in 1823, and proceeded to rebuild the frontage houses and add 11 more at the back to the 10 already put up (completed according to the insurance records by 1829-31).[19] On Thomas's death in 1844, the property was divided, the front 11 houses being bought by George Hubbard and the rear 13 (including those facing South Street) by Joseph Willday;[20] the court books include plans of these sections.[21] About nineteen properties are shown on the 1888 map ('C' in Fig. 38), and by then a large building had also been added along the formerly open rear part of the yard.

Next door, at Cordingleys Yard ('B' in Figs. 37 and 38, a quarter burgage, C10 on the 1786 Plan), development was slower. The Woodruffe family had owned it since 1717, and Joseph, a butcher, inherited the property in 1788. When Joseph insured it in 1790, it seems still to to have been undeveloped but, by 1792, when he mortgaged it for £300, it included six houses, four of them 'lately built and untenanted'. The 1793 rate indicates that the rear properties were empty, but that Woodruffe himself lived in one of the front houses, which was a substantial double-fronted structure.[22] The yard was sold in 1801 and when it was bequeathed in 1824 included six rear houses.

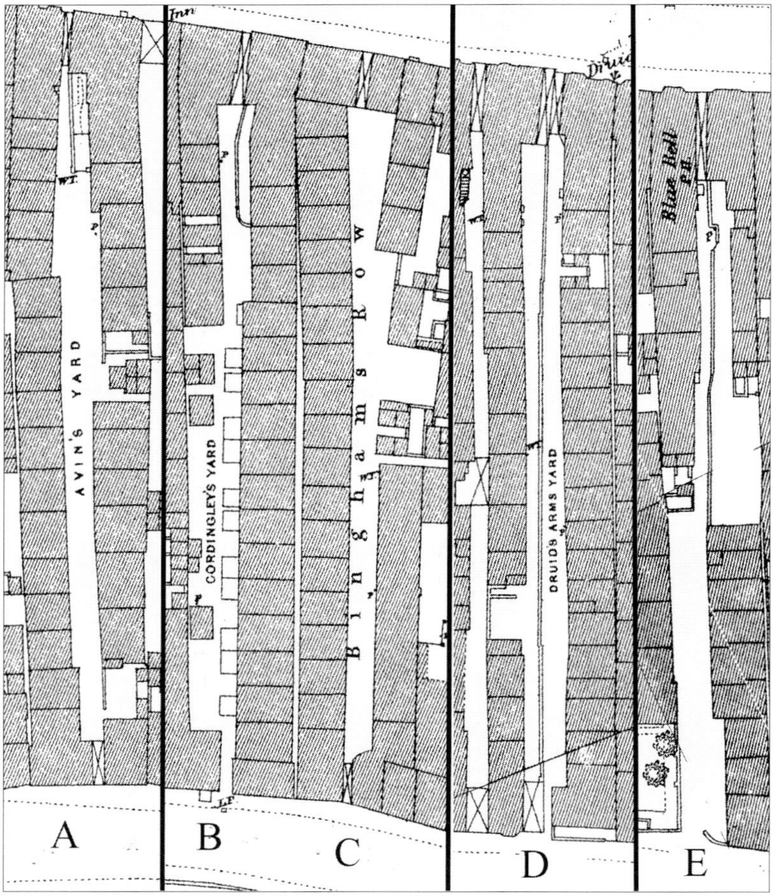

38 *Excerpts from 1888 OS 1:500 map of Atherstone, showing the five yards discussed in detail. (A-E as in Fig. 37).*

39 *Plan of Avins Yard, Atherstone in 1848 overall (top) and detail covering one-and-a-half-storey cottages at the north end (below). South is to the right.*

By 1831, when it was mortgaged for £800, 13 further houses had been built in the yard – these must be the range running back to the rear of the yard visible on the 1888 OS map ('B' in Fig. 38).[23]

For the third case, Avins Yard ('A' in Figs. 37 and 38, a half burgage, C4 on the 1786 Plan), an informative plan was drawn up in 1848, when it was subdivided (and part sold to William Avins), showing the location of the cottages in the yard (*see* Fig. 39).[24]

Development had begun much earlier than this, in about 1745, when what had been one house (presumably on the frontage) was subdivided into four dwellings, to which had been added five small tenements by 1788, when it was mortgaged for £200. By the 1793 rate assessment, much of the yard's development had taken place. This lists 15 back tenants, compared to the 25 cottages, two shops and two stables shown on the 1848 plan. By 1817, it was being described as having about 26 back tenements,[25] and in 1825 the dwellings shared space with a skinner's workshop, a hatter's shop, lime pits, dung hole and hog sty.

The fourth property, Druids Arms Yard ('D' in Figs. 37 and 38, a half burgage, C16 on the 1786 Plan), had belonged to the Rathbone family for half a century before 1785, when it was inherited by Sarah Rathbone. In 1790, she married Michael Soleviol of Castle Bromwich, and they mortgaged the holding for £120. This was increased to £160 in 1792, and three years later they sold it for £500. The surrender on this occasion notes that they had pulled down the old building and erected 14 new dwellings. The 1793 rate shows the development almost complete, with 10 back tenants listed and three vacant houses.[26] Additional details of the sequence of development come from Soleviol's Phoenix Fire Office policies, which are summarised in Table 16.[27]

Date	*Description*	*Occupier*	*£*
24 June 1791	Dwelling house	Mr Bott, victualler	70
	Brewhouse and chamber over, adjoining house		20
	Malthouse adjoining brewhouse		40
	Stable adjoining malthouse		10
	Chamber over the yard, being a dwelling room	Catherine Matts	10
	Hatter's shop adjoining stable	Wm Jennings, hatter	20
	Dwelling house, lean-to & pigsty adjoining	[blank] Buriow, labourer	30
24 June 1792	Dwelling house	Francis Bott, victualler	70
	Brewhouse and chamber over, adjoining house		20
	Malthouse adjoining brewhouse and kiln		40
	Stable adjoining malthouse & 2 bays building used as pigsties		15
	Chamber over the yard, being a dwelling room	Catherine Matts, coal-carrier	10
	Hatter's finishing shop adjoining stable	[blank]	15
	Dwelling house adjoining	Buriows, labourer	30
	A dwelling house} Separate from the above	William Jennings, mason	30
	A dwelling house} buildings but adjoining	[blank] Harrison, bookeeper [*sic*]	30
	A dwelling house}	Benj Twist, bookeeper	
24 June 1793	Dwelling house	Thomas Podmore, victualler	80
	Brewhouse adjoining		10
	12 dwelling houses with offices all adjoining in yard belonging to 1st mentioned dwelling house	[tenants] Richard Collier, William Thompson, Thomas Hawford & others. No hazardous trades	240
		Benjamin Twist, book-keeper	60
	A dwelling house adjoining	Thomas Podmore	30
	2 stables adjoining between said dwelling houses		
	[*added*] One of above stables converted to a dwelling house since		

Table 16 *Michael Soleviol: insurance policies.*

The final example, Blue Bell Yard ('E' in Figs. 37 and 38, a half burgage, C22 on the 1786 Plan), had a more chequered history and, possibly as a result, its development was less typical, with alternating short ranges of back buildings on both sides of the burgage plot. From 1648 to 1789, the half burgage copyholding was the property of the Biddle family, successively George and Suzanna, William and Mary, George and Anne, Robert and Mary.[28] In 1786, this Robert, a barber and maltster, and his wife Mary, mortgaged it to Samuel Stratton, gentleman; then in 1789, Mary, as a widow, sold it outright to Stratton. A few months later, he passed it on to John Taylor, carpenter and joiner, who must have begun the development of the yard. At the latter's death, reported to the court in December 1790, the property was described as 'lately taken down and rebuilt in two tenements'.[29] In the 1793 rate assessment, in addition to the two front houses, it included a rear tenement, a joiner's shop and 'Mr Corbett's casting shop'.[30] In 1796, Taylor's son sold the whole property to Thomas Mottram. He was described as a woolcomber and grocer, but was clearly an entrepreneur with an eye to the best profits, for he was also a 'dealer and chapman'. Mottram then insured the property on 1 July with the Phoenix, when its description indicates that it was principally being used for his wool-combing business (*see* Table 17).[31]

Description	*Occupier*	£
His now dwelling house	Thomas Mottram	200
Household goods, stock in trade as a grocer therein		50
First wool warehouse and brewhouse adjoining		20
Stock therein		150
Combing shop and charcoal house adjoining each other & the last mentioned not communicating – warranted not to have any stove therein		15
Stock therein		20
A large barn, separate, brick & thatched for housing wood	J. Cook, victualler	10
Stables adjoining, brick and tile	William King &	20
A dwelling house adjoining the first mentioned [*house*]	Cook	200
A brewhouse and carpenter's shop adjoining do	[*blank*] Fletcher,	20
A tenement adjoining	labourer	30

Table 17 *Thomas Mottram: insurance policy.*

One side of the yard was occupied by Mottram's business premises and the other by the tenanted second house, probably already known as the *Blue Bell*. However, two years later he split up the holding, selling this second house, the buildings behind it and a plot of land 64 feet long to the then tenant, William Hickling, victualler. Hickling, who was obviously the innkeeper of the *Blue Bell*, then re-insured the house and its description indicates that he was plying more than one trade, since he had converted the carpenter's shop into a slaughter-house.[32]

Two years later, when Mottram seems to have been in financial difficulties, he mortgaged his half for £300. However, in 1802 he was declared bankrupt and the property was sold to William Webster, saddler, for £450. But Webster's tenure, too, was short-lived. He retained it for only a few years before selling it in two portions to William Hood, clock and watchmaker, the front part in 1805 and the rear block two years later. Finally, in 1808, Hood bought the *Blue Bell* from William Hickling.[33]

The range of small houses seen on the OS map ('E' in Fig. 38) was probably built in 1813. In that year, Hood mortgaged the main house and the rear buildings for £300 to one Josiah Shaw, and the *Blue Bell* for another £300 to John Clarke of Tamworth. The first mortgage was transferred in 1820 to Charles Smith of Burbage, by which time the former workshops had clearly been rebuilt as cottages (they were occupied by seven tenants). On a further transfer in 1826, to Thomas Worthington of Mancetter, the sum secured was increased to £495 – Hood's business may by then have been in difficulties.

The later history of Blue Bell Yard was full of incident, though the buildings were now complete. William Hood died in 1828, leaving the *Blue Bell* jointly to his son William and daughter Ann. The adjoining house, where he lived himself, went to his wife Sophia for life, and then to his children. William Hood the younger went bankrupt in 1837, and in 1840 his assignees sold his shares of both parts of the property to his sister. For the *Blue Bell*, she paid only £200, taking into account the fact that money bequeathed to her and William had been provided for the mortgage. The remainder was still subject to Worthington's 1826 mortgage and to Sophia Hood's life interest as well as to Ann's half share, and therefore was deemed to be worth only £16.[34] Ann died in 1841, and eventually (in 1869), her executor sold the property to Edwin Clark, hatter, who was already the tenant. Later still, the *Blue Bell* and the rear of the property was bought by Burton Brewery, who were the owners in 1912 (though they did not own the adjoining house, No. 89, Long Street).[35]

The Character of the Yards

Graphic descriptions of the yards come from reports prepared for Atherstone Rural District Council in 1926 as part of its slum clearance programme,[36] and the report of the Atherstone Medical Officer of Health in 1911.[37]

As a typical example, in 1926, Nos. 1 and 2 in Cordingleys Yard each had a single living room, 13 feet square, with a pantry and coal place. Upstairs were two bedrooms, 13ft x 7ft 6in and 9ft x 10ft. The only rear windows opened onto what was called the 'twitchel', the local dialect word for the little space, one to two feet wide, between the buildings of one yard and the next (*see* Fig. 38).[38] As this was never cleaned out, and it received the run-off from the roofs on both sides without any drainage, it was full of filth and the windows overlooking it were therefore never opened. Furthermore, the house was only 10 feet away from the buildings across the yard, and the houses were very overcrowded. Cordingleys Yard as a whole included 14 houses with 42 rooms – holding 60 people – a density of 382 persons per acre.[39]

The 1911 Report gives a generic description of an even more modest dwelling, with a living room about 15ft x 12ft, a space about six feet square at the head of the stairs used as a children's sleeping place; the only bedroom measured about 12ft x 10ft and was occupied by the parents. It noted, as a characteristic example of overcrowding, that Herbert Evans lived in No. 1 in Cordingleys Yard with his wife and their six children aged from 14 down to one year old.

From a public health viewpoint, the pressure for clearance arose from:

> the lack of a good water-supply, drainage or sewerage,
> the general dirt and squalor,
> the lack of ventilation and adequate light,
> the poor construction, including leaking roofs, rising damp (not surprising from the state of the twitchels),
> the overcrowding.

The clearance orders were regularly challenged by the owners, who put forward proposals for improvement, including combining the houses in pairs and removing intermediate ones, but their interventions were to no avail.[40]

Photographs of the Atherstone Yards

The descriptions of the yards are complemented by a series of some thirty photographs of the yards, taken in the early 1900s, that graphically illustrate the character of their buildings.[41]

40 *Avins Yard, Atherstone (A) looking north, towards Long Street. This and Figs. 41-5 all show courts on the south side of Long Street.*

Fig. 40, of Avins Yard ('A' in Fig. 38), shows a range of one-and-a-half-storey cottages on the left (west side), which are among the smallest identified houses and were probably part of its earliest development *c.*1777 (*see* Fig. 39, bottom). Their plastered façades suggest that they were timber-framed. They face a more typical range of two-storey brick tenements.

41 *Avins Yard, Atherstone (A), looking south.*

Fig. 41 shows the same yard looking south, with the elevations of the brick cottages more clearly visible. The fenestration is characteristic of the yards, with a door and window on the ground floor, but just one window above, set high under the eaves.

42 *Druids Arms Yard, Atherstone (D), looking north, with part of the adjoining Spencers Yard and the dividing wall between them.*

Fig. 42 shows a long range of similar cottages in Druids Arms Yard ('D' in Fig. 38), with a sheet hung out to dry from the nearest house, and more washing further down the yard. This yard, like several others in Atherstone, was built-up on one side only and the dividing wall and part of the adjoining Spencers Yard are visible on the left.

43 *Willdays Terrace, Atherstone (also known as Binghams Row, B), looking north.*

Fig. 43 is of Binghams Row ('C' in Fig. 38), unusual for Atherstone in having houses of three storeys, though the fenestration is similar to houses in the other yards.

44 *Cordingleys Yard, Atherstone (C), looking north.*

Fig. 44, of Cordingleys Yard ('B' in Fig. 38), shows some of the 60 occupants, perhaps including the previously mentioned Herbert Evans and his family (*see* p.178). The 1911 description of the yards indicates that pigs were very often kept there, and the enclosure in the foreground could well be a pigsty – although it could be one of the little iron-fenced gardens that one or two of the residents managed to secure. The single-storey buildings seen in the background were probably communal privies and washhouses.

45 *Blue Bell Yard, Atherstone (E), looking north.*

Fig. 45 gives a general impression of Blue Bell Yard ('E' in Fig. 38), looking north, from a viewpoint beside the main row of cottages, with the arched entry from Long Street just visible at the end. As far as the cottages can be seen, they show the characteristic fenestration pattern. On the left is the back wall of the cottages in the next yard, whose ground-floor windows must have made them slightly more pleasant than some, although they have no bedroom windows; this was perhaps for reasons of privacy, as the further range which does not face any buildings in this yard does have upstairs windows. The lean-to building on the left behind what may be a cart-shed probably contained the privies.

46 *View of the* Blue Bell, *Long Street, at the start of the Atherstone Ball Game, c.1920.*

47 *View of Long Street looking east, from a postcard dated 1903. No. 90 Long Street is the left-most house.*

As these case studies have shown, rebuilding of the yards was often accompanied (or preceded) by rebuilding of the front houses facing Long Street. The late Georgian appearance of many of these houses correlates well with the predominantly *c.*1800 date of the yards. Figs. 46 and 47 illustrate characteristic examples, respectively: No. 69 Long Street (formerly the *Druids Arms*) and a series of houses towards the western end of Long Street. They show the plain brick elevations with 6-over-6 sash windows, simple door-cases and elegant shop fronts that can still be seen on Long Street (though the shop windows have rarely survived 20th-century commercial development) (cf the examples listed in the Gazetteer).

Internal Layout of the Atherstone Houses

The only early plan (*see* Fig. 39, made in 1848) of houses in the yards that shows more than just their footprint is that of Avins Yard, but the internal layout of the houses can be reconstructed with considerable confidence from descriptions and the dimensions noted above: p.178.[42]

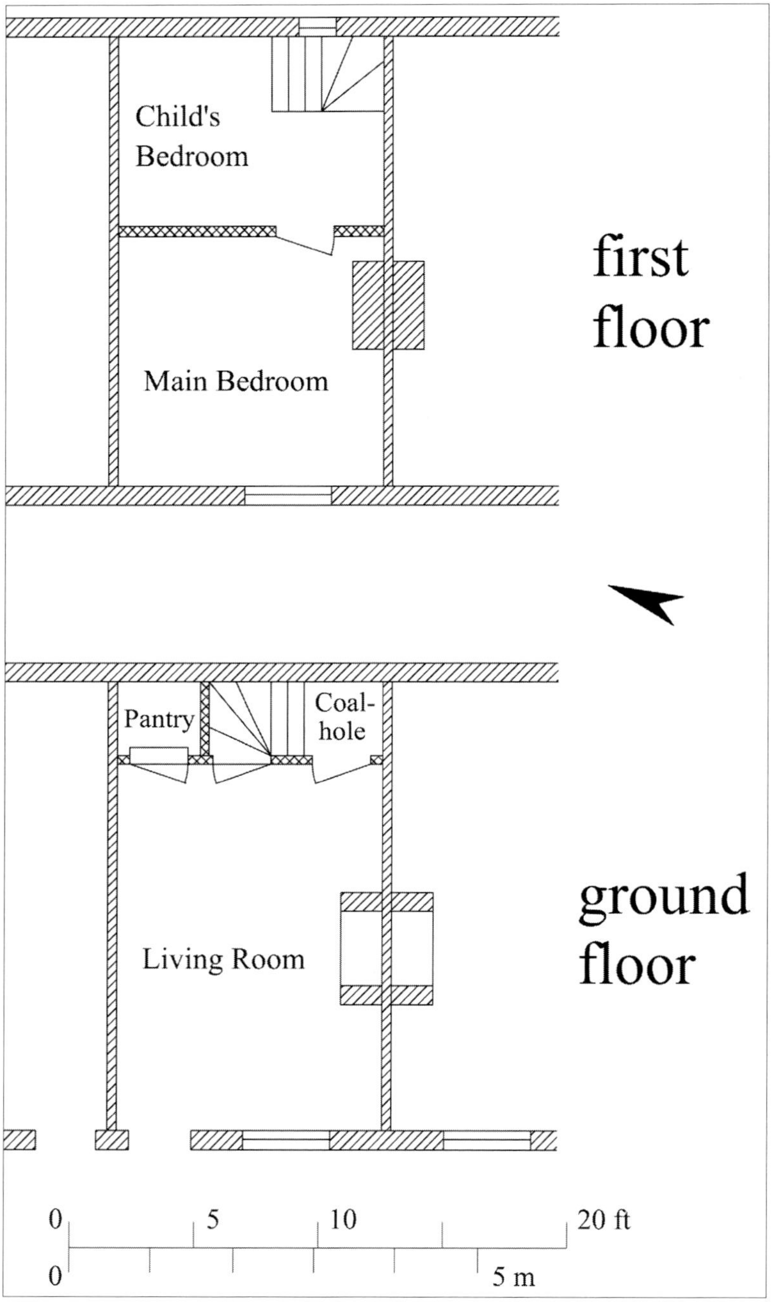

48 *Reconstructed plan of house No. 8 in Cordingleys Yard, Atherstone.*

The houses ranged from 11 to 16 feet in width and were mostly about 15 feet deep with fireplaces on one of the party walls. As a specific example, we can combine the evidence for No. 1 Cordingleys Yard with a verbal description: p.185, and a sketch plan for No. 8.[43] No. 8 was slightly deeper than No. 1, but even narrower, with an overall footprint (measured from the 1:500 map) of 12ft 3in x 19ft 6in, giving internal dimensions of 18ft deep by 11ft 6in wide (compared with 15ft x 13ft for No. 1).[44] The living room occupied almost all of the ground floor. It was entered directly from the yard and had its fireplace on the side wall away from the door (back-to-back with the adjoining house). Probably when built – and certainly by 1900 – it had a small range for cooking, rather than an inglenook fireplace.[45] A stud-and-plaster wall partitioned off the rear of the living room to provide not only a shallow pantry (about three feet wide) but also a boxed-in stair in a space 3-4ft square, with a coal-hole beneath the stair. Larger pantries might include a thrall (stone slab), but this one had only a couple of shelves (sparsely occupied as the family bought their food from day to day at the shops at either end of the yard, or used vegetables from their allotment).

The only rear window in the house, about eighteen inches square, lit the landing at the head of the stair. Of the two bedrooms, the larger front one stretched across the full width of the house and had a window to the court. The smaller bedroom in No. 8 was unlit, but was divided by only a rail from the stairway, so it shared the latter's meagre light. Neither bedroom was heated.[46] Traditionally, the second bedroom was where the children slept.[47]

A parallel description to this reconstruction of Cordingleys Yard was given in 1988 by an elderly woman who lived in Avins Yard as a child.[48] Her house was one of the larger ones in the yard, facing South Street (the upper right-hand house in Fig. 39), atypical in having three bedrooms, a hallway and a separate pantry, as she noted in her reminiscences:

> You'd go into the house. A door opened up a step. There was a step on the front we used to sit on, and then you opened the door at the top and we went upstairs there. It was all closed off, and next door was the coal house. The coal was tipped in under the stairs, inside the house. Next to the stairs. You had to walk into the living room and it was off the living room. It had to be swept in – 12 hundred [weight] of coal, and we used to have pieces of wood across the front to keep it in. So we went across to another door and went into the front room, and upstairs there was three shut-off bedrooms and a square landing, so really it was a nice sized house. You could have had a bathroom made. And then there was a pantry. You turned left into the living room. It was a living room kitchen. The oven was in the grate in there and then a little grate in the front room, just a sitting room grate for the fire. We had a high shelf over the range.

Similar details come from the memories of John Fletcher who lived in Vinraces Row, on the north side of Long Street.[49] He recollected the three doors, with a step down to the pantry which had a thrall, a step up to the stair door, and the third door to the coal place under the stairs. In his extended family, the sleeping arrangements were rather different:

> We had a landing and it wasn't very big but me dad made a bed that just fit the landing. You couldn't walk round, you had to climb over to get in. Me mother and me dad slept there and me gran slept in the little bed in the bedroom and me and me sister slept in another bed in the bedroom. They had no wardrobe, dressing tables, they had a little chester draws [chest of drawers] you know, and that's all they had like. Same as downstairs, they had a table, four chairs and we had a sofa under the window, but somebody had made it like, it weren't one they'd bought, that's all ... You had a black leaded grate

> [and] each side your fireplace you had cupboards, but you had no furniture other than a table and four chairs. We had a stool, a little stool somebody had made and that was it.

Furnishings were sparse but might include rag rugs on the red quarry-tile floors. Washing was done in a puncheon of warm water, with a weekly bath in a zinc tub.

Other reminiscences add to our image of the yards themselves. Each held a pump, though water was also sold by the bucket (½d. each). The privies and wash-houses were shared, and the latter operated by unwritten rules. In Cordingleys Yard, four houses could use it on each allotted day – so almost every day was wash-day for some family, explaining why many of the yard photographs show washing hung out. John Fletcher also commented on these arrangements:

> In the wash-house you had a copper, a cast iron copper which was bricked in the corner with a fire box underneath, and wash day you had to get up at six o'clock in the morning, fill your copper with water, light your fire underneath and get your water boiling, 'cause in those days people always boiled all the whites to get them cleaner. You had a tub, a big wooden tub, a dolly peg to peg your clothes up and down – like punch 'em up and down, finger on the top. By the time the women had done the washing and they had to clean all the floor up, clean the ashes out, wipe the copper round and get all clean for the other people that was going in to do the washing in the afternoon. So, if you was ill or anything or you couldn't do it on your day you had to go and ask somebody if they'd swap with you.

The privies generally drained into the ash-pit. Although some of the early evidence for the yards indicates the presence of pigsties, by the time of these reminiscences, very few had space for them.

Excavation Evidence

In 2005, excavation in advance of redevelopment of the site of Cordingleys Yard and Binghams Row revealed the sites of several of the yard houses.[50]

Fig. 49 shows the excavated plan of houses A-D in Cordingleys Yard, and Figs. 50 and 51 gives two views of house 'C' under excavation. From a correlation of the plan with the 1935 closure order, houses 'A-D' on the plan can be identified with nos. 4-7 in the yard.[51] It is satisfying that the excavation plans correspond very precisely to the reconstruction drawing (Fig. 48). However, some aspects of the buildings are only identifiable by archaeology, including the exact dimensions. As described by Mr Aucott, the party walls (195, 275, 177; Fig. 49) were only one brick thick, though curiously wall 275 and the internal wall 182/202 were built on arched foundations, perhaps because the ground here was unstable because of earlier pits in the back of the burgage plot. Floors were of red bricks originally, repaired in quarry tiles. An unexpected feature was the ash-pit in front of the fireplace (181) (also found in houses in Binghams Row). This was probably used to rake ashes into from the range, rather than taking them outside every time the fireplace was cleaned up; it presumably had a wooden cover.

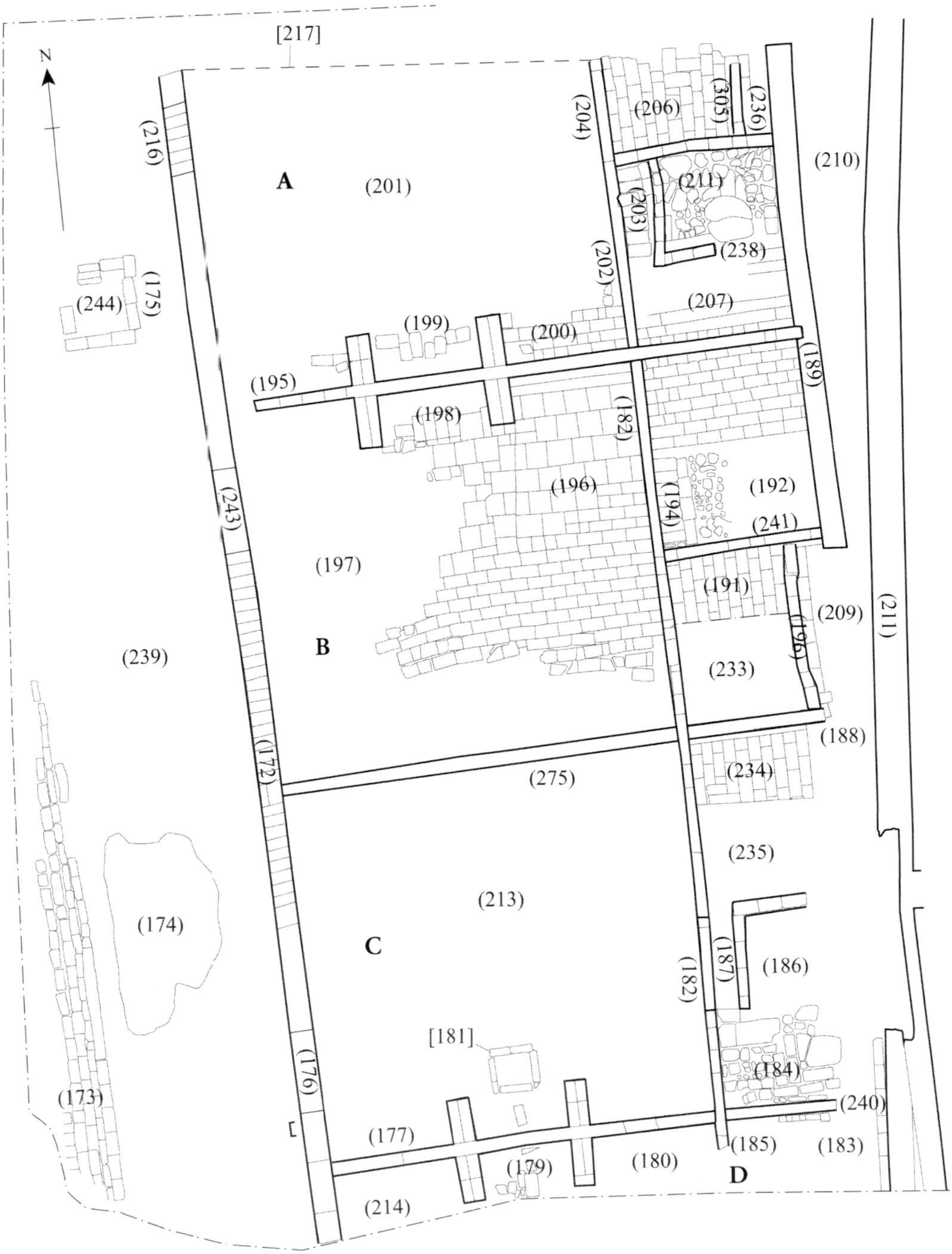

49 *Plan of excavated houses 4-7 (A-D) in Cordingleys Yard.*

50 *Excavated site of house 6 in Cordingleys Yard – general view.*

THE 1851 AND 1901 CENSUSES

The 1851 census enumerations confirm the population density within the yards.[52] Of the 14 houses recorded in Druids Arms Yard, four were lived in only by a husband and wife, the others housing up to nine people. No. 13 was occupied by George Golding, an iron-caster, his wife Margaret, three daughters ranging from 24 to six years old, three sons from 13 to one year, and a young man visiting. In all, the yard was home to 53 people. The six cottages in Blue Bell Yard were occupied by 29 people, ranging from Sophia Lewis and her two-year-old son, and Mary Dutton, a 70-year-old pauper with her granddaughter and two lodgers, to Joseph Harding, cow-leech, his wife and their five children.

For small houses, the 1901 census gives additional information: the number of occupied rooms (when this was less than five). Most of the Druids Arms Yard houses had three rooms, corresponding to the reconstruction discussed above, one having only two and one four rooms – we may hope that George Golding had lived there, though in 1901 the two-room house was occupied by a shoe-repairer, his wife and their three young children. In Avins and Cordingleys Yards, almost all the houses were recorded as having three rooms.

THE DEVELOPMENT OF THE YARDS: COMPARISONS

The Atherstone yards show a pattern of intensive development of the medieval burgage plots that parallels that found in courts in other towns, notably Coventry, Leeds (preceding its better known back-to-back housing), and Nottingham.[53] After a few records of house subdivision from the mid-18th century onwards, the main period for building the yards was in the decades either side of 1800, and the process seems to have been essentially complete by 1830-40.

The individual houses examined measured 12-14ft square overall; dimensions that match those of the many hundred other houses shown on the large-scale maps. They have a characteristic asymmetrical front fenestration that differs from the typical 'single-fronted' terrace house, in having only one first-floor window, normally positioned asymmetrically, above the ground-floor window. This reflects their internal layout, particularly that they are too narrow to have more than one first floor front room. This external appearance parallels that found in Coventry court houses and, interestingly, similar elevations are also seen in rural terraces of the period as, for example, in a row of cottages built by the Reverend Luxmoore in Bridestowe, Devon, in about 1800.[54]

Other studies of industrial housing have emphasised either the development process or the improved housing that slowly followed the numerous improvement acts of the later 19th century.[55] Most are enlivened with a few photographs of courts and back-to-backs, but only include generic descriptions of the houses themselves. The most significant exceptions are

51 *Excavated site of house 6 in Cordingleys Yard – detail at rear of house showing the location of the coal-hole (nearest camera), stair and pantry.*

Jeremy Lowe's study of industrial housing in Wales, and Peter Guillery's of small London houses.[56] These show that among houses surviving to be recorded, the Warwickshire ones are notable for their small number of rooms, being paralleled only by a few of the earliest examples elsewhere. Nationally, the positioning of the common features, the stair and the fireplace, is also remarkably variable. As well as generally being of three or more storeys, London houses often had their stair against the front wall and usually included a small first-floor window lighting it, producing a subtly different fenestration pattern to that described above; only a few of Guillery's London examples show asymmetrically placed first- and second-floor windows. The Welsh houses also often had stairs against the side walls.

The London houses frequently, and the Welsh houses occasionally, combined workshops and dwellings, but this pattern is particularly significant in the north; for example, in Preston, Lancashire, many houses had cellar loom-rooms, providing suitable humidity for cotton-weaving – houses with weaving lofts have been frequently recorded in Yorkshire.[57] In contrast, in Atherstone the workers seem to have worked in the hatters' own premises (as described in Chapter Eight). This may be one factor governing the small size of these houses. In one respect, if not in many others, Warwickshire did not descend to the notoriously lowest level in the hierarchy of slum housing – it included neither the infamous cellar dwellings found in London and some northern towns, nor single room houses.[58]

As elsewhere, too, the memories of those who lived there reflect a very strong sense of community, despite the physical drawbacks of life within the courts; as John Fletcher again testifies:

> What was it like with the neighbours?
> John: Very very good. I can say there was no animosity about …
> [People] all pulled with one another and helped one another out.
> Nobody had got much money but if somebody had come up against hard
> times you know, through some reason, illness or anything, all the neighbours
> would give them a little bit of their little bit and they looked after one another.
> And as regards arguments I can never remember one.

GAZETTEER

Bob Meeson and Mike Trye

The following descriptions of the buildings in Atherstone (as they existed in May 2007) is arranged in two parts, the first relating to the Market Place area of the town, the second to Long Street.

The first part of the tour is fully illustrated by the streetscape drawings (*see* p.69). It follows the order of these drawings and begins on the west side of Church Street, starting at the south end and continuing to the *Angel Inn*. The east side of Market Street is described next, beginning at Chapel House, opposite the east end of the church in Friars Gate, and ending at the junction with Long Street – this is in reverse of the postal addresses, but it allows the entries to be followed left to right in the same order as the streetscape drawings. The first part of the tour continues, in the same order as the drawings, returning north along the west side of Market Street, turning left along the south end of the Market Place, then down the east side of Church Street and finally around the corner onto the section of Long Street between Church and Market Street.

The second part, Long Street, is not illustrated by streetscape drawings, but does run along the street in sequence. It includes all of the buildings along the north side, commencing with Grendon House at the west end and continuing as far as No. 122 in the east. It then returns along the south side of Long Street, from No. 133 all the way back to No. 21, close to the junction with Station Street.

Where commercial names are given, they refer to the town in June 2008.

The Gazetteer links closely to Chapter Five. Many of the buildings are discussed in Bob Meeson's overview of Atherstone's historic buildings, while the locations of the six properties described in that chapter in the Building Histories are indicated.

The Market Place Area: The West Side of Church Street

2 Church Street

The side elevation of 80 Long Street; a modern brick building with bland stretcher bond brickwork, aluminium window frames.

2a Church Street (Curds and Whey)

Single bay of three storeys in Flemish bond brickwork, painted yellow. Modern shop front on the ground floor. On the first floor, the off-centre 6-over-6 sash window is a replacement under an elliptical head. Brick modillion eaves, concrete-tiled roof.

4 Church Street

Modern shop front in mock Victorian style. On the first floor, Flemish bond bricks; the window has a splayed flat lintel with keystone, modern replacement 8-over-8 sash window with horns. Moulded eaves, blue-tiled roof pierced by a hipped dormer containing a modern two-light casement window.

6a Church Street (Bairstow Eaves)

Single-bay brick front in Flemish bond, with two storeys plus attic. The shop front is modern, but in a 19th-century style. On the first floor, a modern replacement sash window, 8-over-8, with horns; chamfered brick sill, splayed stone lintel with keystone. Moulded eaves. Blue tile roof pierced by single hipped dormer, but the two-light casement is modern.

52 *2a Church Street (Curds and Whey)*

6 CHURCH STREET (FORMERLY THE THATCH)

Two storeys plus attic, painted brick, trying to be Flemish bond; two bays plus an entry shared with No. 8. On the ground floor, to the left, a good wooden door-case with Doric pilasters and a canopy over; four-panel door with raised moulded edges – the top two panels now of glass. To the right of the doorway, a multi-pane shop window. The deep string course continues from No. 8. On the first floor, two tripartite windows with pegged wooden frames (two mullions, one transom, a central side-hung casement); splayed brick lintels. The former moulded wooden eaves have been replaced by plain boxing. Single, central, three-light hipped dormer window looks relatively modern. Old blue tiles on pitched roof, red brick stack.

8 CHURCH STREET (FORMERLY JANE STAFFORD)

Flemish bond brick façade of two bays and two storeys. Shallow brick plinth pierced by a cellar-light. The shop doorway and the shop window to its right (now plate glass), are framed by panelled surrounds and a canopy. On the door, the bottom panel has vertical boards with double reeds but the top is now of glass. Another window of the ground floor is smaller, with a central mullion. Above, a deep brick string course. Both first-floor windows have splayed brick lintels and both are mullioned, with two panes in each light; each contains one side-hung casement. Moulded wooden eaves. Inside, on the ground floor, a cast iron corner fireplace complete with fire basket; one late Georgian/Victorian door. In the attic, scant remains of a clasped purlin roof (15th- or early 16th-century).

10 CHURCH STREET (BUTLER'S BOOK EMPORIUM)

Painted stucco three-bay front of three storeys. On the ground floor, a shallow chamfered plinth; central doorway (modern door) under a rusticated round arch with keystone. Shop windows to left and right, now with modern glazing, but the lintels remain, stepped up to a giant keystone. Above, a string course, then three sash windows to the first floor, with stone sills and straight head with giant keystones; broad frames almost flush to the wall, 6-over-6 panes, no horns. On the second floor, 3-over-3 sashes to left and right have been replaced by fixed-light successors; blind aperture in the middle. Moulded eaves, blue tiled roof. Both gables show line of an older, lower roof, more steeply pitched; the entire attic has been raised along the street elevation, so possibly there were originally dormer windows.

12 CHURCH STREET (HOWKINS & HARRISON)

A wide, relatively low brick façade of three bays, the middle bay stepped forward. On the ground floor, three plate glass shop windows, breaking a low stone band; the door in the middle has a glazed top panel and a narrow rectangular over-door light. On the first floor, a stone sill-band; the three windows have splayed lintels, moulded key-blocks, and 2-over-2 sashes with horns. Above, blind false windows with stone sills and lintels with key-stones. Parapet with moulded top, hiding a low, tiled roof.

14 Church Street

Brick gables to the street, laid in Flemish bond. The ground-floor shop-front extends across the premises to the left. A former entry may have been incorporated within the shop-front, then there are big plate glass windows to left and right of a central doorway. On the first floor, each of the two windows has a stone sill and splayed lintels with moulded keystones. The window frames might be Edwardian – 2-over-2 sashes. The gable stands over a plain stone band and contains a single attic window like those below, but now bricked up.

16/20 Church Street (Serenity Hair and Beauty)

A three-storey Flemish bon brick building in two portions, divided by the entry that once served Phoenix Yard; the two portions are described separately:

To the right: ground floor, two shop-fronts, both with canted bay windows. The shop to the right is the narrower of the two, and has a plainer architrave round the doorway; four-panel door, the top two panels now glazed; that to the left includes reeded pilasters rising to a frieze and a moulded canopy. On the first floor, 6-over-6 sash windows with set-back frame, stone sills, splayed stone lintels with key blocks. On the second floor, 2-over-2 sash windows with similar sills and lintels.

The left portion of this building incorporates the Phoenix Yard entry and an altered shop front; the front window is plate glass, but one reveal, bracket, and the moulded canopy might be Victorian. On the upper floors the window sills and lintels are similar to those in the rest of the façade, but the sash windows are now 2-over-2, not older than Edwardian. Plain wood eaves, blue tile roof.

53 *The* Angel Inn *(Building History One).*

The *Angel Inn*

☙ Building History One

Partly medieval, but now with a façade of c.1920-30 with applied plank decoration. The east front (facing the Market Place) is of two gabled bays. On the ground floor, two canted bay windows, each of four lights. There is no entrance on the front elevation; the entrance in the south side of the building was probably by a carriageway through a high arch, but this has been demolished. Two four-light windows on the first floor, then one two-light window in each gable. On the long north elevation, behind the front range, evidence of a lean-to roof at the rear of a now-demolished structure. A substantial beam marks the position of a wide aperture, now bricked up; the beam apparently spanned a single large room set out across the line of the earlier wall. The earliest window in this side of the inn is possibly Georgian, but the top sash has been replaced; the other windows are 19th-century and later.

The East Side of Market Street

Chapel House Hotel and Restaurant, Friars Gate

If style is any guide, the older four-bay façade, now stuccoed, is of the 1720s. The front (west) elevation is divided by a high brick wall between the front and back gardens; the single bay on the north side of the wall is probably an addition. In the corner next to the garden wall, a single Tuscan Doric column carries one corner of an early 19th-century flat portico. The 6-over-6 sash windows have exposed sash boxes and narrow moulded architraves, a moulded eaves cornice, and a blue-tiled roof pierced by flat-topped dormers with casement windows. Originally, there were two good rooms at the front of the house – a big reception room and a more private parlour for the family, and there is a very good staircase with turned balusters. Such internal features as three-quarter-round bead-mouldings on the corners of chimney-breasts and elliptical arches belong to a refurbishment after 1800. A good but steep service stair with turned end-baluster, thin square balusters and a moulded hardwood handrail probably belongs to this time. In the added north bay, the dining room has pretty shaped cornice boards, unlikely to predate 1800.

St Mary's House, Friars Gate

Formerly a rectory; set well back, behind a high brick wall. Three bays of two storeys plus attics, stuccoed. The flush-panelled door in the middle of the ground floor is set under a three-pane over-door light and a bracketed flat canopy. To the left, a canted bay window under a pitched tiled roof. To the right, an 8-over-8 sash window with exposed sash boxes flush to the façade. On the first floor, two 8-over-8 sash windows, and a third in the middle which is 6-over-6; moulded eaves cornice, then a steeply-pitched tiled roof broken by four inserted dormers – early post-war. End-stacks, double-pile plan.

54 *23/25 Market Street, Swan House (Building History Two).*

23/25 MARKET STREET, SWAN HOUSE

BUILDING HISTORY TWO

A later 18th-century inn, with late-Georgian, Victorian/Edwardian alterations. The front elevation is of three bays, all stuccoed, but one of those is taken up by the tall, wide arch over North Street (North Street was cut through it in 1795-7). The two-storeyed bay to the left is an addition, and is lower than the other two. Most of the ground-floor level is taken up by double doors, part-glazed, part-panelled, set between side-lights, all within a chamfered surround and below top-lights and a moulded cornice. Above, a 6-over-6 sash window with stone sill and stuccoed reveals, then a low parapet. The middle bay has 6-over-6 sash windows on the ground and first floors; curiously, on the first floor, the bottom sash has horns on top – suggesting that it might have been turned upside down. Above the arch in the right-hand bay, a 3-over-3 sash window, tucked under the eaves. Blue tile roof. In the reveals of the big arch, adjacent to North Street, a blocked window and doorway, then a five-bay three-storeyed brick range to the east. The first bay beyond the arch contains a doorway under the shadow of a pentice, and with a brick with the inscription 'RB 1795'. The ground- and first-floor windows are 6-over-6 sashes under splayed brick heads. The 3-over-3 sash windows on the second floor are tucked under dentilled eaves. The roof of this range is now covered with modern concrete tiles.

(At the time of the survey, this was The Old Surgery, and Sale, Hill and Davenport, solicitors.)

21 MARKET STREET, *MARKET TAVERN*

BUILDING HISTORY THREE

A 17th-century building with a Georgian brick façade. Situated on the opposite side of the Market Place from the *Angel Inn*, the *Market Tavern* is, at first sight, more evidently Georgian. One has only to step off the street into the bar to find that this was originally two rooms, divided by a close-studded timber-framed wall; the evidence is in the main ceiling beam, deeply chamfered on both sides, but also with closely-spaced double-pegged empty mortices. On each side of this former wall, the ceilings are divided by more deeply-chamfered beams. Just inside the entry to the right there is the tell-tale evidence of a former jetty – a straight joint in the brickwork; part of the original jetty plate appears to remain in situ. On the upper floor, portions of the late medieval timber-framed partition walls and roof trusses might have escaped the Georgian rebuild.

19 MARKET STREET, BEECH HOUSE

BUILDING HISTORY FOUR

One of the best town houses in Warwickshire, built by William Eyre, gentleman, in 1708. Dating from the middle of the reign of Queen Anne, Beech House is the oldest remaining brick house overlooking the Market Square, and it is indisputably the finest, even if it has vernacular undertones.

55 *19 Market Street, Beech House (Building History Four).*

The front elevation is of five bays with a basement, two full storeys and an attic, though it was not designed to the very best proportions that could be achieved at this time. Both doorways, and the windows at each end of the first floor, are sited disproportionately close to the giant corner pilasters.

15/17 Market Street

These two premises each have one big gable on the front elevation. However, not enough could be seen inside to confirm whether they were built separately or as one. The two sides are divided by a pair of substantial brick back-to-back chimneys, probably 17th-century:

No. 17 (Shortland Parsley)

The front elevation, under the left-hand gable, is now pebble-dashed. There are canted bays on each side of the central doorway, which has a three-pane over-door light. The door has a single flat panel below the locking rail, and 2-over-2 panes above. On the first floor, the window has a stone sill and broad frames, but the 2-over-2 sashes with horns might be Edwardian; the barge-boards are modern. Inside, on the ground floor, the second room back from the street has an enormous fireplace with a bressumer behind the mantel shelf. Empty mortices in the soffit of the ceiling beam indicate the line of the former partition wall. The very thick wall at the back of this room marks the original back of the building. The present staircase is an insertion. On the first floor, the partition wall between this and the adjoining building is timber-framed, with several poor studs; the long brace a modern insertion.

56 *No. 17 (Shortland Parsley).*

No. 15 (Howkins and Harrison)

The right-hand gable and the first floor below both display timber-framing. There are doorways at each end of the front elevation; that to the left (with moulded architrave round a plank door with a drop-latch) leads to the passage which now separates the two premises. Between the doorways is a late Victorian or Edwardian shop-front with narrow fielded panels and a canopy surrounding a window topped by a metal ventilation panel, then to the right, the other door, glazed above the locking bar, is set back; it has an over-door light. On the first floor, the timber-framing defines small square panels, late 16th- or 17th-century in character, and this is pierced by two replacement 2-over-2 sash windows. The framing in the big gable has been mocked up.

Inside, behind the passage door, the splayed head of a post survives from the originally jettied front elevation. The front portion of the passage was previously part of the main room; behind this, a narrow barrel-vaulted passage passes between the chimney stacks. On the first floor, some timber framing is visible – all of rather thin scantling, and probably altered. In the yard there is a coal-house, and a laundry/wash house, still with its copper.

11/13 MARKET STREET, THE WORKS HAIRDRESSERS, FORMERLY CHURCH'S RESTAURANT

BUILDING HISTORY FIVE

This building was re-fronted in the early 19th century, but was once a spectacular timber-framed house, with each of the upper floors impressively jettied. There is a door with over-door light and a narrow bow-window to the left, then to the right is a double bow window with central doorway, again with an over-door light, all made together. The left-hand bow is an 8-over-8 sash with reeded architraves; the other bow windows are 16-paned, and these, too, include opening sashes. The door between them has two fielded panels with flush-moulded edges below, and glass panes above. A decorated entablature unites the ensemble. Above, the brick front is laid in

57 *11/13 Market Street: The Works, hairdressers; formerly Church's restaurant (Building History Five).*

Flemish bond. On the first floor, three 6-over-6 sash windows stand on a sill course; they have broad exposed frames set close to the face of the wall, and rusticated flat arches with big key-blocks. Above, on the second floor, three smaller windows with wooden frames and stone or rendered sills, but that in the centre is blind. Above again are moulded eaves and an old tiled roof.

9 Market Street (Ex-Servicemen's Club)

The front elevation is tall and impressive, and the giant pilasters would hark back to the early Georgian period if it were not for the incised lines after the manner of John Soane, which make the building later than about 1800. The stuccoed façade is of five three-storeyed bays over a very shallow plinth. The central doorway has an elliptical fanlight with three radiating glazing bars under a broken pediment. A string course, stopping at the pilasters, divides the first and second floors. The windows have elliptical heads and stone sills. Unfortunately, the symmetry is broken by a doorway to the right, inserted to serve a secondary entry along the south side of the building, and every sash window frame has been replaced by inappropriate successors. Inside, most of the interior has been comprehensively refitted, but on the first floor one room retains a good ceiling with moulded beams.

7 Market Street (Unicorn Cantonese)

Three bays, two storeys, stuccoed. The flat pilasters to left and right are broken by a moulding projected out from the canopy over the shop-front. The latter is now late Victorian, with recessed double doors at the centre, having drop-back lights above. The narrow vented metal grilles along the top of each of the windows suggest that they were designed for a food-store. The three windows on the first floor have replacement brick sills, plain reveals, but instead of 8-over-8 sashes they now have top-hung casements. Fillet, frieze and shaped cornice along the eaves. Slate roof, one end-stack.

3a/5 Market Street

Three bays, three storeys, Flemish-bond brickwork. On the ground floor, one narrow shop to the left and one two-bay shop-front to the right. That on the left (No. 5) has a small multi-pane bay window and a part-glazed door; both are framed by wooden pilasters rising to tiny capitals under a canopy frieze. Still in the first bay, an entry having an elliptical rusticated arch with keystone. Then, right again, a big modern shop-front. On the first floor, three sash windows with stone sills, moulded lintels with bracketed canopies, that to the centre with extra detailing. Three more similar sash windows on the second floor. Unfortunately, all the window frames now have highly inappropriate central pivoting panels. Moulded brick eaves cornice, one blue brick end stack.

1/3 Market Street

Three bays, three storeys, brick laid in Flemish bond. In the left-hand bay, a narrow entry under a shallow segmental brick arch, then a modern shop-front.

To the right, another big, modern shop-front (William Hill). On the first and second floors, three windows with stone sills and shallow segmental brick arches; the sash windows have been replaced by frames having central swivelling sections. Dentilled eaves, concrete tiled roof.

REAR OF 88A LONG STREET, FRONTING ONTO THE SOUTH END OF MARKET STREET

Two bays of three storeys, brick laid in Flemish bond. The ground floor is now all modernity. On the first floor, two windows with stone sills and shallow segmental heads should contain 6-over-6 sashes but these have been replaced by poor frames having central swivelling panels. Similar replacement windows on the top floor. Dentilled eaves, concrete roof-tiles.

THE WEST SIDE OF MARKET STREET

86 LONG STREET

Following the Streetscape drawings, this building is described in two parts (*see* below, p.205, for the Long Street elevation):

Market Street Elevation

Six bays of three storeys, incorporating two modern shop fronts on the ground floor. On the first floor, to the left, an 8-over-8 sash window, set back, in a panel with a narrow moulded surround like those on the front elevation; console brackets support the stone sill. To the right, a circular window, still glazed. On the second floor, a 4-over-4 sash window with similar details, and another glazed roundel. Four more bays have similar sash windows, but without console brackets, and one of the top floor windows is much wider, tripartite, 4-over-4 in the middle and 2-over-2 on each side. Moulded eaves parapet. Some features replaced with plastic.

Corner of Market Street and Derby Lane

A single-storey adjunct to the back of 86 Long Street, with a swept-up parapet, hipped red-tiled roof and a modern flat dormer.

6 MARKET STREET (BATES)

Single-bay rendered three-storey façade. Modern shop front. On the first floor, a 6-over-6 sash window with a stone sill has been replaced by top-hung casements; rusticated lintel with key-block. On the second floor the window sill has been redone, and again the 3-over-3 sash has been replaced by casements. Moulded wood eaves, and a gable parapet to Derby Lane.

8 MARKET STREET (SALON 57)

Single bay, three storeys; Flemish bond red brick; possibly built with No. 6.

The ground-floor window was 6-over-6 sash, but now a top-hung casement, splayed stone lintel with key-block. The window is off-set to the left, so the doorway is probably primary, but the frame and the door are both modern. On the first floor, 6-over-6 sash window replaced by top-hung casement; stone sill, splayed stone lintel with key-block. On the second floor, the 3-over-3 sash has again become a top-hung casement. Moulded wooden eaves, but now the roof has concrete tiles.

10, 10a and 10b Market Street (Fishing 4 U)

Three bays, three storeys, Flemish bond brickwork. On the ground floor, there is no sign that there was ever a central doorway or window aperture. Instead, to the left, there is a bow window and a doorway, both in modern joinery, but plausibly reflecting what was there before. In the right-hand bay, a doorway with moulded architrave and a rectangular over-door light; splayed lintel with keystone. On the first and second floors, the central window recesses are blind. To left and right, all have stone sills, splayed lintels with keystones; originally 6-over-6 sashes on the first floor and 3-over-3 on the top floor, but now all top-hung casements. Moulded wooden eaves, slate roof.

12 Market Street (SEL Estate Agents)

Single bay, three storeys, Flemish bond. Modern shop frontage to ground floor. On the first floor, 6-over-6 sash windows with broad exposed sash boxes nearly flush to the façade; stone sills and splayed lintels with key-blocks. On the second floor, 3-over-3 sashes, primary sash boxes. Moulded wooden eaves, slate roof.

The Side of the Atherstone Electrical (formerly Arragon Properties) Building in Market Street

This building is at the rear of offices now facing the Market Place, but originally it was a separate property in Market Street. Two main bays face the street, plus one narrow bay canted back to the right. Three storeys, Flemish-bonded mottled brown bricks. Shallow plinth with chamfered blue brick top. Originally there was a doorway to the left, but this has been carefully patched in, and there is now a creditably good window to match the others. So now there are three 6-over-6 sash windows to the ground floor, all with stone sills, splayed stone lintels with moulded keystones. In the canted side to the right, the ground-floor window is another insertion, replacing a former doorway. On the first floor, two more 6-over-6 sash windows and, in the canted wall to the right, a 1-over-1 sash. On the second floor the sashes are 3-over-6, with similar sills and lintels. Plain brick eaves, tiled roof (*c.*1800 or earlier?)

The remainder of this street elevation forms the rear of Atherstone Electrical.

THE SOUTH SIDE OF THE MARKET PLACE

ATHERSTONE ELECTRICAL, FORMERLY ARRAGON PROPERTIES

Single-bay brick façade of two-and-a-half storeys. Modern shop front in a big shallow recess which rises to a round arch on the first floor. The rubbed brick arch rises from a decorated band and frames a very good Venetian window with bolection-moulded surround and standing on a string. At eaves level, a moulded string forms the base of a shallow-pitched gable with a moulded top. Standing on the string, a Diocletian window with a 3-over-3 sash at the centre and fixed panes at each side.

The side elevation, in Market Street, has a chamfered plinth and a cellar arch. On the ground floor, there was formerly a doorway to the left, now

58 *Atherstone Electrical, formerly Arragon Properties.*

neatly blocked. Today there is a 6-over-6 sash in broad frame, stone sill, splayed lintel with key-block; to the right, a canted bay window, but the shadow of something else behind it. On the first floor, two good 6-over-6 sashes with keystones. Moulded eaves, tiled roof, tall brick ridge-stack.

16/16a Market Place (Throckmortons and Arragon Properties)

The date 1877 is painted on the first floor of 16a. Uncommonly for Atherstone, it is built in English garden-wall bond, but the left side has been plastered over. Two modern shop fronts. On the first floor, paired sash windows, each pair linked by a chamfered sill and moulded lintel; however, the top lights appear to be fixed, and each has a cusped Gothic head. Moulded cornice, slate roof. More Gothic heads in the dormer windows. Nineteenth-century brick chimney stack with stepped string.

5/7 Church Street (but overlooking the Market Place)

Modern shop fronts. On the first floor, a big tripartite window with stone sill and lintel – the latter with tiny dentils under an ogee-head moulding. More windows to match, but now with top-hung casements. The tiled roof bisects an old sign on the gable wall of the adjacent premises, so it must postdate 1877. Curved wall on the corner of Church Street and Market Place, with brick eaves, concrete tiles on the roof. On the first floor, a square window with stone sill, splayed lintel, but now a modern top-hung casement. A narrow adjunct might be the remnant of a stable with loft over, belonging to New Swan yard.

The East Side of Church Street

New Swan, Church Street

The ground floor of the main street elevation has two bays of windows plus a central doorway; three storeys. Chamfered plinth, then stucco, deeply lined rustication below the string, plain above, except for the quoins at the corners. There are Doric pilasters on each side of a central doorway containing double doors with fielded panels having flush-moulded edges. The bay window is tripartite, with quarter-round ends; the flat central light is an 8-over-8 sash, while the curved ends are 4-over-4. Above, to the right, a bay window, again tripartite, 6-over-6 in the middle, but with straight canted sides containing 2-over-2 sashes (with horns). Another, to the right, with 8-over-8 panes. On the second floor, there are no windows in the Church Street elevation.

On the north elevation, facing the yard, all the windows have been redone, some with top-hung casements. The front range retains evidence of two good Georgian windows having splayed brick heads; one is blocked, and the other has been replaced by a casement window in a square aperture. Two more blocked Georgian windows on the first floor; that nearest to Church Street retains its exposed sash box. In the gable, a 3-over-6 sash window in broad frames set back. Otherwise, just one doorway; 10-pane over-door light, modern door.

On the elevation facing Derby Lane, the rustication to the ground floor returns as far as a sash window framed by Tuscan Doric pilasters and a canopy. The remainder of this elevation is in plain stucco, and there are no quoins on the right-hand corner. The set-back door is modern. To the right, two tripartite windows with pegged frames and top-hung casements – secondary. On the first floor, three 6-over-6 sash windows, set well back.

82 Long Street: side elevation in Church Street (Tags)

In 1878, this was the *Coffee Tavern* – an unusual manifestation of the Temperance Movement. The Church Street elevation of this building is of four bays and three storeys. On the ground floor, a square plate glass window is modern but it may be fitted into an older surround; two brackets under a chamfered sill, moulded reveals, and volutes support the canopy. The doorway has Tuscan pilasters supporting an architrave-cornice and pediment. Next, a smaller window but with similar details to its counterpart. On the first floor, three 2-over-2 sash windows with chamfered stone sills and moulded surrounds. Nearer the corner, double console brackets support a wide chamfered sill under coupled 2-over-2 sash windows with moulded reveals, under a single pediment. On the top floor, three 2-over-2 sash windows with stone sills and moulded surrounds. To the right, two paired console brackets carry the panel with moulded sides that was intended for the *Coffee Tavern* sign.

Long Street: 82-6 (Around the Corner of East Side of Church Street)

82 Long Street: Long Street Elevation

(see *p.201 for the other elevation)*

Modern shop front, and a narrow entry to the right. On the first floor, three windows like those on the side elevation, but the window with pediment in the centre also has eared architraves. The second floor windows stand on a moulded string: 2-over-2 sashes with moulded reveals and straight heads. Projecting eaves over paired console brackets. Hipped tiled roof.

84 Long Street (Natural Nails and Toolbox)

In the late 19th century this (with No. 86), was known as the *Board Inn*. Now two small shops with modern frontages to the ground floor. The first floor is stuccoed, with an eaves parapet. Three 6-over-6 sash windows with horns, but set well back. Red-tiled pitched roof.

86 Long Street (Scope) (also *see* p.201)

Long Street elevation: Stuccoed façade of three bays and three storeys; modern shop front. On the first floor, three 8-over-8 sash windows, set back; that to the left has brackets under the stone sill. On the second floor, to left and right, 4-over-4 sash windows within moulded frame and with stone sills over little consoles. The middle window is tripartite, with a 4-over-4 sash in the centre and 2-over-2 sashes on each side. Moulded cornice and eaves parapet, wrapped around a tight curve on the south-east corner.

Long Street: The North Side of Long Street, West to East

Grendon House

Nineteenth-century stuccoed façade of three bays and three storeys. On the ground floor, a pretty door-case with fluted pilasters and a broken triangular pediment; rectangular over-door light with fancy glazing bars – the door has fielded panels with raised moulded edges. In the middle, a good bow window with fielded panels flat against the wall to left and right. Right of the window, a big low elliptical rusticated archway with key block. On the first floor, three sash windows (6-over-6 and 8-over-8) with stone or rendered sills and flat rusticated heads with key blocks. The second floor has three 3-over-3 sash windows with similar sills and heads. Moulded eaves, old blue tiles, integral brick stack.

59 *Grendon House.*

THE WHITE HART HERITAGE CENTRE

Formerly a public house. A long façade of late 19th-/early 20th-century mock timber-framing. Details on the ground floor include a chamfered plinth, Tuscan flat pilasters, and etched glass pub windows. On the first floor, applied timbers, painted black, and white pebbledash. Coved eaves, then a swept-out red-tiled roof. The roof-lights and dormers are probably 20th-century.

2/6 LONG STREET

Wide early 20th-century façade: the hopper-heads carry the date 1901. The ground floor is of red brick with stone dressings; the windows are of three-lights with big panes, having side-hung casements in the middle. The single unit to the left has its own front door, but the other two are divided by an entry which is marked by a pretty arcade of short Tuscan colonettes. Shaped corbels and a stone band under applied false framing and pebble-dash on the first floor, where there are three four-light windows. Above the eaves, the middle of the façade is marked by an over-sized gable, now with a modern window. Red-tiled roof, brick stacks; one dormer with canted sides looks relatively modern.

8 LONG STREET

Pebble-dashed front of one three-storeyed bay; now with plastic windows and a concrete-tile roof.

10 LONG STREET (NEW IMAGES)

Red bricked façade (Flemish bond) of two three-storeyed bays. The ground floor has been rebuilt. On the first and second floors, both windows now have concrete sills and plastic window-frames, but the reveals are original, with console brackets under flat pediments. Wooden eaves with paired console soffit brackets. Hipped blue-tile roof. Two cottages to the rear have been rebuilt.

60 *10 Long Street (New Images).*

Memorial Hall

The Memorial Hall stands on the site of the Garden Row yard. Opened on 6 September 1962, this flat-roofed building presents a brick and concrete façade to the street, with a tall, narrow glass panel near each corner. The main front is to the east, where eight bays of concrete and glass are broken by a lower block containing the entrance lobby and services.

Library

Flat-roofed building of 1966 in brick and glass, quieter than its neighbour but bland.

32/34 Long Street *(The Clock,* formerly *The White Bear)*

May have originally consisted of three main bays, but now of four, all of three storeys. A straight joint is just apparent between the left-hand bay and the other three, and originally there was an arch to a wide entry here. A chamfered plinth and an entablature define the bottom and top of the ground-floor bays, three of which have paired sash windows over aprons; the doorway in the middle of the main façade is flanked by flat pilasters and contains a three-panelled door and rectangular over-light. All the windows

61 *32/34 Long Street* (The Clock, *formerly* The White Bear).

on the first floor (6-over-6 but all replacements) have flat splayed arches with plain key blocks; the 3-over-3 windows on the second floor have moulded key blocks. The front slope of the roof is in slate, but the back is now tiled. A clock and a pub sign hang on the front wall. The ground floor has been substantially refitted with modern pub fixtures.

36 LONG STREET (PINOCCHIO)

Over-sized modern shop front to ground floor, pebble-dashed above. Two poor-quality softwood-framed windows (after 1960s) to first floor. Of the original front, only the brick eaves are visible. Old blue tiles on the roof. The two-storeyed brick range to the rear is of more interest and historical potential, having five mill-style windows with elliptical heads, but now unfortunately all bricked up at various times.

38 LONG STREET (GOLD AND SILVER)

A former inn: nos. 38 and 40 were once the *George and Dragon*, C112 on the 1786 Plan (*see* Fig. 7). Modern shop front to the ground floor. On the pebble-dashed first floor, three 6-over-6 sash windows (frames set back); rendered sills, flat splayed lintels. Dentilled brick eaves, modern red clay tiles on the pitched roof. The yard to the right is fronted by a gateway with a four-centred arch flanked by pilasters, all of timber. The low brick range along the south side of the yard has blocked apertures with segmental heads – probably stabling or other services associated with the former inn. The south end of the range is now a small shop; some of the detailing complements the gateway.

40 LONG STREET (FOUR SEASONS)

A former inn: nos. 38 and 40 were once the *George and Dragon*, C112 on the 1786 Plan (*see* Fig. 7).

42 LONG STREET (BEAUTIFULLY YOURS)

Modern shop front. On the first floor, a rendered sill band, 2-over-2 sash windows having rusticated splayed heads with key blocks. Moulded bricks along the eaves, old blue-tiled pitched roof with gable parapet to the left.

(There appears to be no number 44.)

46 LONG STREET (ATHERSTONE CARPETS)

Probably built as a small branch of Woolworths in their inter-war style. The building has a new shop front and has been refurbished under a heightened roof. On the first floor, flat pilasters and a good shaped parapet.

50 LONG STREET (NEWS SHOP)

A two-storeyed brick façade below a concrete-tiled pitched roof, now with no stacks. On the ground floor, the plank door to the left is at the front of a narrow extension, plausibly with stairs to the upper floors; the shop front might be Edwardian. On the first floor, one blocked window with a segmental arch and two late Victorian or Edwardian 2-over-2 sash windows with brick sills and moulded lintels.

Behind 50 Long Street (formerly Hatton's Hat Factory)

A group of mill buildings of industrial archaeological interest. The first building along the lane has a good west elevation of four three-storeyed bays. All the windows have brick sills and segmental brick arches. Some of the small-paned iron-framed windows survive; others have been redone in wood. One of the bays has loading doors at each level and a wooden crane jib projects out from the eaves. The south gable wall is of three three-storeyed bays. More industrial buildings to the rear would repay further investigation.

52 Long Street (Country Classics)

Two bays of three storeys, brick in Flemish bond. On the ground floor, an entry or stair-doorway to the left, modern shop front to the right. On both of the upper floors, the windows have stepped lintels with key blocks; the window frames are replacements. Dentilled eaves, tiled roof and two integral end stacks.

54/54a Long Street (First Choice)

Modern shop fronts. On the first floor, good red bricks laid in English bond. Six good 6-over-6 sash windows with broad frames almost flush with the brickwork, chamfered brick sills, barely elliptical heads with soldier-bond bricks. Blue/green slate roof.

56/58 Long Street (Windridge and Connexions)

Ground floor rendered. To the left, an elliptical arch with keystone over an entry, then modern plate glass shop fronts. On the first floor, five bays of 6-over-6 sash windows, unfortunately now redone as top-hung casements; rendered sills, flat splayed heads with key blocks. On the second floor, 3-over-3 sashes, again now with top-hung casements. Moulded eaves, pitched tiled roof.

60 Long Street (S&O Supplies)

Two bays, three storeys, red brick in Flemish bond. On the ground floor, a modern adaptation of an older shop front. The first and second floors are defined by stone sill bands; flat, incised, splayed window-heads with key blocks. The sashes have been replaced by 3-over-6 top-hung casements. Moulded eaves, blue-tiled roof, Victorian stack to left, and a tiny window in the gable.

62 Long Street (Dolphin Fish Bar)

Modern shop front, entry doorway to right. Two bays, three storeys, brick in Flemish bond. The casement window frames are replacements within the original wide rectangular apertures. Pitched roof, blue tiles.

64 Long Street (Goldenbuy)

Single bay, three storeys, brick in Flemish bond. Modern shop front to the ground floor. The first- and second-floor windows have stone sills and volute-bracketed canopies; the window frames have been replaced. Moulded eaves, decorative hopper.

66 Long Street (Ellenkays)

Single bay, three storeys, painted brick. On the ground floor, an entry doorway to the left, set back under an elliptical arch. Late 19th-century shop front with modern adaptations? On the first floor, the sill band is now broken by an enlarged aperture containing a modern window, but the original window arch remains – flat, splayed, rusticated, with a key block. Moulded eaves, blue tile roof.

68/70 Long Street

The fenestration pattern for Nos. 68 and 70 has been altered. Originally they comprised a single building with a façade of five bays:

68 Long Street (Sue & Sallys)

Two bays of three storeys, rendered façade. In the middle of the ground floor, a modern bow window; to the left and right, semi-circular rusticated arches with key blocks; on the right the door fills the arch, but on the left there is an over-door light. On the first floor a lead band is wrapped over the string course; plastic window frames under flat, splayed and rusticated arches with key blocks. The second-floor windows are similar, but with rendered sills. Moulded eaves, shallow-pitched tiled roof, old brick stack to left.

70 Long Street (The Good Life)

On the ground floor, an entry doorway to the left, a modern shop front to the right. On the first floor, a sill band, two windows under flat, splayed heads with key blocks; plastic window frames. On the second floor the windows have rendered sills, flat, splayed heads with key blocks, and plastic windows. Moulded eaves, shallow-pitched tiled roof.

72 Long Street (Cobs and Coffee)

Inter-war (?) brick building, two storeys of two bays, with several horizontal bands. Modern shop front to the ground floor, with an entry doorway to the right. On the first floor, two wide plastic windows.

74 LONG STREET (LEWIS)

Two bays of three storeys – a stuccoed Regency façade. On the ground floor, bay windows and, to the right, an entry doorway with a semi-circular head. On the first floor, two panels are set back under round arches and linked by a string. The windows in each panel have rendered sills and splayed heads with key blocks; 6-over-6 sashes in broad frames. On the second floor, one glazed lunette under a shaped parapet. Pitched tiled roof.

76 LONG STREET (SHIRLEY ANN)

One bay of two storeys plus attic; brick, partly rebuilt. On the ground floor, a late, Victorian or Edwardian shop front with a moulded entablature and an over-light above the door. On the first floor, a replacement 10-over-10 sash window. Moulded eaves, pitched tile roof, replacement gabled dormer with side-hung casements.

78/80 LONG STREET (NATIONWIDE BUILDING SOCIETY)

A modern, bland two-storey façade of stretcher-bond brick, rendered corners, aluminium window frames; deep cornice band under projecting eaves. Tiled roof with hipped end to Church Street.

82/86 LONG STREET

See p.205 after Church Street, east side.

62 *74 Long Street (Lewis).*

88 LONG STREET (PRIMA)

Corner plot, brick to Market Street, ashlar facing to Long Street (*see* p. 201 for the Market Street elevation). The front elevation is three bays of three storeys, but the ground floor is now taken up by a modern shop front. The first floor is marked by a moulded sill band. The three windows are 2-over-2 sashes, set behind projecting moulded reveals and head with flat canopies on brackets. The windows on the second floor also stand on a moulded sill band; bracketed sills, moulded reveals and heads, but no canopies. Above, there is another stone band, then projecting wooden eaves with shaped brackets. The tiled roof is hipped at both ends.

88A LONG STREET (WILLIAM HILL)

Three-storeyed stone-clad façade, with a modern shop front to the ground floor. The first floor is marked by a sill-band with chamfered top. The big, wide tripartite window has a 2-over-2 sash at the centre, flanked by 1-over-1 at each side. The window is articulated by four Doric pilasters, which rise to shaped heads with keystones, and these, in turn, support a moulded head-band. On the second floor, another sill band for two windows with bracketed sills, moulded reveals and head, with 2-over-2 sashes. Above again, another narrow moulded stone band, then projecting wooden eaves with shaped brackets. Hipped roof, red brick stack. Late 19th-century?

90 LONG STREET (BARCLAYS BANK) *(See* Fig. 47)

Painted brick façade in Flemish bond; three bays of three storeys. On the ground floor, some decent replicated brackets under a canopy, but the windows and doorway are modern. On the first floor, the windows stand on a sill band with a moulded top. All three 2-over-2 sash windows have shouldered architraves with mouldings, but that at the centre is distinguished by a segmental pediment over brackets. Another sill band on the second floor has a discrete soffit moulding; three 2-over-2 sash windows have moulded architraves. The projecting eaves with shaped brackets stand on a moulded band. The gabled roof has blue tiles.

92/92A LONG STREET (THE WEDDING CENTRE AND PERSONALLY YOURS)

Three wide bays of three storeys in red/brown bricks laid in Flemish bond, the ground floor having two shop fronts. That to the left retains a central recessed glazed door and over-door light, fronted by a little canopy with diminutive central pediment; above all this, there is a bracketed canopy with integral drop-down awning box. The shop window to the right is modern, with no doorway, the two premises now containing one business. Three windows on the first floor have stone sills, splayed and rusticated lintels with keystones; the sashes with broad frames have lost their glazing bars. The three windows on the second floor have stone sills and lintels without keystones; the modern window frames incorporate top-hung lights. Moulded stone eaves and shallow parapet. Tiled roof, tall brick stack to the left, lower blue-brick stack to the right.

94 Long Street (The Old Bakery)

The applied ashlar façade is three bays wide and three storeys high. On the ground floor, to the left, is an entry doorway with a semi-circular moulded arch. The shop front could be *c.*1900, were it not for the off-centre recessed and glazed door and, above that and the larger shop windows, the glazed frieze of leaded lights – possibly inter-war; there is also a retractable awning box. To the right of the shop window, a stone plinth with moulded top, and an elaborate window. The latter has a stone sill supported by four shaped brackets, blind recessed panels to left and right, and a 2-over-2 sash at the centre, having a low segmental arched head; all of this is topped by a moulded canopy with brackets and finials. On the first floor the sill band has foliate stops at each end. Three 2-over-2 sash windows with segmental heads have shouldered architraves with cable-moulded reveals, shaped keystones and segmental pediments – cranky but very swanky. Three smaller windows on the second floor have shaped, flat-fronted architraves; unfortunately the 2-over-2 frames are now in plastic, and a plastic fascia has been added along the front of the bracketed and moulded eaves. Shallow-pitched, tiled roof with one off-centre stack, and another to the right.

96 Long Street (Lloyds Bank)

Three bays of three storeys in red brick laid in Flemish bond. Modern bank front on the ground floor. On the first floor, three 6-over-6 sashes, standing on a sill band and set back, with simple brick reveals; splayed heads with

63 *94 Long Street (The Old Bakery).*

shaped keystones. On the second floor, the sashes are 3-over-3, with rendered or stone sills, splayed heads with shaped keystones. Moulded eaves and low stone parapet. Clay-tiled shallow-pitched roof, red brick stacks with blue bands. Nineteenth-century.

98/100 Long Street (Keri Ann and Vaughan Davis)

These premises occupy a long street frontage of five bays, having a slightly projecting central portion and recessed corners, probably late-18th-century. On the left side a 20th-century shop front and a doorway to several flats; on the right, the front of an Edwardian post office in good ashlar, with four main panels framed by Tuscan pilasters, all topped by a classical frieze and cornice. In the two bays to the left, the storey band is flush to the brickwork, and on both floors the 2-over-2 sash windows have very simple rendered sills and lintels – either they have been redone or possibly this end of the building was lower status. In the remainder of the façade the storey band projects, and the 2-over-2 sashes have splayed lintels with keystones. Moulded eaves with diminutive parapet; roof not visible from street.

102 Long Street (TNT)

Three bays plus one on the right set slightly back, three storeys, with rendered storey bands; Flemish bond. On the ground floor, a blue brick chamfered plinth. To the left, on the ground floor, a good doorway; two stone steps, Doric pilasters, broken pediment. Bolection moulded and fielded panels on the door and the reveals, and a good semi-circular over-door fanlight. Along the rest of the ground floor, three 6-over-6 sash windows with stone sills, rusticated splayed lintels with keystones. Similar windows on the first and second floors, probably all renewed but well executed. Moulded eaves and low stone parapet, shallow-pitched roof. Eighteenth-century.

106 Long Street (Liberal Club)

Two bays, three storeys, stuccoed. On the ground floor, two 2-over-2 sash windows with shouldered and eared architraves. The narrow doorway squashed in to the left looks like an afterthought, despite the moulding on the lintel; the equally narrow doorway at the extreme right of the façade has an un-moulded head and is almost certainly secondary. Presumably the entrance was formerly off the entry to the right, but there is no way of checking from the building evidence, as the wall there has been rebuilt. A sill band marks the first floor, where two windows with shouldered and eared architraves contain rotting 20th-century casement frames. On the second floor, only the left-hand window is the correct size; it has a moulded wooden architrave and a stone or rendered sill, and now has poor side-hung casements. The window aperture to the right has been deepened, and again has a poor modern frame. Narrow moulded eaves, blue-tiled roof, brick end stacks.

108 Long Street (Formerly Jenkins' Bakery)

Two wide bays of three storeys, stuccoed. On the ground floor, to the left, a narrow entry through an archway with a round head. At the centre, an interesting shop front includes a recessed glazed door to the left and a two-panel window to the right, all under a canopied head. Further right, a shallow plinth below a window with a stone sill, plain surrounds, formerly with two fixed lights but now restored to 8-over-8 sashes. On the first floor, two good 8-over-8 sash windows with horns, stone sills, projecting architraves and elliptical pediments rising from the level of a moulded string. The two windows on the second floor are 4-over-4 sashes with stone sills and plain surrounds. Shallow eaves, blue-tiled roof, off-centre ridge stack. Early 19th-century.

The portion of a massive classical column that stands adjacent to the south east corner of 108 Long Street is all that remains standing of the former Corn Exchange.

Lloyd's Pharmacy

The west corner plot between Long Street and Ratcliffe Street is occupied by a modern building of three tall storeys, brick in stretcher bond, with the main doorway in a big diagonal face.

64 *108 Long Street (Formerly Jenkins' Bakery)*

110 LONG STREET (HSBC BANK)

The east corner of Long Street and Ratcliffe Street is occupied by what is currently the HSBC Bank. Quoins only on the north end of the west elevation and the east end of the south. Between these, the two main stuccoed façades are united by a massive string with soffit moulding which divides the ground and first floors. The west elevation is of three bays. On the first and second floors there are 6-over-6 sash windows with moulded sills and architraves, and flat canopies; those on the first floor also have aprons. A narrow diagonal bay on the corner contains the bank doorway on the ground floor and sash windows above. The south elevation has three bays of similar windows; those on the second floor are 3-over-6. Concrete tile roof, hipped at the corner, shaped and stuccoed stacks. The hopper at the top of one of the rainwater pipes bears the date 1913, but the Listed Building description attributes the building to 1837, by J.A. Hansom.

ALBERT HALL

The large porch at the front of the building has a flat canopy with cyma-moulded edges and is supported on eccentric twin columns, but is it secondary? Behind the porch is the gabled main façade. The brick corner pilasters are heavily rusticated below and panelled above, then, near the top, there are stone plaques with foliate designs. On the first floor, a big tripartite window with round arches and four Gothic columns having composite capitals, then a lattice panel above – Italian Gothic, and lots of fun. Up again, a band of giant nail-head decoration, then a narrow string, and a big date-stone – 1876. Another band, with foliate stops, bears the name of the building. In the gable, which has a moulded stone top, there is a round window with cruciform glazing bars. Blue slate pitched roof.

122 LONG STREET (DENHAM HOUSE)

Four bays, three storeys, Flemish bond red brickwork, once with very fine joints, but re-pointed. The façade looks clean, but the bricks are pock-marked, suggesting that they might have been sand-blasted rather than cleaned by more gentle means. The ground floor has a blue brick chamfered plinth. The front door is in the second bay from the left; modern replica fluted pilasters rise to Ionic capitals and support a flat canopy, a restrained effort devoid of a proper cornice. The door is set within panelled reveals, those at the bottom flush, and those above fielded. To the left and right of the door are 8-over-8 sashes with horns within narrow stone sills, plain reveals and rusticated splayed lintels with stepped giant keystones. Intact folding shutters can be seen within. The right-hand bay retains an elliptical rusticated arch with giant stepped keystone over double doors with flush panels. On the first floor, the four 6-over-6 sash windows have stone sills, plain reveals, and incised splayed lintels with keystones; those on the second floor are 3-over-3 but otherwise similar. Moulded and modillion eaves and a shallow parapet. Blue tiled roof with parapet gables, stack to the left.

Long Street: The South Side of Long Street, East to West

Note: The first two buildings are beyond the limit of the Gazetteer.

155 Long Street, The Conservative Club (Atherstone House)

This impressive late 17th- or early 18th-century building is described by Bob Meeson in Chapter Five (*see* p.55).

175 Long Street (The *Old Swan*)

Building History Six

This has an impressive timber-framed elevation that disguises the complicated history of the building. The only known fragment of a cruck-framed building in the town places its date firmly in the medieval period. The wide frontage masks an extremely complex sequence of alterations, best interpreted by reference to the description in Building History Six.

133 Long Street (Garner Canning & Sale)

Three bays of three storeys; good red brick laid in Flemish bond with narrow joints. Part of a chamfered stone plinth remains to the left, and an entry with a splayed brick flat arch to the right. Between them, a modern shop front, but retaining a possibly original doorway; flat pilasters support a broken pediment, and while the door is now glass, the half-round over-door light is very good – late 18th- or early 19th-century. A plain stone sill band on the first floor, then two 6-over-6 sashes, and one 8-over-8, all set back, with plain brick reveals and below rusticated splayed heads with keystones. Three 3-over-3 sashes on the second floor have stone sills and similar heads to those below. Moulded eaves, tiled roof, end-stacks.

131 Long Street (Anchor Print)

Hard red brick with thin joints. Most of the ground floor is taken up by a big (Edwardian?) shop front incorporating a wide doorway set back behind canted windows. On the shop window surround, foliate corbels carry barley-sugar-twisted colonettes with annulets. To the right of the shop-front, a doorway with rectangular over-door light and a stone lintel. On the first floor are three four-pane sash windows with stone sills and lintels, and with stopped quarter-round mouldings to the reveals. Moulded eaves, blue-tiled roof.

129 Long Street (Bank House)

A handsome façade behind metal railings on a low wall of *c.*1800. The date (1711) on the front elevation is misleading, as the architectural style is somewhat later; the Listed Building Description plausibly suggests *c.*1775 (*See* p.59 and Figs. 15-16).

A long and interesting façade of five three-storeyed bays, that in the centre projecting slightly forward, and those to each side being different widths. The composition is held together by a chamfered plinth; stone sill band to the first floor, moulded eaves and a stone parapet. The walls are of red brick laid in Flemish bond, while the pitched roof is covered with green slates; it has parapet gables and two ridge stacks. In the left-hand bay, an elliptical rusticated arch marks a carriage entrance; the 6-over-6 sash with horns has plain reveals and a splayed brick head. The 3-over-3 sash on the second floor has a stone sill and splayed brick head.

In the middle of the three-bay central portion a good doorway; three stone steps, Tuscan Doric pilasters, but with fluting at the top, and a triangular pediment. There is a good semi-circular fanlight over the six-panel door. On each side of the door, there are tripartite windows with volute-bracketed stone sills, Tuscan Doric architrave and mullions, and a full canopy frieze. The windows in the centre are 6-over-6 sashes, and 2-over-2 at each side. On the first floor, the centre is marked by a more elaborate 6-over-6 window having stone, shouldered architraves, and a fluted flat canopy above. To left and right, there are 6-over-6 sashes with splayed brick heads. On the second floor too, the central window (3-over-3) has stone architraves, but with no canopy. Those to the left and right have stone sills and splayed brick heads. The wide right-hand bay now has a three-part assembly of doorway and two 8-over-8 windows, united between panelled pilasters and beneath a single canopy frieze – probably around 1800. The door has six flush panels and a very good rectangular over-door fanlight. The windows on the first and second floors are similar to those in the left bay.

127 LONG STREET (*WHITE HORSE*)

Edwardian tiled façade to the ground floor, with etched glass pub window. On the first floor, white-painted Flemish bond brickwork, three bays. To left and right, modern side-hung casements; between them, but off-centre, a tripartite casement window. Elaborate brick eaves with dentils and dog-tooth. Blue tile pitched roof with two hipped dormers (casement windows). Brick ridge stack.

65 *127 Long Street* (White Horse).

125 Long Street (Bargain Booze)

On the ground floor, an entry to the left, otherwise a modern shop-front. Above, Flemish bond brickwork with grey headers. On the first floor, two 8-over-8 sash windows, rendered sills, rusticated splayed lintels with key-blocks. On the second floor, 4-over-4 sashes, otherwise as on first floor; also a tiny central window of four small panes. Moulded eaves; slates on shallow-pitched roof with end stacks.

119/123 Long Street (Somerfield)

Modern; three bays, three storeys, flat and bland.

113/117 Long Street (Workforce and 19 Gales)

A wide façade of three bays, three storeys, Flemish bond: possibly around 1820-40. The ground floor probably began as an integrated front with three little shops, each with similar windows. Chamfered stone sill. Under each shop window, there are flat wooden panels with flush-moulded edges. Each shop window is of two large panes divided by slender columns with diminutive capitals; elliptical heads, then above, a bracketed canopy frieze incorporating egg and dart decoration. On the first floor, three 8-over-8 sash windows with nosings, exposed sash boxes, stone sills, incised splayed lintels with keystones. On the second floor, four 8-over-8 sashes, here with quarter-round mouldings. Board eaves, blue tile roof, end stacks rebuilt.

111 Long Street (Hospice Book Shop)

Two narrow bays of three storeys, Flemish bond; 19th-century. On the ground floor, to the right, a four-panel door to the flats above. Next, the shop front in three parts; set back glazed door and two large windows with elliptical heads, divided by a round mullion – picks up the theme of 113/117. On the first floor, two 6-over-6 sash windows with horns; stone sills, quarter-round moulding on the lintels. Second floor probably had 3-over-6 sashes, but now the lower portions are on horizontal pivots. Board eaves. Blue tile roof with fretted red ridge tiles. One brick ridge stack to the left, with dentils.

107/109 Long Street (HBS Household and Snobs)

Three bays, three storeys, red brick in Flemish bond. Victorian Gothic. On the ground floor, a good shop front across both properties, under a canopy with volutes at each end – late 19th century. Originally the outer corners of the shop windows were quarter-round, but only one of them has survived. The two shop-fronts are separated by three big fielded panels with moulded edges. No. 109 has the narrower shop front, the door part-panelled but glazed above, and with a tall rectangular over-door light. No. 107 has the double front. On the first floor, three 6-over-6 sashes with horns (all replacements); stone sills, and the green-painted stone lintels have good hood moulds with foliate stops. On the second floor, replacement 3-over-3 sashes with similar sills and lintels. Flat stone bands at the eaves has incised acanthus leaf motif. Blue tile roof. Red fretted ridge tiles. Brick stacks with yellow bands.

105 Long Street (NFU Mutual)

Two bays, three storeys, Flemish bond. Modern shop front. First floor; 1-over-1 (large pane) sashes; there are upturned volutes on the shouldered architraves, which have round corners – the Victorians are marking the arrival of plate glass. Similarly on the second floor, but the windows rise into bracketed eaves, the latter with a saw-tooth canopy. Shallow-pitched slate roof, no chimney-stacks.

101 Long Street (Martins, formerly Dillons)

On the corner of Coleshill Street, a three-bay, three-storey stuccoed façade. Modern shop front to ground floor. In the right-hand bay, a modern projecting window bay at first- and second-floor level. The other two bays have 2-over-2 sash windows; rendered sills, plain reveals, dentils and shallow ogees on the lintels – Victorian or Edwardian. On the second floor, the sash windows have been replaced by plastic successors. Plain gable. Along Coleshill Street the back range is old brick, but who would now know?

99 Long Street (*Red Lion Hotel*)

A wide frontage of four bays, two storeys. The outer bays project forwards and have steeply-pitched gable parapets. The recessed central portion has a wider gable parapet of lower pitch. The parapets hide a complicated roofscape; one wonders how old it might be. Back on the ground floor, a rendered chamfered sill, and a milestone ('London 100, Lutterworth 17¾, Lichfield 15'). Unlike the building, the latter is listed. In the angle between the left-hand wing and the recessed front, a low metal rail supported by thin round balusters encloses a quarter-round area – not much more than

66 *99 Long Street* (Red Lion Hotel).

three feet wide. Both wings have tripartite windows with rendered or stone sills. In the middle bay, one more tripartite window on the ground floor, and two above, but to the right there is a wide elliptical carriageway arch; modern double doors, one with a wicket.

On the elevation to Coleshill Street, a long back range, part rendered, but then red brick. Two storeys, blue-tiled pitched roof. Various sash windows with stone sills, most with splayed brick lintels; one later tripartite window with chamfered brick sill. The only doorway is secondary. Next along Coleshill Street, a three-bay extension. Rendered plinth; central doorway with etched glass doors. The ground-floor windows have heavy frames under segmental arches. Three 2-over-2 sash windows on the first floor. Late Victorian or Edwardian.

97 Long Street (Lloyd's Pharmacy)

One of the best façades left in Atherstone; mid-18th century. Four bays, two-and-a-half storeys; stuccoed. Rendered, chamfered plinth. To the left, a service doorway having reeded architraves with corner blocks; the door has six fielded panels with flush-moulded edges. Right of this, the main doorway is framed by three-quarter-round Tuscan Doric pilasters, extra blocks at frieze level; the pediment was broken by a round over-door light, although that is now just a board; the panelled arch soffit survives, with beads. Panelled reveals, flush at the bottom, then fielded above, with flush-moulded edges. The door has six panels, flush at the bottom, but fielded above, with reeds on the leading edges. To the right of the doorway, a good two-bay shop front; three-quarter-round wooden corners, and a canopy with thin bands of foliage, part-glazed double doors – good late-Victorian work. On the first floor, four windows have stone sills, simple reveals, exposed sash boxes, 6-over-6 sashes; rusticated splayed heads with big keystones. Swanky eaves band, then an impressive parapet; flat panels between four balustraded sections. Cyma recta and hollow mouldings on the balustrade, and fluted urns at each end. Pitched blue tile roof. To the left, a simple gable with a casement window; but to the right, a shaped gable parapet, now broken by a narrow stack. Before the adjoining building was constructed,

67 *97 Long Street (Lloyd's Pharmacy).*

the gable would have been an impressive marker when seen from along the street to the west. The building now has two gables on the rear elevation but, according to the Listed Buildings description, this arrangement masks what began as an L-shaped plan-form.

95 Long Street (formerly *The Earl of Richmond*)

Lined stucco; three storeys, two main bays. The recessed panel to the left steps out at each floor level – a neat device to accommodate a site plan with an angled front, and respecting the parapet frieze on the adjoining building. There, on the ground floor, a doorway with quarter-round moulded reveals and an over-door light with a round head. Good door with four flat panels, raised moulding and rectangular fillet. On the main front, at ground-floor level, a chamfered plinth. To the left, a stone bay window with canted sides and plate glass sashes with segmental heads. To the right of the bay, a secondary group including a door and two windows with a canopy over. On the first floor, two 2-over-2 sash windows; the stone architraves have shoulders, shaped ears, and segmental heads turned out at the end – 19th-century. The attic is marked by a moulded storey band; two windows with bracketed sills. Modillion eaves, pitched slate roof; gable end stacks.

93 Long Street (The *Three Tuns* Hotel)

Three bays, three storeys. Banded rustication over a chamfered plinth. To the left, Tuscan columns support a canopy over replacement double doors. In the

68 *95 Long Street (formerly* The Earl of Richmond).

middle, a big multi-paned window with a canted recessed centre, a canopy above. The joinery is modern and although it respects the recess, this bears no relationship to what appears in the Listed Building Description. Right again, a wide round arch over an entry under the end of the building. Above the sill band there are quoins at the corners. Three sash windows: 8-over-8 to the left, 6-over-6 to the right; the 8-over-8 in the middle is distinguished by shouldered architraves and a bracketed canopy. On the top floor two 4-over-8 sashes, but the third window is now a 3-over-6 casement. Moulded eaves, pitched slate roof, ridge stack backs onto entry.

91 Long Street (Greggs)

Two bays, three storeys. Modern shop front, modern casements, plastic eaves, concrete tile pitched roof, but stack on left gable is old.

89 Long Street (W.C. Masters and Son)

One bay of three storeys; painted brick in Flemish bond. Modern shop front. On the first and second floors the windows have splayed brick heads, but the sashes have been replaced by casements. Diagonal bricks at the eaves; red tile pitched roof, no stacks.

87 Long Street (Aladdin's Cave)

Two bays, three storeys. Modern shop front. Pebble-dash above. On the first floor, two 6-over-6 sash windows with exposed sash boxes. On the second floor, 2-over-2 sashes with rendered sills and splayed lintels. Diagonal bricks at the eaves. Blue tiles on the pitched roof; a stack to the right.

85 Long Street

Three bays, three storeys, taller than its neighbours. Modern shop fronts; on the right, an entry under a round arch (formerly leading to Gutteridges Yard, between the Hand and Bottle and the Bluebell [Fig. 45]) On the first floor, a sill band; three windows with exposed sash boxes nearly flush to the wall, but the replacement sashes are 1-over-1; rusticated splayed heads with key-blocks. On the top floor, the windows have retained their 3-over-3 sashes; stone sills, rusticated lintels with key-blocks. Shallow wooden eaves parapet, steeply-pitched tiled roof, central stack.

81/83 Long Street (Atherstone Gallery and Raj Mahal)

Three bays, three storeys, stuccoed. Modern shop front on the left. To the right, an older shop front with a two-light window; boarded reveals to the recessed doorway; the door has two fielded panels below, glass above. A central doorway gives access to the flats above. On the first floor, two windows are now plastic; that to the left retains the stone sill and moulded wooden sash boxes, but there is now a top-hung casement. On the top floor, two plastic windows to the right. That to the left has a stone sill, moulded sash boxes, 3-over-3 sashes. Bracketed eaves, pitched tiled roof, no stacks.

79 LONG STREET (SUPERDRUG)

Modern shop front. On the first floor, two casement windows under round arches – three blind roundels above. Plain red brick, plain eaves, red tiled roof; no stack, gable is rendered.

77 LONG STREET

One bay, two storeys, stuccoed. A modern shop front has been inserted between two fluted pilasters which support giant volutes. Modern three-light casement with transom on the first floor. Plain eaves, pitched red tile roof.

75 LONG STREET (EVERY OCCASION)

Wide two-storeyed façade. Modern shop front. On the first floor, two widely separated 8-over-8 sash windows, hidden sash boxes, rendered sills; the heads fit up to the moulded wooden eaves with brackets. Pitched red tile roof, one stack.

THE ARCADE

Built 1985. Modern shops on either side of an arcade with a big glazed panel under a semi-circular arch; yellow and blue brick details.

69 LONG STREET (DAY'S, FORMERLY THE *DRUIDS ARMS* [FIG. 42])

Inter-war (?) shop front, but redolent of Atherstone in its 19th-century heyday; door with four flat panels in the middle. On each side, there are two big four-pane panels, removable; narrow glazed top-lights, then a canopy with brackets at each end. To the right, a four-panel door under a flat lintel and an ogee panel that led to Druids Arms Yard. Painted Flemish bond brickwork on the first floor. Two 8-over-8 sash windows with horns – good recent carpentry. Incised splayed heads with key-blocks under brick eaves with shaped modillions. Pitched roof, blue tiles, end ridge stacks.

67 LONG STREET (FORMERLY VIKING)

Modern shop front. Above, painted brick in Flemish bond. On each of the upper floors there are two windows with moulded stone sills, splayed heads with fluted keystones, 18th-century. The top-hung casements are completely out of character. Good moulded and bracketed eaves, but then a concrete-tiled roof; no stacks. We must ask why this was permitted on a listed building.

69 *63/63a Long Street (Congraves Sweets and Treats, formerly Daniels).*

63/63a Long Street (Congraves Sweets and Treats, formerly Daniels)

A real eye-catcher – an elaborate and expensive ornamental Victorian Gothic façade, bearing the date 1875. Two bays, three tall storeys; one of only two examples of English bond brickwork in Long Street. On the right, the shop front has been adapted, but there are still green-glazed bricks below, and a canopy over. To the left, a pair of doors flanked by corner pilasters and divided by a three-quarter-round pier with annulet; three composite capitals, face masks. Next comes the date-stone, but then there are elaborate mouldings and a band of nail-head, impressively projecting to support a big stone oriel window with canted sides. A sill band is carried round the oriel. The leading corners of the latter are Gothic piers with annulets and foliate capitals, and the large-pane sash windows have tight curves at the top. The oriel has its own eaves and hipped canopy. To the right of all this, a sash window with a stone lintel on the line of a decorated flat band in blue brick, all under a pointed Gothic relieving arch which defines a diaper panel in gauged brickwork. On the top floor, recessed corners to left and right; sill band, two sash windows, then yet another band in blue bricks; stepped and moulded eaves. Steeply-pitched tiled roof, one ridge stack to the left.

59/61 Long Street (Co-Op)

Truly monstrous, obtrusive, overbearing canopy that dominates both the street and what must have begun as two reasonable buildings; plausibly constructed as a pair, as they have the same moulded eaves. On the building to the left, why is the fenestration so odd? On the right, 2-over-2 sash windows under splayed and incised lintels with stepped keystones.

53/57a Long Street (formerly The Bake House, Stewart Davies and The Coffee Bean, now vacant and Milo's Deli)

Row of four shops: possibly 1970s. Stretcher-bond brickwork, concrete tile roof, softwood casement windows, no chimneys.

49/51 LONG STREET (THE HOSPICE SHOP AND GEORGINA)

Two shops: possibly *c.*1980. More stretcher bond, and concrete tiles.

45/47 LONG STREET (ANTIQUES)

Date plaque, 1827. Mottled brick laid in Flemish bond. Three bays, three storeys. No. 47 has glazed double doors to left (set back) within a good shop-front with reeded pilasters rising to a corbelled canopy. To the right, No. 45 – front door now hard against the shop front. Reeded door-case; the door has flush flat panels with beaded edges; now glass above the locking-rail; over-door light flanked by lozenges, and a flat canopy. To the right, a blue brick chamfered plinth pierced by elliptical arched cellar window. Three-light shop window in right-hand bay, having pyramidal corner blocks at each end, all under a canopy. On the first floor, left, a big canted bay window with sashes; flat leaded top. Centre and right, 2-over-2 sash windows with exposed sash boxes, but with horns (i.e. after 1850); stone sills, splayed lintels with big keystone blocks, plain brick reveals. Top floor, three 2-over-2 sash windows with similar sills and lintels. Moulded wooden eaves, pitched blue tile roof, end stacks.

On the rear elevation of No. 45, a canted multi-pane bay window and, to the right, a Victorian door in a blocked wide aperture under an elliptical arch. Above, two casement windows. A back range of two-and-a-half storeys: one remade bay window over brackets and several casement windows under elliptical and flat arches. The next block back is lower, of two storeys, with one loading bay door on the first floor. Yet another building on another side of the yard, part of which is paved with setts.

70 *45/47 Long Street (Antiques).*

33-43 LONG STREET

*c.*1970, flat-fronted block of six shops.

31 Long Street (*Wheatsheaf Inn*)

Two bays, three storeys. Each bay has, on the ground floor, one door and one three-light casement window with high transom. On the first floor, boards applied over brick, two-light casement window. On the second floor, rendered, a two-light casement window under gablets in each bay, low parapet. Late Victorian or Edwardian? Pitched tiled roof, hard red brick end stacks.

27/29 Long Street (Happy Gathering)

Six bays, three storeys, English bond. Ground floor now includes two small shop fronts and two small windows – all 20th-century, but, to right, a rusticated elliptical carriage arch. On the first floor, five of the six bays should be 2-over-2 sashes, stone sills, splayed lintels with key blocks, but three windows now have plastic frames. The sixth is a tripartite window with 2-over-2 sash to centre and a bracketed canopy above. On the second floor, a sill band, then six 2-over-2 sash windows; the splayed lintels rise to the wooden bracketed and moulded eaves. Pitched roof with old tiles, three brick stacks.

25 Long Street (Masterclean)

Three bays, three storeys, stuccoed: possibly Regency. Big, wide shop-front with elaborate bracketed canopy, modernised to its detriment. First floor, right-hand window is blind; the other two have plastic frames but the apertures are intact. There are sunken panels on the window-sills; console-bracketed flat canopies over each window. Second floor – window to right is blind; the other two are like those below, but with bracketed canopies. Moulded eaves, blue tile roof, central brick stack.

71 *31 Long Street* (Wheatsheaf Inn).

23 Long Street (Encore)

Two bays, three storeys, Flemish bond. Modern shop front to ground floor and a small doorway on left, to an entry – wooden lintel painted like a splayed head in front of an elliptical brick rear-arch. On first and second floors, two windows with elliptical heads under lintels with flat tops, now with plastic frames. Modillion eaves, blue tile roof, one small end stack.

21 Long Street (Herbs & Spices)

Two bays, three storeys, brick in Flemish bond. The shop front has canted multi-pane bays on each side of the central doorway. To the right, an eight-panel modern door under a shallow elliptical brick arch fronts an entry. On the first floor, flush stone sills and splayed rusticated lintels with keystones to 6-over-6 windows with horns, but exposed sash boxes. On the second floor, 3-over-3 sashes converted to top-hung casements. Modillion brick eaves, blue tiled roof, one end stack.

Notes

Abbreviations used in the Notes:

BCA	Birmingham City Archives
Dugd.	Dugdale muniments at Merevale Abbey
IGI	International Genealogical Index (on-line)
KCL	King's College, Cambridge, Library
LJRO	Lichfield Joint Record Office
LPL	Lambeth Palace Library
SRO	Staffordshire Record Office
TNA	The National Archives
WCRO	Warwickshire County Record Office

Introduction, pp.viii-ix

1. Edmund Burke, *Reflections on the revolution in France* (1790).

Chapter One, pp.1-12

1. Arden-Close, C.F., 'The centres of England and Wales', *Geog. Journal*, vol. 97 (1941), pp.179-81. In 1941 the mean point was further defined as 300m west north west of the old Nuneaton-Ashby railway bridge on the A5 near MIRA (OS NGR SP36409510).
2. Ordnance Survey, CR 11695/36 (8 April 1971) and private communications to A.F. Cook, from M.L. Cox, 16 November 1994 and 12 May 2000. However, this is a calculation that is constantly shifting, owing to coastal erosion/deposition/mean sea level/ocean levels rising/UK land mass actually changing level after the ice sheets depressed it down into the crustal rock. In 1971 the mean point was given as 500m east south east of the old Nuneaton-Ashby railway bridge, as above (OS NGR SP37229490).
3. We are grateful to Sara Wear, keeper of archaeology at Warwickshire Museum, for advice on this section.
4. Hingley, R., 'Prehistoric Warwickshire: a review of the evidence', *Trans. Birm. Arch. Soc.*, vol. 100 (1996), pp.1-24.
5. Dauncey, K.D.M., *Oldbury Camp Excavation Report* (1949); Ferris, I. and Sterenburg, J., 'Nuneaton Oldbury camp', *West Mids. Arch.*, vol 35 (1992), p.57; Hingley, R., *op. cit.*, pp.1-24.
6. Hill, J.D., 'Hill-forts and the Iron Age of Wessex', *The Iron Age in Britain and Ireland: Recent Trends*, Champion,T.C. and Collis, J.R. (eds.) (1996).
7. Cook, A.F., *Millennium Project (Nuneaton and district)*, vols. 1-2, 4, 6-7, Home Piece (2000).
8. The Bronze Age showed a leap in human complex activity and the data for that time is better than for both Neolithic/Mesolithic and Iron Ages. However, it is possible that such a claim may need to be revisited. Meso- and Neolithic artefact finds are under re-assessment, as some were found to be faked or deliberately planted, while there are suspect Iron-Age sites on aerial photos as yet uninvestigated; they may or may not be of that age.
9. Stukeley, W., *Itinerarium Curiosum or an account of the antiquitys and remarkable curiosities in nature and art observ'd in travels thro' Great Britain*, Illustrated with copper plates, London (1724).
10. Bloxam, M.H., 'On certain mediaeval antiquities found in Warwickshire', a paper read at Rugby School Natural History Society (5 December 1885), pp.1-7; Bloxam, M.H., 'The ancient British, Roman and Anglo-Saxon antiquities of Warwickshire', *Trans. Birm. Arch. Soc.*, vol. 2 (1875-81), pp.25-38 (1875).
11. Records, at the former Warwickshire Sites and Monuments Records (SMR), now HER (Historic Environments Record).
12. Thomas, G. and Taylor, S., Nuneaton Technical College (1965) (ref A.F. Cook).
13. Rivet, A.L.F. and Smith, C., *The place names of Roman Britain* (1979), pp.411-12.
14. Salway, Peter, 'Roman Britain ' in *Oxford History of England*, Clarendon (1987), *see* map VII, pp.100-2, Trent areas.
15. Webster, G., *Boudicca: the British Revolt against Rome AD 60*, Batsford (1978).
16. Webster, G., *op.cit.*
17. *Roman Mancetter*, leaflet produced by Warwickshire Museum; Swan, V.G., *The Pottery Kilns of Roman Britain (supplementary series)*, HMSO (1984). This has a reference (p.99) to Hartley, K.F., 'Excavations, 1973a, and unpublished'.
18. Vose, R.H., *Glass* (1980), pp.132-4 and plate 38, 'Roman glass furnace at Manduessedum'.
19. Codrington, T., *The Roman Roads in Britain*, London (1919); Rowlands, M.B., *The West Midlands from AD 1000*, Longman (1987); Salzman, L.F. (ed.), *Victoria History of the County of Warwick*, vol. 4 University of London & Institute of Historical Research, Oxford University (1947).
20. Webster, G., *op. cit.*
21. Beresford, M.W. and St Joseph, J.K., *Mediaeval England: an aerial survey*, Cambridge University (1979); Beresford, M.W., *Deserted Mediaeval Villages*, Lutterworth Press (1972); Beresford, M.W., *New towns of the Middle Ages*, Lutterworth Press (1967); Beresford, M.W., 'The deserted villages of Warwickshire', *Trans. Birm. Arch. Soc.*, vol. 66, 1950 (1945-6); Bond, C.J., 'Deserted Mediaeval Villages in Warwickshire: a review of field evidence', *Trans. Birm. Arch. Soc.*, vol. 86 (1974).
22. Parkes, S., 'Notice on the Black Oxide of Manganese, south of Warwickshire', *Trans. Geol. Soc.*, series 2, vol. 1, pt.1 (1824), p.168.

23. Hare, L., *Mining in Warwickshire* (Warwickshire Library Committee) (1988); Douglass, D., *A miner's life*, Routledge, Kegan Paul (1983).
24. Cook, A.F., *op. cit.*
25. Worssam, B.C. and Old, R.A., 'Geology of the Country around Coalville', *Mems. Geol. Surv.* (1988), Sheet 155.
26. Jope, E.M., 'The Saxon Building Stone Industries in South and Midland England', *Mediaeval Arch.*, vol. 8 (1964), pp.91-118; Cook, A.F., *op. cit.*; Mann, E., 'Geological expedition to Atherstone and Nuneaton', *Report of Rugby School Natural Hist. Soc.* (1873) pp.19-22; Peacock, D.P.S., *The archaeology of stone*, English Heritage (1998); Knowles, D. and Hadcock, R.N., *Medieval Religious Houses, England and Wales* Longmans Group (1953).
27. Parkes, S., *op. cit.*
28. Taylor, K. and Rushton, A.W.A., 'Pre-Westphalian geology: Warwickshire Coalfield', *IGS Bulletin 35*, HMSO (1971).
29. Drayton, M., *Poly-Olbion* (1612-22). An edition of the text may be found in Hooper, R., *Complete Works of Michael Drayton*, John Russell Smith, Soho Square, London (1876).
30. Dugdale, W., *The Antiquities of Warwickshire, 1656*, 2nd edn, vols. 1-2; Rev., Thomas, W., printed J. Jones (1730).
31. Burton, W., *The description of Leicestershire; containing Matters of Antiquity, History, Armorye and Genealogy*, 2nd edn (1777).
32. Nichols, J., *The History and Antiquities of the County of Leicester*, vol. 4, pts 1-2 (1795-1815).
33. Doubleday, H.A. and Page, W. (eds.), *Victoria History of the County of Warwick*, vol. 1 (1904).
34. Doubleday, H.A. and Page, W. (eds.), *op. cit.*, vol. 2 (1908).
35. Kinvig, R.H. (ed.), *Birmingham and its regional setting:a scientific survey*, British Association for the Advancement of Science (1950); Warwick, G.T., *Birmingham and its Regional Setting: geomorphology and relief and physiographic regions*, British Association for the Advancement of Science (1950).
36. *The character of England: landscape, wildlife and natural features*, English Nature and the Countryside Commission (1996).
37. Whitfield, W.A.D., and Beard, G.R., 'Soils in Warwickshire 4; Sheet SP29/39 (Nuneaton)', *Soil Survey Record No. 66*, Harpenden (1980).
38. DEFRA *Agricultural Land Classification:* 'Grade 3a and 3b = Land with moderate limitations that restrict the choice of crops and/or reduce yield and/or demand careful management.'
39. Bridge, D. McC., Carney, J.N., Lawley, R.S. and Rushton, A.W.A., 'Geology of the country around Coventry and Nuneaton', *Memoir for 1:50,000 geological sheet 169*, HMSO (1998); Downing, R.A., 'The Hydrogeology of the Trent River Basin', *Water Supply Papers, IGS No. 5* (1970).
40. 'Misfit/superimposed' are the correct technical words to use because no one has yet coined a specialist term for this type of river. In the case of the Anker, it is literally a *mis-fit* (too small for the job it appears to have done); the present-day river did not shape or create the big valley in which it lies. Today's trickling, meandering Anker could never have eroded this large valley. Its present day meandering course appears to have been *superimposed* on an old landscape with which it had little connection. That large valley was shaped by an older river, the Proto-Soar/Bytham River. The Proto-Soar ceased to exist after the ice sheets had melted 425,000 years ago (and dumped millions of tons of silt, sand and gravel everywhere). The post-glacial river systems were created by rainfall and snowfall running down the new slopes that existed. In the end, of course, they became permanently established, as did the River Anker.
41. Hadfield, C., *The canals of the West Midlands*, vol. 5, 3rd edn, David & Charles (1985).
42. Richardson, L., 'Wells and Springs of Warwickshire', *Mems. Geol. Surv.* (1928).
43. National Coal Board, Coal Survey Laboratory, Birmingham, *Folios, Maps and Diagrams of the Warwickshire Coalfield* (1957); Environment Agency, Nov. 1999, and environmental overview, Mar. 2000, *Local Environment Agency Plan. Burton, Nuneaton and Tamworth, consultation drafts.*

Chapter Two, pp.13-16

1. Bassett, S., 'Anglo-Saxon Birmingham', *Midland History 25* (2000), 1-27; Slater, T.R., *A Century of Celebrating Christ. The Diocese of Birmingham, 1905-2005*, Chichester, Phillimore (2005), pp.14-16.
2. Gover, J.E.B., Mawer, A., Stenton, F.M. and Houghton, F.T.S., *The Place-names of Warwickshire*, Cambridge, Cambridge University Press (1936), p.77.
3. Morris, R., *Churches in the Landscape*, London, Dent (1989).
4. Gelling, M., *The West Midlands in the Early Middle Ages*, Leicester, Leicester University Press (1992).
5. Stenton, F.M., *Anglo-Saxon England*, Oxford, Clarendon Press, 2nd edn (1947), pp.247-59.
6. Hill, D., *An Atlas of Anglo-Saxon England*, Oxford, Blackwell (1981), pp.40-61.
7. Gelling, *op. cit.*, Fig. 54.
8. Stenton, *op. cit.*, pp.321-6.
9. Gelling, *op.cit.*, pp.146-53.
10. Morris, J., *Domesday Book Warwickshire*, Chichester, Phillimore (1976), note 1.6; Finberg, H.P.R., *Gloucestershire Studies*, Leicester, Leicester University Press (1957), pp.17-51.
11. Morris, J., *op cit.*, 15.2, 15.3.
12. Hooke, D., *The Anglo-Saxon Landscape. The Kingdom of the Hwicce*, Manchester, Manchester University Press (1985), pp.190-227; Gelling, *op. cit.*, pp.172-83.

Chapter Three, pp.17-28

1. Salzman, L.F., *Victoria History of Warwickshire IV, Hemlingford Hundred*, London, Oxford University Press (1947) pp.126-30 (hereafter VCH).
2. Dugdale, Sir W., *The Antiquities of Warwickshire Illustrated II*, 2nd edn, London (1730), pp.1,076-86.
3. For the 18th-century fields, *see* Chapter Seven; for the 15th- and 16th-century fields, *see* Chapter Four and Chapter Six.
4. WCRO, P7, 'A Plan of Atherston Feildes, Parcell of the Estate of Abraham Bracebridge Gent. in the County of Warwick taken in the year 1716 by Robert Hewitt'.
5. WCRO, P7.
6. Holt, R., *The Mills of Medieval England*, Blackwell, Oxford (1988), pp.172-4.
7. Hooke, D., *The Landscape of Anglo-Saxon England*, London, Leicester University Press (1998).
8. Letters, S., *Online Gazetteer of Markets and Fairs in England and Wales to 1516*, www.history.ac.uk/cmh/gaz/gazweb2.html, Warwickshire (27 June 2006).
9. Morris, R., *Churches in the Landscape*, Duckworth, London (1989).
10. Letters, *op cit.*, provides details of the local markets at Tamworth (founded 913, Saturday); Coleshill (founded 1207, Sunday); Ashby de la Zouche (founded 1219, Wednesday) Market Bosworth (founded 1224, Wednesday); Nuneaton (founded 1226, Tuesday) and Polesworth (founded 1242, Thursday).
11. Morgan, M. (1946), *The English Lands of the Abbey of Bec*, Oxford University Press, Oxford (1946), pp.94-5.
12. Morgan, *ibid.*
13. *See* Note 5 to Chapter Nine (The early records are rolls. The later bound volumes comprising the manor court records are nevertheless often referred to as manor court 'rolls'.)
14. Vanderzee, George, *Nonarum Inquisitiones in Curia Scaccarii: temp. regis Edwardi III*, HMSO (1807), p.442.
15. Cooper, W., *Henley-in-Arden, an Ancient Market Town*, Birmingham (1946); Slater, T.R. and Bartley, G., *Rural Settlements in Warwickshire*, Coventry, Birmingham Branch of the Geographical Association (1981).
16. I am grateful to Nat Alcock for providing me with a copy of his transcript of the survey.
17. WCRO, Z 484, 'Plan of Atherstone 1786'.
18. VCH, *op. cit.*, p.128.
19. Dugdale, *op. cit.*, p.1,079; TNA, SC 12/28/13, Survey of Warwickshire Guild and Chantry properties 1547x49'; I am grateful to Nat Alcock for supplying me with a copy of this survey.
20. VCH, *op. cit.*, p.127.
21. VCH, *op. cit.*, p.129.
22. Beresford, M.W., *New Towns of the Middle Ages*, Lutterworth, London (1967); Palliser, D.M., Slater, T.R. and Dennison, E.P., 'The topography of towns 600-1300', in D.M. Palliser (ed.), *The Cambridge Urban History of Britain*

I, 600-1540, Cambridge University Press, Cambridge (2000), pp.153-86.
23. Slater, T.R., 'Planning English medieval street towns: the Hertfordshire evidence', *Landscape History* 26 (2004), pp.19-36.
24. For Stratford *see* Slater, T.R., 'Domesday village to medieval town: the topography of medieval Stratford-upon-Avon', in Bearman R. (ed.), *The History of an English Borough: Stratford-upon-Avon, 1196-1996*, Suttons, Stroud (1997), pp.30-42; for Henley *see* Slater and Bartley *op. cit.*
25. *See* Conzen, M.R.G., *Alnwick, Northumberland. An Essay in Town-plan Analysis*, London Publications of the Institute of British Geographers No. 27 (1960); Slater, T.R., 'Ideal and reality in English episcopal medieval town planning', *Transactions, Institute of British Geographers*, NS 12 (1987), pp.191-203; Lilley, K.D., 'Mapping the medieval city', *Urban History* 27 (2000), pp.5-30.
26. Ordnance Survey, Warwickshire, 1:500 First Edition 1888 (Surveyed 1877), Sheets VI.II.16-17, 21-3.
27. Jones, E.L., Porter, S. and Turner, M., *A Gazetteer of English Urban Fire Disasters 1500-1900*, Norwich, Historical Geography Research Series 13 (1984); Farr, M. (ed.), *The Great Fire of Warwick*, Dugdale Society Warwickshire Record Series 36 (1992).
28. However, in 1779 the Horse Fair was located in the open area directly in front of the manor house (WCRO, HR36/1).
29. *See* Building History Two: Swan House for the complicated circumstances of this improvement.
30. For a more detailed example *see* Slater (1987), *op. cit.*
31. For Stratford *see* Slater (1987), *op. cit.*; for Beaumaris *see* Beresford, *op. cit.*, p.50; for Thame *see* Bond, C.J., 'Central place and medieval new town: the origins of Thame, Oxfordshire', in Slater, T.R. (ed.), *The Built Form of Western Cities*, Leicester, Leicester University Press (1990), pp.83-108.
32. For the techniques of metrological analysis *see* Slater, T.R., 'English medieval towns with composite plans: evidence from the Midlands', in T.R. Slater (ed.) *Built Forms, op. cit.* (1990), pp.60-82.
33. Adams, I.H., *Agrarian Landscape Terms: a Glossary for Historical Geography*, London, Institute of British Geographers Special Publication No. 9 (1977), pp.1-2, 6-9, 64, 93.

Chapter Three: Appendix, pp.29-36

1. Two contemporary copies of the survey survive, WCRO, L2/86 (lacking the final 30 tenants) and Lambeth Palace CM XX/1 (complete; cited as Lambeth). Extracts of a court roll from the reign of Edward VI (1547-53) are transcribed in Benjamin Bartlett, *History and Antiquities of the Parish of Mancetter*, London (1791); since it names Henry Grey as Duke of Suffolk, it must date to 1551-4. This includes a summary listing of the customary tenants and their rents, corresponding closely to the survey; it seems that Bartlett's text must have been damaged, since the transcript has a number of gaps and several apparent mis-readings (such as Rolf for Altoft).
2. WCRO, L2/86, p.12 (entries 42-3); Roman numerals have been converted to Arabic.
3. Bartlett's text includes 'rents resolute' [i.e. quit rents] paid to the Duke of Suffolk by tenements held by 13 other people, which apparently represent the freeholdings (absent from the other texts).
4. First series starting with guild property No. 7 in the survey; second series starting with property 55 of William Hodgekens.
5. The following calculations ignore all burgages which are associated with additional land, that might have altered the rent paid. The rent of only 4d. paid for one full burgage is also ignored; this holding (property 25 of Mr Lewas) was clearly anomalous, with abuttals that do not match those of any other holdings, and described as 'called the garrette howses'.
6. For one ½ burgage, the rent is omitted. The total rent given in the survey is £36 15s. 7½d., which includes the demesne land as well.
7. Dugd., 566.
8. Even the earliest surviving manor court roll, for 1334, contains several surrenders of what must be copyhold property.
9. Although these are not listed in the survey, they probably can be identified with the 13 additional rents listed in Bartlett's transcript. It seems that many of these former Merevale properties were grouped together at the west end of Long Street on the north side (the later F39-F61), which explains why the survey does not include the expected 30-36 freehold abuttals.
10. BCA 168242. A rental of Merevale Abbey for 1497 lists 12 cottage tenants (TNA, E315/283, f.8). It probably omits the principal tenants who held by lease, and indeed three such leases survive dating from 1525 to 1535 (E303/17, nos. 297, 320, 322).
11. These rents would have been extinguished after the manor was granted to William Devereux in 1554, as he would not need to pay rent to himself. In 1649, a survey of Crown property (TNA, E317/Wark/8) lists nine properties, most of which can be located among the later freeholds; they are derived from former property of the Guild of Mancetter which was never re-sold, as noted in a series of summaries of Crown property (TNA, SC12/26/33; /27/43, 45, dating from 1592 to *c.*1640; thus, they are included among the Guild's copyholds in the 1547 survey.
12. They are described in the Particulars for Grant to Harry Cartwrighte (TNA, E318/7/248); although the two tenements are not precisely located, one of them can be identified with the later F42, standing between the church and the Market Place.
13. Most of the manorial rents are listed in BCA 168242 and E315/283; a significant number have values of 15d. and 7½d., probably for ½ and ¼ burgages respectively.
14. cf. Note 11.
15. Dugd. 1658, 26 June 1649. The purchaser in October was the sitting tenant (Dugd. 2657). The former Merevale estate passed from Walter to William Devereux in 1550, and from him to his nephew, Robert Devereux, Earl of Essex (unlike his manor of Atherstone, which was inherited by William's daughters). Robert's grand-daughter, Frances, married William Seymour, Marquess of Hertford.
16. The original enfranchisement deed has not been found, but it is referred to in WCRO, CR258/14. The number of properties covered is estimated from the disappearance of copyholds from the court books.
17. TNA, MAF 9/355.
18. Several copies of the 1786 map survive, most accessibly in WCRO, P26. An updated version of it also exists, dated 1815, which is at Merevale Abbey, with a copy at WCRO, Z484(u).
19. The court books record the rents only irregularly.

Chapter Four, pp.37-48

1. I am greatly indebted to Christopher Dyer for his expertise and advice in the preparation of this chapter. *See:* Dyer, C., 'How Urban was Medieval England', *History Today*, 67 (1997), pp.37-44; Hilton, R.H., 'Small Town Society before the Black Death', *Past and Present*, 20 (1984), pp.53-72; Hilton, R.H., 'Towns in Societies', *Urban History Yearbook* (1982), pp.9-10; Dyer, C., *Making a Living in the Middle Ages*, London (2002), pp.187-96.
2. For general background on the economy of the forest of Arden at this time *see*: Dyer, C., *Warwickshire Farming 1349-c.1520* (Dugdale Society Occasional Paper, 27, 1981); Dyer, C., 'The West Midlands' in Miller, E. (ed.), *The Agrarian History of England and Wales*, 3, Cambridge (1991), pp.77-91, 222-37, 636-47; Watkins, A., 'Cattle Grazing in the forest of Arden in the later middle ages', *Agricultural History Review*, 37 (1989), pp.17-23; Watkins, A., 'The Woodland Economy of the forest of Arden in the later middle ages', *Midland History*, 18 (1993), pp.19-32; Watkins, A., 'Peasant Economy in the forest of Arden' in Britnell, R.H. (ed.), *Daily Life in the Late Middle Ages*, Stroud (1998), pp.83-102; Watkins, A., 'Merevale Abbey in the late 1490s', *Warwickshire History*, 9 (1994), pp.87-104; *Victoria County History of Warwickshire* (VCH), II, pp.219-20. For the background to western

Leicestershire *see*: King, E., 'The East Midlands' in *Agrarian History of England and Wales*, 3, pp.210-22; Hilton, R.H., 'Medieval Agrarian History' in *Victoria County History of Leicestershire*, 2, pp.182-93.

3. LPL, CM XX/1; Dugdale, W., *The Antiquities of Warwickshire* (second edition revised W. Thomas, London 1730), 1,084.
4. Morgan, M., *The English Lands of the Abbey of Bec*, London (1946), pp.9-12, 128ff.
5. Chibnall M. (ed.), *Select Documents of the English Lands of the Abbey of Bec*, Camden Society, series 3, 73 (1951), pp.103-5.
6. Hilton, R.H., *The Social Structure of Rural Warwickshire in the Middle Ages*, Dugdale Society Occasional Paper, 9 (1950).
7. *Calendar of the Charter Rolls*, 1226-57, p.307; Baker, W.A., 'Warwickshire Markets', *Warwickshire History*, 6 (1986), pp.87-104; Watkins, A., *Small Towns in the Forest of Arden in the 15th Century*, Dugdale Society Occasional Papers, No 38 (1998), pp.4-5.
8. Beresford, M.W., 'The Origins of Medieval Boroughs in Warwickshire: an additional note Atherstone', *Warwickshire History*, 1(3) (1970), pp.28-9; *Select Documents of the English Lands of the Abbey of Bec*, pp.105-6; Dyer, C., *Making a Living*, pp.97-8, 219.
9. Wellstood, F.C. (ed.), *Warwickshire Feet of Fines*, volume I, 1195-1284, Dugdale Society, 11 (1932), 62. A similar concord from the following year can be seen, *ibid.*, 99. But, as is noted above (p.20), these supposedly free tenants were really copyholders.
10. Morgan, M., *op. cit.*, p.94.
11. Watkins, A., *Small Towns in the Forest of Arden*, p.5; *Select Documents of the English Lands of the Abbey of Bec*, pp.125-6; Dyer, C., *Making a Living*, pp.197-8, 219; Morgan, M., *op. cit.*, p.94. Neither Beresford nor Morgan fully appreciated the extent to which Atherstone developed as a town because they were unaware of the evidence contained in the court rolls.
12. Placita de Quo Warranto, London (1818), p.780; Dugdale, *Antiquities of Warwickshire*, pp.1,083-4.
13. *Select Documents of the English Lands of the Abbey of Bec*, pp.105-6; Carter W.F. (ed.), *Lay Subsidy for Warwickshire 6 Edward III*, Dugdale Society, 6 (1926), p.40; Salter J.L. (ed.), *Atherstone*, Warwickshire County Library (1985), p.6; McClure, P., 'Patterns of Migration in the late Middle Ages: the evidence of English Place-Name Surnames', *Economic History Review*, 32, 2nd series (1979), pp.167-82; Carus-Wilson, E.M., 'The First Half-Century of the Borough of Stratford-upon-Avon', *Economic History Review*, 17, 2nd series (1965), pp.46-63; Watkins, A., 'The Development of Coleshill in the Later Middle Ages', *Warwickshire History*, 5 (1983-4), pp.167-84.
14. Watkins, A., *Small Towns in the Forest of Arden*, pp.10-3; Austin, J.D., *Hats, Coal and Bloodshed*, Friends of Atherstone Heritage (2005); Watts B. and Winyard, E., *The History of Atherstone*, Mercia Publications (1988), p.14; LPL, CM XX/1; SRO, D641/1/2/269; WCRO, MR13/31.
15. WCRO, MR13/15, MR13/30, MR13/2, MR13/24. A *pipe* varied in size according to the contents, but was equivalent to two hogsheads (approximately 100 gallons).
16. Watkins, A., 'Merevale Abbey in the late 1490s', pp.99-100. By this period, Matthew Corviser's surname (meaning 'shoemaker') would have been inherited, though no doubt adopted by an ancestor because of his trade.
17. Dyer, C., 'Market Towns and the Countryside in Late Medieval England', *Canadian Journal of History*, 31 (1996), pp.17-35; Melbourne Hall, Melbourne, Derbyshire, X94 Lothian Box 34/3 (I am indebted to Dr Jane Laughton for this reference); LJRO Register of Wills (1516-26), p.48; Watkins, A., *Small Towns in the Forest of Arden*, pp.14-15; SRO, D641/1/2/269.
18. *Calender of Patent Rolls* (1317-21), p.327; *ibid.* (1330-32), p.259; *ibid.* (1343-5), p.3; Dugdale, *Antiquities of Warwickshire*, p.1084; Watkins, A., 'Merevale Abbey in the late 1490s', pp.87-92.
19. WCRO, MR13 for this period.
20. *See* the Appendix to Chapter Three for an account of the copyhold system.
21. Watkins, A., *Small Towns in the Forest of Arden*, pp.7-8; WCRO, MR 13/1; MR13/20/ MR13/21; MR13/27; MR13/30; MR13/34.
22. Watkins, A., *Small Towns in the Forest of Arden*, pp.8-9; WCRO, MR13/34.
23. Watkins, A., *Small Towns in the Forest of Arden*, pp.8-9; WCRO, MR13/3, MR13/5, MR13/6, MR13/11, MR13/12, MR13/16, MR13/21, MR13/22; Hutton, R., *The Rise and Fall of Merry England*, Oxford (1994), pp.19, 57.
24. KCL, Atherstone Court Rolls; VCH, IV, 122-3, 129; Roth, P., *English Austin Friars, 1249-1538*, New York (1966), pp.1, 85-6, 240-1; 2, 268-77; Hunt, J., 'Ralph VIII, Lord Basset of Drayton and Coventry Whitefriars', *Trans. Birmingham Warwickshire Archaeol. Soc.*, 104 (2000), p.95; TNA, PROB 11/3 f. 27, PROB 11/4 f. 128; LJRO, Register of Wills (1516-26), p.48; Dugdale, *Antiquities of Warwickshire* (1086).
25. VCH, pp.4, 122-3, 129.
26. Watkins, *Small Towns in the Forest of Arden*, pp.9-10; WCRO, MR13/23; Calendar, of Patent Rolls (1452-61), p.475; Watts and Winyard, *History of Atherstone*, p.11. On the bequests and properties of the Mancetter gild *see* WCRO, MR13/23, MR13/26, MR13/27, MR13/29, MR13/33; MR13/35; LJRO, Register of Wills (1516-26), p.40; LPL, CM XX/1.
27. WCRO, MR 13/26; LPL, CM XX/1.
28. VCH, pp.2, 356-7; WCRO, MR13/13.
29. Hilton, R.H., 'Lords, Burgesses and Hucksters', *Past and Present*, 97 (1982), p.7; Dyer, C., *Making a Living*, pp.202-3; Ross, A.S.C., 'Assize of Bread and Ale', *Economic History Review*, 9, 2nd series (1950), p.323; Bolton, J.L., *Medieval English Economy*, London (1980), pp.123, 139-40.
30. Bennett, J.M., *Ale, Beer and Brewsters in England*, Oxford (1996), pp.43-50; Hilton, R.H., 'Women Traders in Medieval England', *Women's Studies*, 2 (1984), pp.139-55; Watkins, *Small Towns in the Forest of Arden*, pp.16-7; WCRO, MR13/3, MR13/5, MR13/6, MR13/8, MR13/13, MR13/15, MR13/16, MR13/17, MR13/19, MR13/20, MR13/21, MR13/22.
31. For the public houses in Atherstone *see* Austin, J.D., *Hats, Coal and Bloodshed*. Judy Vero has identified the earliest references to named inns in the Manor Court Rolls, using references from the 1786 Plan for buildings, and MCR references, but none of those names can be traced to earlier than the mid-17th century. However, *The Swan* (F33 on Fig.7) was owned by Edward Drayton, vintner in 1555; his inventory, 1625, shows it in use as an inn (*see* p.85); and the *Angel Inn* (C108) was probably an inn from medieval times. *See* Chapter Six, Note 30.
32. WCRO, MR13/13, MR13/16; Watkins, A., *Small Towns in the Forest of Arden*, pp.15-16.
33. Probably one big enough to bake bread made with five 'measures' (perhaps bushels or stricks) of corn at a time.
34. Watkins, *Small Towns in the Forest of Arden*, pp.16-17; SRO, D641/1/2/269, D641/1/2/271, D641/1/2/272, D641/1/2/273; LPL, CM XX/1.
35. Watkins, *Small Towns in the Forest of Arden*, pp.17-18; WCRO, MR13/6, MR13/15, MR13/13.
36. Dyer, C., 'The Consumption of Freshwater Fish in Medieval England', in Dyer, C., *Everyday Life in Medieval England*, London (1994), pp.77-100; Watkins, A., *Small Towns in the Forest of Arden*, p.18; WCRO, MR13/27.
37. Hilton, R.H., 'Lord, Burgesses and Hucksters', *Past and Present*, 97 (1982), pp.3-15; Hilton, R.H., 'Women Traders in Medieval England', pp.143-46; Watkins, A., *Small Towns in the Forest of Arden*, pp.18-19; WCRO, MR 13/21, MR13/25.
38. Morgan, M., *English Lands*, pp.47-52, 94, 114-5.
39. Either side of Coleshill Road, approximately 200 metres beyond the south back way, stretching as far as the Outwoods (note supplied by J. Vero).
40. SRO, D641/1/2/269, D641/1/2/271, D641/1/2/272, D641/1/2/273.
41. Dyer, C., *Warwickshire Farming*, pp.22-3; Watkins, A., 'Peasant Economy in the forest of Arden', p.90; Salter, J.L., *Atherstone*, p.12. Chapters Three, Six and Seven also give references to the field system.
42. Field names are given in SRO, D641/1/2/269, D641/1/2/271, D641/1/2/272, D641/1/2/273; TNA, E 101 519/31; LPL, CM XX/1; Salter, J.L., *Atherstone*, p.12; KCL, ATH 29; WCRO, P7; Dyer, C., Warwickshire Farming, p.11; Watkins, A., 'Cattle Grazing in the forest

of Arden', pp.17-23; Watkins, A., 'The Woodland Economy of the forest of Arden', pp.19-32; Watkins, A., 'Merevale Abbey in the late 1490s', pp.87-104; Watkins, A., 'Maxstoke Priory in the 15th century: the development of an estate economy in the forest of Arden', *Warwickshire History*, 10 (1996), pp.3-18; Salter, J.L., *Atherstone*, p.12.
43. TNA, E101 519/31.
44. LJRO, Register of Wills (1516-26), 40, 48, Richard Knyght of Atherstone, 8 March 1536/7.
45. LPL, CM XX/1.
46. The Washbrook appears to be the Innage Brook, at the west end of town. An area nearby was called the Washpad, presumably where women did the washing. This name persists into the 19th century, with Washpad Yard (F1) in the 1851 Census. This yard clearly ran along the eastern side of the Innage Brook, and it is interesting to note that one of the occupants of the seven houses was Mary Bates, 'laundress'. The back way was linked to Long Street only after the railway goods yard was built in 1847. Washpad Yard must have been demolished to make way for Melbourne House. It was occupied by Thos. Jennings, tanner, in 1649 (Dugd. 1658). C2 includes a 'water place', WCRO, L2/3 p.119 (1757). This is the end of the burgage plot on a corner that abuts the Innage Brook. (Note supplied by J. Vero).
47. LPL, CM XX/1; WCRO, MR13/10, MR13/13, MR13/16, MR13/19, MR13/30, MR13/35.
48. Lay Subsidy for Warwickshire 6 Edward III, 40; Sheail, J., 'The Regional Distribution of Wealth in England as indicated in the 1524/5 Lay Subsidy Returns', Ph.D. thesis, University of London (1969).

Chapter Five, pp.49-67

1. Pevsner, Nikolaus, with Wedgwood, A., *Architectural Guide to Warwickshire*, Yale University Press (1966).
2. Salzman, L.F. (ed.), *Victoria County History: a history of the County of Warwick: Volume IV*, p.129, n.64, Oxford University Press (1947).
3. Salzman (ed.), *op.cit.*
4. Pevsner, *op.cit.*
5. Ogilby, John, *Britannia* (1675).

The Streetscapes, pp.68-75

1. The HART project provided the pre-1851 information, analysed by Judy Vero; later evidence was researched by Mike Trye.

Building Histories

Nat Alcock provided valuable support for these studies.

Building History One, pp.77-82

1. Tite, G., 'From the Acorn to the Woolpack'. *Context: The Journal of the Association of Conservation Officers* (now the Institute of Historic Building Conservation), Issue number 46, March 1995.
2. WCRO, P7, Hewitt, R., 'A Plan of Atherston Feildes' (1716).
3. WCRO, L2/5, p.54, 26 March 1794: 'now Abraham Bracebridge lately pulled down and now used as a road'.
4. A beam with similar mouldings at Little Harts Heath, Staplehurst (Kent) has been ascribed a felling-date of 1507: *see* Pearson, S., *Medieval Houses of Kent* (1994), p.159. Similar mouldings on a beam at 65 The Kings House, Salisbury have been ascribed by RCHME to the last quarter of the 15th century.
5. WCRO, L2/15, p.32.
6. WCRO, L2/15, pp.30-33.
7. WCRO, L2/16, p.45v.
8. Vero, J., *Hatting and the Bracebridges of Atherstone, 1612-1872*, Warwick (1995), p.46; WCRO, MR9/37, Miscellaneous documents relating to the manor of Atherstone, *c.*1692.
9. WCRO, CR258/259, Will of John Walmisley (1712).
10. WCRO, CR258/259, Will of John Walmisley (1712).
11. LJRO, Inventory of John Walmisley, 1721.
12. F29 on 1786 Plan.
13. Both messuages bequeathed to the Cotterells were occupied by Widow Weston. The second is unidentified and may have stood at the rear of F29.
14. WCRO, L2/1, p.170.
15. WCRO, L2/1, p.257.
16. WCRO, L2/1, pp.167-70, 215, 257; L2/3, pp.92-3, 125.
17. WCRO, L2/1, pp.167-70, 215, 257; L2/3, pp.92-3, 125.
18. WCRO, L2/4, pp.325-7.
19. WCRO, HR38/1.
20. WCRO, CR1039/1.
21. The Rate Book for 1825 (Dugd. 504) shows the property divided, for the occupier of the back dwelling was then Benjamin Payne, a baker, who is listed as having, 'House, Bakehouse, Stable and Gardens.'
22. WCRO, L2/5, p.54 (abuttal information).
23. WCRO, L2/8. pp.89-91.
24. Pigot's Directory, 1828/9, p.765.
25. WCRO, CR1039/4. Chapter Eight, also, has references to the fire risks of the hatting industry.
26. WCRO, L2/8, pp.92-3.
27. Kelly's Directory, 1896, p.25.

Building History Two, pp.83-90

1. LJRO, Will of Edward Drayton 1625; WCRO, L2/14, p.11.
2. A plan of the yard drawn in 1797 shows how it ran back between two stables, two chaise houses, a shed for carriages, post stable for six horses, a pump and a cistern. It was only 13ft 4in wide at the entrance between the gateposts (WCRO, HR36).
3. TNA, PROB 11/37, Will of Christopher Draiton, butcher of Atherstone, 1556.
4. WCRO, MR13/37.
5. This is the property known as St Mary's House today, F41 on 1786 Plan. It served as the schoolmaster's and boarding house, whilst the grammar school was accommodated in the chancel of the church opposite.
6. C103 on 1786 Plan. *See also* WCRO, L2/11, 10 Aug 1602, admittance of William Foxe to ½ burgage 'between the tenements of Edward Draiton on one side and William Allsopp on the other side.' William Allsopp's house is C102 (Beech House). From these references, we can tentatively build up the occupation of the east side of Market Street at the end of the 16th century.
7. WCRO, MR13/37. The property is sometimes described as one burgage, sometimes as ¾. The missing ¼ burgage seems to have been land at the back of the main house which was in the same ownership but handled differently.
8. LJRO, Will of Edward Drayton, 1625. His property includes, 'house at the Castle Gate', new house, with land, 'spring wood called Mancetter Park.'
9. LJRO, Inventory of Edward Drayton, 1625.
10. The possession of a wine license identifies Edward as one of the major merchants in Warwickshire.
11. WCRO, L2/13, pp.1-2. This concerns the surrender in 1645 of ½ yardland by Joyce Goare, the widow of 'Thomas Goare of Tamworth, gent.' to John Ensor, innholder. No will has yet been discovered for Thomas Goare, nor any reference to him in the records. The name Goare is spelt variously, 'Gore', 'Goe' or 'Geare.'
12. The 'Taynter Croft' was a plot of land sometimes attached to Swan House, sometimes surrendered separately. It was usually described as ¼ burgage adjoining the messuage abutting on Spicer Lane (WCRO, L2/16, 8 Jun 1677).
13. LJRO, Inventory of Jonathan Griffith, 1650. Fortunately, its identification with the Swan is clear from the text.
14. WCRO, L2/15, p.133. A number of transactions must have taken place in the intervening years, for which the court records are lost. We are therefore uncertain about the precise relationship between the apparent owners in 1660 and Edward's daughters. *See* WCRO, L2/14, pp.39v, 45, and L2/15, pp.44, 153. Richard Grey, who owned the house opposite Swan House, also had an interest in the property (TNA, PROB 11/313, Will of Richard Gray, Atherstone, gent.).
15. LJRO, Will of Jonathan Griffith [Griffin], 1650. Bequeaths to 'Elizabeth Bauldwin my Daughter in Law Twenty shillings'. At this period, 'In law' was often used to denote a step-relationship.
16. WCRO, L2/15, p.135; D7/4/7 B64.
17. WCRO, Hearth Tax Returns for Warwickshire.

18. WCRO, L2/16, p.85; B321.
19. WCRO, L2/17, p.10.
20. WCRO, L2/17, p.23.
21. WCRO, L2/17, p.23.
22. WCRO, B313. Anne Wood was the widow of Lewis Wood, a brasier. They kept the *Red Lion* until his death in 1696 (LJRO, Will of Lewis Wood). Anne was the sister of George Clare, surgeon, who occupied the *Red Lion* in 1707 (LJRO, Will of George Clare 1707).
23. TNA, PROB11/589, Will of William Salisbury, 1722.
24. WCRO, L2/1, p.181.
25. WCRO, L2/1, p.222.
26. WCRO, CR258/482, Assessment for Poor Relief.
27. WCRO, CR1039/1.
28. John Byng, *Torrington Diaries*, 1789, Eyre Spottiswood (1935), vol. II, p.97.
29. WCRO, CR1039/1.
30. Universal British Directory, 1793.
31. WCRO, CR1039/1. This records that 'Mr William Carter, Ath, Innholder, insures for £600, Household Goods £200, Utensils & Stock in his said Dwellinghouse £150, White China & Glass £100, Live & Dead Stock in his Stables & out Buildings adjoining his House in the Market Place, £150.'
32. WCRO, HR36.
33. WCRO, L2/4, p.318 (abuttal information).
34. WCRO, L2/7, p.187. For a discussion of the town's four 'Swans', *see* Building History Six, the *Old Swan*.
35. Deeds to 23 Market Street, kindly loaned by Martin Shaw.

BUILDING HISTORY THREE, PP.91-4

1. It is given as ¼ burgage in 1703 (WCRO, L2/20 p.36), but when next mentioned in 1738 (L2/1, p.420), it appears as a half burgage. It may perhaps have been enlarged in the interval by adding some land at the back, but no direct evidence of this has been found.
2. WCRO, L2/10, p.36. William Fox is shown as a neighbour of 19 Market Street.
3. TNA, PROB 11/169, Will of Thomas Draper, 1635.
4. WCRO, Hearth Tax Returns.
5. LJRO, Inventory of Thomas Draper, 1684.
6. WCRO, L2/20, p.39.
7. WCRO, L2/1, p.420.
8. WCRO, L2/26, pp.12-13.
9. WCRO, L2/4, p.318; HR38/1.
10. WCRO, L2/5, pp.531-5.
11. CR1039/4, Christmas 1811.
12. CR1039/4, Christmas 1823.
13. The 'equity of redemption' is the right of a mortgagor to redeem the property he has mortgaged; this right could be granted to someone else who would then own the property outright if he repaid the mortgage (Alcock, N.W., *Old Title Deeds*, Chichester (1986), p.122). For a similar example, *see* Building History Five.
14. WCRO, L2/7, p.187.
15. TNA, PROB11/1931, Will of John Sanders, 1840.
16. WCRO, L2/8, p.513.
17. *Post Office Directory for Warwickshire* (1845), p.594.
18. *Morris & Co's Commercial Directory and Gazetteer of Warwickshire* (1866), p.686.
19. Kelly's Directory for Warwickshire (1896), p.26.
20. Watts, B. and Winyard, E., *The History of Atherstone*, Mercia Publications (1988), p.238.
21. J.N. Roper's Diary, John Oxley Library, Brisbane (copy at WCRO).
22. A letter from Edward Smith of Atherstone to R. Smith, Jnr.M of Upper Hall, Droitwich, dated 1840. Sold as Lot 230 by Madeley Auctions, December 2004.
23. Kelly's Directory for Warwickshire (1912), p.35.

BUILDING HISTORY FOUR, PP.95-9

1. According to the architectural historian, Lyndon F. Cave.
2. The scrapbook of Charles Hanson Sale (kindly lent by his descendant, Jim Beechey) records William Eyre as the builder.
3. Parallels in Sussex,Yorkshire and Surrey within these date brackets are illustrated in Alcock N.W., and Hall L., *Fixtures and fittings in dated houses 1567-1763*, Practical handbook in archaeology 11, CBA (1994), pp.2-3.
4. LJRO, Will of William Alsoppe, 1551. After the dissolution of the guild, their property was bought en-bloc by middle-men and then resold to individuals.
5. LJRO, Will of John Alsoppe, 1582.
6. LJRO, Inventory of John Allsoppe, 1582. Wright, a chandler, lived to the south, probably in the present 15/17 Market Street, which has changed very little in its external appearance.
7. WCRO, L2/10, pp.32, 79.
8. WCRO, L2/10, p.79
9. LJRO, Inventory of William Allsoppe, 1634.
10. WCRO, Mancetter Parish Register, Marriages, 9 February 1636/7.
11. WCRO, L2/15, p.62.
12. WCRO, L2/15, pp.102-6.
13. WCRO, L2/16, p.37v.
14. WCRO, L2/16, p.39v.
15. TNA, PROB11/337, Will of John Chamberlaine, 1671.
16. WCRO, L2/17, p.38.
17. TNA, PROB11/395, Will of John Chamberlaine, 1689.
18. TNA, PROB11/456, Will of Matthias Ward, 1700. At some point, he must have bought the house from Robert Smith, but this transaction has not been identified.
19. TNA, PROB11/498, Will of Prudentia Ward, 1707.
20. WCRO, L2/20, p.101.
21. Coventry City Archives, PA/101/7/268-270.
22. On corner of Long Street and Ratcliffe Street. F29 on 1786 Plan.
23. WCRO, L2/1, p.192, C29, C100, C101 and C102 on 1786 Plan.
24. TNA, PROB3/22/157, the inventory of goods at Beech House taken on William Eyre's death.
25. WCRO, L2/1, p.192.
26. Elizabeth died a spinster two years later. WCRO, L2/1, p.416.
27. When Littleton died there is evidence that she and her second husband, Francis Soden disputed his will. Coventry City Archives, PA/101/7/171, 4 Oct 1748.
28. TNA, PROB11/800; Will of Fisher Littleton Esq. The will is dated 1746, but was not proved until 1753, so Dorothy Wolferstan could have been said to be premature in claiming her inheritance before the will was proved.
29. WCRO, L2/3, p.100
30. A chronology of the ownership of Beech House from 1708 until 1866 is included in C.H. Sale's scrapbook.
31. C105 on the 1786 Plan.
32. She was married to Thomas Handford, a surgeon, who owned the adjacent property.
33. C105 on the 1786 Plan.
34. Chronology of ownership in C.H. Sale's scrapbook.

BUILDING HISTORY FIVE, PP.100-8

1. WCRO, L2/14, p.4v. C54 on 1786 Plan.
2. This was known as a nuncupative will – dictated on a death-bed.
3. TNA, PROB11/165, Will of Richard Warwick, 1634.
4. One of the houses was Richard Warwick's own house in Long Street (C54 on 1786 Plan); the other appears to have been a neighbouring house in the occupation of William Musson (presumably Elizabeth Musson was his wife or daughter.). The dates of the previous surrenders were 15 December 1633 and 10 April 1634 (WCRO, L2/14, p.5). These took place during a period when the records have not survived.
5. WCRO, L2/14, f.5
6. The Charities of the County of Warwick (1839), pp.969-70.
7. I am grateful to Canon Adrian Mairs for a transcript of memorials in St Peter's Church, Mancetter, prepared by the Birmingham and Midland Society for Genealogy (1985).
8. TNA, PROB11/197, Will of Hester Warwick, 1646.
9. The two houses in Market Street are C100 and C101 on the 1786 Plan. The third property was a a piece of land

described as 'garden, orchard, barn & hovell [*operimento*] & piece of land of 12ft length to lay dong or cowpass upon [*fimum et sterquilium*] with free ingress & egress in & through the gatehouse & yard late belonging to the mansion house of William Power, deceased lying to the lands of Drayton of London, Samuell Bracebridge, Richard Goodall & the lands in the tenure of William Symonds.' (WCRO, L2/14. p.4.v) This land was behind the properties on the corner of Market Street and Long Street. It abutted F32, C92, C93, C94, C98, C99, C100,and was accessed from Long Street, via C93.

10. WCRO, L2/14, p.6 & 6v. records Jonathan Grew as the occupier previous to Charles Careswell, i.e. during the time that Hester Warwick owned the house.
11. Olof, P. and Wallin, E., *The Family of Symonds: Descendants of Richard Symonds and Grace Brookes*, married in 1605 at Nuneaton (Stockholm, 1993, privately published).
12. WCRO, L2/15, p.106.
13. WCRO,L2/16, p.8v.
14. WCRO, L2/16, p.47v.
15. TNA, PROB11/383, Will of William Symonds, 1686.
16. It is likely that one exists but more work is needed before the link can be proven.
17. WCRO, Hearth Tax assessments.
18. Details of these books can be found in Chapter Six.
19. *Foxe's Book of Martyrs* was first published in 1563 and records in graphic detail the sufferings of the Protestant martyrs, two of which, Robert Glover and Joyce Lewis, lived in Mancetter.
20. TNA, PROB11/449, Will of Joshua Symonds, 1699.
21. WCRO, L2/1, p.9.
22. Today Beech House, C102 on the 1786 Plan.
23. On corner of Long Street and Ratcliffe Street, F29 on the 1786 Plan. He appears to have sold the *Bear Inn* some time after 1710. His other properties appear on the 1786 Plan as C29, C100, C101, C102, F61.
24. Elizabeth was the widow of Charles Harcourt Esq. of Rowden, Leics.
25. Coventry City Archives, PA/101/7/268-9; Lease and settlement, 6 Jan 1706/7.Coventry City Archives, PA/101/7/261-2.
26. Coventry City Archives, PA/101/7/268-270.
27. TNA, PROB 3/22/157, C11/736/42.
28. Coventry City Archives, PA/101/141/15, 16 Nov 1706, concerns house in Coventry formerly owned by Vademont Eyre, possibly his brother: BCA, MS917/2490, 2 September 1713, and 2491, 7 July 1716, concerning lands in Nether Whitacre, Warwickshire.
29. WCRO, L2/1, p.192.
30. WCRO, L2/1, p.416.
31. Coventry City Archives, PA/101/7/171, 4 Oct 1748.
32. *See* Note 28, Building History Four. WCRO, L2/23, p.5. A note is added to the entry 'half rests with Lord of Manor; co-owned with Soden & wife.'
33. F61 on 1786 Plan.
34. WCRO, L2/3, p.100.
35. LRJO, Administration of Francis Fitzgerald, 23 Oct 1760. (He died intestate).
36. WCRO, L2/4, p.62.
37. WCRO, L2/4, p.81.
38. WCRO, L2/4, p.87.
39. C92 on the 1786 Plan (*see* Fig. 7).
40. WCRO, L2/4, p.114.
41. TNA, PROB 11/1178.
42. TNA, PROB 11/1294.
43. WCRO, L2/5, p.183.
44. WCRO, L2/5, p.389.
45. CRO L2/5, pp.382-4.
46. This was the south section of 15/17 Market Street.
47. On the 1887 OS map, this pump can be seen at the rear of the south side of 15/17 Market Street.
48. This was part of 11/13 Market Street, which was not included in the sale.
49. *See* the description of 15/17 Market Street, pp.54, 99.
50. WCRO, L2/6, pp.27-9.
51. The 'equity of redemption' is the right of a mortgagor to redeem the property he has mortgaged, even if the due time for repayment has passed; this right could be granted to someone else. (Alcock, N.W., *Old Title Deeds*, Chichester (1986), p.122.)
52. WCRO, L2/8, p.127-130.
53. WCRO, L2/8, p.526.
54. Census for 1851.
55. WCRO, L2/8, p.550.
56. Account books of Johnsons, saddlers, 1919-1946, in possession of Friends of Atherstone Heritage.
57. Kelly's Directory for Warwickshire (1932).

BUILDING HISTORY SIX, PP.109-12

1. F38 on the 1786 Plan, Fig. 7.
2. There was also a Swan with Two Necks in Long Street, on the site of today's 49 and 51 Long Street (C12, Fig. 7).
3. Alcock, N.W., Meeson, R.A. and E.J., *Polesworth Abbey Gatehouse: a documentary history and an historic building survey and analysis*, Report 0706, Jan. 2007, Warwickshire County Council.
4. A number of surrenders in the manor court rolls of the 1590s relate to property abutting C49 (occupied by John Power). F12 immediately to the east is one (WCRO, L2/10, p.61). Further to the east, William Roberts owned at least two further properties. L2/10, pp.60v-61v records six surrenders of mostly adjoining properties to his use, one of which may be the *Old Swan*.
5. WCRO, L2/14 pp.31 & 37. Perhaps Katherine had some dower rights.
6. WCRO, Hearth Tax assessments for Warwickshire, also printed: Walker, M., ed., *Warwick County Records: Hearth Tax Returns*, volume I, Warwick (1957), p.250.
7. WCRO, L2/16, p.28.
8. *See* Appendix to Chapter Three.
9. C50 on 1786 Plan.
10. C49 on 1786 Plan.
11. LJRO, Will of John Power, 1677.
12. In Ford's own will of 1709, through his executors he 'humbly' requested his landlord to allow his wife to take over the lease, and after her death for it to be passed to his grandson. But sadly he died in debt, and the executors renounced their right to the execution of the will and granted administration to Samuel Bracebridge as the principal creditor. (LJRO, B/C/11: Will of Jeremiah Ford 1709, includes papers relating to condition, and executors' renunciation of their duties.)
13. LJRO, Inventory of Richard Bancks, 1708, including condition and bond.
14. C96 on 1786 Plan.
15. WCRO, CR1039/1, 29 Sept 1786.
16. WCRO, CR2511/22.
17. WCRO, QS36/14-16: Winters; WCRO, QS36/17: Wm Alcock. A note of caution has to be applied to this identification; it is not entirely clear that the transfer of the name took place before rather than after Alcock became the inn-keeper of the *Old Swan*.
18. Pigot's Directory for Warwickshire, p.765.
19. Dugd., 504, Rate Book 1825. An estate map drawn up by the Bracebridges in 1822 shows a small gap between the *Old Swan* and the houses to the west in Long Street, WCRO, CR258/342-3. The site at the time was described as 'Buildings Garden & Croft', and was just over an acre in extent.
20. WCRO, CR2511/22.
21. Watts, B. & Winyard, E., *History of Atherstone*, Mercia Publications (1988), p.286.

CHAPTER SIX, PP.113-38

1. WCRO, L2/86. Survey of the Manor of Atherstone, dated 10-11 May 1547. *See* the Appendix to Chapter Three.
2. The 'Commission of Inquiry Touching Enclosures 1517' examined how many houses and buildings had been pulled down and how great lands which were in tillage were then converted to pasture (Fisher, H.E.S. and Jurica, A.R.J. (eds.),

Documents in English Economic History 1000-1760 [1977]), p.120; Enclosure Riots in the East Midlands 1607-08, *ibid.*, p.132.

3. For more on the field system, *see* Chapter Four, under 'Agriculture'.
4. The site of the battlefield is currently (2008) the subject of an ongoing study by The Battlefields Trust and Leicestershire County Archaeology Services..
5. At this time Atherstone Manor was in the hands of Mount Grace Priory in Yorkshire but the closure of this Priory would have had less immediate impact locally.
6. Elton, G.R., *England Under the Tudors* (1974), pp.120, 200. Henry VIII wanted moderate orthodoxy with some of the old practices removed and never envisaged the spread of Protestantism which his break with Rome encouraged.
7. WCRO, DR130/1, Mancetter Parish Register; LJRO, Probate Documents; WCRO, L2; MR13.
8. Richardson, John, *The Local Historian's Encyclopaedia* (1986), p.71, Sec. D20.
9. *Cattel* or *Cattle* here does not mean 'livestock' but is an old word for personal property, wealth or goods.
10. *See* Note 5 to Chapter Nine. The bound volumes comprising the manor court records are nevertheless often referred to as manor court 'rolls'.
11. Sheail, J., 'The Regional Distribution of Wealth in England as indicated in the 1524/5 Lay Subsidy Returns', Ph.D. thesis, University of London (1969). Until the end of the 18th century, the number of households in Atherstone is more reliable than the number of inhabitants. Household sizes in the 4.5 to 5.0 range are generally considered to be appropriate for the 16th-17th centuries. Here, for simple comparison, 5.0 is adopted.
12. LPL, CM XX/1; P. Clark and J. Hosking, *Population Estimates of English Small Towns 1550-1851*, Centre for Urban History, University of Leicester, Working paper, 5 (1993), pp.153-6. However, the 1563 returns have been criticised for under-recording, so not too much weight can be put on this apparent decline.
13. Gregg, Pauline, *Black Death to Industrial Revolution: a social and economic history of England* (1976), Ch.16.
14. Clark, Peter and Slack, Paul, *English Towns in Transition 1500-1700* (1976), p.90; Coleman, D.C., *The Economy of England, 1450-1750* (1977), p.14.
15. For the parish of Mancetter, only two inventories survive for the 1560s and five for the 1570s; all are for Oldbury and Hartshill, which perhaps escaped the worst of the infection.
16. Arkell, T. and Alcock, N.W. (eds), *The Warwickshire Hearth Tax*, Dugdale Society, forthcoming.
17. Bartlett, Benjamin, *Manduessedum Romanorum* (1796); Foxe, John, *Actes and Monuments* (1572) (known as *The Book of Martyrs*); Richens, B., *Narrative of persecutions and sufferings of the two martyrs, Robert Glover and Mrs Lewis of Mancetter*, 2nd edn. (1836) (WCRO, C 284 Ric).
18. The title, *Sir*, was normal for clergymen and does not imply knighthood.
19. Orpen, P.K., 'Recruitment patterns of the schoolmaster in the 17th century – a study of Warwickshire schools', *Warwickshire History*, 4 (3), lists a school at Mancetter.
20. William Symonds was fined in 1678 for holding a conventicle in his house at Atherstone. WCRO, Quarter Sessions.
21. Probably an astrological symbol [OED sub *notory* and *notary*].
22. The rent would be 14s. 1d. while the value given to the property would be £10.
23. For more on the field system, *see* Chapter Four, under 'Agriculture'.
24. WCRO, CR 258/335; P7. Survey of the Manor of Atherstone (1716), including map (*see* Fig. 3).
25. Hoskins, W.G., *The Making of the English Landscape* (1957), p.155.
26. Paines of The Manor of Atherstone. WCRO, L2/3, p.22. 'A paine made that no person shall have any fireplace in any such building as is thacked appearing dangeruos and not parged nor in any working shop nor work by candlelight in any room on paine of £1 19s. 4d.'
27. Two further sons, Thomas and Christopher, were also to receive the same and Thomas an additional £3. His daughters, Mary, Agnes and Ellen were also bequeathed £6, and his married daughter, Alice Robinson, three quarters (84lbs) of malt. These sums were to be paid by sons John and Thomas out of their legacies. John, together with his mother Margaret, was joint executor of the will, although Thomas was probably the eldest as he also received a further £3. Unfortunately, most of the family were born before the Parish Register began; only Ralph, born in 1580 and Mary, born in 1585, are recorded. John married Alice Abell within a year of his father's death. An overseer of the will was Richard Robinson, possibly his son in law; a further family member mentioned was his cousin Bickley.
28. Steer, F.W., *Farm and Cottage Inventories of Mid Essex 1635-1749* (1969), p.32; Malting is a process applied to cereal grains, in which the grains are made to germinate and then are quickly dried before the plant develops; this produces sugar that can then be fermented into beer, etc. A malting, sometimes called maltings or malting floor, is a building that houses the process of converting barley into malt, for use in the brewing or distilling process, and a malt kiln is a building used for the drying process.
29. Defoe, Daniel, *A Tour Through the Whole Island of Great Britain* (1972 edition), p.88.
30. Nicols, J., *The history and antiquities of the county of Leicester* (1815); For the public houses in Atherstone *see* Austin, J.D., *Hats, Coal and Bloodshed*. Furthermore, looking ahead to the 18th century, Judy Vero has compiled the following notes on the earliest references to named inns in the Manor Court Rolls, using references from the 1786 Plan for buildings, and MCR references: C24, *The Three Tuns* (1764), L2/6, p.78; C26, *Red Lion* (1711), L2/1, p.28; C33, *White Horse*, pre-1763 was *Kings Arms*, L2/26, p.57; C57, *Sign of the Cock* (1746), L2/3, p.22; C58 (incorrectly marked C56 on plan), also F16; was held by Goodere Hunt as innholder in 1672, L2/26, p.12, also will of 1671. He appears to have run as inns buildings at the extreme ends of the town ... prime sites given the importance of catching your customers as they enter the town ... as did the *Angel* to the north. C61, *Sign of the Flower Pot* (1802), L2/5, p.225; C70, *Black Horse* (1811), L2/5, p.518; C80, *Hat and Beaver* (1835), L2/7, p.443 ('for many yrs used as a public house'); F29, *Bear Inn* (1705), L2/20, p.66; C120, *White Hart* 1760 L2/26, p.8 (held by Goodere Hunt from 1647, L2/14, p.14); F33, *Sign of the Swan* (1710), L2/12, p.7, owned by Ed Drayton, vintner; his inventory (1625) shows its use as an inn. C108, the *Angel Inn* (1721), L2/1, p.167 (but probably an inn from medieval times). F12, *Old Swan*, No early evidence that it was an inn. The name *Old Swan* seems to have been transferred to this building from the Market Place in the 1820s. William Alcock probably first innkeeper (he took out a victualler's bond for '*Old Swan Inn*' in 1824 and 1827. Recorded as innkeeper of *Old Swan* in 1828.
31. Spavold, J. and Brown, S., *Ticknall Pots and Potters*, Landmark Publishing (2005). Pages 51 and 170 give an account of Thos. Hanson, potter, who moved to Atherstone.
32. Thos. Bayton's inventory, valued in total at £100 15s. 6d., lists: In Ye Chamber 2 strikes of maslin, 3 strikes of barley 10 quarters of mault dried and to dry£15.0.0. His crop of corn growing in the fields was valued at £14.0.0, and his eight cows, one bull and four calves were valued at £24.0.0. He also had twenty cheeses, and wool, yarn and wood in the yard – but no indication of lantern-making.
33. Morgan, Paul, *Warwickshire Apprentices in the Stationers' Company of London, 1563-1700*.

Chapter Seven, pp. 139-54

For references below to the 1786 Plan, *see* Fig. 7.

1. Beech House, Market Street, C102 on 1786 Plan. *See* Building History Four.
2. C33 on 1786 Plan.
3. WCRO, L2/3, p.22. *See also* Chapter Three, and Chapter Six.
4. In an 'open' settlement there were a number of freeholders and the lord of the manor had limited power. This

contrasts with the 'closed' settlement where there were few freeholders and the lord of the manor was firmly in control. The importance of weak seigniorial control to the growth of industry has been highlighted by A. Rogers and D.R. Mills; *See* A. Rogers, 'Rural Industries and Social Structure: the Framework Knitting Industry of South Nottinghamshire 1670-1840', pp.7-35, and D.R. Mills, 'Rural Industries and Social Structure: Framework Knitters in Leicestershire, 1670-1851,' pp.183-203, both in *Textile History*, 13 (1982); For an account of trade and agriculture in Atherstone in the 17th century, *see* Chapter Six.

5. Vero, J., *A Concern in Trade: Hatting and the Bracebridges of Atherstone, 1612-1872*, Warwick (1995), pp 72-75.
6. C44 on 1786 Plan, today the Conservative Club.
7. WCRO, L2/4, p.74.
8. WCRO, L2/4, pp.74, 244.
9. C54 and C55 on 1786 Plan.
10. *See* Note 5 to Chapter Nine. The bound volumes comprising the later manor court records are nevertheless often referred to as 'rolls'.
11. WCRO, L2/10, p.64v.
12. Today the area is lawned, but the depression where the pool used to be can still be seen.
13. WCRO, L2/11, 7 June 1602.
14. F17 on Plan of 1786.
15. Unpublished research of Bill Grimke-Drayton.
16. C55 on 1786 Plan. Abel Roper also owned C32.
17. BCA, Aylesford Collection. Obverse of portrait of Abel Roper.
18. WCRO, DR322/67, 1-223, settlement certificates for Atherstone.
19. C92 on 1786 Plan WCRO, L2/1, p.330.
20. C93 on 1786 Plan WCRO, L2/26, p.25.
21. C100 on 1786 Plan WCRO, L2/4, p.62. *See* Building History Five.
22. Chapter Eight, p.160, makes reference to the bankruptcy of Edmund Simonds.
23. A cottager was a rural labourer who lived in a cottage which either he, or his employer, owned but which did not include farm-land.
24. WCRO, HR35/25. The Case of Atherstone concerning Inclosure of Common Fieldes as drawn up by Mr Baxter and Others, January 1738.
25. WCRO, P7.
26. Information on strip holdings is taken from the Plan of 1716, WCRO, P7, which numbers each strip and has a key for each holding. Though the strips varied in size, the average was an acre. (Fig. 3 shows the central part of the 1716 open-field estate map of Atherstone parish, redrawn.)
27. Vero, *op.cit.*, p.23.
28. A haberdasher of hats was a merchant who purchased materials, put them out to cottage hatmakers, paid them for their labour and sold the hats. In London, the right to do this had previously been the preserve of the Haberdashers until the feltmakers achieved Incorporation in 1604. *See also* Chapter Eight.
29. WCRO, L2/16, p.50.
30. WCRO, HR35/25. HR35/44, written in 1763, reflects on the cost of a yardland in 1740, 'Mr Bracebridge may recollect, or has the means in his power to know that his Father purchas'd of Mr Ragdale in 1740, when the Inclosure was formerly depending, one Yard Land for £252 15s. od., containing 22 to 23 acres.' By 1763 the price had risen to £350 for a yardland.
31. WCRO, 1716 Field Map, P7.
32. WCRO, HR35/25.
33. WCRO, HR35/9.
34. WCRO, HR35/1-60. A concise account of Atherstone's battle can be found in Thompson, E.P., *Customs in Common*, London (1991), pp.152-8.
35. WCRO, HR35/10.
36. Tammy is a rough-textured woollen cloth.
37. WCRO, HR35/10.
38. WCRO, HR35/15.
39. WCRO, HR35/15.
40. Although the horse race has long gone, the site is commemorated in 'Racemeadow Road', to the north of the town.
41. WCRO, HR35/25.
42. WCRO, CR2511/20, copy of Atherstone Inclosure Award, 1765.
43. WCRO, HR35/47 & 48, August 1764.
44. WCRO, HR35/46.
45. WCRO, CR2511/24.
46. Watts, B. and Winyard, E., *The History of Atherstone*, Mercia Publications (1988), p.37.
47. Martin, J.M., *Warwickshire and the Parliamentary Movement*, PhD Thesis, University of Birmingham (1965), WRO, C 631 MAR, Appendix XXV. Quoted in Watts & Winyard, *op.cit.*, p.37.
48. C52 on 1786 Plan; WRO L2/4, p.254.
49. WCRO, L2/7, p.354.
50. C56 on 1786 Plan; WRO L2/4, p.369.
51. WCRO, L2/7, p.245.
52. C60 on 1786 Plan; L2/5, p.31.
53. WCRO, L2/7, p.233.
54. WCRO, L2/7, p.245.
55. WCRO, L2/8, p,282.
56. WCRO, L2/8, p.452
57. WCRO, L2/8, p.485.
58. Brown,Richard, *Society and Economy in Modern Britain 1700-1750*, London and New York (1991), p.189.
59. WCRO, L2/3 p.116. C93 on 1786 Plan.
60. Mathias, Peter, *The First Industrial Nation: The Economic History of Britain 1700-1914*, London and New York (1983), p.135.
61. WCRO, L2/3, p.122, L2/26, p.23. C31 on 1786 Plan.
62. I am grateful to Tom Arkell for his unpublished transcript of the 1670 list.
63. This is the 'surrender' of copyhold property, recorded in the manor court rolls.
64. WCRO, L2/15, p.60; C9 on 1786 Plan.
65. WCRO, L2/15, C37 on 1786 Plan.
66. C9, C21, C114, C115, C118, C119 and F58 on the 1786 Plan.
67. Nat Alcock also discusses Haddon in Chapter Nine, p.173.
68. WCRO, L2/4, p.259.
69. Richard Davies appears in abuttal information, *see* WRO, L2/2, p.147, L2/3, p.55, L2/26, p.42. His 14 houses are referred to as Davissus Houses in insurance records, *see* WRO, CR1039/1, 24 Jun 1786. C19 on 1786 Plan, later to become the *Nelson Inn*.
70. WRO, CR1039/1, 29 Sep 1790.
71. Though there were claims that the cost of this work could be more than the land was worth, a document related to Enclosure, WCRO, HR35/60, may indicate otherwise. It includes a quotation for November 1764. 'To cut ditch 3ft wide and proportionable depth, with one row of Quicksetts, 1s 6d and each acre of post and rails with Double rails, 2s 6d.'
72. C5 on 1786 Plan.
73. C4 on 1786 Plan.
74. C42 on 1786 Plan, *see also* Note 2.
75. WCRO, L2/4, p.36.
76. WCRO, L2/6, p.276.
77. C34 on 1786 Plan.
78. C36 on 1786 Plan.
79. WCRO, L2/37, p.4.
80. WCRO, L2/5, p.117.
81. WCRO, L2/5, pp.145-7.
82. WCRO, L2/5, pp.328-36.
83. WCRO, L2/5, p.491.
84. WCRO, L2/5, p.334.
85. WCRO, L2/5, p.368.
86. WCRO, L2/8, p.212.
87. WCRO, L2/6, p.604. William Pinchback, Luke Smith, George Davis, James Pinchback, William Hall, Samuel Boyard, James Bryan, John Haddon, Charles Smith, William Sylvester, Thomas Dexter, William Symonds, William Burbage, Thomas Cooke, Richard Broadley, William Thompson.
88. WCRO, CR2511/19.
89. WCRO, CR2511/19, 13 May 1826.

CHAPTER EIGHT, PP.155-70

For references below to the 1786 Plan, *see* Fig. 7.

1. *See* Note 5 to Chapter Nine.
2. WCRO, L2/1-77.
3. In a few cases ownership has been traced from as early as 1584, but for the majority, our information begins inthe 1640s; for selected properties, also, the evidence has been extended to the end of the court book series in 1871.
4. Probate material for the Parish of Mancetter (of which Atherstone was a part), is kept at the Lichfield Joint Record Office. It was first transcribed by a group of volunteers led by Marion Alexander in the 1980s. The wills of the most affluent or those who had property in more than one county are to be found at The National Archives.
5. WCRO, CR1039/1-12. *See also* Chapter Nine, Note 7.
6. I am grateful to Clive Orton for this anecdote.
7. The author recollects that a substantial quantity were dug up from this deep trench. Some bones, horns (and a medieval shoe) were also found at the far west end of Long Street near to the Innage Brook.
8. WCRO, CR258/452.
9. These premises are C9 to C15 on the 1786 Plan of Atherstone.
10. *See* p.164 under 'Willday's Hat Manufactory' for more on the water supply.
11. WCRO, CR1130/5.
12. WCRO, P8.
13. This is the area where the Foxes and Walmsleys had their business, discussed under 'The early development of Atherstone's hatting'. I am told by local residents that some houses in the town still have water cisterns beneath their ground floor.
14. Smith, J.H., 'The development of the English Felt and Silk Hat Trades 1500-1912', Ph.D. thesis, University of Manchester (1980), p.9.
15. For an account of the Coventry capping trade, *see*, King, Peter, *The Mystery of The Coventry Cappers*, London and New York (2000).
16. Weinstein, Rosemary, *The History of the Worshipful Company of Feltmakers 1604-2004*, Chichester (2004), pp.29-32; Workman, Christine, 'The Hat Industry', in *Rural Industries of the Lune Valley*, Winstanley (ed.), University of Lancaster (2000), p.106; McKnight, Penny, *Stockport Hatting*, Stockport (2000), p.4; King, Peter, *op.cit.*, p.74.
17. Vero, J., *A Concern in Trade: Hatting and the Bracebridges of Atherstone 1612-1872*, Warwick (1995).
18. Marion Alexander in Chapter Six raises the possibility that John Abell's barrel of soap is indicative of participation in the hat trade (p.125).
19. WCRO, CR258/261.
20. Plots C70 and C76 on the 1786 Plan.
21. LJRO, Will of Kathrine Fox, 1682.
22. A 'tod' is a unit for weighing wool, 2 stone (28 pounds) equal to approximately 13 kilos.
23. C70 on 1786 Plan, today 156 Long Street.
24. WCRO, L2/15, p.119.
25. LJRO, Will of Anne Walmsley, 1690.
26. This is the hatters' spelling of the word 'basin.' It is used in most of the primary sources and P.M. Giles spells it this way in 'The felt-hatting industry, *c.*1500-1850 with particular reference to Lancashire and Cheshire' in *Transactions of the Lancashire & Cheshire Antiquarian Society*, vol. 69 (1959), p.114.
27. The family home was a freeholding, F59 on the 1786 Plan.
28. LJRO, Will of John Ragdale, 1702.
29. John appears to have been one of the few property owners in the town, apart from the Bracebridges, to enfranchise his property so that in the mid-18th century this house became freehold. It is F55 on the 1786 Plan.
30. LJRO, Will of Asael Ragdale, 1729.
31. As noted in the Introduction to this chapter, during the study period of 1640 to 1850, as many as 50 of the town's burgage plots are recorded as having hatting activities upon them at some time or other.
32. Fig. 34 is from Tomlinson, Charles, *Illustrations of Useful Arts and Manufactures*, SPCK, London (1858).
33. Vero, J., *op cit.*, There is more on the field system in earlier centuries in Chapter Three, Chapter Four, Chapter Six and Chapter Seven.
34. WCRO, CR1039/1, 29 Sep 1784.
35. C38 on the 1786 Plan.
36. WCRO, CR1039/1, [29] Sep 1796.
37. WCRO, CR1039/1, 29 Sep 1798.
38. WCRO, L2/6, p.212 1 Mar 1817; p.232 1 May 1817.
39. WCRO, L2/7, pp.527-33, 18 Nov 1836. However, Tanner may have received further money from the sale of Power's possessions.
40. At F40 on the 1786 Plan.
41. WCRO, CR1039/2, 11 Mar 1802.
42. L2/6, pp.285-289.
43. C65 on the 1786 Plan.
44. Hatters' Gazette, 1 Nov 1866, quoted in J.H. Smith, Ph.D thesis, p.164.
45. Reynolds was the owner. WRO, L2/5, p.32, 19 Jun 1793 (C60).
46. Vero, J., *op.cit.*, pp.74-75.
47. TNA, E317/Wark/8 [Parliamentary survey] Dec. 1649. Richard was tenant of what had been Crown property, one of the unsold properties that had formerly belonged to the Guild of Atherstone (*see* Note 11 in Appendix to Chapter Three). Abuttal information is given in WCRO, L2/14, p.31v, 21 Jun 1649; L2/16 p.88, 10 Oct 1677.
48. Vero, J., *op.cit.*, p.66.
49. Abuttal information WCRO, L2/17, p.41 20 Oct 1687; L2/19, p.6, 2 Jan 1695. F11 on the 1786 Plan.
50. Logwood was widely used in Atherstone to dye hats. It was imported from America in logs approximately three feet long and was prepared in mills. The log was fed against a set of rotating blades to reduce it to small chips. After drying, the chips were ground to a powder in an edge-mill under grit millstones. *See* Raistrick, Arthur, *Industrial Archaeology*, London (1972), Paladin edition (1986), p.107.
51. Vero, J., *op.cit.*, p.66.
52. WCRO, L2/2, p.147, 30 Sep 1742; L2/26, pp.69-70, 6 Sep 1764. C19 on 1786 Plan.
53. WCRO, L2/2, p.148, 30 Sep 1742. C30 on 1786 Plan.
54. WCRO, L2/1, 6 Oct 1733, C105 in 1786 Plan.
55. WCRO, L2/1, pp.359-360, 6 Oct 1733. C13 on the 1786 Plan.
56. Vero, J., *op.cit.*, p.75.
57. C14 in 1766 and C15 in 1771.
58. WCRO, CR1039/1 25 Mar 1797. While others of the town's hatters had premises dedicated to hatting before this date, there is no insurance record of John Willday's operation until 1797. It may be that he had previously insured with a company whose records have not survived.
59. WCRO, CR1039/2. Insurance record for 11 Mar 1802.
60. *The Applause of the Jury, 1782-85*, Heinemann (1981), from the Yale Editions of the Private Papers of James Boswell (I am grateful to John D. Austin for this reference.)
61. WCRO, L2/5, p.5, 19 May 1792, L2/5, p.33, 20 Jul 1793, L2/5, p.62, 7 Mar 1795 and L2/5 p.268, 1 Mar 1803. The property is C119 on the 1786 Plan. It was sold to William Hood in 1803, but the Willdays bought it back in 1809.
62. There were a number of hatting businesses in Pennsylvania at this time, though it is not known if that was the purpose of Willday's interest in the State.
63. TNA, PROB11/1480, Will of John Willday, 1808.
64. C13, C14, C15 on 1786 Plan.
65. WCRO, CR1039/4, Order Book New Fire Office, 1810-1833. The numbered plan has not survived.
66. WCRO, CR258/452 *See* this chapter, p.156.
67. WCRO, CR258/452.
68. The dye recipe for black wool felt contained logwood, copperas and verdigris. (Dye and Proof Recipes, 1853, Vero & Everitt Archive).
69. There were various recipes for proof, usually based on shellac. Naptha, sandric, mastic, resin, turpentine, were some of the other ingredients. (Dye and Proof Recipes, 1853, Vero & Everitt Archive).
70. C11 on 1786 Plan. Insurers were also wary of stoves for drying hats on account of the high risk of fire, which was not unfounded, as the leaflet of Fig. 35 demonstrates.
71. WCRO, CR1039/4.
72. C9 on the 1786 Plan. Binghams Yard is discussed in Chapter Nine, *passim*.

73. Vero, J., *op.cit.*, p.89.
74. WCRO, L2/7, p.414.
75. WCRO, CR1039/5.
76. Although the first abolition bill was passed by the House of Lords in 1807, a bill abolishing slavery in the British Empire was not passed until 1833, and it was 1838 before the last vestige of slavery was abolished.
77. *Post Office Directory of Warwickshire* (1845), p.593.
78. WCRO, CR3056/1, *Select Vestry Minute Book* (1828-36).
79. WCRO, CR1039/4.
80. 'You will be surprised but not sorry to hear that my old and unflinching enemy, Mr Jos Willday, Hatter, died at 7 o'clock tonight.' (William Vero, hatter, writing to his son in Australia, 27 October 1852, quoted in Vero, J., *op.cit.*, p.92).
81. WCRO, CR1039/5.
82. An application for listing was rejected by English Heritage in 2006, though as the building is in a conservation area it will probably survive.
83. Watts, B. and Winyard, E., *The History of Atherstone*, Mercia Publications (1988) p.324.
84. TNA, PROB 11/2162, Will of Joseph Willday.
85. WCRO, CR1108, 26 June 1861: Lease by Catherine Whitby to Charles Phillips of manufactory.
86. WCRO, CR1108.
87. *Umbrella and Portmanteau Trades Review*, 1 Dec 1880, p.609.
88. Watts & Winyard, *op.cit.*, p.340.
89. C13 on 1786 Plan.
90. C14 and C15 on 1786 Plan.
91. C11 and C12 on 1786 Plan.
92. Surrender 1 June 1894 by Ebenezer Brown of Copyhold Factory hereditaments in Station Street, Atherstone, and admittance of Charles Vero. Vero & Everitt archives.
93. Vero & Everitt's factory at the west end of Station Street has been re-developed as a supermarket, and Ball & Company's factory in Owen Street is now the site of flats. W.A. Hatton's factory stands to the north of 50 Long Street. Austin Aspden (formerly Denham & Hargrave)'s factory stood at 120-126 Long Street; only the office on the street front now survives. Part of F.J. Eliot ('The Tannery') survives behind Wainwright's Garage on South Street. Wilson & Stafford's Britannia Works is on Coleshill Road beside the Coventry Canal.

CHAPTER NINE, PP.171-90

1. HART and especially its secretary, Judy Vero, have provided invaluable support for the present study. John Austin told me of the key part played in the clearance of the courts by Dr John Herring, the Atherstone Medical Officer of Health from 1909-17. Herring's 1911 Report is particularly informative (Wellcome Library, Provincial MOH Reports 1911, ABR-BAT; copy held by HART). This present study was initially presented at the conference held in Oxford in November 2003, *Housing the Masses*, organised by the Vernacular Architecture Group and OUDCE, and is in part included in N. W. Alcock, 'Housing the urban poor in 1800: courts in Atherstone and Coventry, Warwickshire', *Vernacular Architecture*, 36 (2005) 49-60.
2. The 1:500 OS map of the same date (WCRO) shows the individual houses in the yards in greater detail, but its large scale makes reproduction difficult; this map is used as the basis for the plans in Fig. 38. The laying out of the burgage plots on which the yards were built is discussed in Chapter Three.
3. One copy of the original map is WCRO, CR2511/21, with a modern reproduction at P26; it was updated in 1815, showing the frontage lengths of the burgage plots, but only a reduced photostat is available of this version (WCRO, Z484(u)) and the dimensions are almost illegible on the photostat. The original at Merevale Hall could not be found in 2003. According to their size (and presumably the rent they paid), the plots were counted as full burgages or ¾, ½ or ¼ of a burgage.
4. The yards were generally named either from their owners or from the public houses that frequently stood on their Watling Street frontages; these names are given in the 1851 census and incompletely on the 1:500 scale map of 1888; Watts, B. & Winyard, E., in *History of Atherstone*, Mercia Publications (1988) cite the names of 60 yards from the 1911 Medical Officer of Health Report.
5. WCRO, L2. The manor court records are referred to variously in the chapters of this book, as manor court rolls and manor court books. The earlier records are rolls. The main later sequence is a series of large volumes lettered 'A' to 'I', running from 1710 to 1871 (L2/1-9. Regrettably, although a further volume 'J' is referred to (and there may have been later ones as well), it has not survived in the collection. These volumes are supplemented by a series of less formal court books, continuous from 1645 to 1871.
6. WCRO, HR38/1. Another poor-rate assessment, for 1833, is CR2511/22.
7. WCRO, CR1039/1, New Fire Office (1784-99); /2-9, Phoenix Fire Office (1790-1899).
8. North Warwickshire Borough Council, Atherstone (Environmental Health Department) holds an incomplete run of the MOH reports, but a copy of the key report for 1911 could only be found at the Wellcome Medical Library, London. (*See* Note 1).
9. E.g. Beresford, M.W., *East End, West End*, Leeds (1988); Thoresby Soc, pp.60-61 [Leeds]; Caffyn, Lucy, *Workers' Housing in West Yorkshire, 1750-1920*, London (1986); Chapman, S.D. (ed.), *The History of Working Class Housing*, Newton Abbot (1971); Girouard, M., *The English Town*, London (1995) [Nottingham].
10. These were more usually called 'courts' (e.g. in Coventry), but in Atherstone, they were generally 'yards', or occasionally 'rows', when the burgage plots were too narrow to accommodate more than one row of houses.
11. E.g. Beresford, *op. cit.*
12. Watts and Winyard, *op. cit.*
13. As reported by the Medical Officer of Health in 1911 (Wellcome Library, 1911 MOH report for Atherstone). His calculation was somewhat flawed, as he compared the density within an individual yard with that of a complete ward in Birmingham.
14. *Victoria County History, Warwickshire II* (1908), 185, 185n. The 1671-2 population is based on the 257 households listed in the Hearth Tax.(*See* note 16, Chapter Six) A population of c.750 has been suggested for 1730, based on the number of houses reported in that year (Dr Thomas (ed.), W. Dugdale, *Antiquities of Warwickshire*, 2nd edn; London: 1730) by Martin, J.M., 'Warwickshire and the Parliamentary Enclosure Movement', PhD thesis, Birmingham University (1955), 215. A comparison with the census figures led Martin to conclude that the population expansion in Atherstone in the later 18th century was greater than in any of the other places examined. However, the figure for 1671-2 must be considered more reliable than that for 1730, casting doubt on this conclusion.
15. C9 on the 1786 Plan. As well as the court entries, a deed bundle survives in private hands, from 1766 onwards. The property is first recorded in the court books in 1655, when it was in the hands of the Pettie family; it passed to Matthew Goodwin in 1670, Thomas Goode in 1706, John Hodges in 1709, John Liptrot in 1745, followed by his daughter Mildred, who sold it to Thomas Haddon in 1756 (L2/15, 60; L2/16, 23, 30,78v, 88v; L2/20, 68, 91; L2/1, 41, 293-4; L2/3, 17, 53, 107).
16. WCRO: L2/4, pp.264, 275. The dispute in Chancery concerned whether his real or personal estate should be used to pay his debts: PRO C12/2306/15 (bill); C12/2037/22 (answers); C12/2313/5 (interrogatories including information about Hadden's business debts).
17. WCRO, CR1039/1.
18. WCRO, HR38/1.
19. WCRO, CR1039/4.
20. Two of the frontage houses were bought by Harry Roe, the owner of the adjoining property.
21. WCRO, L2/8, pp.248, 270, 275. Separate copies of two of the plans are in L2/99/1-2. Curiously, the second plan appears not to match the layout of the site, although the description is unambiguous
22. WCRO, L2/4, p.358; L2/5, p.40; HR38/1.
23. WCRO, L2/5, pp.112, 213; L2/7, pp.24, 279. The sale in 1801 was to William Nurthall and, confusingly, on his death

in 1824, he left it to his nephew, another Joseph Woodroffe – probably the son of the previous owner; William Nurthall had married Mary Woodroffe in 1795 (IGI).

24. WCRO, L2/8, p.424.
25. WCRO, L2/3, p.50; L2/4, pp.151, 339; L2/6, p.265. A mortgage for £100 had been already taken out in 1777 (L2/4, pp.151-2). An insurance memorandum of 1784 (CR1039/1) mentions five houses, but the then owner, William Nurthall, also owned the adjoining burgage (C5), so it is possible that this covered both properties.
26. WCRO, L2/2, p.161; L2/4, p.428; L2/5, pp.8, 71; HR38/1.
27. WCRO, CR 1039/2, pp.10, 14.
28. WCRO, L2/14, f.24v; /15, f.101; /17, f. 64; /20, f.135; L2/3, pp.97, 104; L2/4, pp.310, 351-3, 389.
29. WCRO, L2/4, pp.389, 400, 432.
30. WCRO, HR 38/1.
31. WCRO, CR 1039/2, p.20.
32. Ibid., p.26.
33. WCRO, L2/5, pp.114, 154, 210, 249, 258, 349, 408, 432. The first part (¼ burgage) was described as a messuage with shop, back buildings and garden extending 183ft back from Watling Street, with free access to the back lane. The rear part (one-eighth burgage) was a 'part messuage with two back buildings or shops'. Hickling's part had previously been described as ¼ burgage, but was later described as one-eighth burgage. Fig. 58 (E) indicates approximately the divisions of the plot at this period.
34. WCRO, L2/8, p.57. The mortgage had been transferred in 1826 to the executors of Joshua Frone of Ashby Parva, who had lent the money from his estate. The bequest took effect when William and Ann reached the age of 21, so by 1837 was effectively paid off, as they were lending the money to themselves. The surrender and admission is notable, because one of the executors, Seth Clarke, formerly of Sharnford, was now living in Great Bend, Susquehanna County, Pennsylvania, from where he sent his letter of attorney. William Hood the elder had married Mary Frone in 1804 in Croft, Leicestershire, and Ann and William were born in 1807 and 1812 respectively, and baptised in the Atherstone Congregational Chapel (IGI).
35. WCRO, L2/9, pp.148, 217, 463, 587. The sale to the brewery must have taken place after 1871, but their ownership is recorded in the '1910 Domesday', WCRO, CR1978/2/8.
36. WCRO: CR1546/145/pt ii. The descriptions are most detailed for Cordingleys and Binghams (then called Willdays) Yard, though other yards were also included in this phase of clearance. Although the reports refer to a plan, this seems not to have survived.
37. *See* Note 1; cited in Watts and Winyard, *op. cit.*, particularly pp.208-12.
38. OED defines *twitchel* as a narrow passage or footway, though those in Atherstone seem to have had no through access, and indeed if the maps are to be believed, no access at all in some cases.
39. Similar figures for Binghams Row are given in the 1911 Report. It measured 78 x 14yds (1,092 sq yds) and included 22 houses occupied by 123 people.
40. WCRO, CR1546/145/pt ii. The progress of clearance is described in Watts and Winyard, *op.cit.*, and the confirmation orders are in TNA, HGL23 (dated 1935-7).
41. Several sets exist, including one at Warwickshire County Record Office, PH213. The illustrations used here were kindly provided as scans by Judy Vero, from a set in her possession, but they have been referenced according to the PH213 numbering.
42. The overall dimensions shown should be reasonably accurate as the plan was prepared to accompany the division of the property. Some Atherstone RDC building plans have survived from the 1870s onwards (WCRO, CR2662) but none relate to houses in the yards.
43. The description and plan have been provided by Mr Dennis Aucott, a retired builder, who as a child of eight in about 1931 visited his grandparents in this house (personal communication, 2005).
44. These dimensions, derived from the map footprint, differ somewhat from those reported in the Atherstone Clearance Orders, which describe living rooms in Nos. 3-19 (all identical on the map) measuring 12ft x 13ft. From Mr Aucott's information, the front and rear walls were of 9in brickwork, but the party walls were only 4½in thick.
45. The fireplace of a house in Court 33, Much Park Street, Coventry (just north of St John's Street) in the early 20th century was described as 'old-fashioned ... with hobs on each side and an oven on one side which took up the whole of one wall of the room. ... water was heated in a huge iron pot on a sort of grid across the fire', The Women's Research Group, *Hurdy Gurdy Days* (Coventry, 2001). Mr Aucott described the range in No. 8 Cordingleys Yard in similar terms.
46. By contrast, several of the restored back-to-backs in Inge Street, Birmingham have grates in their upper rooms.
47. As indicated in the 1911 MOH report and confirmed by Mr Aucott.
48. Recorded by Judy Vero from Doris Warner (nee Clark), at the time in her late 70s, on 23 June 1988.
49. *The Atherstone Yards Project*, Atherstone Public Library, typescript of recordings made in January 1995, quoted with permission. Other details come from *Spoken Memories*, a compilation made in 1985 by Richard Margoschis, from an extensive series of interviews. Regrettably, his original recordings have not come to light.
50. Gilbert, David, 'Excavations at Station Street, Atherstone, Warwickshire 2005-2006', Birmingham and Warwickshire Archaeol. Soc. Trans. 111 (2007), pp.97-132.
51. TNA, HLG23/4119.
52. Transcript of 1851 census from HART records. 1901 census: PRO: RG13/2898, f.43ff.
53. N.W. Alcock, 'Housing the urban poor in 1800: courts in Atherstone and Coventry, Warwickshire', *Vernacular Architecture*, 36 (2005) pp.49-60. Beresford, M.W., *op. cit.*; Girouard, M., *op.cit.*
54. Alcock, *op. cit.* The Bridestowe houses are described and illustrated in Charles Vancouver, *General View of the Agriculture of Devon*, London (1808); reprinted, Newton Abbot (1969), pp.94-7. I thank Dr John Broad for this reference, which he included in his lecture 'Housing the Masses', at the conference in November 2003 (*see* note 1 above).
55. E.g. Gauldie, Enid, *Cruel Habitations*, London (1974); Rodger, Richard, *Housing in Urban Britain 1780-1914*, Cambridge (1989); Burnett, John, *A Social History of Housing*, Newton Abbot (1978).
56. Lowe, Jeremy, *Welsh Industrial Workers Housing 1775-1875*, Cardiff (1985); Guillery, Peter, *The Small House in Eighteenth-Century London*, New Haven and London (2004); for Club Row, Bethnal Green, *see* p.68.
57. Papers by Giles, Colum and Timmins, Geoffrey, in Barnwell, P., Palmer, M. and Airs, M (eds.), *The Vernacular Workshop: from Craft to Industry, 1400-1900*, CBA Research Report 140, York (2004), pp.75-89, 90-100.
58. Cf. Burnett, *op. cit.*, pp.58-61. Coventry did include many lodging houses, with single rooms occupied by numbers of unrelated individuals.

Index

Note: Buildings listed in the Gazetteer, but not otherwise referred to, are not indexed separately.

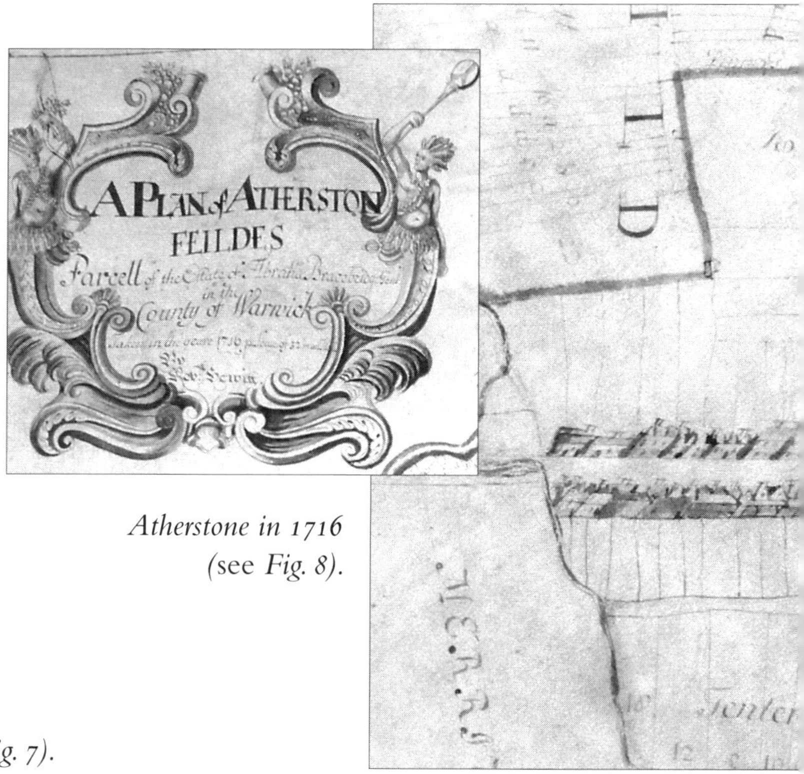

Atherstone in 1716 (see Fig. 8).

Atherstone in 1786 (see Fig. 7).

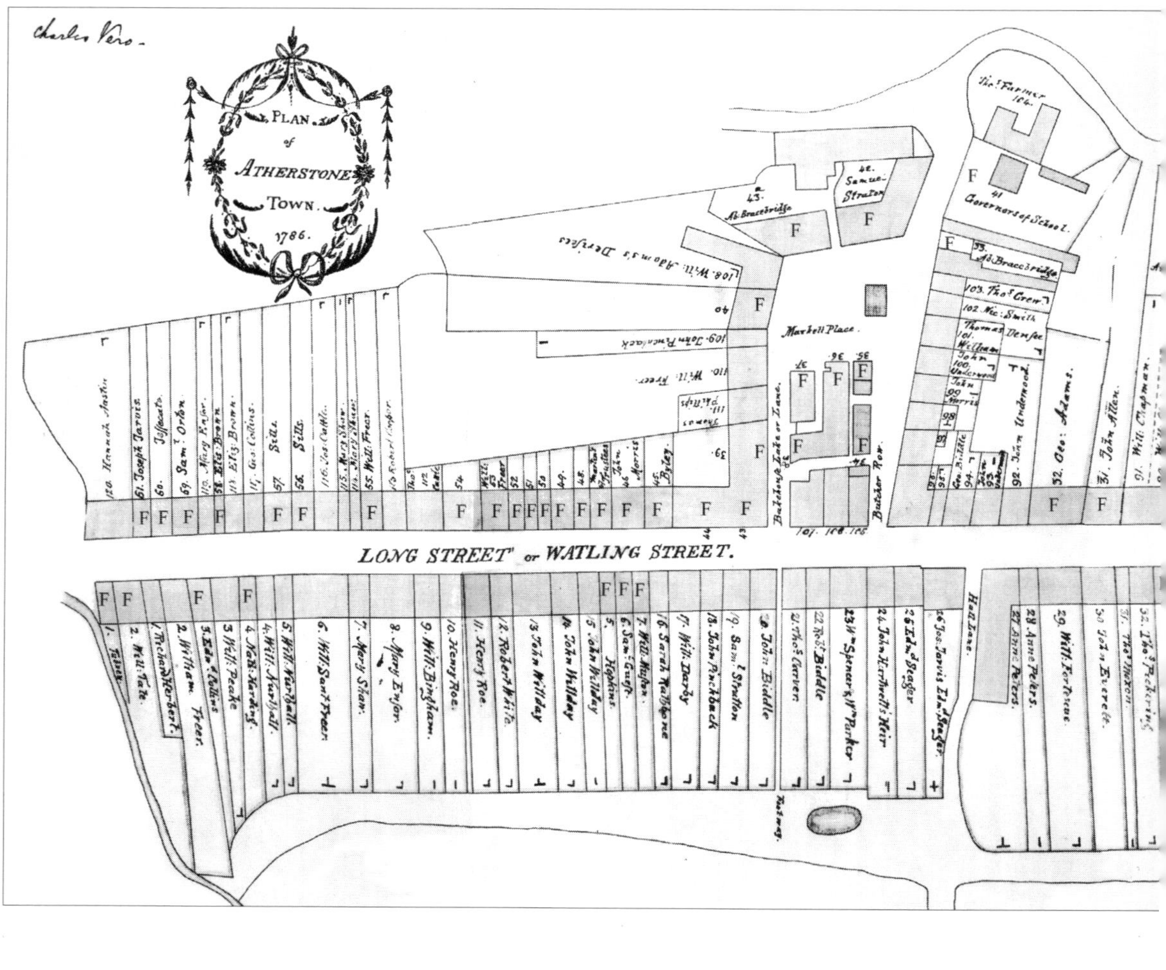